The Costs and Benefits
of Price Stability

A National Bureau
of Economic Research
Conference Report

The Costs and Benefits of Price Stability

Edited by Martin Feldstein

The University of Chicago Press

Chicago and London

MARTIN FELDSTEIN is the George F. Baker Professor of Economics at Harvard University and president of the National Bureau of Economic Research.

The University of Chicago Press, Chicago 60637
The University of Chicago Press, Ltd., London
© 1999 by the National Bureau of Economic Research
All rights reserved. Published 1999
08 07 06 05 04 03 02 01 00 99   1 2 3 4 5
ISBN: 0-226-24099-1 (cloth)

Library of Congress Cataloging-in-Publication Data

The costs and benefits of price stability / edited by Martin Feldstein.
       p.   cm.—(A National Bureau of Economic Research conference report)
    Papers presented at an NBER conference held at the Federal Reserve Bank of New York on Feb. 20–21, 1997.
    Includes bibliographical references and index.
    ISBN 0-226-24099-1 (cloth : alk. paper)
    1. Prices—Government policy—Congresses.   2. Price regulation—Congresses.   3. Monetary policy—Congresses.   4. Inflation (Finance)—Congresses.   I. Feldstein, Martin S.   II. Series: Conference report (National Bureau of Economic Research)
    HB236.A3 C63   1999
    338.5'26—dc21   98-43630
                                                                      CIP

The Costs and
Benefits of
Price Stability

Edited by   Martin Feldstein

The University of Chicago Press

Chicago and London

MARTIN FELDSTEIN is the George F. Baker Professor of Economics at Harvard University and president of the National Bureau of Economic Research.

The University of Chicago Press, Chicago 60637
The University of Chicago Press, Ltd., London
© 1999 by the National Bureau of Economic Research
All rights reserved. Published 1999
08 07 06 05 04 03 02 01 00 99   1 2 3 4 5
ISBN: 0-226-24099-1 (cloth)

Library of Congress Cataloging-in-Publication Data

The costs and benefits of price stability / edited by Martin Feldstein.
     p. cm.—(A National Bureau of Economic Research conference report)
  Papers presented at an NBER conference held at the Federal Reserve Bank of New York on Feb. 20–21, 1997.
  Includes bibliographical references and index.
  ISBN 0-226-24099-1 (cloth : alk. paper)
  1. Prices—Government policy—Congresses.   2. Price regulation—Congresses.   3. Monetary policy—Congresses.   4. Inflation (Finance)—Congresses.   I. Feldstein, Martin S.   II. Series: Conference report (National Bureau of Economic Research)
    HB236.A3 C63   1999
    338.5'26—dc21   98-43630
                                              CIP

Contents

Preface   ix

Introduction   1
Martin Feldstein

1.   **Capital Income Taxes and the Benefit of
Price Stability**   9
Martin Feldstein
Comment: Stanley Fischer
Discussion Summary

2.   **Price Stability versus Low Inflation in Germany:
An Analysis of Costs and Benefits**   47
Karl-Heinz Tödter and Gerhard Ziebarth

3.   **A Cost-Benefit Analysis of Going from Low
Inflation to Price Stability in Spain**   95
Juan J. Dolado, José M. González-Páramo,
and José Viñals

4.   **Some Costs and Benefits of Price Stability
in the United Kingdom**   133
Hasan Bakhshi, Andrew G. Haldane, and Neal Hatch
Comment (on chaps. 2, 3, and 4): Andrew B. Abel
Comment (on chaps. 2, 3, and 4): Rudiger Dornbusch
Discussion Summary (for chaps. 2, 3, and 4)

5.   **Inflation and the User Cost of Capital:**
            Does Inflation Still Matter?   199
            Darrel Cohen, Kevin A. Hassett,
            and R. Glenn Hubbard
            Comment: Alan J. Auerbach
            Discussion Summary

6.   **Excess Capital Flows and the Burden of Inflation**
            in Open Economies   235
            Mihir A. Desai and James R. Hines Jr.
            Comment: Jeffrey A. Frankel
            Discussion Summary

7.   **Identifying Inflation's Grease and Sand Effects**
            in the Labor Market   273
            Erica L. Groshen and Mark E. Schweitzer
            Comment: Laurence Ball
            Discussion Summary

8.   **Does Inflation Harm Economic Growth?**
            Evidence from the OECD   315
            Javier Andrés and Ignacio Hernando
            Comment: Frederic S. Mishkin
            Discussion Summary

            Contributors   349

            Author Index   351

            Subject Index   357

Preface

The success of the Federal Reserve and other countries' central banks during the past decade in lowering inflation to less than 3 percent in virtually every major industrial country now focuses attention on the appropriate monetary policy in a low-inflation environment. While there is widespread agreement within the economics profession and among policy officials that monetary policy should not permit the kinds of high inflation that characterized the 1970s in the United States and in many other industrial countries, there is much less agreement about the right long-run goal for monetary policy, about the price that a nation should be willing to pay to achieve that goal, and about the short-run actions to be taken in pursuit of that goal.

This volume is a research contribution to that ongoing discussion. It contains the papers prepared for an NBER project on the costs and benefits of going from the existing low rate of inflation to full price stability. The starting point for this project was a paper that I wrote for an earlier NBER project on inflation organized by Christina Romer and David Romer (chap. 3 in *Reducing Inflation: Motivation and Strategy,* ed. C. Romer and D. Romer [Chicago: University of Chicago Press, 1997]). That paper developed a framework for calculating the gains in economic welfare associated with going from 2 percent inflation to price stability and comparing those gains with the cost of disinflation.

An unusual feature of the current project was the decision to replicate the same analysis of the costs and benefits of reducing inflation in three other countries: Germany, Spain, and the United Kingdom. The central banks of each of those countries collaborated in the study with members of their staffs preparing the three country studies. I am grateful to those researchers and to the directors of economics at the central banks (Ottmar Issing of the Deutsche Bundesbank, José Viñals of the Bank of Spain, and Mervyn King of the Bank of England) for their interest and participation in this project. The researchers

met at the NBER during the project to review the details of the analysis and the specific assumptions that are needed to implement the comparative analysis in the separate countries. We were joined by Mihir Desai (Harvard University), Liam Ebrill (World Bank), James Hines (University of Michigan and NBER), Glenn Hubbard (Columbia University and NBER), Erzo Luttmer (Harvard University), and Torsten Persson (Stockholm). The discussions in this group also modified the framework developed in my earlier paper and helped to shape the research presented in the chapters in this volume by Desai and Hines and by Cohen, Hassett, and Hubbard.

The research papers were presented and discussed at an NBER conference held at the New York Federal Reserve Bank on 20–21 February 1997. The conference brought together a mixture of macroeconomists and public finance specialists with the expertise needed to discuss these complex issues on the border between macroeconomics, taxation, and welfare economics. The volume contains the discussants' prepared remarks and a brief summary of the general discussion of each paper prepared by Erzo Luttmer, a graduate student at Harvard.

I am grateful to Frederic Mishkin, then chief economist of the New York Federal Reserve Bank, and to William McDonough, president of the New York Federal Reserve Bank, for agreeing to host the conference at the New York Federal Reserve and for their participation in the conference itself.

Kirsten Foss Davis and the members of her conference department at the NBER provided their usual expert services in advance of the New York meeting. The staff of the New York Federal Reserve Bank provided excellent facilities and services. Norma MacKenzie in my office and Deborah Kiernan of the NBER publications department have guided the manuscript of this book. I am grateful to all of them.

Martin Feldstein

Introduction

Martin Feldstein

During the past decade, the United States and most of the countries of western Europe have experienced substantial declines in their rates of inflation. Since 1992, the annual rates of increase of consumer prices in the United States have been 3 percent or less. Inflation rates in many European countries and in Japan have been even lower.

But low inflation is not the same as price stability. The Federal Reserve and other central banks repeatedly state that "price stability" is their goal. Even allowing for measurement bias in the official inflation statistics, price stability would require a U.S. inflation rate as measured by the consumer price index (CPI) of 1 or 2 percent.

The issue for the Federal Reserve and other central banks is therefore whether to take steps to lower inflation even more until full price stability is achieved. Similarly, the central banks face the question of how to respond if an adverse price shock should raise the inflation rate from current levels to, say, 3.5 or 4 percent.

In keeping with our NBER tradition, the papers in this volume do not offer specific policy advice. Our goal is rather to provide information that can help policy officials at the Federal Reserve and others who are interested in this question to reach a more informed decision.[1]

There are of course many ways in which going from low inflation to full price stability confers benefits on an economy. The primary focus of the present volume is on the gains that would result from price stability because of the

Martin Feldstein is the George F. Baker Professor of Economics at Harvard University and president of the National Bureau of Economic Research.

1. For a recent discussion of the policy issues involved in setting price stability as a goal of monetary policy, see *Achieving Price Stability*, the 1996 annual conference of the Federal Reserve Bank of Kansas City. My own policy views are presented there in a brief statement (Feldstein 1997b).

interaction between inflation and the tax system. Even in the absence of inflation, the tax systems of the United States and western Europe cause losses of
economic efficiency by distorting individuals' choices between current and future consumption and by inducing overinvestment in owner-occupied housing.
These tax distortions are exacerbated by inflation; the higher the rate of inflation, the greater the tax bias against future consumption and the greater the tax
bias in favor of owner-occupied housing. Because inflation increases the existing tax distortions, the resulting welfare loss from even low rates of inflation
can be quite substantial. More formally, the deadweight losses that result from
inflation are not just "small triangles" (i.e., second-order effects) but are potentially much larger "trapezoids" (i.e., first-order losses of economic welfare).

The welfare gain from reducing the rate of inflation is a permanent one.
Indeed, because the welfare loss caused by inflation is proportional to the level
of GDP, the annual welfare gain from reducing inflation grows over time in
proportion to the growing level of GDP. In contrast, standard economic theory
implies that the cost of going from low inflation to price stability is the temporary cost of moving down the short-run Phillips curve. Because of this contrast
between the permanent gain and a temporary loss, even a relatively large temporary output loss incurred to reduce inflation can be more than offset by the
present value of the permanent and growing gain of lower inflation.

I first explored this contrast between the short-run cost of disinflation and
the permanent gain of lower inflation in a paper that focused just on the reduced distortion in the demand for money (Feldstein 1979). That paper emphasized that although the annual welfare gains from reducing the distortion in the
demand for money are very small, they can be enough to justify a large cost
of disinflation if the discount rate used to calculate the present value of the
future welfare gains is low enough.

Although I had written extensively on the interaction of taxes and inflation,[2]
it was only in 1996, as part of an NBER project organized by Christina and
David Romer, that I presented an analysis based on that research to evaluate
the welfare gain that would result from going from low inflation to price stability (see Feldstein 1997a). I found there that the gain associated with the tax-
inflation interaction is very much larger then the potential gain from reducing
the distortion in money demand. I estimated that going from a 2 percent rate
of inflation to price stability raises annual economic welfare by an amount
equal to about a 1 percent rise in real GDP. Even with a relatively high real
discount rate, the present value of this permanent and growing stream of welfare gains could substantially outweigh the output loss required to go from low
inflation to price stability.

This finding raised the important question of whether this relatively large
welfare gain from moving to price stability is a special feature of the U.S. tax
system or whether it would occur in other industrial countries, each with its

2. See my papers on this subject collected in Feldstein (1983).

own tax rules. If the potential tax-inflation gain that I had calculated is unique to the United States, it might be possible to achieve the same gain by shifting the U.S. tax system in the direction of the tax systems of other major countries. But if the tax-inflation interaction is a source of significant welfare loss in all countries, the prospect of limiting that loss by feasible tax reforms would be less promising. The potential gain from going from low inflation to price stability in other countries would of course also be important to the monetary authorities of those countries.

To explore this issue, I invited the Deutsche Bundesbank, the Bank of Spain, and the Bank of England to participate in an NBER project to refine and replicate my earlier analysis. The results of our combined efforts are presented in the first four chapters of this volume. These results show that differences in national tax rules do cause differences in the gain from disinflation but that in each country there would be a significant gain from shifting from 2 percent inflation to full price stability.

In their analysis of the German economy, Karl-Heinz Tödter and Gerhard Ziebarth found that the gain from reducing inflation by 2 percentage points was equivalent to a perpetuity of 1.4 percent of GDP, about 40 percent greater than the basic estimate for the United States. The difference is concentrated in the effect of the inflation-tax interaction on the timing of consumption. Although the complex differences between U.S. and German laws make it difficult to pinpoint the reason for the difference in welfare effects, I suspect that it is the higher marginal rate of tax in the German case that is the primary reason for the difference.

The Spanish analysis by Dolado, González-Páramo, and Viñals also found a larger gain from achieving price stability than the U.S. numbers imply. Their calculations imply that the gain from a 2 percentage point inflation reduction would be about 1.7 percent of GDP, about 70 percent more than the estimate for the United States. The principal source of the difference is the much higher deadweight loss associated with the increased demand for housing in Spain. According to those authors, this reflects the fact that in Spain the tax privileges associated with owner-occupied housing are quite generous and the size of the housing stock is also relatively large.

While the calculations for Britain also show a significant gain from reducing inflation, the gain is very much less than in the other countries, only about one-fifth of the U.S. value, or about 0.2 percent of GDP a year. This lower level of loss reflects the substantial differences between the tax systems of the United Kingdom and the other countries, particularly the ways in which U.K. investors can reduce the tax on investment income and the limited tax advantage of home mortgages. Britain indexes capital gains for inflation, eliminating one significant source of the tax-inflation interaction that penalizes postponed consumption. There are also many more opportunities for middle and upper income individuals to save in untaxed forms in Britain, implying that the tax-inflation interaction does not distort the timing of consumption for these individuals.

Finally, deductible mortgage borrowing is much more limited in Britain, reducing the effect of inflation on the tax subsidy to owner-occupied housing.[3]

My 1996 analysis had several potentially important omissions. Two of these gaps have been filled by papers in the current volume. Darrel Cohen, Kevin Hassett, and Glenn Hubbard have studied the effect of inflation on the net-of-tax profitability of different kinds of business assets: equipment versus structures and short-lived assets versus long-lived assets. They find that inflation raises the user cost of capital, thus exacerbating the distortion that the tax system would cause in the absence of inflation, but that the magnitude of the effect and the resulting welfare consequence are very small.

Mihir Desai and James Hines filled the second gap by extending the earlier analysis to an open economy with international capital flows. They show that in this context the tax-inflation interaction distorts international capital flows and that this extra dimension of behavior can cause the gain from achieving price stability to be substantially larger than it would be in a closed economy. In an important case that they examine, the gain from price stability would be about twice as large as it would be in a closed economy.

There are two further interrelated tax-inflation issues that remain to be examined: the effect of inflation on the debt-equity mix of household portfolios (since inflation raises the tax on debt relative to the tax on equity) and the effect of inflation on the financing mix of firms (since inflation lowers the cost of debt finance relative to the cost of equity finance). Although neither of these welfare effects is likely to be of the same order of magnitude as the issues assessed in the analyses that have been done, it would be desirable to explore these additional questions.

A more fundamental issue is the assumption that a shift to price stability changes the level of real GDP (including the change in deadweight losses) but does not alter the economy's rate of economic growth. There is substantial evidence that high rates of inflation (exceeding 10 percent per year) do reduce economic growth (Barro 1995; Bruno and Easterly 1995; Fischer 1993; Sarel 1996), but those studies have found no evidence that single-digit rates of inflation permanently affect the rate of economic growth. The paper in this volume by Andrés and Hernando analyzes the experience of OECD countries during a period of relatively low inflation and finds that even low inflation has an important negative temporary effect on the long-term growth rate; that is, it permanently lowers the level of real incomes (by reducing investment and the efficiency with which factor inputs are used). Their careful econometric analysis suggests that reducing the permanent rate of inflation by 1 percentage point

3. Although the study has been done with great care and attention to the details of the British tax system, there are unresolved issues about just how much of the favorable tax treatment of saving affects *marginal* saving. Because the saving incentives are subject to limits, many individuals may face the full tax rate at the margin even though they face lower average tax rates on investment income. Since the welfare effects depend on the marginal tax rates, the impact of lower inflation may be greater than the authors of this study calculate.

would permanently raise the level of real income by between 0.5 and 2.0 percent. This finding that there is a level effect but not a rate-of-growth effect is consistent with the assumption made in the analyses in the other papers. Although the Andrés-Hernando estimate seems substantially larger than the estimates obtained in the four country studies, it is important to bear in mind that they are looking at the level of income and not at the change in economic welfare. If each generation of individuals saves more when they are young, the capital stock will be permanently larger and real incomes higher. The utility gains to the individuals will, however, be less than the rise in income since they have accepted lower levels of consumption during their younger years to achieve this.

The studies in this volume also assume that the shift to price stability requires a temporary rise in unemployment but that price stability, once it is achieved, can be sustained without a permanently higher rate of unemployment, that is, that there is a short-run Phillips curve but that the long-run Phillips curve is vertical. This long-established conclusion about the nature of the inflation-unemployment relation has recently been challenged by Akerlof, Dickens, and Perry (1996), who believe that a downward-sloping long-run Phillips curve (associating higher unemployment with lower inflation) exists at very low rates of inflation because of the difficulty of achieving reductions in nominal wages. The essence of their argument is that the reductions in real wages for particular employees or firms that are occasionally needed to maintain employment can be achieved by reducing the rate of increase of nominal wages when there is moderate inflation but cannot be achieved when there is price stability because such real wage cuts would require lowering the level of nominal wages.

Since the United States has not yet experienced price stability, there is no way to test this directly. It is clear, however, that the recent experience with very low inflation provides no support for the Akerlof-Dickens-Perry view since very low inflation has been accompanied by low and declining rates of unemployment; in the five years since the rate of CPI inflation fell to 3 percent or less (i.e., since 1992) the unemployment rate has fallen from 7.5 percent to less than 5.0 percent.[4] One possible reason for this favorable relation is the finding of Groshen and Schweitzer (in chap. 7 of this volume) that reducing inflation decreases the kind of wage variability that makes labor markets less efficient at matching jobs and job seekers.

My own view is that the resistance to nominal wage reductions would gradu-

---

4. This experience should also raise questions about the possible importance of "hysteresis effects" in this context, i.e., the proposition that a "temporarily" higher rate of unemployment will become permanently higher because unemployment causes workers to lose their skills and their commitment to work. While this may be relevant in the context of Europe's high rates of unemployment and very long unemployment spells, in the United States with our much lower rates of unemployment and much shorter unemployment spells hysteresis effects seem much less likely a priori and are clearly not supported by the experience after the recession that ended in 1991.

ally disappear in a sustained period of price stability as such changes become more common. In addition, the current tendency to make bonuses a part of annual compensation even for lower paid workers provides a way of reducing total compensation by cutting the bonus without the psychologically more difficult action of reducing the individual's official wage rate.

There are of course other advantages of price stability that have not been explored in this volume. Price stability may bring a "credibility bonus" that allows the monetary authority to offset adverse inflation shocks with less loss of output. Price stability also makes financial planning easier, even for apparently sophisticated financial investors. These issues are discussed briefly in my own chapter in this volume.

Because of the importance of the tax-inflation interaction as a source of welfare loss, some participants in the conference suggested that the gain from price stability could be achieved by changing the tax law instead of by reducing inflation. Although the proposals for "fundamental tax reform" that would completely eliminate the personal and corporate income taxes and substitute taxes on wages or consumption would eliminate the distorting effects of inflation, such tax rules have not been enacted anywhere in the world and now show no sign of being adopted in the United States. Indexing all aspects of the measurement of taxable income (including capital gains, interest payments and receipts, and depreciation) for inflation would be another way to eliminate the current distorting effects of the tax-inflation interaction. But it is again noteworthy that no major industrial country has adopted such indexing.[5] In Feldstein (1997a, sec. 3.8) I discuss the technical, legal, and administrative reasons that are likely to prevent such comprehensive tax indexing from ever being enacted.

In any case, the Federal Reserve (and every other central bank) must decide how to conduct monetary policy and what inflation rate to seek. It does not have the option of changing the structure of the tax system. While economists may offer advice about ways in which the economy's performance can be improved by changes in labor market institutions, social insurance rules, and tax regulations, the central bank must make monetary policy in the institutional context that it finds.

There is finally the question of whether a negative rate of inflation would be better than price stability. The logic of the tax-inflation calculation implies that the welfare gain that would result from going from low inflation to price stability would be increased further by going to a negative inflation rate. Deciding whether that would be a desirable goal in practice would require balancing such tax-inflation gains against not only the costs associated with getting to

---

5. Although the influential chairman of the House Ways and Means Committee has long been an advocate of indexing capital gains and succeeded in getting such a provision incorporated into the 1997 tax bill passed by the House of Representatives, the strong opposition of the White House and the lack of strong support among Senate Republicans kept it from becoming part of the final 1997 tax legislation.

such a rate of disinflation but also the effect of a negative inflation rate on the quality of individual decision making, on the "credibility bonus" usually associated with price stability, and on the possible psychological effect of disinflation on managers and other investors.

For the past several years, the U.S. economy has been enjoying a remarkable combination of low inflation and low unemployment. There is clearly no public or political support at this time for a deliberate policy to increase the unemployment rate in order to reduce further the rate of inflation. Similarly, there is no support for a policy of deliberately raising the inflation rate in order to reduce unemployment. The Federal Reserve must nevertheless continue to focus on setting a goal for the long-term rate of inflation. More specifically, the members of the Federal Reserve's Open Market Committee should be asking themselves three kinds of questions, listed here in what may be the order of increasing difficulty: First, how should the Federal Reserve respond if some nonmonetary force causes a rise in inflation? Second, how should it respond if economic activity slows, pointing to a rise in unemployment and a further decline in inflation? And, third, what risk of excess tightening and resulting economic decline should the Federal Reserve be willing to take as it contemplates the probability that the current low rate of unemployment (now 4.9 percent) is below the level that is consistent with stable inflation? I hope that the studies presented in this volume will help the Federal Reserve (as well as other central banks) to deal with these questions.

References

Akerlof, George, William Dickens, and George Perry. 1996. The macroeconomics of low inflation. *Brookings Papers on Economic Activity*, no. 1: 1–59.

Barro, Robert. 1995. Inflation and economic growth. NBER Working Paper no. 5326. Cambridge, Mass.: National Bureau of Economic Research, October.

Bruno, Michael, and William Easterly. 1995. Inflation crises and long-run growth. NBER Working Paper no. 5209. Cambridge, Mass.: National Bureau of Economic Research, August.

Feldstein, Martin. 1979. The welfare cost of permanent inflation and optimal short-run economic policy. *Journal of Political Economy* 87 (4):749–68.

———. 1983. *Inflation, tax rules, and capital formation*. Chicago: University of Chicago Press.

———. 1997a. The costs and benefits of going from low inflation to price stability. In *Reducing inflation: Motivation and strategy*, ed. C. Romer and D. Romer, 123–56. Chicago: University of Chicago Press.

———. 1997b. Price stability. In *Achieving price stability*. Kansas City: Federal Reserve Bank of Kansas City.

Fischer, Stanley. 1993. The role of macroeconomic factors in growth. *Journal of Monetary Economics* 32:485–512.

Sarel, Michael. 1996. Nonlinear effects of inflation on economic growth. *IMF Staff Papers* 43:199–215.

1 Capital Income Taxes and the Benefit of Price Stability

Martin Feldstein

The fundamental policy question of whether to go from a low inflation rate to price stability requires comparing the short-run cost of disinflation with the permanent gain that results from a sustained lower rate of inflation. Since that permanent gain is proportional to the level of GDP in each future year, the real value of the annual gain grows through time at the rate of growth of real GDP.[1]

If this growing stream of welfare gains is discounted by a risk-based discount rate like the net rate of return on equities, the present value of the future gain is equal to the initial annual value of the net gain (G) divided by the difference between the appropriate discount rate (r) and the growth rate of total GDP (g): thus $PV = G/(r - g)$. With a value of r equal to 5.1 percent (the real net-of-tax rate of return on the Standard & Poor's portfolio of equities from 1970 to 1994) and a projected growth rate of 2.5 percent, the present value of the gain is equal to almost 40 times the initial value of the gain.[2]

Martin Feldstein is the George F. Baker Professor of Economics at Harvard University and president of the National Bureau of Economic Research.

The current paper builds on my earlier study "The Costs and Benefits of Going from Low Inflation to Price Stability," which was distributed as NBER Working Paper no. 5469 and published in C. Romer and D. Romer, eds., *Reducing Inflation: Motivation and Strategy* (Chicago: University of Chicago Press, 1997). I am grateful for comments on the earlier paper and for discussions about the current work with participants in the 1997 NBER conference, *Reducing Inflation,* to the authors of papers in the current project who served as members of the project working group, and to Erzo Luttmer and Larry Summers.

1. This assumes that going from low inflation to price stability does not permanently affect the rate of economic growth. The unemployment and output loss associated with achieving a lower rate of inflation were discussed in section 3.2 of Feldstein (1997). That analysis assumed that there is a short-run Phillips curve but not a long-run Phillips curve. Both of those assumptions have been called into question and will be discussed in more detail in papers in this volume. I present my own view of this controversy in the introduction to this volume.

2. In an earlier analysis of the gain from reducing inflation (Feldstein 1979), I noted that with a low enough discount rate the present value of the gain would increase without limit as the time horizon was extended.

The analysis developed below implies that the annual gain that would result from reducing inflation from 2 percent to zero would be equal to between about 0.76 percent of GDP and 1.04 percent of GDP. The present value of this gain would therefore be between 30 and 40 percent of the initial level of GDP. The evidence cited in Ball (1994) implies that inflation could be reduced from 2 percent to zero with a one-time output loss of about 6 percent of GDP. Although these estimates of the benefits and costs are subject to much uncertainty, the difference between benefits and costs leaves little doubt that the aggregate present value benefit of achieving price stability substantially exceeds its cost.

The paper begins by estimating the magnitude of the two major favorable components of the annual net gain that would result if the true inflation rate were reduced from 2 percent to zero:[3] (1) the reduced distortion in the timing of consumption and (2) the reduced distortion in the demand for owner-occupied housing. Each of these calculations explicitly recognizes not only that the change in inflation alters household behavior but also that it alters tax revenue. Those revenue effects are important because any revenue gain from lower inflation permits a reduction in other distortionary taxes while any revenue loss from lower inflation requires an increase in some other distortionary tax.[4]

Even a small reduction of inflation (from 2 percent to zero) can have a substantial effect on economic welfare because inflation increases the tax-induced distortions that would exist even with price stability. The deadweight loss associated with 2 percent inflation is therefore not the traditional "small triangle" that would result from distorting a first-best equilibrium but is the much larger "trapezoid" that results from increasing a large initial distortion.

These adverse effects of the tax-inflation interaction could in principle be eliminated by indexing the tax system or by shifting from our current system of corporate and personal income taxes to a tax based only on consumption or labor income. As a practical matter, however, such tax reforms are extremely unlikely. Section 3.8 of Feldstein (1997) discusses some of the difficulties of shifting to an indexed tax system in which capital income and expenses are measured in real terms. Although such a shift has been advocated for at least two decades, there has been no legislation along those lines.[5] It is significant, moreover, that no industrial country has fully (or even substantially) indexed its taxation of investment income. Moreover, the annual gains from shifting to price stability that are identified in this paper exceed the costs of the transition

3. I assume that the official measure of the rate of inflation overstates the true rate by 2 percentage points. The text thus evaluates the gain of going from a 4 percent rate of increase of the consumer price index (CPI) to a 2 percent rate of increase.

4. Surprisingly, such revenue effects are generally ignored in welfare analyses on the implicit assumption that lost revenue can be replaced by lump-sum taxes.

5. Most recently, the indexing of capital gains was strongly supported by the Republican majority in the House of Representatives in the 1997 tax legislation but was opposed with equal vigor by the White House and was not part of the final legislation.

within a very few years. Even if one could be sure that the tax-inflation distortions would be eliminated by changes in the tax system 10 years from now, the present value gain from price stability until then would probably exceed the cost of the inflation reduction.

There are also some countervailing disadvantages of having price stability rather than continuing a low rate of inflation. The primary advantage of inflation that has been identified in the literature is the seigniorage that the government enjoys from the higher rate of money creation. This seigniorage revenue reduces the need for other distortionary taxes and therefore eliminates the deadweight loss that such taxes would entail. This seigniorage gain in money creation must of course be measured net of the welfare loss that results from the distortion in money demand. In addition, the real cost of servicing the national debt varies inversely with the rate of inflation (because the government bond rate rises point for point with inflation but the inflation premium is then subject to tax). Both of these effects are explicitly taken into account in the calculations presented in this paper.

As I noted in the introduction to this volume, there are several papers in this volume that go beyond the original analysis of Feldstein (1997). The paper by Cohen, Hassett, and Hubbard presented in chapter 5 estimates how reducing inflation affects the efficiency of business's choices among different types of capital investments (structures and equipment of different durabilities). The paper by Desai and Hines (chap. 6) shows how the closed economy analysis of this paper can be extended to an open economy with flows of trade and capital. The study by Groshen and Schweitzer (chap. 7) discusses the behavior of the labor market at low inflation, and the research by Andrés and Hernando (chap. 8) examines the effect of reducing inflation on the sustained rate of growth.

Absolute price stability, as opposed to merely a lower rate of inflation, may bring a qualitatively different kind of benefit. A history of price stability may bring a "credibility bonus" in dealing with inflationary shocks. People who see persistent price level stability expect that it will persist in the future and that the government will respond to shocks in a way that maintains the price level. In contrast, if people see that the price level does not remain stable, they may have less confidence in the government's ability or willingness to respond to inflation shocks in a way that maintains the initial inflation rate. If so, any given positive demand shock may lead to more inflation and may require a greater output loss to reverse than would be true in an economy with a history of stable prices.

A stable price level is also a considerable convenience for anyone making financial decisions that involve future receipts and payments. While economists may be very comfortable with the process of converting nominal to real amounts, many people have a difficult time thinking about rates of change, real rates of interest, and the like. Even among sophisticated institutional investors, it is remarkable how frequently projections of future returns are stated in nomi-

Table 1.1   **Net Welfare Effect of Reducing Inflation from 2 Percent to Zero (changes as percent of GDP)**

Source of Change	Direct Effect of Reduced Distortion (1)	Welfare Effect of Revenue Change		Total Effect	
		$\lambda = 0.4$ (2)	$\lambda = 1.5$ (3)	$\lambda = 0.4$ (4)	$\lambda = 1.5$ (5)
Consumption timing					
$\eta_{sr} = 0.4$	**1.02**	−0.07	−0.26	**0.95**	**0.76**
$\eta_{sr} = 0$	0.73	−0.17	−0.64	−0.56	0.08
$\eta_{sr} = 1.0$	1.44	0.09	0.33	1.53	1.77
Housing demand	0.10	0.12	0.45	0.22	0.55
Money demand	0.02	−0.05	−0.19	−0.03	−0.17
Debt service	n.a.	−0.10	−0.38	−0.10	−0.38
Total					
$\eta_{sr} = 0.4$	**1.14**	−0.10	−0.38	**1.04**	**0.76**
$\eta_{sr} = 0$	0.85	−0.20	−0.76	0.65	0.08
$\eta_{sr} = 1.0$	1.56	0.06	0.21	1.62	1.77

Note: A 2 percent inflation rate corresponds to a rise in the CPI at 4 percent a year. The welfare effects reported here are annual changes in welfare. n.a.: not applicable.

nal terms and based on past experience over periods with very different rates of inflation.

I will not attempt to evaluate these benefits of reducing inflation even though some of them may be as large as the gains that I do measure. For the United States, the restricted set of benefits that I quantify substantially exceed (in present value at any plausible discount rate) the cost of getting to price stability from a low rate of inflation.

Table 1.1 summarizes the four types of welfare changes that are discussed in the remaining sections of the paper. The specific assumptions and parameter values will be discussed there. With the parameter values that seem most likely, the overall total effect of reducing inflation from 2 percent to zero, shown in the lower right-hand corner of the table, is to reduce the annual deadweight loss by between 0.76 percent of GDP and 1.04 percent of GDP.

1.1   Inflation and the Intertemporal Allocation of Consumption

Inflation reduces the real net-of-tax return to savers in many ways. At the corporate (or, more generally, the business) level, inflation reduces the value of depreciation allowances and therefore increases the effective tax rate. This lowers the rate of return that businesses can afford to pay for debt and equity capital. At the individual level, taxes levied on nominal capital gains and nominal interest also cause the effective tax rate to increase with the rate of inflation.

A reduction in the rate of return that individuals earn on their saving creates

a welfare loss by distorting the allocation of consumption between the early years in life and the later years. Since the tax law creates such a distortion even when there is price stability, the extra distortion caused by inflation causes a first-order increased deadweight loss.

As I emphasized in an earlier paper (Feldstein 1978), the deadweight loss that results from capital income taxes depends on the resulting distortion in the timing of consumption and not on the change in saving per se. Even if there is no change in saving (i.e., no reduction in consumption during working years), a tax-inflation-induced decline in the rate of return implies a reduction in future consumption and therefore a deadweight loss. The current section calculates the general magnitude of the reduction in this welfare loss that results from lowering the rate of inflation from 2 percent to zero.[6]

To analyze the deadweight loss that results from a distortion of consumption over the individual life cycle, I consider a simple two-period model of individual consumption. Individuals receive income when they are young. They save a portion, S, of that income and consume the rest. The savings are invested in a portfolio that earns a real net-of-tax return of r. At the end of T years, the individuals retire and consume $C = (1 + r)^T S$. In this framework, saving can be thought of as expenditure (when young) to purchase retirement consumption at a price of $p = (1 + r)^{-T}$.

Even in the absence of inflation, the effect of the tax system is to reduce the rate of return on saving and therefore to increase the price of retirement consumption. As inflation increases, the price of retirement consumption increases further. Before looking at specific numerical values, I present graphically the welfare consequences of these changes in the price of retirement consumption. Figure 1.1 shows the individual's compensated demand for retirement consumption C as a function of the price of retirement consumption at the time that saving decisions are made (p).

In the absence of both inflation and taxes, the real rate of return implies a price of p_0, and the individual chooses to save enough to generate retirement consumption of C_0. With no inflation, the existing structure of capital income taxes at the business and individual levels raises the price of retirement consumption to p_1 and reduces retirement consumption to C_1. This increase in the price of retirement consumption causes the individual to incur the deadweight loss shown as the shaded area A; that is, the amount that the individual would have to be compensated for the rise in the price of retirement consumption in order to remain at the same initial utility level exceeds the revenue collected by the government by an amount equal to the area A. Raising the rate of inflation from zero to 2 percent increases the price of retirement consumption to p_2

---

6. Fischer (1981) used the framework of Feldstein (1978) to assess the deadweight loss caused by the effect of inflation on the return to savers. As the current analysis indicates, the problem is more complex than either Fischer or I recognized in those earlier studies.

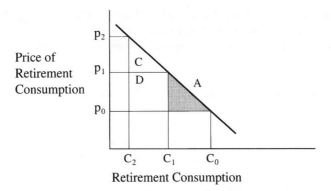

$$\Delta \text{ DWL} = (p_1 - p_0)(C_1 - C_2) + 0.5 \, (p_2 - p_1)(C_1 - C_2)$$
$$\Delta \text{ REV} = (p_1 - p_0)(C_1 - C_2) - (p_2 - p_1) \, C_2$$

Fig. 1.1   Retirement consumption

and reduces retirement consumption to C_2. The deadweight loss now increases by the trapezoidal area

$$C + D = (p_1 - p_0)(C_1 - C_2) + 0.5(p_2 - p_1)(C_1 - C_2).$$

The revenue effect of such tax changes are generally ignored in welfare analyses because it is assumed that any loss or gain in revenue can be offset by a lump-sum tax or transfer. More realistically, however, we must recognize that offsetting a revenue change due to a change in inflation involves distortionary taxes and therefore each dollar of revenue gain or loss has an additional effect on overall welfare. The net welfare effect of reducing the inflation rate from 2 percent to zero is therefore the combination of the traditional welfare gain (the trapezoid $C + D$) and the welfare gain (loss) that results from an increase (decrease) in tax revenue. I begin by evaluating the traditional welfare gain and then calculate the additional welfare effect of the changes in tax revenue.

1.1.1   Welfare Gain from Reduced Intertemporal Distortion

The annual welfare gain from reduced intertemporal distortion is

$$(p_1 - p_0)(C_1 - C_2) + 0.5(p_2 - p_1)(C_1 - C_2)$$
$$= [(p_1 - p_0) + 0.5(p_2 - p_1)](C_1 - C_2).$$

The change in retirement consumption can be approximated as

$$C_1 - C_2 = (dC/dp)(p_1 - p_2) = C_2(p_2/C_2)(dC/dp)(p_1 - p_2)/p_2$$
$$= C_2 \varepsilon_{Cp}[(p_1 - p_2)/p_2],$$

where $\varepsilon_{Cp} < 0$ is the compensated elasticity of retirement consumption with respect to its price (as evaluated at the observed initial inflation rate of 2 percent). Thus the gain from reduced intertemporal distortion is[7]

$$
(1) \quad \begin{aligned} G_1 &= [(p_1 - p_0) + 0.5(p_2 - p_1)]C_2\varepsilon_{Cp}[(p_1 - p_2)/p_2] \\ &= [(p_1 - p_0)/p_2 + 0.5(p_2 - p_1)/p_2]p_2C_2\varepsilon_{Cp}[(p_1 - p_2)/p_2]. \end{aligned}
$$

Note that if there were no tax-induced distortion when the inflation rate is zero ($p_1 = p_0$), G_1 would simplify to the traditional triangle formula for the deadweight loss of a price change from p_1 to p_2.

To move from equation (1) to observable magnitudes, note that the compensated elasticity ε_{Cp} can be written in terms of the corresponding uncompensated elasticity η_{Cp} and the propensity to save out of exogenous income σ as[8]

$$
(2) \quad \varepsilon_{Cp} = \eta_{Cp} + \sigma.
$$

Moreover, since saving and retirement consumption are related by $S = pC$, the elasticity of retirement consumption with respect to its price and the elasticity of saving with respect to the price of retirement consumption are related by $\eta_{Cp} = \eta_{Sp} - 1$. Thus

$$
(3) \quad \varepsilon_{Cp} = \eta_{Sp} + \sigma - 1
$$

and

$$
(4) \quad G_t = [(p_1 - p_0)/p_2 + 0.5(p_2 - p_4)/p_2][(p_2 - p_1)/p_2]S_2(1 - \eta_{Sp} - \sigma),
$$

where $S_2 = p_2C_2$, the gross saving of individuals at the early stage of the life cycle.

To evaluate equation (4) requires numerical estimates of the price of future consumption at different inflation rates and without any tax, as well as estimates of gross saving, of the saving elasticity, and of the propensity to save out of exogenous income.

Inflation Rates and the Price of Retirement Consumption

To calculate the price of retirement consumption, I assume the time interval between saving and consumption is 30 years; for example, the individual saves on average at age 45 and then dissaves at age 75. Thus $p = (1 + r)^{-30}$, where the value of r depends on the tax system and the rate of inflation. From 1960 through 1994, the pretax real return to capital in the U.S. nonfinancial corpo-

---

7. This could be stated as the difference between the areas of the two deadweight loss triangles corresponding to prices p_1 and p_2, but the expression used here presents a better approximation.

8. This follows from the usual Slutsky decomposition: $dC/dp = (dC/dp)_{COMP} - C (dC/dy)$, where dC/dy is the increase in retirement consumption induced by an increase in exogenous income. Multiplying each term by p/C and noting that $p(dC/dy) = dp C/dy = dS/dy = \sigma$ yields eq. (2).

rate sector averaged 9.2 percent.[9] Ignoring general equilibrium effects and taking this as the measure of the discrete-time return per year that would prevail in the absence of taxes implies that the corresponding price of retirement consumption is $p_0 = (1.092)^{-30} = 0.071$.[10]

Taxes paid by corporations to federal, state, and local governments equaled about 41 percent of the total pretax return during this period, leaving a real net return before personal taxes of 5.4 percent (Rippe 1995). I will take this yield difference as an indication of the combined effects of taxes and inflation at 2 percent (i.e., measured inflation at 4 percent) even though tax rules, tax rates, and inflation varied over this 35-year interval.[11] The net-of-tax rate of return depends not only on the tax at the corporate level but also on the taxes that individuals pay on that after-corporate-tax return, including the taxes on interest income, dividends, and capital gains. The effective marginal tax rate depends on the form of the income and on the tax status of the individual. I will summarize all of this by assuming a marginal "individual" tax rate of 25 percent. This reduces the net return from 5.4 to 4.05 percent. The analysis of the gain from reducing the equilibrium rate of inflation is not sensitive to the precise level of this return or the precise difference between it and the 9.2 percent pretax return since our concern is with the effect of a difference in inflation rates on effective tax rates. Similarly, the precise level of the initial effective tax rate is not important to the current calculations since our concern is with the change in the effective tax rate that occurs as a result of the change in

9. This 9.2 percent is the ratio of profits before all taxes (including property taxes as well as income taxes) plus real net interest payments to the replacement value of the capital stock. Feldstein, Poterba, and Dicks-Mireaux (1983) describe the method of calculation, and Rippe (1995) brings the calculation up to date. Excluding property taxes would reduce this return by about 0.7 percentage points; see Poterba and Samwick (1995).

10. An increase in the capital stock would depress the marginal product of capital (ρ) from its currently assumed value of 0.092. That means a smaller gain from the reduced intertemporal distortion. The effect, however, is so small that given the approximations used throughout the analysis, it does not seem worth taking this into account. The following calculation shows that with an elasticity of saving with respect to the real interest rate of 0.4 (i.e., $\eta_{sr} = 0.4$) and a Cobb-Douglas technology, the marginal product of capital only falls from 0.092 to 0.089.

To see this, note that (as shown later in the text) the net return to savers at 2 percent inflation when the pretax yield is 9.2 percent is $0.4425(0.092) = 0.0407$. The analysis in the text also shows that reducing inflation to zero raises the net return to $0.4425\rho + 0.0049$, where ρ is the marginal product of capital at the higher saving rate.

If the saving rate (s) is a constant elasticity function of the expected net real return equal to 0.4, then $s_1/s_0 = [(0.4425\rho + 0.0049)/0.0407]^{0.4}$, where s_1 is the saving rate with price stability and s_0 is the saving rate at a 2 percent rate of inflation.

A Cobb-Douglas technology implies $y = k^b$ and therefore that $\rho = bk^{b-1}$. In long-run equilibrium, $sy = nk$, where s is the saving rate and n is the growth of population and technology. Thus $\rho = bns^{-1}$. More specifically, the observed marginal product of capital is 0.092 and satisfies $0.092 = bns_0^{-1}$ while $\rho = bns_1^{-1}$ defines the marginal product of capital with the saving rate that prevails when there is price stability.

It follows that $0.092/\rho = s_1/s_0 = [(0.4425\rho + 0.0049)/0.0407]^{0.4}$. Solving this gives $\rho = 0.0889$, or only about 3 percent below the value of 0.092 with the initial capital stock. Even with a saving response elasticity of 1, the marginal product of capital is 0.0866.

11. The average rate of measured inflation during this period was actually 4.7 percent, implying an average "true" inflation rate of 2.7 percent.

the equilibrium rate of inflation.[12] The price of retirement consumption that corresponds to this net return of 4.05 percent is $p_2 = (1.0405)^{-30} = 0.304$, where the subscript 2 on the price indicates that this represents the price at an inflation rate of 2 percent.

Reducing the equilibrium inflation rate from 2 percent to zero lowers the effective tax rate at both the corporate and individual levels. At the corporate level, changes in the equilibrium inflation rate alter the effective tax rate by changing the value of depreciation allowances and by changing the value of the deduction of interest payments. Because the depreciation schedule that is allowed for calculating taxable profits is defined in nominal terms, a higher rate of inflation reduces the present value of the depreciation and thereby increases the effective tax rate.[13] Auerbach (1978) showed that this relation can be approximated by a rule of thumb that increases taxable profits by 0.57 percentage points for each percentage point of inflation. With a marginal corporate income tax rate of 35 percent, a 2 percentage point decline in inflation raises the net-of-tax return through this channel by $0.35(0.57)(0.02) = 0.0040$, or 0.40 percentage points.[14]

The interaction of the interest deduction and inflation moves the after-tax yield in the opposite direction. If each percentage point of inflation raises the nominal corporate borrowing rate by 1 percentage point,[15] the real pretax cost of borrowing is unchanged but the corporation gets an additional deduction in calculating taxable income. With a typical debt-capital ratio of 40 percent and a statutory corporate tax rate of 35 percent, a 2 percent decline in inflation raises the effective tax rate by $0.35(0.40)(0.02) = 0.0028$, or 0.28 percentage points.

The net effect of going from a 2 percent inflation rate to price stability is therefore to raise the rate of return after corporate taxes by 0.12 percentage points, from the 5.40 percent calculated above to 5.52 percent.[16]

12. Some explicit sensitivity calculations are presented below.

13. See Feldstein, Green, and Sheshinski (1978) for an analytic discussion of the effect of inflation on the value of depreciation allowances.

14. It might be argued that Congress changes depreciation rates in response to changes in inflation in order to keep the real present value of depreciation allowances unchanged. But although Congress did enact more rapid depreciation schedules in the early 1980s, the decline in inflation since that time has not been offset by lengthening depreciation schedules and has resulted in a reduction in the effective rate of corporate income taxes.

15. This famous Irving Fisher hypothesis of a constant real interest rate is far from inevitable in an economy with a complex nonneutral tax structure. E.g., if the only nonneutrality were the ability of corporations to deduct nominal interest payments and all investment were financed by debt at the margin, the nominal interest rate would rise by $1/(1 - \tau)$ times the change in inflation, where τ is the statutory corporate tax rate. This effect is diminished, however, by the combination of historic cost depreciation, equity finance, international capital flows, and the tax rules at the level of the individual (see Feldstein 1983, 1994; Hartman 1979). Despite the theoretical ambiguity, the evidence suggests that these various tax rules and investor behavior interact in practice in the United States to keep the real pretax rate of interest approximately unchanged when the rate of inflation changes (see Mishkin 1992).

16. Note that although the margin of uncertainty about the 5.5 percent exceeds the calculated change in return of 0.12 percent, the conclusions of the current analysis are not sensitive to the precise level of the initial 5.5 percent rate of return.

Consider next how the lower inflation rate affects taxes at the individual level. Applying the 25 percent tax rate to the 5.52 percent return net of the corporate tax implies a net yield of 4.14 percent, an increase of 0.09 percentage points in net yield to the individual because of the changes in taxation at the corporate level. In addition, because individual income taxes are levied on nominal interest payments and nominal capital gains, a reduction in the rate of inflation further reduces the effective tax rate and raises the real after-tax rate of return.

The portion of this relation that is associated with the taxation of nominal interest at the level of the individual can be approximated in a way that parallels the effect at the corporate level. If each percentage point of inflation raises the nominal interest rate by 1 percentage point, the individual investor's real pretax return on debt is unchanged but the after-tax return falls by the product of the statutory marginal tax rate and the change in inflation. Assuming the same 40 percent debt share at the individual level as I assumed for the corporate capital stock[17] and a 25 percent weighted average individual marginal tax rate implies that a 2 percentage point decline in inflation lowers the effective tax rate by $0.25(0.40)(0.02) = 0.0020$, or 0.20 percentage points.

Although the effective tax rate on the dividend return to the equity portion of individual capital ownership is not affected by inflation (except, of course, at the corporate level), a higher rate of inflation increases the taxation of capital gains. Although capital gains are now taxed at the same rate as other investment income (up to a maximum capital gain rate of 28 percent at the federal level), the effective tax rate is lower because the tax is only levied when the stock is sold. As an approximation, I will therefore assume a 10 percent effective marginal tax rate on capital gains. In equilibrium, each percentage point increase in the price level raises the nominal value of the capital stock by 1 percentage point. Since the nominal value of the liabilities remains unchanged, the nominal value of the equity rises by $1/(1 - b)$ percentage points, where b is the debt-capital ratio. With $b = 0.4$ and an effective marginal tax on nominal capital gains of $\theta_g = 0.1$, a 2 percentage point decline in the rate of inflation raises the real after-tax rate of return on equity by $\theta_g[1/(1 - b)]d\pi = 0.0033$, or 0.33 percentage points. However, since equity represents only 60 percent of the individual's portfolio, the lower effective capital gains tax raises the overall rate of return by only 60 percent of this 0.33 percentage points, or 0.20 percentage points.[18]

Combining the debt and capital gains effects implies that reducing the inflation rate by 2 percentage points reduces the effective tax rate at the individual investor level by the equivalent of 0.40 percentage points. The real net return

17. This ignores individual investments in government debt. Bank deposits backed by noncorporate bank assets (e.g., home mortgages) can be ignored as being within the household sector.
18. The assumption that the share of debt in the individual's portfolio is the same as the share of debt in corporate capital causes the $1/(1 - b)$ term to drop out of the calculation. More generally, the effect of inflation on the individual's rate of return depends on the difference between the shares of debt in corporate capital and in the individual's portfolio.

to the individual saver is thus 4.54 percent, up 0.49 percentage points from the return when the inflation rate is 2 percentage points higher. The implied price of retirement consumption is $p_1 = (1.0454)^{-30} = 0.264$.

Substituting these values for the price of retirement consumption into equation (4) implies[19]

$$(5) \qquad G_t = 0.092S_2(1 - \eta_{Sp} - \sigma).$$

Saving Rates and Saving Behavior

The value of S_2 in equation (5) represents saving during preretirement years at the existing rate of inflation. This is, of course, different from the national income account measure of personal saving since personal saving is the difference between the saving of younger savers and the dissaving of retired dissavers.

One strategy for approximating the value of S_2 is to use the relation between S_2 and the national income account measure of personal saving in an economy in steady state growth. In the simple overlapping generations model with saving proportional to income, saving grows at a rate of $n + g$, where n is the rate of population growth and g is the growth in per capita wages. This implies that the saving of young savers is $(1 + n + g)^T$ times the dissaving of older dissavers.[20]

Thus net personal saving (S_N) in the economy is related to the saving of the young (S_y) according to

$$(6) \qquad S_N = S_y - (1 + n + g)^{-T}S_y.$$

The value of S_2 that we need is conceptually equivalent to S_y. Real aggregate wage income grew in the United States at a rate of 2.6 percent between 1960 and 1994. Using $n + g = 0.026$ and $T = 30$ implies that $S_y = 1.86S_N$. If we take personal saving to be approximately 5 percent of GDP,[21] this implies that $S_2 = 0.09\text{GDP}$.[22]

19. To test the sensitivity of this result to the assumption about the pretax return and the effective corporate tax rate, I recalculated the retirement consumption prices using alternatives to the assumed values of 9.2 percent for the pretax return and 0.41 for the combined effective corporate tax rate. Raising the pretax rate of return from 9.2 to 10 percent only changed the deadweight loss value in eq. (5) from 0.092 to 0.096; lowering the pretax rate of return from 9.2 to 8.4 percent lowered the deadweight loss value to 0.090. Increasing the effective corporate tax rate from 0.41 to 0.50 with a pretax return of 9.2 only shifted the deadweight loss value in eq. (5) from 0.092 to 0.096. These calculations confirm that the effect of changing the equilibrium inflation rate is not sensitive to the precise values assumed for the pretax rate of return and the effective baseline tax rate.

20. Note that the spending of older retirees includes both the dissaving of their earlier savings and the income that they have earned on their savings. Net personal saving is only the difference between the saving of savers and the dissaving of dissavers.

21. Some personal saving is of course exempt from personal income taxation, particularly savings in the form of pensions, individual retirement accounts, and life insurance. What matters, however, for deadweight loss calculations is the full volume of saving and not just the part of it that is subject to current taxes. Equivalently, the deadweight loss of any distortionary tax depends on the marginal tax rate, even if some of the consumption of the taxed good is exempt from tax or is taxed at a lower rate.

22. This framework can be extended to recognize that the length of the work period is roughly twice as long as the length of the retirement period without appreciably changing this result.

If the propensity to save out of exogenous income (σ) is the same as the propensity to save out of wage income, $\sigma = S_2/(\alpha * \text{GDP})$, where α is the share of wages in GDP. With $\alpha = 0.75$, this implies $\sigma = 0.12$.

The final term to be evaluated in order to calculate the welfare gain described in equation (5) is the elasticity of saving with respect to the price of retirement consumption. Since the price of retirement consumption is given by $p = (1 + r)^{-T}$, the uncompensated elasticity of saving with respect to the price of retirement consumption can be restated as an elasticity with respect to the real rate of return: $\eta_{Sr} = -rT\eta_{Sp}/(1 + r)$. Thus equation (5) becomes

(7) $$G_1 = 0.092S_2[1 + (1 + r)\eta_{Sr}/rT - \sigma].$$

Estimating the elasticity of saving with respect to the real net rate of return has proved to be very difficult because of the problems involved in measuring changes in expected real net-of-tax returns and in holding constant in the time-series data the other factors that affect saving. The large literature on this subject generally finds that a higher real rate of return either raises the saving rate or has no effect at all.[23] In their classic study of the welfare costs of U.S. taxes, Ballard, Shoven, and Whalley (1985) assumed a saving elasticity of $\eta_{Sr} = 0.40$. I will take this as the benchmark value for the current study. In this case, equation (7) implies (with $r = 0.04$)

(8)
$$G_1 = 0.092S_2[1 + (1 + r)\eta_{Sr}/rT - \sigma]$$
$$= 0.092(0.09)(1 + 0.42/1.2 - 0.12)\text{GDP} = 0.0102\text{GDP}.$$

The annual gain from reduced distortion of consumption is equal to 1.02 percent of GDP. This figure is shown in the first row of table 1.1.

To assess the sensitivity of this estimate to the value of η_{Sr}, I will also examine two other values. The limiting case in which changes in real interest rates have no effect on saving, that is, in which $\eta_{Sr} = 0$, implies[24]

(9)
$$G_1 = 0.092S_2[1 + (1 + r)\eta_{Sr}/rT - \sigma]$$
$$= 0.092(0.09)(1 - 0.12)\text{GDP} = 0.0073\text{GDP},$$

that is, an annual welfare gain equal to 0.73 percentage points of GDP.

If we assume instead that $\eta_{Sr} = 1.0$, that is, that increasing the real rate of return from 4.0 to 4.5 percent (the estimated effect of dropping the inflation rate from 2 percent to zero) raises the saving rate from 9 to 10.1 percent, the welfare gain is $G_1 = 0.0144\text{GDP}$.

These calculations suggest that the traditional welfare effect on the timing of consumption of reducing the inflation rate from 2 percent to zero is probably

23. See among others Blinder (1975), Boskin (1978), Evans (1983), Feldstein (forthcoming), Hall (1988), Makin (1987), Mankiw (1987), and Wright (1969).

24. This is a limiting case in the sense that empirical estimates of η_{Sr} are almost always positive. In theory, of course, it is possible that $\eta_{Sr} < 0$.

bounded between 0.73 percent of GDP and 1.44 percent of GDP. These figures are shown in the second and third rows of table 1.1.

1.1.2   Revenue Effects of a Lower Inflation Rate Causing a Lower Effective Tax on Investment Income

As I noted earlier, the traditional assumption in welfare calculations and the one that is implicit in the calculation of subsection 1.1.1 is that any revenue effect can be offset by lump-sum taxes and transfers. When this is not true, as it clearly is not in the U.S. economy, an increase in tax revenue has a further welfare advantage because it permits reduction in other distortionary taxes while a loss of tax revenue implies a welfare cost of using other distortionary taxes to replace the lost revenue. The present subsection calculates the effect on tax revenue paid by the initial generation of having price stability rather than a 2 percent inflation rate and discusses the corresponding effect on economic welfare.

Reducing the equilibrium rate of inflation raises the real return to savers and therefore reduces the price of retirement consumption. The effect of this on government revenue depends on the change in retirement consumption. Calculating how the higher real net return on saving affects tax revenue requires estimating how individuals respond to the higher return. In particular, it requires deciding whether the individuals look ahead and take into account the fact that the government will have to raise some other revenue (or reduce spending) to offset the lower revenue collected on the income from savings.

I believe that the most plausible specification assumes that individuals recognize the real after-tax rate of return that they face but that those individuals do not take into account the fact that the government will in the future have to raise other taxes to offset the revenue loss that results from the lower effective tax on investment income. They in effect act as if "someone else" (the next generation?) will pay the tax to balance the loss of tax revenue that results from the lower inflation rate. This implies that the response of saving that is used to calculate the revenue effect of lower inflation should be the uncompensated elasticity of saving with respect to the net rate of return (η_{sr}).[25]

At the initial level of retirement consumption, reducing the price of future consumption from p_2 to p_1 reduces revenue (evaluated as of the initial time) by $(p_2 - p_1)C_2$. If the fall in the price of retirement consumption causes retirement consumption to increase from C_2 to C_1, the government collects additional revenue equal to $(p_1 - p_0)(C_1 - C_2)$. Even if $C_2 < C_1$, the overall net effect on revenue, $(p_1 - p_0)(C_1 - C_2) - (p_2 - p_1)C_2$, can in theory be either positive or negative.

In the present case, the change in revenue can be calculated as

25. If individuals believed that they face a future tax liability to replace the revenue that the government loses because of the decline in the effective tax rate, the saving response would be estimated by using the compensated elasticity. This was the assumption made in the earlier version of these calculations presented in Feldstein (1997).

$$d\text{REV} = (p_1 - p_0)(C_1 - C_2) - (p_2 - p_1)C_2$$

(10)
$$= (p_1 - p_0)(dC/dp)(p_1 - p_2) - (p_2 - p_1)C_2$$

$$= (p_1 - p_0)(p_1 - p_2)(dC/dp)(p_2/C_2)(C_2/p_2) - (p_2 - p_1)C_2$$

$$= (p_1 - p_0)(p_1 - p_2)\eta_{Cp}(C_2/p_2) - (p_2 - p_1)C_2.$$

Replacing $p_2 C_2$ by S_2 and recalling from equation (3) that $\eta_{Cp} = \eta_{Sp} - 1$ yields

(11) $d\text{REV} = S_2\{[(p_1 - p_0)/p_2][(p_2 - p_1)/p_2](1 - \eta_{Sp}) - (p_2 - p_1)/p_2\}.$

Substituting the prices derived in the previous section ($p_0 = 0.071$, $p_1 = 0.264$, and $p_2 = 0.304$) implies

(12)
$$d\text{REV} = S_2[0.0836(1 - \eta_{Sp}) - 0.1316]$$

$$= \{0.0836[1 + (1 + r)\eta_{Sr}/rT] - 0.1316\}.$$

The benchmark case of $\eta_{Sr} = 0.4$ implies $d\text{REV} = -0.019S_2$ or, with $S_2 = 0.09\text{GDP}$ as derived above, $d\text{REV} = -0.0017\text{GDP}$.

The limiting case of $\eta_{Sr} = 0$ implies $d\text{REV} = -0.0043\text{GDP}$, while $\eta_{Sr} = 1.0$ implies $d\text{REV} = 0.0022\text{GDP}$.

Thus, depending on the elasticity of saving with respect to the rate of interest, the revenue effect of shifting from 2 percent inflation to price stability can be either negative or positive.

1.1.3   Welfare Gain from the Effects of Reduced Inflation on Consumption Timing

We can now combine the traditional welfare gain (G_1 of eqs. [8] and [9]) with the welfare consequences of the revenue change ($d\text{REV}$ of eqs. [11] and [12]). If each dollar of revenue that must be raised from other taxes involves a deadweight loss of λ, the net welfare gain of shifting from 2 percent inflation to price stability is

(13a) $G_2 = (0.0102 - 0.0017\lambda)\text{GDP}$ if $\eta_{Sr} = 0.4$.

Similarly,

(13b) $G_2 = (0.0073 - 0.0043\lambda)\text{GDP}$ if $\eta_{Sr} = 0$,

and

(13c) $G_2 = (0.0144 + 0.0022\lambda)\text{GDP}$ if $\eta_{Sr} = 1.0$.

The value of λ depends on the change in taxes that is used to adjust to changes in revenue. Ballard et al. (1985) used a computable general equilibrium model to calculate the effect of increasing all taxes in the same proportion and concluded that the deadweight loss per dollar of revenue was between 30

and 55 cents, depending on parameter assumptions. I will represent this range by $\lambda = 0.40$. Using this implies that the net welfare gain of reducing inflation from 2 percent to zero equals 0.95 percent of GDP in the benchmark case of $\eta_{S_r} = 0.4$. The welfare effect of reduced revenue (-0.07 percent of GDP) is shown in column (2) of table 1.1 and the combined welfare effect of 0.95 percent of GDP is shown in column (4) of table 1.1.

In the two limiting cases, the net welfare gains corresponding to $\lambda = 0.4$ are 0.56 percent of GDP with $\eta_{S_r} = 0$ and 1.53 percent of GDP with $\eta_{S_r} = 1.0$. These are shown in the second and third rows of column (4) of table 1.1.

The analysis of Ballard et al. (1985) estimates the deadweight loss of higher tax rates on the basis of the distortion in labor supply and saving. No account is taken of the effect of higher tax rates on tax avoidance through spending on deductible items or receiving income in nontaxable forms (fringe benefits, nicer working conditions, etc.). In a recent paper (Feldstein 1995a), I showed that these forms of tax avoidance as well as the traditional reduction of earned income can be included in the calculation of the deadweight loss of changes in income tax rates by using the compensated elasticity of taxable income with respect to the net-of-tax rate. Based on an analysis of the experience of high-income taxpayers before and after the 1986 tax rate reductions, I estimated that elasticity to be 1.04 (Feldstein 1995b). Using this elasticity in the NBER TAXSIM model, I then estimated that a 10 percent increase in all individual income tax rates would cause a deadweight loss of about \$44 billion at 1994 income levels; since the corresponding revenue increase would be \$21 billion, the implied value of λ is 2.06.

A subsequent study (Feldstein and Feenberg 1996) based on the 1993 tax rate increases suggests a somewhat smaller compensated elasticity of about 0.83 instead of the 1.04 value derived in the earlier study. Although this difference may reflect the fact that the 1993 study is based on the experience during the first year only, I will be conservative and assume a lower deadweight loss value of $\lambda = 1.5$.

With $\lambda = 1.5$, equations (13a), (13b), and (13c) imply a wider range of welfare gain estimates: reducing inflation from 2 percent to zero increases the annual level of welfare by 0.63 percent of GDP in the benchmark case of $\eta_{S_r} = 0.4$. With $\eta_{S_r} = 0$ the net effect is a very small gain of 0.08 percent of GDP, while with $\eta_{S_r} = 1.0$ the net effect is a substantial gain of 1.77 percent of GDP. These values are shown in columns (3) and (5) of table 1.1.

These are of course just the annual effects of inflation on savers' intertemporal allocation of consumption. Before turning to the other effects of inflation, it is useful to say a brief word about nonsavers.

1.1.4   Nonsavers

A striking fact about American households is that a large fraction of households have no financial assets at all. Almost 20 percent of U.S. households with heads aged 55 to 64 had no net financial assets at all in 1991, and 50 percent

of U.S. households had assets under $8,300; these figures exclude mortgage obligations from financial liabilities.

The absence of substantial savings does not imply that individuals are irrational or unconcerned with the need to finance retirement consumption. Since social security benefits replace more than two-thirds of after-tax income for a worker who has had median lifetime earnings and many employees can anticipate private pension payments in addition to social security, the absence of additional financial assets may be consistent with rational life cycle behavior. For these individuals, zero savings represents a constrained optimum.[26]

In the presence of private pensions and social security, the shift from low inflation to price stability may cause some of these households to save, and that increase in saving may increase their welfare and raise total tax revenue. Since the calculated welfare gain that I reported earlier in this section is proportional to the amount of saving by preretirement workers, it ignores the potential gain to current nonsavers.

Although the large number of nonsavers and their high aggregate income imply that this effect could be important, I have no way to judge how the increased rate of return would actually affect behavior. I therefore leave this out of the calculations, only noting that it implies that my estimate of the gain from lower inflation is to this extent undervalued.

1.1.5   Relation between Observed Saving Behavior and the Compensated Elasticity

Subsection 1.1.1 estimates the compensated elasticity of demand for retirement consumption with respect to its price in terms of forgone preretirement consumption (ε_{C_p}) from the relation between the "observable" elasticity of saving with respect to the net-of-tax rate (η_{S_r}) and the value of ε_{C_p} implied by utility theory in a life cycle model. More specifically, the analysis uses a life cycle model in which income is received in the first period of life and is used to finance consumption during those years and during retirement.

This is of course not equivalent to assuming that all income is received at the *beginning* of the working years. The assumption in the calculations is that the time between the receipt of earnings and the time when retirement consumption takes place is $T = 30$ years, essentially treating income as if it occurs in the middle of the working life at age 45 and dissaving as if it occurs in the middle of the retirement years at age 75. These may be reasonable approximations to the "centers of gravity" of these life cycle phases.

It can be argued, however, that many individuals also receive a significant amount of exogenous income during retirement (social security benefits) and

---

26. The observed small financial balances of such individuals may be precautionary balances or merely transitory funds that will soon be spent. It would be desirable to refine the calculations of this section to recognize that some of the annual national income account savings are for precautionary purposes. Since there is no satisfactory closed-form expression relating the demand for precautionary saving to the rate of interest, I have not pursued that calculation further.

that taking this into account changes the relation between the "observed" η_{Sr} and the implied value of ε_{Cp}. In thinking about this, it is important to think about the group in the population that generates the deadweight losses that we are calculating. This group excludes those who do no private saving and depend just on their social security retirement benefits to finance retirement consumption. More generally, in deciding on the importance of social security benefits relative to retirement consumption (the key parameter in the adjustment calculation that follows), we should think about a "weighted average" with weights proportional to the amount of regular saving that the individuals do. This implies a much lower value of benefits relative to retirement consumption than would be obtained by an unweighted average for the population as a whole. I have not done such a calculation but think that an estimate of social security benefits being 25 percent of total retirement consumption may be appropriate for this purpose.

To see how this would affect the results, we use the basic Slutsky equation $\varepsilon_{Cp} = \eta_{Cp} + \sigma$ (where ε_{Cp} is the compensated elasticity of retirement consumption with respect to its price in terms of forgone consumption during working years, η_{Cp} is the corresponding uncompensated elasticity, and σ is the propensity to save) and the retirement period budget constraint $C = S/p + B$ (where C is the retirement consumption, S is the saving during working years, p is the price of retirement consumption in terms of forgone consumption during the working years, and B is social security benefits). Taking derivatives of the retirement period budget constraint with respect to the price of retirement consumption implies $[(C - B)/C]\eta_{Sp} = \eta_{Cp} + [(C - B)/C]$.[27]

Combining this with the Slutsky equation implies $\varepsilon_{Cp} = [(C - B)/C](\eta_{Sp} - 1) + \sigma$. Shifting from the price elasticity to the interest rate elasticity using $\eta_{Sp} = -(1 + r)\eta_{Sr}/rT$ leads finally to

$$-\varepsilon_{Cp} = [(C - B)/C][(1 + r)\eta_{Sr}/rT + 1] - \sigma.$$

To see how taking this exogenous income into account alters the implied estimate of ε_{Cp}, consider the following values based on the standard assumptions that $r = 0.04$, $T = 30$, and $\sigma = 0.12$:

| | Implied Value of $-\varepsilon_{Cp}$ | |
Benefit-Consumption Ratio	$\eta_{Sr} = 0$	$\eta_{Sr} = 0.4$
Zero	0.88	1.227
0.25	0.6	0.89

Thus the assumption that the individual receives exogenous income during retirement that finances 25 percent of retirement consumption reduces the implied value of the compensated elasticity of demand by about one-fourth.

27. When there are no social security benefits, this reduces to the familiar relation $\eta_{Sp} = \eta_{Cp} + 1$.

Table 1.2   **Net Welfare Effect of Reducing Inflation with Exogenous Retirement Income (changes as percent of GDP)**

Source of Change	Direct Effect of Reduced Distortion	Welfare Effect of Revenue Change		Total Effect	
		$\lambda = 0.4$	$\lambda = 1.5$	$\lambda = 0.4$	$\lambda = 1.5$
Total					
$\eta_{Sr} = 0.4$	**0.86**	-0.10	-0.38	**0.76**	**0.48**
$\eta_{Sr} = 0$	0.64	-0.20	-0.76	0.44	-0.12
$\eta_{Sr} = 1.0$	1.18	0.06	0.21	1.24	1.39

Note: Calculations relate to reducing inflation from 2 percent to price stability (i.e., from a 4 percent annual increase in the CPI to a 2 percent annual increase). Exogenous retirement income is 25 percent of retirement consumption among the relevant group of individual savers.

This reduces the implied welfare gain in one category of table 1.1, the "direct effect of reduced consumption distortion." To see the magnitude of this reduction, rewrite equation (7) as

$$(7')\qquad G_1 = 0.092 S_2\{[(C - B)/C][1 + (1 + r)\eta_{Sr}/rT] - \sigma\}.$$

With $B/C = 0.25$ and $\eta_{Sr} = 0.4$, this implies $G_1 = 0.0074\text{GDP}$ instead of the value of 0.0102GDP obtained for $B = 0$. Similarly, with $\eta_{Sr} = 0$ the value of G_1 declines from 0.0073GDP to 0.0052GDP, while with $\eta_{Sr} = 1$ the decline is from 0.0144GDP to 0.0106GDP. These results are summarized in table 1.2, which corresponds to the three summary lines at the bottom of table 1.1.

1.2   Inflationary Distortion of the Demand for Owner-Occupied Housing

Owner-occupied housing receives special treatment under the personal income tax. Mortgage interest payments and local property taxes are deducted, but no tax is imposed on the implicit "rental" return on the capital invested in the property. This treatment would induce too much consumption of housing services even in the absence of inflation.[28]

Inflation reduces the cost of owner-occupied housing services in two ways. The one that has been the focus of the literature on this subject (e.g., Rosen 1985) is the increased deduction of nominal mortgage interest payments. Since the real rate remains unchanged while the tax deduction increases, the subsidy increases and the net cost of housing services declines. In addition, inflation increases the demand for owner-occupied housing by reducing the return on investments in the debt and equity of corporations.

Reducing the rate of inflation therefore reduces the deadweight loss that

28. This section benefits from the analysis in Poterba (1984, 1992) but differs from the framework used there in a number of ways.

results from excessive demand for housing services. In addition, a lower inflation rate reduces the loss of tax revenue; if raising revenue involves a deadweight loss, this reduction in the loss of tax revenue to the housing subsidy provides an additional welfare gain.

1.2.1   Welfare Gain from Reduced Distortion of Housing Consumption

In the absence of taxes, the implied rental cost of housing per dollar of housing capital (R_0) reflects the opportunity cost of the resources:

$$(14) \qquad\qquad R_0 = \rho + m + \delta,$$

where ρ is the real return on capital in the nonhousing sector, m is the cost of maintenance per dollar of housing capital, and δ is the rate of depreciation. With $\rho = 0.092$ (the average pretax real rate of return on capital in the nonfinancial corporate sector between 1960 and 1994), $m = 0.02$, and $\delta = 0.02$,[29] $R_0 = 0.132$; the rental cost of owner-occupied housing would be 13.2 cents per dollar of housing capital.

Consider in contrast the corresponding implied rental cost per dollar of housing capital under the existing tax rules for a couple who itemize their tax return:

$$(15) \quad RI = \mu(1 - \theta)i_m + (1 - \mu)(r_n + \pi) + (1 - \theta)\tau_p + m + \delta - \pi,$$

where RI is the rental cost of an itemizer, μ is the ratio of the mortgage to the value of the house, θ is the marginal income tax rate, i_m is the interest rate paid on the mortgage, r_n is the real net rate of return available on portfolio investments, τ_p is the rate of property tax,[30] m and δ are as defined above, and π is the rate of inflation (assumed to be the same for goods in general and for house prices). This equation says that the annual cost of owning a dollar's worth of housing is the sum of the net-of-tax mortgage interest payments $\mu(1 - \theta)i_m$ plus the opportunity cost of the equity invested in the house $(1 - \mu)(r_n + \pi)$ plus the local property tax reduced by the value of the corresponding tax deduction $(1 - \theta)\tau_p$ plus the maintenance m and depreciation δ less the inflationary gain on the property π.

In 1991, the year for which other data on housing used in this section were derived, the rate on conventional mortgages was $i_m = 0.072$ and the rate of inflation was $\pi = 0.01$.[31] The assumption that $di_m/d\pi = 1$ implies that i_m would be 0.082 at an inflation rate of $\pi = 0.02$.[32] Section 1.1 derived a value of $r_n = 0.0405$ for the real net return on a portfolio of debt and equity securities when

---

29. These values of m and δ are from Poterba (1992).
30. Following Poterba (1992) I assume that $\tau_p = 0.025$.
31. The CPI rose by 3.1 percent from December 1990 to December 1991, implying a "true" inflation rate of 1.1 percent. While previous rates were higher, subsequent inflation rates have been lower.
32. The assumption that $di_m/d\pi = 1$ is the same assumption made in section 1.1. See n. 15 above for the reason that I use this approximation.

$\pi = 0.02$. With a typical mortgage-to-value ratio among itemizers of $\mu = 0.5$,[33] a marginal tax rate of $\theta = 0.25$, a property tax rate of $\tau_p = 0.025$, $m = 0.02$, and $\delta = 0.02$, the rental cost per dollar of housing capital for an itemizer when the inflation rate is 2 percent is $RI_2 = 0.0998$. Thus the combination of the tax rules and a 2 percent inflation rate reduces the rental cost from 13.2 cents per dollar of housing capital to 9.98 cents per dollar of housing capital.

Consider now the effect of a decrease in the rate of inflation on this implicit rental cost of owner-occupied housing:

$$(16) \quad dRI/d\pi = \mu(1 - \theta)di_m/d\pi + (1 - \mu)d(r_n + \pi)/d\pi - 1.$$

Section 1.1 showed that if each percentage point increase in the rate of inflation raises the rate of interest by 1 percentage point, the real net rate of return on a portfolio of corporate equity and debt decreases from $r_n = 0.0454$ at $\pi = 0$ to $r_n = 0.0405$ at $\pi = 0.02$; that is, $dr_n/d\pi = -0.245$ and $d(r_n + \pi)/d\pi = 0.755$. Thus with $\theta = 0.25$, $dRI/d\pi = 0.75\mu + 0.755(1 - \mu) - 1$. For an itemizing homeowner with a mortgage-to-value ratio of $\mu = 0.5$, $dRI/d\pi = -0.25$. Since $RI_2 = 0.0998$ at 2 percent inflation, $dRI/d\pi = -0.25$ implies that $RI_1 = 0.1048$ at zero inflation. The lower rate of inflation implies a higher rental cost per unit of housing capital and therefore a smaller distortion.

Before calculating the deadweight loss effects of the reduced inflation, it is necessary to derive the corresponding expressions for homeowners who do not itemize their deductions. For such nonitemizers mortgage interest payments and property tax payments are no longer tax deductible, implying that[34]

$$(17) \quad RN = \mu i_m + (1 - \mu)(r_n + \pi) + \tau_p + m + \delta - \pi.$$

The parametric assumptions made for itemizers, modified only by assuming a lower mortgage-to-value ratio among nonitemizers of $\mu = 0.2$, implies $RN_2 = 0.1098$ and $RN_1 = 0.1137$. Both values are higher than the corresponding values for itemizers, but both imply substantial distortions that are reduced when the rate of inflation declines from 2 percent to zero.

Figure 1.2 shows the nature of the welfare gain from reducing inflation for taxpayers who itemize. The figure presents the compensated demand curve relating the quantity of housing capital demanded to the rental cost of such housing. With no taxes, $R_0 = 0.132$ and the amount of housing demanded is H_0. The combination of the existing tax rules at zero inflation reduces the rental cost to $R_1 = 0.1048$ and increases housing demand to H_1. Since the real pretax

33. The relevant μ ratio is not that on new mortgages or on the overall stock of all mortgages but on the stock of mortgages of itemizing taxpayers. The Balance Sheets for the U.S. Economy indicate that the ratio of home mortgage debt to the value of owner-occupied real estate increased to 43 percent in 1994. I use a higher value to reflect the fact that not all homeowners are itemizers and that those who do itemize are likely to have higher mortgage-to-value ratios. The results of this section are not sensitive to the precise level of this parameter.

34. This formulation assumes that taxpayers who do not itemize mortgage deductions do not itemize at all and therefore do not deduct property tax payments. Some taxpayers may in fact itemize property tax deductions even though they no longer have a mortgage.

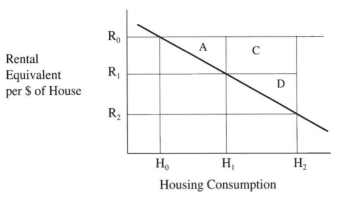

Fig. 1.2 Homeownership investment

cost of providing housing capital is R_0, the tax-inflation combination implies a deadweight loss shown by area A, that is, the area between the cost of providing the additional housing and the demand curve. A rise in inflation to 2 percent reduces the rental cost of housing further to $R_2 = 0.0998$ and increases the demand for housing to H_2. The additional deadweight loss is the area C + D between the real pretax cost of providing the increased housing and the value to the users as represented by the demand curve.

Thus the reduction in the deadweight loss that results from reducing the distortion to housing demand when the inflation rate declines from 2 percent to zero is

$$(18) \qquad G_3 = (R_0 - R_1)(H_2 - H_1) + 0.5(R_1 - R_2)(H_2 - H_1).$$

With a linear approximation,

$$
\begin{aligned}
(19) \qquad G_3 &= (R_0 - R_1)(dH/dR)(R_2 - R_1) \\
&\quad + 0.5(R_1 - R_2)(dH/dR)(R_2 - R_1) \\
&= -(R_2/H_2)(dH/dR)\{[(R_0 - R_1)/R_2][(R_1 - R_2)/R_2] \\
&\quad + 0.5(R_1 - R_2)^2 R_2^{-2}\}R_2 H_2.
\end{aligned}
$$

Writing $\varepsilon_{HR} = -(R_2/H_2)(dH/dR)$ for the absolute value of the compensated elasticity of housing demand with respect to the rental price (at the observed values of R_2 and H_2) and substituting the rental values for an itemizing taxpayer yields

$$
\begin{aligned}
(20) \qquad GI_3 &= \varepsilon_{HR}[(0.273)(0.050) + 0.5(0.050)^2]RI_2 HI_2 \\
&= 0.0149\varepsilon_{HR} RI_2 HI_2.
\end{aligned}
$$

A similar calculation for nonitemizing homeowners yields

(21) $$GN_3 = 0.0065\varepsilon_{HR} RN_2 HN_2.$$

Combining these two equations on the assumption that the compensated elasticities of demand are the same for itemizers and nonitemizers gives the total welfare gain from the reduced distortion of housing demand that results from reducing equilibrium inflation from 2 percent to zero:

(22) $$G_3 = \varepsilon_{HR}(0.0149 RI_2 HI_2 + 0.0065 RN_2 HN_2).$$

Since the calculations of the rental rates take into account the mortgage-to-value ratios, the relevant measures of HI_2 and HN_2 are the total market values of owner-occupied housing of itemizers and nonitemizers. In 1991, there were 60 million owner-occupied housing units and 25 million taxpayers who itemized mortgage deductions.[35] Since the total 1991 value of owner-occupied real estate of $6,440 billion includes more than just single-family homes (e.g., two-family homes and farms), I take the value of owner-occupied homes (including the owner-occupiers' portion of two-family homes) to be $6,000 billion. The Internal Revenue Service reported that tax revenue reductions in 1991 due to mortgage deductions were $42 billion, implying approximately $160 billion of mortgage deductions and therefore about $2,000 billion of mortgages. The mortgage-to-value ratio among itemizers of 0.5 implies that the market value of housing owned by itemizers is $HI_2 = \$4,000$ billion. This implies that the value of housing owned by nonitemizers is $HN_2 = \$2,000$ billion.

Substituting these estimates into equation (22), with $RI_2 = 0.0998$ and $RN_2 = 0.1098$, implies that

(23) $$G_3 = \$7.4\varepsilon_{HR} \text{ billion.}$$

Using Rosen's (1985) estimate of $\varepsilon_{HR} = 0.8$ implies that this gain from reducing the inflation rate is $5.9 billion at 1991 levels. Since 1991 GDP was $5,723 billion, this gain is 0.10 percent of GDP.

1.2.2 Revenue Effects of Lower Inflation on the Subsidy to Owner-Occupied Housing

The G_3 gain is based on the traditional assumption that changes in tax revenue do not affect economic welfare because they can be offset by other lump-sum taxes and transfers. The more realistic assumption that increases in tax revenue permit reductions in other distortionary taxes implies that it is important to calculate also the reduced tax subsidy to housing that results from a lower rate of inflation.

The magnitude of the revenue change depends on the extent to which the

---

35. The difference between these two figures reflects the fact that many homeowners do not itemize mortgage deductions (because they have such small mortgages that they benefit more from using the standard deduction or have no mortgage at all) and that many homeowners own more than one residence.

reduction in inflation shifts capital from owner-occupied housing to the business sector. To estimate this I use the compensated elasticity of housing with respect to the implicit rental value,[36] $\varepsilon_{HR} = 0.8$. The 5 percent increase in the rental price of owner-occupied housing for itemizers from $RI_2 = 0.0998$ at $\pi = 0.02$ to $RI_1 = 0.1048$ at zero inflation implies a 4 percent decline in the equilibrium stock of owner-occupied housing, from \$4,000 billion to \$3,840 billion (at 1991 levels). Similarly, for nonitemizers, the 3.6 percent increase in the rental price from $RN_2 = 0.1098$ at $\pi = 0.02$ to $RN_1 = 0.1137$ at zero inflation implies a 2.9 percent decline in their equilibrium stock of owner-occupied housing, from \$2,000 billion to \$1,942 billion (at 1991 levels).

Consider first the reduced subsidy on the \$3,840 billion of remaining housing stock owned by itemizing taxpayers. Maintaining the assumption of a mortgage-to-value ratio of 0.5 implies total mortgages of \$1,920 billion on this housing capital. The 2 percentage point decline in the rate of inflation reduces mortgage interest payments by \$38.4 billion and, assuming a 25 percent marginal tax rate, increases tax revenue by \$9.6 billion.

The shift of capital from owner-occupied housing to the business sector affects revenue in three ways. First, itemizers lose the mortgage deduction and property tax deduction on the \$160 billion of reduced housing capital. The reduced capital corresponds to mortgages of \$80 billion and, at the initial inflation rate of 2 percent, mortgage interest deductions of 8.2 percent of this \$80 billion, or \$6.6 billion. The reduced stock of owner-occupied housing also reduces property tax deductions by 2.5 percent of \$160 billion of forgone housing, or \$4 billion. Combining these two reductions in itemized deductions (\$10.6 billion) and applying a marginal tax rate of 25 percent implies a revenue gain of \$2.6 billion.

Second, the increased capital in the business sector (\$160 billion from itemizers plus \$58 billion from nonitemizers) earns a pretax return of 9.2 percent but provides a net-of-tax yield to investors of only 4.54 percent when the inflation rate is zero. The difference is tax collections of 4.66 percent on the additional \$218 billion of business capital, or \$10.2 billion of additional revenue.

Third, the reduced housing capital causes a loss of property tax revenue equal to 2.5 percent of the \$218 billion reduction in housing capital, or \$5.4 billion.

Combining these three effects on revenue implies a net revenue gain of \$16.9 billion, or 0.30 percent of GDP (at 1991 levels).

---

36. The use of the compensated elasticity is a conservative choice in the sense that the uncompensated elasticity would imply that reduced inflation causes a larger shift of capital out of housing and therefore a larger revenue gain for the government. The compensated elasticity is appropriate because other taxes are adjusted concurrently to keep total revenue constant. This is different from the revenue effect of the tax on saving where the revenue loss takes place in the future and can plausibly be assumed to be ignored by taxpayers at the earlier time when they are making their consumption and saving decisions.

1.2.3   Welfare Gain from the Housing Sector Effects
of Reduced Equilibrium Inflation

The total welfare gain from the effects of lower equilibrium inflation on the housing sector is the sum of (1) the traditional welfare gain from the reduced distortion to housing consumption, 0.10 percent of GDP, and (2) the welfare consequences of the $16.9 billion revenue gain, a revenue gain of 0.30 percent of GDP. If each dollar of revenue raised from other taxes involves a deadweight loss of λ, this total welfare gain of shifting from 4 percent inflation to 2 percent inflation is

$$(24) \qquad G_4 = (0.0010 + 0.0030\lambda)GDP.$$

The conservative Ballard et al. (1985) estimate of $\lambda = 0.4$ implies that the total welfare gain of reducing inflation from 2 percent to zero is 0.22 percent of GDP. With the value of $\lambda = 1.5$ implied by the behavioral estimates for the effect of an across-the-board increase in all personal income tax rates, the total welfare gain of reducing inflation from 2 percent to zero is 0.55 percent of GDP. These are shown in row 4 of table 1.1.

Before combining this with the gain from the change in the taxation of savings and comparing the sum to the cost of reducing inflation, I turn to two other ways in which a lower equilibrium rate of inflation affects economic welfare through the government's budget constraint.

1.3   Seigniorage and the Distortion of Money Demand

An increase in inflation raises the cost of holding non-interest-bearing money balances and therefore reduces the demand for such balances below the optimal level. Although the resulting deadweight loss of inflation has been the primary focus of the literature on the welfare effects of inflation since Bailey's (1956) pioneering paper, the effect on money demand of reducing the inflation rate from 2 percent to zero is small relative to the other effects that have been discussed in this paper.[37]

This section follows the framework of sections 1.1 and 1.2 by looking first at the distortion of demand for money and then at the revenue consequences of the inflation "tax" on the holding of money balances.

---

37. Although the annual effect is extremely small, it is a perpetual effect. As I argued in Feldstein (1979), in a growing economy a perpetual gain of even a very small fraction of GDP may outweigh the cost of reducing inflation if the appropriate discount rate is low enough relative to the rate of aggregate economic growth. In the context of the current paper, however, the welfare effect of the reduction in money demand is very small relative to the welfare effects that occur because of the interaction of inflation and the tax laws.

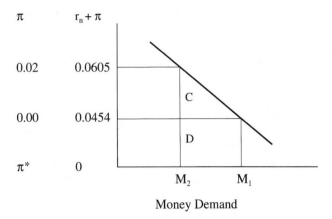

Fig. 1.3   **Money demand and seigniorage**

1.3.1   Welfare Effects of Distorting the Demand for Money

As Milton Friedman (1969) has noted, since there is no real cost to increasing the quantity of money, the optimal inflation rate is such that it completely eliminates the cost to the individual of holding money balances; that is, the inflation rate should be such that the nominal interest rate is zero. In an economy with no taxes on capital income, the optimal inflation rate would therefore be the negative of the real rate of return on capital: $\pi^* = -\rho$. More generally, if we recognize the existence of taxes, the optimal inflation rate is such that the nominal after-tax return on alternative financial assets is zero.

Recall that at $\pi = 0.02$ the real net return on the debt-equity portfolio is $r_n = 0.0405$ and that $dr_n/d\pi = -0.245$. The optimal inflation rate in this context is such that $r_n + \pi = 0.$[38] Figure 1.3 illustrates the reduction in the deadweight loss that results if the inflation rate is reduced from $\pi = 0.02$ to zero, thereby reducing the opportunity costs of holding money balances from $r_n + \pi = 0.0605$ to the value of r_n at $\pi = 0$, that is, $r_n = 0.0454$. Since the opportunity cost of supplying money is zero, the welfare gain from reducing inflation is the area $C + D$ between the money demand curve and the zero opportunity cost line:

(25)
$$
\begin{aligned}
G_5 &= 0.0454(M_1 - M_2) + 0.5(0.0605 - 0.0454)(M_1 - M_2) \\
&= 0.0530(M_1 - M_2) \\
&= -0.0530[dM/d(r_n + \pi)](0.0151) \\
&= 0.00080\varepsilon_M M(r_n + \pi)^{-1},
\end{aligned}
$$

38. If $dr_n/d\pi$ remains constant, the optimal rate of inflation is $\pi^* = -0.060$. Although this assumption of linearity may not be appropriate over the entire range, the basic property that $r_n > \pi^* > -\rho$ is likely to remain valid in a more exact calculation, reflecting the interaction between taxes and inflation.

where ε_M is the elasticity of money demand with respect to the nominal opportunity cost of holding money balances and $r_n + \pi = 0.0605$.

Since the demand deposit component of M1 is now generally interest bearing, non-interest-bearing money is now essentially currency plus bank reserves. In 1994, currency plus reserves were 6.1 percent of GDP. Thus $M = 0.061\text{GDP}$. There is a wide range of estimates of the elasticity of money demand, corresponding to different definitions of money and different economic conditions. An estimate of $\varepsilon_M = 0.2$ may be appropriate in the current context with money defined as currency plus bank reserves.[39] With these assumptions, $G_5 = 0.00016\text{GDP}$. Thus, even when Friedman's standard for the optimal money supply is used, the deadweight loss due to the distorted demand for money balances is only 0.0002GDP.

1.3.2   Revenue Effects of Reduced Money Demand

The decline in inflation affects government revenue in three ways. First, the reduction in the inflation "tax" on money balances results in a loss of seigniorage and therefore an associated welfare loss of raising revenue by other distortionary taxes (Phelps 1973). In equilibrium, inflation at rate π implies revenue equal to πM. Increasing the inflation rate raises the seigniorage revenue by

$$d\text{Seigniorage}/d\pi = M + \pi(dM/d\pi)$$

$$(26) \qquad\qquad = M + \pi[dM/d(r_n + \pi)][d(r_n + \pi)/d\pi]$$

$$\qquad\qquad = M\{1 - \varepsilon_M[d(r_n + \pi)/d\pi]\pi(r_n + \pi)^{-1}\}.$$

With $M = 0.061\text{GDP}$, $\varepsilon_M = 0.2$, $d(r_n + \pi)/d\pi = 0.755$, $\pi = 0.02$, and $r_n + \pi = 0.0605$, equation (26) implies that $d(\text{Seigniorage})/d\pi = 0.058\text{GDP}$. A decrease of inflation from $\pi = 0.02$ to $\pi = 0$ causes a loss of seigniorage of 0.116 percent of GDP.

The corresponding welfare loss is 0.116λ percent of GDP. With $\lambda = 0.4$, the welfare cost of the lost seigniorage is 0.046 percent of GDP. With $\lambda = 1.5$, the welfare cost of the lost seigniorage is 0.174 percent of GDP.

The second revenue effect is the revenue loss that results from shifting capital to money balances from other productive assets. The decrease in business capital is equal to the increase in the money stock, $M_1 - M_2 = [dM/d(r_n + \pi)](0.0151) = 0.0151\varepsilon_M M(r_n + \pi)^{-1} = 0.30$ percent of GDP. When these assets are invested in business capital, they earn a real pretax return of 9.2

---

39. In Feldstein (1979) I assumed an elasticity of one-third for non-interest-bearing M1 deposits. I use the lower value now to reflect the fact that non-interest-bearing money is now just currency plus bank reserves. These are likely to be less interest sensitive than the demand deposit component of M1. The assumption that $\varepsilon_M = 0.2$ when the opportunity cost of holding money balances is approximately 0.06 implies that a 1 percentage point increase in $r_n + \pi$ reduces M by approximately $0.2(0.01)/0.06 = 0.033$, a semielasticity of 3.3. Since the Cagan (1953) estimates of this semielasticity ranged from $F = 3$ to $F = 10$, the selection of $\varepsilon_M = 0.2$ in the current context may be quite conservative.

percent, but a net-of-tax return of only 4.54 percent. The difference is corporate and personal tax payments of 4.66 percent. Applying this to the incremental capital of 0.30 percent of GDP implies a revenue loss of $0.0466(0.30) = 0.014$ percent of GDP. The welfare gain from this extra revenue is 0.014λ percent of GDP. With $\lambda = 0.4$, the welfare loss from this source is 0.006 percent of GDP, while with $\lambda = 1.5$, the loss is 0.021 percent of GDP.

The final revenue effect of the change in the demand for money is the result of the government's ability to substitute the increased money balance of $M_1 - M_2$ for interest-bearing government debt. Although this is a one-time substitution, it reduces government debt service permanently by $r_{ng}(M_1 - M_2)$, where r_{ng} is the real interest rate paid by the government on its outstanding debt net of the tax that it collects on those interest payments. A conservative estimate of r_{ng}, based on the observed 1994 ratio of interest payments to national debt of 0.061, an assumed tax rate of 0.25, and a 1994 inflation rate of 2.7 percent is $r_{ng} = 0.75(0.061) - 0.027 = 0.018$. The reduced debt service cost in perpetuity is thus $0.018(M_1 - M_2) = 0.000054$GDP. The corresponding welfare gains are 0.002 percent of GDP at $\lambda = 0.4$ and 0.008 percent of GDP at $\lambda = 1.5$.

Combining these three effects yields a net welfare loss due to decreased revenue of 0.05 percent of GDP if $\lambda = 0.4$ and of 0.19 percent of GDP if $\lambda = 1.5$.

Although all of the effects that depend on the demand for money are small, the welfare loss from reduced seigniorage revenue is much larger than the welfare gain from the reduced distortion of money demand and the shift of assets to taxpaying business investments. When considering this small reduction in inflation, the Phelps revenue effect dominates the Bailey money demand effect.

1.4 Debt Service and the Government Budget Constraint

The final effect of reduced inflation that I will consider is the higher real cost of servicing the national debt that results from a reduction in the rate of inflation. This higher debt service cost occurs because inflation leaves the real pretax interest rate on government debt unchanged while the inflation premium is subject to tax at the personal level. A lower inflation rate therefore does not change the pretax cost of debt service but reduces the tax revenue on government debt payments. This in turn requires a higher level of other distortionary taxes.[40]

To assess the effect of inflation on the net cost of debt service, note that the increase in the outstanding stock of government debt (B) can be written as

40. Note that the effect of inflation on business tax revenue (through the tax-inflation interaction on depreciation and corporate debt) has been counted in the above discussion of taxes and saving. This ignores the role of retained earnings and the effect of changes in the mixture of corporate investment on the overall tax revenue.

(27) $\Delta B = (r_g + \pi)B + G - T - \theta_i(r_g + \pi)B,$

where $r_g + \pi$ is the nominal pretax interest rate of government debt and θ_i is the effective rate of tax on such interest payments. Thus $(r_g + \pi)B$ is the gross interest payment on the government debt and $(1 - \theta_i)(r_g + \pi)B$ is the net interest on that debt. G is all other government spending, and T is all tax revenue other than the revenue collected from taxing the interest on government debt.

In equilibrium, the stock of government debt must grow at the same rate as nominal GDP; that is, $\Delta B = B(n + g + \pi)$, where n is the rate of growth of population and g is the rate of growth of per capita output. Combining this equilibrium condition with equation (27) implies

(28) $T/\text{GDP} = G/\text{GDP} + [(1 - \theta_i)r_g - n - g - \theta_i\pi]B/\text{GDP}.$

Thus $d(T/\text{GDP})/d\pi = -\theta_i(B/\text{GDP}).$

Reducing the inflation rate from 2 percent to zero increases the real cost of debt service (i.e., increases the level of taxes required to maintain the existing debt-GDP ratio) by $0.02\theta_i B$. With $\theta_i = 0.25$ and the current debt-GDP ratio of $B/\text{GDP} = 0.5$, the 2 percentage point reduction would reduce tax revenue by 0.25 percent of GDP and would therefore reduce welfare by 0.25λ percent of GDP. The welfare cost of increased net debt service is therefore between 0.10 percent of GDP and 0.38 percent of GDP, depending on the value of λ. These figures are shown in row 6 of table 1.1.

1.5   Net Effect of Lower Inflation on Economic Welfare

Before bringing together the several effects of reduced inflation that have been identified and evaluated in sections 1.1 through 1.4, it is useful to comment on some changes in income that should not be counted in evaluating the welfare gain.

First, if lower inflation causes an increase in saving, there will be more retirement consumption. Although it is tempting to count all of this extra income as a benefit of lower inflation, part of it is just a shift along an intertemporal indifference curve. It is only because we start from a second-best situation in which taxes distort consumption timing that a shift to more retirement consumption constitutes a gain in well-being. Moreover, it is only this welfare gain and not the portion of the extra income that is just a shift along the indifference curve that should be counted. Subsection 1.1.1 correctly counts the welfare gain and does not include the additional retirement income that is just balanced by lower preretirement consumption.

Second, the increase in the capital stock that results if saving rises causes the marginal product of labor to rise and labor incomes to increase. This should not be counted because, at least to a first-order approximation, it is balanced by a corresponding decrease in capital income. To see this, consider again the

Cobb-Douglas assumption of subsection 1.1.1 ($y = k^b$ and $sy = nk$, where s is the saving rate and n is the growth of population and technology). This implies that $y = (s/n)^{b/(1-b)}$. The level of national income therefore rises in the same proportion as the ratio of the saving rates raised to the power $b/(1 - b)$. With $\eta_{Sr} = 0.4$, the level of real income in equilibrium rises by a factor of $(1.035)^{0.333} = 1.0115$, or by 1.15 percent. This includes both labor and capital income.

Consider first the extra labor income. With a Cobb-Douglas technology and a labor coefficient of $b = 0.75$, the extra labor income (pretax) that results as the increased capital stock raises the marginal product of labor is 75 percent of the 1.15 percent of GDP, or 0.008625GDP. But now consider what happens to the preexisting capital income as the increased capital intensity drives down the marginal product of capital. That preexisting capital income was 25 percent of GDP. Footnote 10 showed that the marginal product of capital falls from 0.0920 to 0.0889. This reduces the pretax capital income on the existing capital stock by 0.0031/0.0920 of its original value, that is, by (0.0031/0.092)0.25GDP = 0.00842GDP. Except for rounding errors, this just balances the extra labor income.

I return now to table 1.1, which summarizes the four effects assessed in sections 1.1 through 1.4, distinguishing the direct effects of reduced distortion and the indirect effects that occur through the change in revenue. Separate values are given for the alternative saving demand elasticities ($\eta_{Sr} = 0.4$, $\eta_{Sr} = 0$, and $\eta_{Sr} = 1.0$) and for the alternative estimates of the deadweight loss per dollar of revenue raised through alternative distorting taxes ($\lambda = 0.4$ and $\lambda = 1.5$).

These relatively large gains from reduced inflation reflect primarily the fact that the existing system of capital taxation imposes large deadweight losses even in the absence of inflation and that these deadweight losses are exacerbated by inflation.

Reducing these distortions by lowering the rate of inflation produces annual welfare gains of 1.14 percent of GDP in the benchmark saving case where there is a very small positive relation between saving and the real net rate of interest ($\eta_{Sr} = 0.4$). The deadweight loss distortions in the other two cases, also shown at the bottom of column (1), are 0.85 percent of GDP and 1.56 percent of GDP.

The additional welfare effects of changes in revenue, summarized at the bottom of columns (2) and (3), can be either negative or positive but on balance are smaller than the direct effects of reduced distortion. In the benchmark case of $\eta_{Sr} = 0.4$, the total revenue effects reduce welfare but the reductions are relatively small (between -0.10 at $\lambda = 0.4$ and -0.38 at $\lambda = 1.5$).

The total welfare effect of reducing inflation from 2 percent to zero is therefore a gain in the benchmark saving case of between 0.76 percent of GDP a year and 1.04 percent of GDP a year. A higher saving response increases the net gain while a lower saving response reduces it.

If the cost of reducing the inflation rate from 2 percent to zero is a one-time cumulative loss of 6 percent of GDP, as Ball's (1994) analysis discussed in

section 3.2 of Feldstein (1997) implies, the estimated gains in the benchmark case would offset this cost within six to eight years. If saving is more responsive, the gain from price stability would offset the cost even more quickly. Only if saving is completely interest inelastic and revenue raising has a high deadweight loss does the estimated total effect imply that the welfare gains would take more than a decade to exceed the lost GDP that is required to achieve price stability. Even in this case, the present value of the annual benefits of eliminating inflation exceeds 10 percent of the initial GDP if the growing benefit stream is discounted by the historic real return on the Standard & Poor's portfolio.

1.6 Summary and Conclusion

The calculations in this paper imply that the interaction of existing tax rules and inflation causes a significant welfare loss in the United States even at a low rate of inflation. More specifically, the analysis implies that shifting the equilibrium rate of inflation from 2 percent to zero would cause a perpetual welfare gain equal to about 1 percent of GDP a year. The deadweight loss of 2 percent inflation is so large because inflation exacerbates the distortions that would be caused by existing capital income taxes even with price stability.

To assess the desirability of achieving price stability, the gain from eliminating this loss has to be compared with the one-time cost of disinflation. The evidence summarized in Feldstein (1997) implies that the cost of shifting from 2 percent inflation to price stability is estimated to be about 6 percent of GDP. Since the 1 percent of GDP annual welfare gain from price stability continues forever and grows at the same rate as GDP (i.e., at about 2.5 percent a year), the present value of the welfare gain is very large. Discounting the annual gains at the rate that investors require for risky equity investments (i.e., at the 5.1 percent real net-of-tax rate of return on the Standard & Poor's portfolio from 1969 to 1994) implies a present value gain equal to more than 35 percent of the initial level of GDP. The benefit of achieving price stability therefore substantially exceeds its cost.

This welfare gain could in principle also be achieved by eliminating all capital income taxes or by indexing capital income taxes so that taxes are based only on real income and real expenses. Feldstein (1997, sec. 3.8) discusses the technical and administrative difficulties that are likely to keep such indexing from being adopted, an implication borne out by recent legislative experience. The magnitude of the annual gain from reducing inflation is so large that the expected present value of the gain from disinflating from 2 percent inflation to price stability would be positive even if there were a 50 percent chance that capital income taxes will be completely eliminated or the income tax completely indexed after 10 years.

The analysis of this paper does not discuss the distributional consequences of the disinflation or of the reduced inflation. Some readers may believe that

the output loss caused by the disinflation should be weighted more heavily than the gain from low inflation because the output loss falls disproportionately on lower income individuals and does so in the form of the large individual losses associated with unemployment. It would, however, take very large weights to overcome the difference between the 5 percent of GDP output loss of disinflation and the 35+ percent of GDP present value gain from lower inflation.

References

Auerbach, Alan. 1978. Appendix: The effect of inflation on the tax value of depreciation. In Inflation and taxes in a growing economy with debt and equity finance, by Martin Feldstein, Jerry Green, and Eytan Sheshinki. *Journal of Political Economy* 86, no. 2, pt. 2 (April): S68–S69.

Bailey, Martin. 1956. The welfare cost of inflationary finance. *Journal of Political Economy* 64:93–110.

Ball, Laurence. 1994. What determines the sacrifice ratio? In *Monetary policy,* ed. N. G. Mankiw. Chicago: University of Chicago Press.

Ballard, Charles, John Shoven, and John Whalley. 1985. General equilibrium computations of the marginal welfare cost of taxes in the United States. *American Economic Review* 75 (March): 128–38.

Blinder, Alan. 1975. Distribution effects and the aggregate consumption function. *Journal of Political Economy* 83 (3): 447–75.

Boskin, Michael. 1978. Taxation, saving and the rate of interest. *Journal of Political Economy* 86, no. 2, pt. 2 (April): S3–S27.

Cagan, Phillip. 1953. The monetary dynamics of hyperinflation. In *Studies in the quantity theory of money,* ed. M. Friedman. Chicago: University of Chicago Press.

Evans, O. 1983. Tax policy, the interest elasticity of saving, and capital accumulation. *American Economic Review* 73, no. 3 (June): 398–410.

Feldstein, Martin. 1978. The welfare cost of capital income taxation. *Journal of Political Economy* 86, no. 2, pt. 2 (April): S29–S51.

———. 1979. The welfare cost of permanent inflation and optimal short-run economic policy. *Journal of Political Economy* 87 (4): 749–68.

———. 1983. *Inflation, tax rules, and capital formation.* Chicago: University of Chicago Press.

———. 1994. Tax policy and international capital flows. *Weltwirtshaftliches Archiv* 4:675–97. (NBER Working Paper no. 4851. Cambridge, Mass.: National Bureau of Economic Research, September 1994.)

———. 1995a. The effect of marginal tax rates on taxable income: A panel study of the 1986 Tax Reform Act. *Journal of Political Economy* 103 (3): 551–72.

———. 1995b. Fiscal policies, capital formation and capitalism. *European Economic Review* 39:399–420.

———. 1997. The costs and benefits of going from low inflation to price Stability In *Reducing inflation: Motivation and strategy,* ed. C. Romer and D. Romer, 123–56. Chicago: University of Chicago Press.

———. Forthcoming. Tax avoidance and the deadweight loss of the income tax. *Review of Economics and Statistics.* (NBER Working Paper no. 5055. Cambridge, Mass.: National Bureau of Economic Research, 1995.)

Feldstein, Martin, and Daniel Feenberg. 1996. The effect of increased tax rates on tax-

able income and economic efficiency: A preliminary analysis of the 1993 tax rate increases. In *Tax policy and the economy,* ed. J. Poterba. Cambridge, Mass.: MIT Press.

Feldstein, Martin, Jerry Green, and Eytan Sheshinski. 1978. Inflation and taxes in a growing economy with debt and equity finance. *Journal of Political Economy* 86, no. 2, pt. 2 (April): S53–S70.

Feldstein, Martin, James Poterba, and Louis Dicks-Mireaux. 1983. The effective tax rate and the pretax rate of return. *Journal of Public Economics* 21 (2): 129–58.

Fischer, Stanley. 1981. Towards an understanding of the costs of inflation, II. *Carnegie-Rochester Conference Series on Public Policy* 15:15–42.

Friedman, Milton. 1969. The optimum quantity of money. In *The optimum quantity of money and other essays.* Chicago: Aldine.

Hall, Robert. 1988. Intertemporal substitution in consumption. *Journal of Political Economy* 96, no. 2 (April): 339–57.

Hartman, David. 1979. Taxation and the effects of inflation on the real capital stock in an open economy. *International Economic Review* 20 (2): 417–25.

Makin, John. 1987. *Saving, pension contributions and real interest rates.* Washington, D.C.: American Enterprise Institute.

Mankiw, N. G. 1987. Consumer spending and the after-tax real interest rate. In *The effects of taxation on capital accumulation,* ed. M. Feldstein. Chicago: University of Chicago Press.

Mishkin, Frederic. 1992. Is the Fischer effect for real? *Journal of Monetary Economics* 30:195–215.

Phelps, Edmund. 1973. Inflation in the theory of public finance. *Swedish Journal of Economics* 75:67–82.

Poterba, James. 1984. Tax subsidies to owner occupied housing: An asset market approach. *Quarterly Journal of Economics* 99:729–45.

———. 1992. Taxation and housing: Old questions, new answers. *American Economic Review* 82 (2): 237–42.

Poterba, James, and Andrew Samwick. 1995. Stock ownership patterns, stock market fluctuations, and consumption. *Brookings Papers on Economic Activity,* no. 2: 295–357.

Rippe, Richard. 1995. Further gains in corporate profitability. *Economic Outlook Monthly* (Prudential Securities, Inc.), August.

Rosen, Harvey. 1985. Housing subsidies: Effects on housing decisions, efficiency and equity. In *Handbook of public economics,* vol. 1, ed. M. Feldstein and A. Auerbach. Amsterdam: North Holland.

Wright, C. 1969. Saving and the rate of interest. In *The taxation of income from capital,* ed. M. J. Bailey. Washington, D.C.: Brookings Institution.

Comment   Stanley Fischer

I very much appreciate the opportunity offered by the invitation to discuss this paper of Martin Feldstein's, whose recent work on the benefits of reducing inflation has attracted so much attention.

Stanley Fischer is first deputy managing director of the International Monetary Fund.
Views expressed are those of the author and not necessarily of the IMF.

Over a decade ago, an estimate that a reduction of the inflation rate from 10 percent to zero could bring net benefits equal to about 2 percent of GDP was regarded as high (Fischer 1981)—and that estimate included a variety of costs due to the greater uncertainty about future price levels associated with higher inflation rates. Now we have the startling claim that the benefits of reducing inflation from 2 percent to zero amount to 1 percent of GDP, currently about $70 billion per annum. As table 1.1 shows, this is the sum of four partial effects, in which by coincidence the total welfare effects are approximately equal to those arising from the single effect of the distortion to the timing of consumption caused by the reduction in the after-tax return to saving associated with higher inflation.

The Basic Model

The distortion is that individuals consume too much while young. If inflation were lower (by 200 basis points), (1) the net corporate rate of return would rise by 12 basis points from 5.40 to 5.52 percent and (2) the net return to the individual saver would rise by 49 basis points from 4.05 to 4.54 percent. Feldstein estimates that saving by individuals who save (as opposed to those who are dissaving in the second period of their lives) amounts to 9 percent of GDP.

It follows that with an uncompensated interest elasticity of saving of 0.4, the welfare gain from the reduction in inflation amounts to 1.02 percent of GDP. Corresponding to the increase in saving is an impressive 5 percent increase in the steady state capital stock.

To understand this result, note that there is also a significant welfare gain, amounting to 0.73 percent of GDP, even with a zero uncompensated income elasticity of saving. This benefit arises from the higher return on saving, which makes higher second-period consumption possible even though there is no increase in first-period saving.

The basic result is startling, especially for macroeconomists used to thinking about the costs of inflation in terms of such easy metaphors as menu and shoe leather costs. Feldstein's paper requires us to change gears and think about the plausibility of a two-period model in which the key parameters are unfamiliar and have no easy empirical counterparts. For instance, we need to consider whether (1) the relevant interest elasticity of saving in the first (30-year) period of life is 0.4 and (2) the basic intertemporal distortion in consumption in the U.S. economy is one in which consumption later in life is too low relative to that earlier in life.

Let me address the second point and suggest that factors omitted from the Feldstein analysis may create an opposite distortion. Specifically, it is often argued that the young face liquidity constraints and cannot consume as much early in life as they would like. Perhaps the right model should include three periods, starting with a period of no or low earning in which individuals would like to consume more than their income. Second, it is more frequently argued that the elderly consume more than they should rather than less. Thus it is far

from clear that the two-period model set up in this paper is the right one for calculating the costs of the intertemporal distortion caused by capital income taxation; and it is quite likely that the analysis overstates the costs of the intertemporal distortion.

Most important, we should note that this paper is entirely an argument for reducing capital taxation. Inflation is essentially incidental to the argument— reducing inflation is simply a means of reducing capital income taxation. Why not make the argument for reducing capital income taxation directly? In part that may be because the analytic arguments in favor of reducing capital income taxation seem to have run out of steam, for reasons that I will have to leave to experts in the field to elaborate.

Other Considerations

Several other points need to be taken into account in appraising Feldstein's striking result.

1. The paper gives short shrift to the argument, recently developed further by Akerlof, Dickens, and Perry (1996), that because of downward wage inflexibility, there is a significant nonlinearity in the long-term Phillips curve at zero inflation. I do not believe that the Akerlof-Dickens-Perry argument would hold in the longest of long runs because downward wage inflexibility is only a convention, not a structural feature of the economy. But I do believe that because economies have operated for so long with positive inflation, it will take a long time for downward wage flexibility to develop in response to high unemployment at a zero inflation rate.

There is a second important argument supporting the view that the average rate of inflation should be above zero. It is that when a recession threatens, it may be useful to have a negative real interest rate. Since the nominal interest rate cannot fall below zero, the real interest rate can be lower when the expected inflation rate is around 2 percent than when it is zero. This may sound like a theoretical issue, but I believe that such considerations are relevant to recent Japanese experience.

2. Feldstein makes much of the argument that the output costs of disinflation are transitory while the welfare gains from reducing the taxation of saving are permanent. However, this is misleading in a model in which the period length is about 30 years. The welfare gains to which Feldstein refers are garnered only when consumption in the second period of life rises. Taken literally, that means after 30 years, long after the output costs of disinflation have been incurred. Indeed, in the early period—the first 30 years—consumption either does not rise or falls when the return to saving rises. Thus the overall welfare impact measured for, say, the first 10 or 20 years would likely be negative, not positive.

3. The paper is a surprising combination of sweeping statements and complicated calculations. Feldstein says—and it is hard to disagree—that there is

a surprising amount of money illusion among market participants. But it is precisely these money-illusioned market participants who are supposed to be increasing their saving in response to a *decline* in the nominal rate of return on saving, albeit one that corresponds to a real increase.

4. It is possible that there is a political economy equilibrium that determines the rate of taxation of capital income. Quite possibly an inflation-induced decline in capital taxation would lead to an offsetting increase in explicit tax rates on capital income.

5. Inevitably, inflation will fluctuate around its average value. This means that so long as the tax system is nominal, the effective rate of taxation of capital will vary with inflation. The distortions do not balance out over the cycle, and they will be present so long as capital income taxation is not indexed. *The right answer to the Feldstein analysis is to index capital income taxation.* The argument for indexation of capital income taxes has been made repeatedly in the United States—and rejected just as often.[1] But the same could have been said until 1996 about the argument for government issue of an indexed bond. And the topic of indexation of capital gains is once again actively on the table in the current budget talks.

6. Finally, let me note that this is the second paper by Feldstein developing this line of argument. But it is not logically the last, for there is nothing in the analysis of this paper that suggests the optimal rate of inflation *in this framework* is zero. Rather, given the substantial gains from reducing inflation to zero, there are certainly further gains from shifting to negative inflation rates. Another paper could be written in this series, arguing for the benefits of, say, inflation of minus 2 or 3 percent or perhaps minus 4.5 percent.

If that paper were written, it would have to confront the questions of why economies have almost always behaved poorly in periods of very low inflation or deflation, and whether the best way of reducing the taxation of capital is by changing the average inflation rate.

References

Akerlof, George A., William T. Dickens, and George L. Perry. 1996. The macroeconomics of low inflation. *Brookings Papers on Economic Activity,* no. 1: 1–59.
Fischer, Stanley. 1981. Towards an understanding of the costs of inflation, II. *Carnegie-Rochester Conference Series on Public Policy* 15:15–42.
Fischer, Stanley, and Lawrence H. Summers. 1989. Should governments learn to live with inflation? *American Economic Review Papers and Proceedings* 99, no. 2 (May): 382–87.

---

1. The merits of that argument are not considered here, but some relevant considerations are discussed in Fischer and Summers (1989).

Discussion Summary

Martin Feldstein thanked Stanley Fischer for his insightful remarks and made the following comments in response.

If some individuals are prevented from consuming as much as they want because of liquidity constraints, they will appear in the data as nonsavers. As the paper notes, reducing the effective marginal tax rate for such individuals would either have no effect (because the constraint would continue to bind) or would be sufficient to induce those individuals to save. To the extent that the constraints would remain binding, the current welfare analysis is correct to ignore those individuals. If some would respond to lower inflation by saving more, the analysis understates the gain from shifting to price stability.

Although the model literally implies that the optimal level of inflation is negative, the policy option to be examined is price stability, not negative inflation. Price stability has the special property that it is the only inflation rate that eliminates the necessity to distinguish between real and nominal changes. While economists have no trouble with this, in reality the distinction leads to confusion and misjudgments. Moreover, negative inflation rates are simply not politically feasible.

While Congress could in principle reduce taxes on capital income to achieve the same efficiency gains as would be achieved by eliminating inflation, as a practical matter Congress is not likely to do this in the foreseeable future. The Federal Reserve must take the tax law (and other institutional arrangements) as given when it makes monetary policy. As economists evaluating monetary policy, we must also take into account the existing institutional arrangements that affect the costs and benefits of different Federal Reserve actions.

Alan Auerbach noted that the analysis appears to imply that inflation is too low if one only considers seigniorage benefits and shoe leather costs of inflation and wondered if this corresponds to findings in the literature. *Feldstein* responded that Edmund Phelps has calculated the optimal rate of inflation, provided that only shoe leather and revenue effects are taken into account, and found that it is indeed higher than current rates.

Auerbach also remarked that the magnitude of the benefits that are based on lower effective capital income taxes seems inconsistent with the simulation results of Auerbach and Kotlikoff and wondered what could explain the discrepancy. He also inquired about the effects of the relative costs of housing and nonhousing capital. A lower tax on nonhousing capital has two effects: it raises saving and it draws capital from the housing sector into the nonhousing sector. The effect on the stock of housing capital seems ambiguous, so why is the welfare gain in the housing sector so large? He then questioned the rationale for Feldstein's use of an uncompensated saving elasticity to calculate the revenue effect on capital income taxes and the statement that using an uncompensated elasticity leads to a smaller revenue loss than using a compensated

elasticity. Finally, he wondered why Feldstein did not use underlying utility function parameters rather than observed saving behavior.

Stephen Cecchetti remarked that the results depend largely on the sophistication of people to react to the fact that price stability lowers effective capital income taxes. The analysis assumes that people are smart and react to lower effective capital income taxes but that Congress will not increase capital income taxes to keep the effective rate the same. He wondered how long it would take, in practice, for Congress to react.

Laurence Ball noted that the author estimated that the benefits of price stability outweigh the costs of disinflation if the benefits exceed 0.16 percent of GDP per annum. In his opinion, this hurdle is too low. The loss of GDP in a disinflation underestimates the social costs of a recession because the costs of a recession are distributed unequally.

Andrew Abel remarked that adding up costs and benefits of partial equilibrium calculations poses no problem in the present analysis, a fact confirmed by the general equilibrium calculations that he presented as the discussant of Feldstein (1997). He also noted that the optimal negative inflation rate equalizes the return on money holdings to the after-tax return of capital. Hence, it would be on the order of minus 5 percent rather than minus 9 percent.

Laurence Meyer raised the issue of how to deal with the effect of inflation on the real interest rate. The impact should depend on the saving elasticity, but in Martin Feldstein's analysis the real interest rate faced by firms is fixed by assumption. In the general equilibrium analysis by Andrew Abel, the real after-tax interest rate is fixed by the structure of the model. One should therefore be careful about critical assumptions that may drive results. He also wondered whether the capital income tax rates used in the paper overstate the effective average marginal capital income tax rates because of the prevalence of tax-preferred savings vehicles such as 401(k)s and individual retirement accounts (IRAs).

Benjamin Friedman noted that the tax system has features, such as 401(k)s, IRAs, loss offset, and stepped-up basis, that lower effective capital income taxes. In other words, the tax system may be moving in the right direction from the perspective of Feldstein's paper. He also suggested that the preferential treatment of owner-occupied housing may be an intentional feature of the tax system because society really may have a desire to stimulate owner-occupied housing.

Feldstein replied to the last two comments by noting, first, that such tax-preferred saving is only relevant if it is the marginal form of saving for the individual. He explained that the correct tax rate to use is a weighted average marginal tax rate, where the average is weighted by the amount of saving done. Because most saving is done by people who save a relatively large amount, most saving is done by those for whom IRAs and 401(k)s are inframarginal. Therefore, these tax-preferred savings vehicles are only of minor importance

to the analysis. Moreover, even saving that is not taxed at the individual level is subject to tax at the corporate level.

Feldstein further noted that the favorable tax treatment of housing increases not only the fraction of the population that chooses to own but, more important, the average amount of housing capital among those who do own. Even if public policy wants to encourage homeownership, there are large distortions in the amount of housing capital.

Anna Schwartz questioned the ability of a central bank to deliver a certain inflation rate with any precision.

Juan Dolado said he would like to know what can be learned from recent experience in Japan, which has had a zero inflation rate.

Stanley Fischer observed that not everyone faces a marginal return to saving of 4.2 percent and wonders how this can be incorporated. He also noted that Andrew Abel's general equilibrium model differs substantially from Martin Feldstein's model because in Abel's model people do not derive utility from housing capital. Hence, the observation that Abel's and Feldstein's calculations yield similar results does not imply that a sum of partial equilibrium results is a good approximation to a general equilibrium result. *Feldstein* noted in reply that Abel's calculation does cause housing capital to raise individual utility because it produces the "income" that individuals consume.

In response to the question about the use of the uncompensated saving elasticity, Feldstein said that he believes this is the most realistic way of modeling people's responses. However, for the final results, it makes little difference whether a compensated or uncompensated elasticity is used in the revenue calculation. The model is calibrated using the uncompensated saving elasticity rather than an underlying preference parameter such as the elasticity of intertemporal substitution because we have a better knowledge about the magnitude of the saving elasticity than about underlying preference parameters.

On the issue of possible political adjustments to capital income taxation in response to lower inflation, Feldstein noted that we still do not index taxes for inflation. Moreover, changes to the corporate income tax constitute only a very crude way of adjusting for the effects of inflation on capital income taxes. Looking at the past, he could not discern a clear relation between capital income tax reform and inflation.

In response to the comment by Ball, Feldstein noted that his calculations imply that the benefits of price stability would easily outweigh the costs even if the social costs of disinflation are twice Ball's original estimate of 0.16 percent of GDP per year.

2 Price Stability versus Low Inflation in Germany: An Analysis of Costs and Benefits

Karl-Heinz Tödter and Gerhard Ziebarth

Are the benefits of disinflation worth the costs?
—Croushore (1992)

2.1 Price Stability: Too Much of a Good Thing?

The notion that price stability should be the priority target of monetary policy has nowadays become widely accepted. This is due to the perception that high and volatile inflation rates distort economic allocation and reduce long-term growth potential (Barro 1995), whereas lasting monetary stability is conducive to economic growth, social welfare, and social cohesion alike. By contrast, the consensus regarding assessment of the "excess burden" associated with a moderate inflation rate, and of the cost (the "sacrifice ratio") of correcting such a rate, is much more fragile.[1] In other words, are the benefits of price stability and the costs of disinflation still in reasonable proportion to one another, or should a moderate pace of inflation—rather than undue zeal in fighting inflation—be tolerated or even aimed at by economic policymakers?[2]

In the context of an in-depth analysis of the functions of money, Konieczny

Karl-Heinz Tödter is deputy head of the Division of Econometrics in the Department of Economics of the Deutsche Bundesbank. Gerhard Ziebarth is head of the Division of Business Cycle Analysis and National Accounts in the Department of Economics of the Deutsche Bundesbank.

The opinions expressed in this paper are not necessarily consistent with the official position of the Deutsche Bundesbank. The authors thank the participants of an NBER workshop; S. P. Chakravarty, University of Bangor; F. Seitz, Fachhochschule Amberg-Weiden; and colleagues in the Economics Department of the Deutsche Bundesbank, especially G. Coenen, H. Hansen, P. Heinelt, and P. Lämmel, for their valuable comments and suggestions. All remaining errors are the authors'.

1. In this connection, it should not be entirely overlooked that the costs of a disinflation could at bottom be charged to the preceding inflation and would have to be offset against its gains.

2. Stanley Fischer, for instance, argues: "The evidence points to an inflation range of 1–3% as being optimal. . . . Once lower inflation is attained, the challenge for policy is to preserve those gains" (1994a, 40). Akerlof, Dickens, and Perry argue along similar lines: "Comparing low inflation rates with a zero inflation rate, we are convinced that the unemployment costs outweigh the costs of tax distortions. We fully appreciate the benefits of stabilizing inflation at a low rate, and advocate that as an appropriate target for monetary policy. But the optimal inflation target is not zero" (1996, 52).

comes to the following conclusion regarding the optimality of an inflation rate of zero: "The review of the theoretical arguments leads me to conclude that the optimal rate of inflation is zero" (1994, 34). He emphasizes especially the adverse effects of inflation on the role of money as a unit of account:

> The uniqueness of zero arises from the accounting role of money: it is, simply, infinitely easier to divide by one than by any other number. Only when the price level is stable can money perform properly its role as a stable unit of account and standard of value. The desirability of a stable standard of measurement is evident from other arrangements: without exception, societies have chosen all other units of measure to be of constant value. Uniquely among all numbers, the credibility of zero can be defended on the grounds that "it makes a pound (£) just like a pound (lb)." (32)

What is to be understood by "price stability" has been expressed in different ways. Alan Greenspan, chairman of the Federal Reserve Board in the United States, defines stable prices as "price levels sufficiently stable so that expectations of [price level] change do not become major factors in key economic decisions" (1989). Decisions with a very short time horizon would probably turn out no different with an inflation rate of 2 to 3 percent from what they would be with price stability. On the other hand, decisions involving a long-term commitment or a long planning horizon must indeed take due account of the effects even of moderate inflation rates, and an average inflation rate of zero will actually impinge on decision making if that rate is accompanied by high volatility. It also has to be borne in mind that the threshold for the perception of inflationary processes depends on past experience and therefore may differ from country to country.

Anyway, inflation rates have been declining all over the world for a number of years. As measured by the consumer price index, the inflation rate in the G-7 countries averaged 3.9 percent per annum between 1960 and 1973. In the wake of oil price hikes and an accommodating monetary policy on the part of some central banks, it rose to 9.7 percent per annum between 1973 and 1979. During the eighties the average inflation rate still came to 5.5 percent per annum. But by 1995 the inflation rate of the G-7 countries was averaging 2.5 percent, and of the 27 OECD nations, 18 registered an inflation rate of less than 3 percent in 1995. Besides the globally higher sensitivity to inflation as a result of the globalization of the financial markets (Issing 1996a), in the member states of the European Union this trend probably also owes something to the envisaged monetary union.

Against this background, and in the light of the forthcoming debate on the operative objectives of monetary policy in the context of a monetary union in Europe, the important economic policy question arises for many countries: *Do the benefits of price stability warrant the costs of any further disinflation?* In a comprehensive study for the United States, Feldstein put this question into concrete shape as follows: "If the true and fully anticipated rate of inflation

(i.e., the measured rate of inflation minus 2 percentage points) has stabilized at 2%, is the gain from reducing inflation to zero worth the sacrifice in output and employment that would be required to achieve it?"[3]

Even though our experience of inflation in the Federal Republic of Germany is different from that in the United States and the institutional framework here shows specific features, monetary policy in this country has to face the same issue. The purpose of this paper is therefore to provide an empirically supported answer for Germany to the question raised by Feldstein. Against the background of the monetary policy strategy pursued by the Bundesbank, we first consider, in section 2.2, the *costs of disinflation;* in quantifying the sacrifice ratio we draw on recently published empirical investigations. With regard to the *benefits of price stability,* there have hitherto been no analyses for Germany as detailed as that by Feldstein for the United States. The focal point of this paper is therefore section 2.3, in which, building on the methodological foundation of Feldstein's approach, we examine the implications for macroeconomic welfare of the interaction of even moderate rates of inflation with the distorting effects of the tax system.[4] First of all, we address, as part of an intertemporal approach, the impact of inflation on the allocation of consumption and saving. Then we investigate the implications of inflation for demand for owner-occupied housing. Thereafter, we consider the distorting effects of inflation on money demand, which ever since Bailey's (1956) paper have been at the center of the literature on the welfare effects of inflation. Finally, we contemplate the effects of inflation on public revenue from the money creation process (seigniorage) and on government debt service. Section 2.4 offers a summary and some concluding remarks.

> Economists should be circumspect when attempting to estimate the costs of reducing the inflation rate.
> —Lucas (1990)

2.2   On the Costs of Disinflation

The costs of a lasting reduction in the rate of inflation depend on nominal and real rigidities in the overall goods and labor markets. Other significant factors are the stance of fiscal policy, the monetary policy strategy pursued by the central bank, and the degree of stability already reached. The Bundesbank's monetary policy has been based on a monetary targeting strategy for over 20 years. With the aid of this policy stance, it has proved possible (despite oil price hikes, monetary upheavals, and tensions in the wake of German unification) to

---

3. Feldstein (1997, 123–24). In the following we refer to this paper without any further details.
4. The fact that, for various reasons, the underlying tax systems play a particular part in the assessment of inflation effects has been stressed in a number of papers; see, e.g., Feldstein, Green, and Sheshinski (1978), Tanzi (1980), King and Fullerton (1983), Sinn (1987), and Sievert et al. (1989).

limit the average rate of inflation in those two decades to about 3 percent per annum, and thus well below the average level of the other industrial countries (5.5 percent).

2.2.1 Monetary Growth and Inflation

Partly owing to deregulation of the financial markets and to financial innovations, a number of countries have dispensed with the traditional monetary aggregates as indicators and intermediate targets of monetary policy. Even so, there continues to be a broad consensus that over the long term, inflation is a monetary phenomenon.[5] Pursuant to the quantity equation, the product of the money stock (M) and the velocity of circulation (V) equals the product of the price level (P) and the real gross domestic product (Y). Written logarithmically, the following applies:[6]

$$(1) \qquad\qquad m + v = p + y.$$

On the basis of this quantity equation, Hallman, Porter, and Small (1989) define the equilibrium price level (P^*) as the money stock per unit of real production potential (Y^*) at the equilibrium velocity of circulation (V^*):

$$(2) \qquad\qquad p^* = m + v^* - y^*.$$

If a stable long-term money demand function

$$(3) \qquad\qquad m - p = \beta_0 + \beta y + \varepsilon$$

exists,[7] with β_0 being either constant or a function of stationary variables and the random variable ε, with expectation zero, measuring deviations from long-term money demand, then the equilibrium velocity of circulation can be expressed as[8]

$$(4) \qquad\qquad v^* = -\beta_0 + (1 - \beta)y^*.$$

The equilibrium price level can now be written

---

5. In the shorter to medium term, trends in the general price level may certainly depart from the path marked out by the growth of the money stock. Nonmonetary price stimuli, temporary changes in the velocity of circulation of money, or cyclical fluctuations in real income may be superimposed on the key relationships for a considerable period. But this does not alter the basic fact that a process of sustained erosion of the purchasing power of money is a monetary phenomenon, for which economic policy is accountable.

6. In this subsection, lowercase letters denote logarithms of variables and the symbol Δ stands for differences, i.e., $x = \ln X$ and $\Delta x = x - x_{-1}$.

7. For Germany it can be assumed that even after unification, there is a stable long-term money demand function; see Issing and Tödter (1995), Scharnagl (1996a, 1996b), and the references therein.

8. Issing and Tödter (1995) estimate the income elasticity of money demand (β) in Germany at 1.43. Given a growth rate of real production potential averaging 2.2 percent per annum, this implies a trend decline in the velocity of circulation of just under 1 percent per annum.

Table 2.1   **Monetary Growth and Inflation in Germany (average growth rates of M3, in percent per annum)**

Period	Δm3	Δy^*	Δp^{*a}	Δp
1970:1–79:4	10.4	3.2	5.8	5.5
1980:1–89:4	6.1	2.1	3.1	2.8
1990:1–96:2[b]	7.6	3.6	2.5	2.5

Source: Issing and Tödter (1995) and authors' calculations.
[a]$\Delta p^* = \Delta$m3 $- 1.43 \Delta y^*$.
[b]Including the increase in M3 and in potential production due to unification.

$$(5) \qquad p^* = m - \beta_0 - \beta y^*.$$

As table 2.1 shows, the growth rates of equilibrium prices over fairly long periods agree pretty well with the actual inflation rates. The price gap, that is, the difference between the equilibrium price level and the actual price level, is composed of two components, viz., the degree of utilization of production potential (output gap) and the degree of liquidity (velocity gap):

$$(6) \qquad p^* - p = (y - y^*) + (v^* - v) = \beta(y - y^*) + \varepsilon.$$

In other words, pressure on prices is felt whenever production capacities are being heavily utilized or whenever cash holding is higher than is consistent with long-term money demand.

As empirical investigations for Germany show, the equilibrium price level and the actual price level are cointegrated (see Tödter and Reimers 1994; Scharnagl 1996a). It follows from this that differences between the two variables are of a temporary nature and that disequilibria that have arisen will disappear again over time. The course of price movements can then be described (as is done here in stylized form) by an error correction equation:

$$(7) \qquad \Delta p = \Delta p^e + \lambda(p^* - p) = \Delta p^e + \lambda\beta(y - y^*) + \lambda\varepsilon.$$

The smaller the parameter λ, the more sluggishly prices respond to (goods and money market) disequilibria, and the higher real rigidity is. The expected inflation rate may be specified in this connection as a learning process in which inflation expectations adjust to changes in equilibrium prices,

$$(8) \qquad \Delta p^e = \gamma \Delta p_{-1} + (1 - \gamma)\Delta p^*,$$

where the parameter γ is a measure of nominal rigidity.

2.2.2   The Bundesbank's Monetary Targeting Strategy

The Bundesbank's monetary targeting strategy primarily serves the objective of price stability. This strategy is geared to the long-term relationship between money and prices, a relationship that is soundly based on the quantity theory

and supported empirically.[9] Since 1988 the Bundesbank has used the money stock in the definition M3 as the indicator and intermediate target of its monetary policy.[10] The annual target for the growth rate of the money stock (μ) is derived in accordance with a normative figure for the rate of inflation aimed at over the medium term (π), after taking due account of forecasts of the growth of production potential (Δy^*) and of the trend change in the velocity of circulation (Δv^*):

$$(9) \qquad \mu = \pi + \Delta y^* - \Delta v^* = \pi + \beta \, \Delta y^*.$$

If the Bundesbank succeeds in getting the money stock to grow in line with this target ($\Delta m = \mu$), then the equilibrium price level and—after the expiration of dynamic adjustment reactions—the actual price level increase at the rate $\Delta p^* = \Delta p = \pi$.

If the Bundesbank wanted to reduce the target inflation rate from π to zero, it would durably have to lower the growth rate of the money stock to $\mu = \beta \, \Delta y^*$. In the event of uncertainty about the level of inflation, however, a distinction must be made between an *inflation target* and a *price level target*. To illustrate the difference between the two targets, let it be assumed that the central bank manages to attain the inflation target of zero, except for an identically and independently distributed random variable v_t with expectation zero and variance σ_v^2. The price level ($p_t = p_{t-1} + v_t$) then follows a random walk process with variance $\sigma_v^2 T$ after T periods. Even though the expected inflation rate for the next period is zero, the uncertainty about the price level in the more distant future may be very high. If, by contrast, the central bank is pursuing the target of stability of price level, the variance of the price level is σ_v^2, regardless of the time horizon. The difference between the two strategies resides in the fact that in the case of an inflation target, the central bank does not need to respond to a temporary positive price shock, whereas in the case of a price-level target, it is forced to usher in a period of deflation (see also Scarth 1994; Fischer 1994a; Hagen and Neumann 1996).

2.2.3   Evidence on the Sacrifice Ratio

The potential costs of disinflation consist in output and employment losses during the period of running down inflation. The level of the costs depends on the slope of the Phillips curve (or the slope of the macroeconomic supply function). If the long-term Phillips curve has negative slope, any reduction in inflation results in lasting losses of output and employment; if the curve is vertical, the output and employment losses are temporary.

9. On the theoretical and empirical foundations of monetary policy, see Issing (1992); on past experience of the monetary targeting strategy, see Issing (1995) and König (1996).

10. M3 is currency in circulation and sight deposits, time deposits for less than four years, and savings deposits at three months' notice held by domestic nonbanks—other than the federal government—at domestic credit institutions.

In the above P^* model, just as in neoclassical models, there need not be any disinflation costs at all if the central bank announces the target of disinflation credibly and if expectations respond immediately. Monetarist and neoclassical models exhibit a vertical Phillips curve in the long run, and thus temporary disinflation costs. The Keynesian models of the sixties postulated a lasting negative trade-off. According to neo-Keynesian theory, too, changes in monetary policy exert effects in real terms on account of rigidities in wage and price movements.[11] The idea of a permanent trade-off between inflation and unemployment is, however, nowadays rejected by most economists: "There is a general acceptance among economists that the medium, and longer, term Phillips curve is vertical. Hence, there is no trade-off in the longer run between growth and inflation. Consequently, there is now also a consensus that the primary macro-policy objective of a central bank should be price stability."[12]

In the literature, it is customary to express the costs of disinflation in terms of what is known as the "sacrifice ratio." The "output sacrifice ratio" (σ) measures the cumulative output loss associated with a decline in the inflation rate. The "unemployment sacrifice ratio" (σ_u) denotes the corresponding rise in the unemployment rate. A link between the two concepts can be effected by the "Okun gap." The simplest way of determining sacrifice ratios is to measure for concrete historical periods of disinflation the cumulative output loss in relation to its trend movement or to the cumulative change in the unemployment rate. By this method, Schelde-Andersen (1992) computes sacrifice ratios for 16 OECD countries. He selects the time span from 1979 to 1982 as a common period of disinflation in all countries. For Germany, the ratio relative to the unemployment rate works out at $\sigma_u = 6.4$, whereas the indicator measured in terms of output yields the value $\sigma = 2.2$.[13] Ball (1994) uses a similar method but identifies specific disinflation periods for each country. For Germany he obtains a ratio of $\sigma = 3.6$ on the basis of quarterly figures for the period 1980:1–86:3.[14] In a similar way to Ball, but with a different approach to estimating production potential, Herrmann (1996) computes a value of roughly $\sigma = 2.6$ on the basis of quarterly data for the period 1981:4–86:4, whereas

11. In simulations with small empirical models for the United States, Croushore comes to the conclusion: "In a comparison of disinflation costs across the different models, the Monetarist-type model shows the lowest cost (actually a negative cost), the New-Classical-type model shows zero cost, the Keynesian-type model shows a high cost, and the PSTAR+ model shows a cost in between the high and low costs of the other models" (1992, 13).

12. Goodhart (1992, 332). Taylor argues along similar lines: "But if there is any change in the paradigm of macro-economics that most economists would agree with, it is that the trade-off view was mistaken" (1992, 13). On the other hand, Akerlof et al. argue that lasting real costs of disinflation exist on account of a "deeply rooted downward nominal wage rigidity" in the economy: "The unemployment costs are not one-time but, rather, permanent and substantial" (1996, 52).

13. For the longer periods from 1979 to 1985 or 1988, the values for σ were actually lower, 1.2 and 1.6, respectively. This suggests that the costs of disinflation are temporary and decrease over time.

14. With annual data for the period 1980–86 he arrived at the value 2.1.

the ratio for the most recent period of disinflation 1992:1–95:4 works out at $\sigma = 2.2$.

More analytically oriented approaches to the estimation of the costs of disinflation are mostly based on Phillips-type relations for wage or price inflation. In the context of the P^* model (eqs. [7] and [8]) the output sacrifice ratio can be measured as the relation between the coefficients of nominal and real rigidity (see Schelde-Andersen 1992, 112):

$$(10) \qquad\qquad \sigma = \gamma/\lambda\beta.$$

In this model, a decline in monetary growth by 1 percentage point leads directly to an equally large decrease in the growth rate of equilibrium prices and ultimately also of the actual inflation rate. The expected inflation rate, however, initially declines by only $1 - \gamma$, in line with equation (8). Hence, a gap of γ percent between the actual decrease in the inflation rate and the expected decrease comes into being on account of nominal rigidities. In order to close this gap, the degree of capacity utilization must drop by $\gamma/\lambda\beta$ percentage points. In the long run, that is, after expectations have come into line with the reduced monetary growth, output and the unemployment rate revert to their equilibrium values.

On the basis of price equations similar to equation (7), Schelde-Andersen (1992) estimates the value of $\sigma = 3.3$ for the output sacrifice ratio for Germany. A Phillips relationship for the wage inflation rate yields $\sigma_u = 4.4$ for the unemployment sacrifice ratio. These estimates also take account of the possibility of permanent disinflation costs, which might derive from the presence of hysteresis effects on the labor market.[15]

It is conspicuous that in these studies the costs of disinflation as estimated for Germany lie distinctly above the OECD average (see table 2.2). In a comparison by Schelde-Andersen (1992) on the basis of the sacrifice ratios he estimated for 16 OECD countries, Germany comes last, as the country with the highest disinflation costs. One possible "explanation" might be that disinflation costs appear to be higher, the lower the initial inflation rate: "A high initial rate of inflation seems to reduce the sacrifice ratio, thus suggesting that inflation is more costly to reduce when it is already very low."[16]

As the above remarks have illustrated, empirical estimates of sacrifice ratios involve a high degree of uncertainty. The results depend crucially on the method, the frequency of the data used, and a number of other factors. This is why simulations with a macroeconometric structural model form an alternative

15. Schelde-Andersen (1992, 159) rejects the hypothesis of extreme hysteresis on the basis of estimates of the Phillips relationship for all countries except the United Kingdom. On the other hand, the null hypothesis that the unemployment rate follows a random walk process cannot be rejected for any of the 16 countries under review.

16. Schelde-Andersen (1992, 129). Other reasons for high disinflation costs relevant for Germany may have been a high real exchange rate (i.e., an unfavorable international competitive position) and low flexibility of the wage-bargaining process.

Table 2.2   **Estimates of the Sacrifice Ratio for Germany**

Method and Author	Period or Data	Sacrifice Ratio Unemployment (σ_u)	Output (σ)
Period analysis			
Schelde-Andersen 1992	1979–82	6.4	2.2
Ball 1994	1980:1–86:3	–	3.6
Herrmann 1996	1981:4–86:4	–	2.6
Herrmann 1996	1992:1–95:4	–	2.2
Unweighted OECD average			
Schelde-Andersen 1992	Annual data	2.5	1.6
Ball 1994	Quarterly data	–	1.5
Ball 1994	Annual data	–	0.8
Phillips approach			
Schelde-Andersen 1992	1960–90	4.4	3.3
Model simulation			
Jahnke 1996	1997:1–2004:4	–	4.0

to such partial analytical estimates.[17] Using the Bundesbank's multicountry econometric model Jahnke (1998) simulated a permanent increase in short-term interest rates that leads to a permanent decline in the inflation rate.[18] The estimation period for the forecasts of behavioral equations in the model extends from 1975:1 to 1995:4, and the simulation period covers the time span from 1997:1 to 2004:4. Over that span of eight years the sacrifice ratio, measured in terms of output, works out at about $\sigma = 4$; this value is above the estimates obtained by partial analytical approaches (see table 2.2).

Altogether, the available empirical evidence suggests that in the past the output sacrifice ratio for Germany can hardly have been above $\sigma = 4$.[19] At that level it would have been about two to three times as high as the average of the other OECD countries. The empirical estimates suggest that the costs of disinflation (C) do not simply depend linearly on the disinflation rate but rather rise disproportionally fast:

$$(11) \qquad\qquad C = \sigma\pi^{1+\varphi}, \qquad \varphi > 0.$$

According to this equation, a reduction of the inflation rate by 1 percentage point—regardless of φ—would imply an output loss amounting to 4 percent

17. Schelde-Andersen argues in favor of the model simulation approach: "Analytically, this is by far the most satisfactory method as it is comprehensive and exogenous factors are isolated. The sensitivity of costs to changes in the lag structure of the price and wage formation process can be estimated and it is also possible to illustrate the effect of changes in credibility" (1992, 122).

18. Documentation for the Bundesbank model is included in Deutsche Bundesbank (1994a, 1996c).

19. Feldstein uses an output sacrifice ratio for the United States of 2 to 3 in his calculations.

of GDP. Assuming $\varphi = 0.5$, a reduction of the inflation rate by 2 percentage points, by contrast, would be associated with an output loss of 11.3 percent.[20]

The available evidence suggests that the costs of disinflation are temporary and are incurred over a comparatively short period.[21] By contrast, the benefits of price stability (G), expressed as a percentage of GDP, are permanent. To compare costs and benefits, we consider the present value of the benefits in all future periods. Given a discount rate of ρ, the present value of the benefits works out at G/ρ. The reduction of inflation is beneficial if the permanent benefits of price stability exceed the annualized costs of disinflation:[22]

$$(12) \qquad\qquad G > \rho\sigma\pi^{1+\varphi}.$$

Given a discount rate of $\rho = 2.5$ percent per annum[23] and the above-mentioned values for the other parameters ($\sigma = 4$, $\pi = 2$, $\varphi = 0.5$), the breakeven point works out at $G = 0.28$. Hence, to summarize the result of this section, the lasting benefits of price stability would have to be greater than 0.28 percent of GDP to warrant the costs of disinflation by 2 percentage points. In section 2.3 we shall turn to the calculation of the benefits of price stability.

> This is real money.
> —Lucas (1994)

2.3 Benefits of Price Stability

The interaction between the tax system and inflation has repercussions on many areas of economic activity. In this section, we are concerned with estimating the welfare-theoretical benefits of price stability. In this context, we consider the steady state effects on the following economic activities: (1) the intertemporal allocation of consumption and saving, (2) the demand for owner-occupied housing, (3) money demand and seigniorage, and (4) government debt service.

We base our quantification of the benefits of price stability on a steady state with a stable and fully anticipated inflation rate of 2 percent per annum[24] and

20. The reduction of inflation by 3 percentage points (from 4.5 to 1.5 percent per annum) between 1992 and 1995 was accompanied by an output loss of 6 to 7 percent. However, starting from this lower level, any further reduction in inflation is likely to involve higher costs.

21. Ball (1994) finds evidence suggesting that rapid disinflation is more favorable, whereas King (1996a) argues in favor of a gradual disinflation process.

22. We are well aware in this context that this criterion derived from a present value concept treats the future worse than the present. Hence, there is a risk that too little importance is attached to future benefits and hence to future generations. This is why the discount rate, in cases of doubt, should tend to be set low, even though this remains ethically questionable from the point of view of intergenerational equity; see Issing (1996b).

23. This rate is roughly in line with the difference between the real rate of interest under conditions of price stability and the growth rate of real potential production (see section 2.3).

24. What is meant is an effective inflation rate of 2 percent, i.e., an inflation rate after adjustment for statistical measuring errors.

examine the comparative static effects of lowering that rate to zero. We take into account both the direct benefits of reducing inflation-induced distortions and the indirect welfare effects emanating from the change in tax revenue owing to the lowering of the inflation rate given the prevailing expenditure stance of the public authorities.

Other advantages of price stability are not included in our computations, although we certainly do not deem them to be insignificant (see the survey in Edey 1994; Fischer 1994b; King 1996b). The avoidance of distortions due to inflation is accompanied by enhancement of performance incentives and more efficient operation of economic processes. This includes the greater informative value of relative prices, a better balanced financing structure, improved economic efficiency, and higher productivity. Furthermore, redistribution processes and redistribution conflicts due to inflation would be avoided, and the wastage of scarce resources in order to sidestep the adverse effects of inflation would cease. In addition, under conditions of price stability the uncertainty engendered by inflation would diminish.[25] The extent to which such improved underlying conditions influence the long-term *growth* path is outside the scope of our investigation. But as is shown in models of the new growth theory, price stability can also contribute to lastingly stronger economic growth (Black, Macklem, and Poloz 1994).[26]

In computing the welfare effects, we are largely following the approach adopted by Feldstein, although we have made a number of modifications to take account of the special features of the German tax system. Moreover, in calculating the indirect revenue effects, we do not set the parameter that measures the deadweight loss of the tax system exogenously but derive it from the model.

2.3.1 Intertemporal Allocation of Consumption and Saving

The taxation of capital and of the earnings accruing from it involves welfare losses. The existing tax system admittedly gives rise to such distortions even if price stability obtains. However, the interaction of inflation and distortionary taxation results in an additional welfare loss, a "deadweight loss," that derives from the fact that inflationary processes drive a "tax-inflation wedge" between the gross yield and the net return on capital. This—as we shall show—reduces the real return on investment, impairs saving, and distorts the intertemporal allocation of consumption. Similarly, the elimination of a positive inflation rate is associated with deadweight gains.

25. This uncertainty depends, as mentioned above, in part on whether the central bank is aiming at the target of an inflation *rate* of zero or at price *level* stability; see subsection 2.2.2.

26. Even a small increase in the pace of growth would generate a huge effect over time. If, in the event of a decline in the inflation rate of 2 percentage points, the real growth rate rose by 0.2 percentage points (this is the magnitude that Grimes [1991] ascertained empirically in a cross-sectional analysis for 27 countries), given a difference of 2.5 percentage points between the real rate of interest and the real growth rate in the starting period, the present value of the increase in real output amounts to three times current GDP.

Welfare-Theoretical Approach

The starting point of the analysis is a two-period overlapping generations model. In this model the following fundamental relationship exists between the savings of the young generation (S) and their later consumption in old age (C):

(13) $S = pC.$

In this intertemporal budget equation, p denotes the price of future consumption. Given a real net payment of interest on savings at a rate r over a period of T years (i.e., over one generation), the price of future consumption, expressed in terms of units of present consumption, is

(14) $p = (1 + r)^{-T}$,   with $\varepsilon_{pr} = -T\dfrac{r}{1 + r}$.

As the elasticity ε_{pr} indicates, an increase in the real net yield on savings leads to a decline in the price of retirement consumption. The price-quantity combinations in the three scenarios under investigation are designated as follows:

No tax, no inflation (p_0, C_0)

Tax, no inflation (p_1, C_1)

Tax and (2%) inflation (p_2, C_2)

As is explained in more detail in appendix A and illustrated by figure 2A.1, under the welfare-theoretical approach to the quantification of the benefits of price stability, the following quantities (areas) are relevant:

(15) $A = \frac{1}{2}(p_1 - p_0)(C_0 - C_1),$

(16) $B = (p_1 - p_0)(C_1 - C_2),$

(17) $C = \frac{1}{2}(p_2 - p_1)(C_1 - C_2),$

(18) $D = (p_1 - p_0)C_2,$

(19) $E = (p_2 - p_1)C_2.$

In the absence of taxes and inflation, an economic agent may save the amount S_0 at the price p_0 in order to achieve the consumption level C_0 in old age. By the introduction of a tax on investment income, the real yield declines and the price of consumption rises to p_1, while the consumption level falls to C_1. As a result the consumers' surplus decreases to the extent of the area A + B + D, and a tax yield amounting to the area B + D comes into being. The difference between the two areas, viz., the (Harberger) *triangle* A is, in terms of welfare economics, a deadweight loss of taxation.

If, under the existing tax system, inflation is added (i.e., if the inflation rate rises from zero to, say, $\pi = 2$ percent), then the *interaction of distortionary taxes and inflation* leads, as will be demonstrated below, to a decline in the real

net yield and a further rise in the price of future consumption to p_2, whereas the level of consumption falls to C_2. Hence the consumers' surplus drops by the area C + E, whereas the tax yield changes by B − E. The difference is again a deadweight loss, but its magnitude is no longer in line only with the "small triangle" of traditional welfare theory, which arises through the "disruption" of a "first best" equilibrium. The deadweight loss of inflation is rather the *trapezoid* B + C, which may be much bigger and which comes into being through the extension, due to inflation, of the already existing tax-induced distortion. On the return to price stability, there arises a correspondingly large deadweight gain.

As will be demonstrated below, the change in the tax yield at zero inflation as measured by the area B − E is negative; that is, a shortfall in tax revenue occurs owing to the disappearance of inflation. Generally, it is assumed that the changed tax revenue is offset by a lump-sum tax, with a neutral effect in terms of welfare accounting. This, however, is an unrealistic assumption. In actual fact, it is to be expected that the shortfall in tax revenue is offset by the introduction, or raising, of other taxes (at a given level of expenditure), which in their turn are associated with welfare-theoretical deadweight losses. If these offsetting taxes involve a deadweight loss per deutsche mark of tax revenue amounting to λ, the welfare gain of price stability will decrease to the extent of $\lambda(B − E)$.[27] The overall benefit of a reduction in inflation then constitutes the sum of the direct deadweight gain and the indirect income effect:

$$(20) \qquad G_C = (B + C) + \lambda(B − E).$$

However, the form in which the tax losses due to the reduction in inflation would be offset, and the associated welfare effects, remain an open question. Feldstein assumes that $\lambda = 0.4$ would be a reasonable "benchmark" value for the shadow price of taxation. By contrast, we calculate the parameter λ directly from our model. More precisely, we approximate the deadweight loss of the German tax system by the ratio

$$(21) \qquad \lambda_C = A/(B + D),$$

which is the deadweight loss of capital income taxation per deutsche mark tax revenue in the regime of price stability. The overall inefficiency of the regime with tax and inflation is also of interest. It can be expressed by

$$(22) \qquad \lambda_{C+\pi} = (A + B + C)/(D + E),$$

while the marginal inefficiency of inflation-induced taxes is defined by

$$(23) \qquad \lambda_\pi = (B + C)/(E − B)$$

(see fig. 2A.1 in appendix A).

---

27. The parameter λ can therefore be regarded as a measure of inefficiency of taxation; in the best case, i.e., in one with offsetting neutral taxes (lump-sum taxes), λ would equal zero.

The above-mentioned areas are, in each case, the product of a price component and a quantity component, which will have to be measured in the next subsections.

Interest Rate and Price Effects

Given a real yield before tax of r_0 and a tax rate on investment income of Θ, in the event of an inflation rate of zero the real net yield amounts to

$$(24) \qquad r_1 = r_0(1 - \Theta).$$

Given a positive inflation rate ($\pi = 2$ percent), investment income is composed of a nominal and a real component. If the simple Fisher theorem applies, and if both components of investment income are taxed at the same rate, then the real net yield, in the case of inflation, is approximately[28]

$$(25) \qquad r_2 = (r_0 + \pi)(1 - \Theta) - \pi = r_1 - \pi\Theta.$$

That is to say, the real rate of interest is reduced owing to inflation by the amount $\pi\Theta$.[29] In principle, this adverse effect of inflation on real net interest rates could be prevented or lessened by indexing the tax system. But it is also conceivable that market adjustment reactions might ensure that the nominal interest rate (R) not only increases to the extent of the inflation rate, as in the simple Fisher theorem, but also responds disproportionately fast: $dR/d\pi > 1$.[30] To take this into account, we write the real net interest rate in the case of inflation as

$$(26) \qquad r_2 = \left(r_0 + \frac{1 - \omega}{1 - \Theta}\pi\right)(1 - \Theta) - \pi = r_1 - \pi\omega.$$

The parameter ω, which will be very important hereafter, reflects the decline in the real yield after tax that would result if the inflation rate were increased by 1 percentage point; it can be interpreted as the effective marginal tax rate on the inflation-induced component of investment income. If $\omega = \Theta$, the real and the inflation-induced components of investment income are treated alike in tax terms, and inflation exerts an unabated impact on the real net yield. If $\omega = 0$, inflation has no effect on the real net yield. After the insertion of equation (24), equation (26) can also be expressed as

28. Furthermore, it is assumed that the gross real interest rate does not include any inflation-induced risk premium and that a Tobin effect (asset substitution between fixed capital and money on account of inflation), if any, can be disregarded.

29. E.g., given a gross yield of 10 percent and a tax rate of 50 percent, the net yield under conditions of price stability would be 5 percent. With 2 percent inflation, the nominal gross yield would rise to 12 percent, but the real net yield would fall to 4 percent. It should be borne in mind in this connection that the coupon is subject to tax, with the result that if the buying rate is above par, the net real interest rate on final maturity decreases even further (and vice versa).

30. See Darby (1975) and Feldstein (1976). Given $dR/dp = 1/(1 - \Theta)$, the effect of inflation on the real net yield would be eliminated entirely.

(27) $$r_2 = r_0(1 - t),$$

where t is the effective average tax rate under conditions of inflation:

(28) $$t = \Theta + \frac{\omega}{r_0}\pi.$$

For Germany, the average real gross yield on fixed capital between 1991 and 1995 works out at $r_0 = 10.8$ percent, according to internal computations by the Bundesbank.[31]

The profits of German corporations distributed to domestic individuals are subject to a variety of taxes: trade tax (on returns and capital), corporation tax, investment income tax, property tax, income tax, and the solidarity surcharge (to finance German unification).[32] But in contrast to the situation in the United States, corporation tax and investment income tax (as well as the applicable solidarity surcharge) are set off against income tax, in the form of a *tax credit*. As can be seen from appendix table 2D.1, the average tax burden in this model calculation amounts to $t = 60.7$ percent.[33] Thus it follows from equation (27) that the real net yield is $r_2 = 10.8(1 - 0.607) = 4.24$ percent.

This yield was achieved with an average inflation rate of 3.3 percent between 1991 and 1995. If it is assumed that the inflation rates recorded in the statistics overstate the actual increases in prices,[34] then it is possible to calculate for the period in question, as Feldstein did for the United States, an average effective inflation rate of $\pi = 2$ percent. The real net yield that would result in the absence of inflation can now be computed from equation (26):

(26') $$r_1 = r_2 + \pi\omega.$$

In order to determine the effective tax rate on nominal investment income (ω), we take account of the *depreciation* and the *interest paid* in the corporate sector and the *interest received* in the private sector.[35]

(29) $$\omega = \tau z - \tau b + \tau'b'.$$

---

31. The gross income of nonfinancial enterprises (excluding also the housing sector, agriculture, and fishery, as well as imputed entrepreneurs' earnings) in relation to net fixed capital at replacement costs is used as an indicator of the fixed capital yield. In order to prevent distortions on account of German unification, we will henceforth use western German data (old Länder) for the period 1991–95 where necessary.

32. The following calculations refer to the stylized tax regulations prevailing in 1995 and 1996. Starting in 1997 the investment income tax was cancelled; furthermore, the abolition of the trade tax on capital is envisaged.

33. The average tax burden on the retained profits of a domestic corporation works out at 64.3 percent, and that on the earnings of a partnership at a calculated rate of 55.3 percent.

34. The consumer price index is likely to be upwardly distorted on account of a product substitution bias, a quality bias, a new goods bias, and an outlet substitution bias (see Edey 1994).

35. In the private sector Feldstein also takes account of the effect of taxing capital gains, but this plays only a subordinate role under German tax legislation (in income taxation there are so-called speculation periods of six months and two years, respectively, for securities transactions and real property transactions).

In this equation, τ is the marginal tax rate for distributed corporate profits and τ' is the (weighted) marginal income tax rate, including the solidarity surcharge. Moreover, z denotes the present value of tax depreciation, b the debt ratio of enterprises (the ratio of borrowed capital bearing interest at market rates to total capital), and b' the ratio of shares and debt securities in households' portfolios.

Since the depreciation is effected in order to calculate the taxable earnings on the basis of historical purchase prices (and not of replacement costs), inflation reduces the present value of depreciation (z) and thus increases the effective tax rate. Auerbach (1978) showed that capital costs increase by the amount τz if the inflation rate rises by 1 percentage point. The present value depends on the write-off period for tax purposes of the asset in question (T_s), as well as on the depreciation method used and the discounting factor (nominal market interest rate after tax). As an approximation to the customary depreciation allowances, we use the formula

$$(30) \qquad z = \frac{2/T_s}{r_2 + \pi + 2/T_s}.$$

As appendix table 2D.1 shows, with the assumptions underlying our considerations the marginal tax burden on the distributed profits of a domestic corporation amounts to $\tau = 48$ percent.[36] If, moreover, one assumes an average write-off period of $T_s = 10$ years, given a real net yield of $r_2 = 4.24$ percent, as calculated above, and an inflation rate of 2 percent, the present value of tax depreciation works out at $z = 0.76$; that is to say, the reduction of the inflation rate by 1 percentage point would increase the real yield by $\tau z = 0.37$ percentage points.

This positive effect on the real yield is counteracted by the tax deductibility of nominal interest costs. If every percentage point of inflation increases the nominal cost of corporate indebtedness by 1 percent (see Feldstein 1997, 133–34; Mishkin 1992), then the real interest costs remain unchanged whereas the enterprise obtains an additional deduction option when calculating its taxable profits. In the case of an inflation rate of zero, this relief of earnings would disappear. Given a corporate debt ratio of $b = 45$ percent,[37] the reduction of the inflation rate by 1 percentage point leads to a decline in the real yield of $\tau b = 0.22$ percentage points.

In the private sector, income taxes are likewise related to nominal interest income, which gives rise to taxation of fictitious profits. Hence, a reduction in the inflation rate lowers the effective tax rate and raises the real net yield. If the real gross yield is independent of the level of the inflation rate, then the

---

36. The distributed profits of a partnership are subject to a marginal tax burden of identical size. On the other hand, the marginal tax burden on the retained profits of a corporation, at 57 percent, is actually even higher (see appendix table 2D.1).

37. This figure refers to the average corporation's liabilities other than its provisions (see Deutsche Bundesbank 1994b, 16).

real net yield falls to the extent of the marginal tax rate. On the basis of a ratio of shares and debt securities to households' net financial assets of $b' = 43$ percent,[38] and on the assumption of a weighted marginal income tax rate (including the solidarity surcharge) of $\tau' = 37.6$ percent,[39] in the event of a decline in the inflation rate of 1 percentage point, a rise in real net interest rates of $\tau'b' = 0.16$ percentage points occurs.

If one combines these three components, the outcome is an effective marginal tax rate on inflation-induced capital income of $\omega = 0.31$. The upshot of this, in accordance with equation (26'), for the real net yield with an inflation rate of zero is $r_1 = 4.24 + 2*0.31 = 4.87$ percent. According to this estimate, the real net yield would rise by 0.63 percentage points on account of the disappearance of an inflation rate of 2 percent.[40]

If one assumes a time span of $T = 27$ years for the average period elapsing between the saving of the young generation and their consumption in old age,[41] the following prices result from equation (14) for retirement consumption in the three aforementioned scenarios:

Scenario	Interest Rate (%)	Price
No tax, no inflation	$r_0 = 10.80$	$p_0 = 0.0627$
Tax, no inflation	$r_1 = 4.87$	$p_1 = 0.2771$
Tax and (2%) inflation	$r_2 = 4.24$	$p_2 = 0.3255$

A First Approximation

Given the interest rates and price changes between the two regimes derived above, we are now able to give a first and rough estimate of the benefits of price stability. For this purpose we need an approximation of the change in retirement consumption $(C_1 - C_2)$. From equation (13) the following expression for the consumption reaction can be derived:

(31) $$dC = \frac{S}{p}\frac{dp}{p}\varepsilon_{Cp}, \quad \text{or } C_1 - C_2 = \frac{p_1 - p_2}{p_2}C_2\varepsilon_{Cp},$$

where ε_{Cp} denotes the compensated elasticity of retirement consumption with respect to its price.[42]

Using the Slutsky decomposition and equations (13) and (14), the unobservable compensated price elasticity of retirement consumption (ε_{Cp}) and the un-

---

38. The net financial assets are calculated without mortgage debts (see Deutsche Bundesbank 1996a; 1996b, 25–47).

39. This rate results from a (weighted) income tax rate of 35 percent and a solidarity surcharge of 7.5 percent (see appendix table 2D.1).

40. For the United States, Feldstein ascertains a rise of 0.49 percentage points in the real net yield.

41. For the United States, Feldstein assumes a period of 30 years.

42. Regarding the compensated demand function, see Silberberg (1978) and Varian (1984).

compensated interest rate elasticity of the saving of the young generation (η_{Sr}) are related through

(32) $\varepsilon_{Cp} = -(1 - \sigma_y - \eta_{Sp})$,   with $\eta_{Sp} = -\eta_{Sr}\dfrac{1 + r}{rT}$,

where σ_y is the income effect caused by a change in the interest rate; it is measured by the ratio of the saving of the young generation to their (exogenous) wage and salary income. In this subsection, we assume that saving is completely interest inelastic and we ignore the income effect, resulting in $\varepsilon_{Cp} = -1$.

As equation (B9) of appendix B shows, in the overlapping generations model the following link exists between the saving of the young generation (S_2) and aggregate private saving (S):

(33) $S = S_2(1 - q)$,   where $q = (1 + n + g)^{-T}$.

In this equation, $n + g = 2.2$ percent is the longer term average growth rate of real wages and salaries (and at the same time of the real domestic product) between 1986 and 1994.[43] If one also bears in mind that private saving accounts for a share $S = 9.3$ percent in GDP, the saving of the young generation is estimated as $S_2 = 20.9$ percent of GDP, giving $C_2 = S_2/p_2 = 64.1$ percent of GDP.[44]

Plugging this value into equation (31) and recalling from the previous section that we estimated the relative change of the price for retirement consumption as $(p_1 - p_2)/p_2 = 14.9$ percent, we obtain the following increase in retirement consumption: $C_1 - C_2 = 9.55$ percent of GDP. In conjunction with equations (16) and (17) we obtain $2.05 + 0.23 = 2.28$ percent of GDP as a rule-of-thumb estimate of the trapezoid area $B + C$.

To make the factors behind this calculation more explicit, we may alternatively use the following simple but instructive formula:

(34)
$$B + C \approx S_2 \frac{p_1 - p_0}{p_1} \cdot \frac{p_2 - p_1}{p_2}$$
$$= 0.209 * 0.774 * 0.149 = 2.4\% \text{ of GDP},$$

which largely confirms the result derived above. Equation (34) decomposes the welfare gains of price stability into three factors. The first, saving of the young, is the base for capital income taxation. The second factor is the change in the price of retirement consumption due to capital income taxation. The third fac-

---

43. In this case, the average rate of the last five years is distorted downward owing to German unification, which is why we use a 10-year average here.

44. Alternatively, the saving of the young generation can also be determined using eq. (B5) of appendix B. In this way, the estimated value of the share of saving of the young generation in the gross domestic product likewise works out at $S_2 = 20.9$ percent.

tor measures the price increase due to (2 percent) inflation. This factor itself can be decomposed approximately into the rate of (dis)inflation (π), the implicit inflation tax rate (ω) defined in equation (26), and the average number of years until retirement (T):

(34′)
$$\frac{p_2 - p_1}{p_2} \approx \pi \omega T.$$

Hence, the welfare costs of inflation tend to be high if the saving rate is high, if capital income is taxed heavily, or if the tax system is not indexed. All of these factors apply to the German economy and may explain—besides still deeply rooted historical experiences with hyperinflation and more recent inflation periods in the seventies and early eighties—the pronounced inflation aversion and stability culture of the German population.

· Thus on the basis of this first approximation we may conclude that the elimination of a low inflation rate of 2 percent produces a direct welfare gain of more than 2 percent of GDP. This ready-reckoner admittedly neglects any substitution effects and income effects of the change in interest rates. Moreover, the welfare effects of compensatory tax revenue changes are not yet included. This is the subject of the next subsection.

Quantity Effects

For a more exact calculation of the quantity effects we need the uncompensated interest elasticity of saving (η_{Sr}) as well as the saving ratio of the young generation (σ_y). As outlined in more detail in appendix B, from the overlapping generations model we obtain $\eta_{Sr} = 0.25$ for the uncompensated saving elasticity, implying $\eta_{Sp} = -0.228$. Since on average gross wages account for 56 percent of GDP, we get $\sigma_y = S_y/GDP = 0.209/0.56 = 0.374$. Therefore, equation (32) yields the value $\varepsilon_{Cp} = -[1 - 0.374 - (-0.228)] = -0.854$ for the price elasticity of retirement consumption. This in turn yields $C_1 - C_2 = (-0.149)*0.642*(-0.854) = 8.16$ percent of GDP for the change in retirement consumption and, by the same procedure, $C_0 - C_1 = 49.9$ percent of GDP. Finally, equation (13) provides the value $C_2 = 64.3$ percent of GDP.[45] Combining the estimated price and quantity effects, areas A to E can now be quantified from equations (15) through (19):

A = 5.35 percent of GDP
B = 1.75 percent of GDP
C = 0.20 percent of GDP
D = 13.79 percent of GDP
E = 3.11 percent of GDP

---

45. This assumes that the share of saving of the young generation is roughly the same under both regimes, i.e., both with and without inflation.

Owing to the disappearance of the distortions in the intertemporal allocation of consumption and saving alone, the direct welfare gain of price stability amounts to $B + C = 1.95$ percent of GDP.

However, tax revenue would decrease by $B - E = -1.36$ percent of GDP. The deadweight loss per deutsche mark of tax revenue on the taxation of investment income is estimated at $\lambda_C = A/(B + D) = 5.35/15.54 = 0.34$. If one assumes that the above-computed tax loss in the case of price stability is offset by raising taxes with a similar shadow price, then the overall benefit of reducing inflation amounts on balance, pursuant to equation (20), to

$$G_C = 1.95 + 0.34 * (-1.36) = 1.48\% \text{ of GDP.}$$

The Problem of Indexation

The shadow price of capital income taxes under conditions of inflation $\lambda_{C+\pi} = (A + B + C)/(D + E) = 0.43$, as calculated from equation (22), is distinctly higher than under price stability, which is $\lambda_C = 0.34$. The reason is the exceptionally high shadow price of the implicit inflation tax, defined in equation (23), which turns out to be $\lambda_\pi = (B + C)/(E - B) = 1.43$, demonstrating yet again that inflation is an extremely inefficient way of generating government revenue. Hence, the principle of causation as well as welfare analysis suggests that monetary policy and not tax policy should be primarily responsible for eliminating the highly inefficient inflation tax.

Nevertheless, it is sometimes argued that the welfare gain deriving from the reduction of inflation could be accomplished equally well by indexing the tax system. This argument is correct only in principle. To attain the same real yield under conditions of inflation as in a state of price stability—that is, r_1—the tax rate would have to be made dependent on the inflation rate. The taxation of capital income would have to be shaped in such a way that the effective average tax rate is a diminishing function of the (true, not necessarily the measured) inflation rate; that is, the following equation would have to apply:

$$(28') \qquad \Theta = t - \frac{\omega}{r_0}\pi = 0.607 - 2.87\pi.$$

Given an inflation rate of 2 percent, the average tax rate of $t = 60.7$ percent would have to fall by 5.7 percentage points to $\Theta = 55$ percent in order to attain the same effective taxation as in the case of price stability. Since r_0 is not necessarily constant, and since ω likewise hinges on variables rather than constants, the indexation formula would have to be adjusted continually. That is only one of many reasons why indexation is not a practicable alternative to price stability.[46] In the absence of inflation, however, the lower effective tax rate would materialize "of its own accord."

---

46. A more detailed discussion of the problems posed by the indexation of the tax system can be found in Feldstein (1997, 150–53).

The Effect of Social Security Contributions

The analysis so far has implicitly assumed that a fully funded system is in place for providing old-age pensions. This assumption allows us to keep the model relatively simple. However, it would be interesting to check whether the results obtained above survive if we take into account that actually many retirees receive a significant amount of exogenous income through an unfunded ("pay as you go") system.

For this purpose we assume that the young pay a fraction of their gross wages as contributions to the social security system (γW), receiving $\gamma W/q$ when retired, where $q = (1 + n + g)^{-T}$ and $n + g$ is the implicit rate of return in a pay-as-you-go system. (In a fully funded system the rate of return would be r.) Moreover, we assume that the old generation leaves "indirect bequests" (R) to the government and the young generation receives transfers (Z) from the government that are not directly linked to R. As explained in appendix C, the budget constraint of the extended overlapping generations model linking savings (S) of the young to their retirement consumption (C) changes from equation (13) to

$$(13') \qquad\qquad S = pC - \frac{p}{q}(\gamma W - R).$$

From national accounts data for the period 1991–95 we get the value $\gamma = 0.15$. The parameter $R = 0.10\text{GDP}$ was calibrated such that the model approximately reproduces the income and expenditure account of the private sector for the stated period.

Perhaps surprisingly, these extensions leave the results practically unchanged. The reduced distortion of intertemporal allocation of consumption yields benefits amounting to

$$G_C = 1.87 + 0.40*(-0.91) = 1.50\% \text{ of GDP},$$

which is almost the same result as that obtained on the basis of the simpler model.

2.3.2   Demand for Owner-Occupied Housing

Owner-occupied dwellings are given preferential treatment in income taxation, although they are fundamentally regarded as a consumer good.[47] Nevertheless, some parts of the acquisition costs are allowed to be deducted from taxes, while the notional rental value (which represents implied investment income) is not subject to taxation. (In contrast to the situation in the United

---

47. The following comments are based on former tax legislation up to 1995, excluding the tax relief on loan interest (which was limited to three years) up to the end of 1994 as well as the special assistance measures in eastern Germany. The system of assistance for residential property that was reformed by the Owner-Occupied Housing Allowance Act of 1 January 1996 has not been taken into consideration.

States, however, debt interest cannot be deducted from taxes.) This results in a subsidy-induced distortion of the demand for residential property as well as in a major shortfall in tax revenue.[48]

For reasons similar to those in subsection 2.3.1 with regard to the dead-weight loss of inflation, the following trapezoid measures the inflation-induced deadweight loss in the case of owner-occupied housing:

$$(35) \qquad G_{H_1} = [(R_0 - R_1) + \frac{1}{2}(R_1 - R_2)](H_2 - H_1),$$

where H is the demand for owner-occupied housing and R represents the user costs per deutsche mark of invested capital.

The Price and Quantity Component

In the absence of taxes and inflation, the implicit rental costs of residential property would amount to

$$(36) \qquad R_0 = r_0 + m + \delta,$$

where $m + \delta$ is the sum of maintenance costs and depreciation per deutsche mark of employed capital, which we put at 4 percent. Given a real gross rate of return in the enterprise sector of $r_0 = 10.8$ percent, the user costs amount to $R_0 = 14.8$ percent. By contrast, under present tax legislation the following calculation is relevant for a married couple given inflation:[49]

$$(36') \qquad R_2 = \mu i_m + (1 - \mu)(r_2 + \pi) + (m + \delta) - \tau' h - \pi,$$

where μ designates the share of the mortgage debt in the value of the house, i_m the nominal mortgage rate, and h the tax concession per deutsche mark of invested capital. Accordingly, the annual user costs of owner-occupied housing are the sum of the (non-tax-deductible) interest payments on the mortgage debt, the opportunity costs of the invested capital, and the maintenance and depreciation costs. The tax saving due to the possibilities of deduction for tax purposes and the inflation-induced increase in the value of the property are to be counted against this.

Under the previous form of Section 10 of the Income Tax Code, 6 percent of the (maximum DM 330,000) acquisition costs of owner-occupied dwellings (which were completed in 1992 or later) may be deducted for tax purpose for

---

48. A further benefit of price stability is the prevention of the "front loading" problem. This liquidity effect makes the acquisition of residential property more difficult since—given positive inflation—the real debt service is highest at the start of the period and later decreases; see the report of the Expert Commission on Housing Policy (Expertenkommission zur Wohnungspolitik 1994, 162 ff.). Given price stability, the real burden would, by contrast, be equally high throughout the period of the mortgage. Croushore (1992) estimates the benefit of this effect alone—assuming a reduction of inflation by 2 percentage points—to be between 0.06 and 0.12 percent of GDP.

49. Owner-occupied houses until 1996 were, in principle, also subject to general (net) wealth tax. Because of the low values to be assessed and the nominal value of the mortgage debts to be counted against them, however, very little wealth tax or none at all was due. Profits from sales are basically negligible in terms of income tax legislation.

an initial period of four years and 5 percent for a further four years.[50] Over eight years this assistance adds up DM 145,200. In addition, the home buyers' child benefit of DM 1,000 per child is deducted from liable tax. In the case of two children, this produces an amount of DM 16,000, which—given a tax rate of $\tau' = 37.6$ percent—corresponds to a gross deductible amount of around DM 42,600. In total, this produces a reduction in the tax base of DM 187,800 for the entire period in which assistance is granted. If average acquisition costs are assumed to be DM 373,000,[51] this corresponds to around 50 percent of the acquisition costs. Both marriage partners can make use of this assistance once. This is taken into account by halving the useful economic life of the property to 25 years. Spread over that period, the tax-deductible amount is $h = 50/25 = 2$ percent per annum of the acquisition costs. Given a share of borrowing in capital spending on housing construction of $\mu = 60$ percent and a nominal annual mortgage rate of 8.5 percent (at 2 percent inflation), equation (36) results in $R_2 = 0.6*8.5 + (1 - 0.6)*(4.24 + 2) - 0.376*2 + 4 - 2 = 8.85$ percent.

Assuming that the simple Fisher relationship $(di_m/d\pi = 1)$ applies to the mortgage rate, and also considering the fact that according to equation (26) $dr_2/d\pi = -\omega$, it follows from equation (36) that $dR_2/d\pi = -\omega(1 - \mu)$. This assumes that h is independent of the inflation rate. Given a lack of inflation, the user costs would hence rise to

(37) $$R_1 = R_2 + \pi\omega(1 - \mu).$$

Since $\omega = 0.31$ was calculated above, it follows that $R_1 = 8.84 + 2*0.31*(1 - 0.6) = 9.09$ percent; that is, the elimination of an inflation rate of 2 percent would increase the user costs of owner-occupied housing by 0.24 percentage points. The welfare effect (34) becomes $G_{H_1} = 0.0583(H_2 - H_1)$. The increase in user costs that are distorted downward by inflation results in a decline in the demand for housing, which leads to a corresponding reduction of capital misallocation. We approximate this quantity effect by

(38) $$H_2 - H_1 = \frac{R_1 - R_2}{R_2} H_2 \varepsilon_{HR},$$

where ε_{HR} is the compensated interest rate elasticity of capital spending on housing construction. Döpke (1996) estimates a long-term value of 0.14 for the uncompensated interest rate elasticity. This corresponds to a compensated

50. Since 1991, an income limit for a single/couple of DM 120,000/240,000 has applied to basic assistance and home buyers' child benefit.
51. Between 1991 and 1995, pure construction costs amounted to an average of DM 2,500 per square meter. This gives construction costs of around DM 305,000, assuming an average floor area of 122m². Furthermore, DM 50,000 in real estate costs are added to this, assuming that a property has an area of 200m² and a real estate price of DM 250 per square meter. Finally, assuming ancillary costs of around 5 percent of the acquisition costs results in the above-mentioned value of DM 373,000.

elasticity of around $\varepsilon_{HR} = 0.25.$[52] A ratio of 1.7 between the value of the owner-occupied housing stock and GDP thus gives $H_2 - H_1 = 1.20$ percent of GDP. In conjunction with the price effect, the direct benefit of price stability with owner-occupied housing is $G_{H_1} = 0.07$ percent of GDP.

The Indirect Revenue Effect

The indirect revenue effect is defined as

$$(39) \qquad G_{H_2} = (H_1 - H_2)r_0\Theta.$$

A fall in demand for owner-occupied housing of 1.20 percent of GDP was produced by equation (38). The capital stock in the enterprise sector increases by the same amount and generates a gross rate of return of $r_0 = 10.8$ percent and a net yield (without inflation) of $r_1 = 4.87$ percent. This corresponds to an effective average rate of taxation of $\Theta = 55$ percent; that is, $G_{H_2} = 1.20*0.108*0.55 = 0.07$ percent of GDP. If the deadweight loss per deutsche mark of tax revenue calculated above is likewise put at $\lambda_C = 0.34$ here, a net benefit is produced on balance (given price stability) of

$$G_H = G_{H_1} + \lambda_C G_{H_2} = 0.07 + 0.34*0.07 = 0.09\% \text{ of GDP.}$$

2.3.3   Money Demand and Seigniorage

The Direct Welfare Effect

Inflation increases the alternative costs of holding non-interest-bearing money balances and lowers the real demand for money below its optimal level. Since the real costs of an increase in the money stock are virtually nil, the optimal money stock, according to Friedman (1969), is that in which the opportunity costs of cash holdings are zero, that is, $r(\pi^*) + \pi^* = 0.$[53]

With the current system of taxation and given 2 percent inflation, the opportunity costs of cash holdings are $r_2 + \pi = 4.24 + 2.0 = 6.24$ percent. Given a zero inflation rate, these costs fall to $r_1 = 4.87$ percent. A Harberger analysis of the money demand produces the following trapezoid as the welfare gain due to a lowering of the inflation rate from effectively 2 percent to zero:

---

52. The relationship $\varepsilon = \eta + \Xi*(H/Y)$ applies between the compensated (ε) and uncompensated (η) elasticity, where Ξ is the income elasticity of the capital spending on housing construction and H/Y is the ratio of capital spending on housing construction to disposable income. With the income elasticity of 1.26 estimated by Döpke (1996) and a ratio of capital spending on housing construction to disposable income of 10 percent, this gives $\varepsilon = 0.14 + 1.26 * 0.10 \cong 0.25$ for the compensated elasticity.

53. The value $r_1 = 4.87$ percent has been determined for the real return given a zero inflation rate. Assuming for the sake of simplicity that the real yield is a linear function of the inflation rate, to which $dr/d\pi = -\omega$ applies, the optimal inflation rate according to Friedman is produced as the solution of $r_1 - 0.31\pi^* + \pi^* = 0$; i.e., $\pi^* = -7$ percent. If there are no lump-sum taxes, it is theoretically possible, however, that the inflation rate is positive as part of an optimal tax mix provided that money is regarded as an end good and not as an intermediate good. See also the papers by Phelps (1973) and Chari, Christiano, and Kehoe (1991).

(40) $G_{M_1} = [(r_1 - 0) + \frac{1}{2}(r_2 + \pi - r_1)](M_1 - M_2);$

that is, $G_{M_1} = 0.0556(M_1 - M_2)$. The change in the money demand can be approximated by

(41) $M_1 - M_2 = \dfrac{r_2 + \pi - r_1}{r_2 + \pi} \varepsilon_{Mi} M_2 .$

According to our estimations, the interest rate elasticity of the demand for money (currency in circulation and required reserves) is $\varepsilon_{Mi} = 0.25$ in absolute value. Given a 9 percent share of these monetary components in GDP, it follows that $M_1 - M_2 = 0.50$ percent of GDP. The product of the price and the quantity effect gives the direct welfare gain of price stability in the money demand; it amounts to just $G_{M_1} = 0.03$ percent of GDP.

The Indirect Revenue Effect

The indirect revenue effect of reduced money demand is made up of three components. First, the reduction of the "inflation tax" to real money balances (M) leads to a loss of monetary seigniorage. This implies a welfare loss since other distorting taxes have to be increased. The (active) seigniorage to the amount of[54]

(42) $S = \pi M$

reacts to changes in the inflation rate in accordance with $dS/d\pi = M + \pi(dM/d\pi)$. After some transformations using $d(r_2 + \pi)/d\pi = 1 - \omega$, this may be written as

(43) $dS = \left[1 - \varepsilon_{Mi}(1 - \omega)\dfrac{\pi}{r_2 + \pi}\right]M\pi .$

Assuming a ratio of money balances (currency in circulation and minimum reserves) to GDP of 9 percent and an interest rate elasticity of money demand in absolute terms of $\varepsilon_{Mi} = 0.25$, the loss of seigniorage if there is price stability comes to $dS = 0.17$ percent of GDP.

Second, an income effect results from the fact that less capital and more real money balances are held if there is price stability. The value $M_1 - M_2 = 0.50$ percent of GDP has been determined above for the rise in the money demand. In the enterprise sector this capital earns a gross return of $r_0 = 10.8$ percent and is subject (given price stability) to taxation at $\Theta = 55$ percent. The loss of income is thus

(44) $dK = (M_1 - M_2)r_0\Theta;$

that is, $dK = 0.03$ percent of GDP.

---

54. Seigniorage also arises in a growing economy independent of the rate of inflation (passive seigniorage).

Third, the government is in a position to reduce interest-bearing debt instruments to the amount of the increased cash holdings. Although this is a one-off effect, it permanently reduces the government's debt service by

$$(45) \qquad dB \; = \; r_{ng}(M_1 \; - \; M_2),$$

where

$$(46) \qquad r_{ng} \; = \; (1 \; - \; \tau')\gamma \; - \; \pi$$

is the real rate of interest on the public debt. Assuming that the ratio of debt service to public debt is $\gamma = 7.8$ percent, and given a rate of taxation of $\tau' = 37.6$ percent, there is a real interest rate of $r_{ng} = 2.87$ percent. The income effect thus comes to $dB = 0.01$ percent of GDP. The total loss of government income if there is price stability is therefore

$$(47) \qquad G_{M_2} \; = \; - dS \; - \; dK \; + \; dB;$$

that is, $G_{M_2} = -0.19$ percent of GDP. Using the same shadow price of taxation as before yields a small negative benefit of money demand under price stability:

$$G_M \; = \; G_{M_1} + \lambda_C G_{M_2} \; = \; 0.03 \; + \; 0.34 * (-0.19) \; = \; -0.04\% \text{ of GDP.}$$

2.3.4   Government Debt Service

This subsection considers the welfare effect that results from the fact that higher real rates of interest also increase the real costs of the government's debt service. A fully anticipated inflation leaves the real gross interest rate on the public debt unchanged, whereas the inflation premium is subject to income tax. A lower inflation rate hence does not reduce the pretax cost of debt service—that is, it does not produce a direct advantage—but it does reduce the tax revenue accruing from the (eligible) interest rate payments on the public debt. This requires a compensatory increase of other taxes.

The starting point for quantifying this effect is the following budget equation for the change in the level of debt (D):

$$(48) \qquad \Delta D \; = \; G \; - \; T \; + \; (r_g + \pi)(1 \; - \; \tau')D,$$

where r_g is the real gross interest rate on the public debt and τ' is the marginal rate of taxation. In equilibrium the public debt grows at the same rate as nominal GDP; that is, $\Delta D = D(n + g + \pi)$. Combining this equilibrium condition with the above budget equation produces the following expression for the tax revenue:

$$(49) \qquad T \; = \; [(1 \; - \; \tau')(r_g + \pi) \; - \; (n \; + \; g \; + \; \pi)]D \; + \; G.$$

Differentiation of this budget constraint with respect to the inflation rate gives the reaction of tax revenue if there is a change in the inflation rate:

Table 2.3   **Benefits of Price Stability: Reducing Inflation from 2 Percent to Zero
(change as percent of GDP)**

| | Welfare Effect | | | Memo Item: |
Item	Direct	Indirect	Overall	United States
Consumption timing	1.95	−0.47	1.48	0.95
Housing demand	0.07	0.02	0.09	0.22
Money demand	0.03	−0.06	−0.04	−0.03
Debt service	−	−0.12	−0.12	−0.10
Overall benefit	2.04	−0.63	1.41	1.04
Memo item: United States	1.14	−0.10		

$$(50) \qquad dT = -\tau'D\,d\pi.$$

Given government debt of $D = 48$ percent of GDP on average over the years 1991–95, $d\pi = 2$ percentage points produces a change of $dT = 0.36$ percent of GDP. This fall in tax revenue resulting from the elimination of inflation must be offset by compensatory tax increases, which gives rise to a (negative) benefit:

$$G_D = 0.34*(-0.36) = -0.12\% \text{ of GDP.}$$

2.3.5   Overall Benefit of Price Stability

The benefits of a zero inflation rate from the intertemporal allocation of consumption (G_C), the demand for owner-occupied housing (G_H), the demand for money (G_M), and the government's debt service (G_D) are combined in table 2.3.

Accordingly, the reduction of an (anticipated, equilibrium, and effective) inflation rate from 2 percent to zero results in a benefit of 1.41 percent of GDP year by year. This benefit is primarily the outcome of preventing inflation-induced distortions in the intertemporal allocation of consumption and saving (1.48 percent of GDP). The correction of the distortions in the demand for owner-occupied housing makes a net contribution amounting to 0.09 percent of GDP. The slight benefit in the case of money demand is overcompensated by the associated shortfalls in government income, resulting on balance in costs amounting to 0.04 percent of GDP. The lack of the alleviating financing effect of inflation in the servicing of public debt leads by itself to further costs, which are estimated at 0.12 percent of GDP. Just under one-third of the direct welfare gains amounting to 2.04 percent of GDP is used up again by indirect revenue shortfalls.

During the years 1991–95 the statistically measured inflation rate in Germany came to an average of 3.3 percent. On account of the lack of precision in statistical measuring, it is not possible to state beyond doubt whether this corresponds to an effective inflation rate of 2 percent. There is hence some

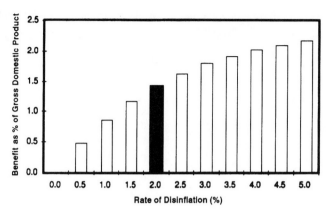

Fig. 2.1   Benefits of price stability

amount of uncertainty regarding the actual size of the "disinflation potential." As figure 2.1 shows, the benefit of price stability is a nonlinear function of the size of reduction in inflation. Assuming a reduction in inflation of 3 percentage points (which would then roughly correspond to a measured inflation rate of zero), rather than of 2 percentage points, the benefit increases from 1.41 to 1.78 percent of GDP. Conversely, a reduction in the inflation rate by only 1 percentage point would still produce a sizable benefit of 0.85 percent of GDP. By way of approximation, the relationship between the size of the reduction in inflation (π) and the benefit as a percentage of GDP (G) may be expressed by

(51) $$G = \pi^{\zeta}, \qquad \zeta > 0,$$

where $\zeta = 0.5$ describes this relationship quite well.

Comparing the results for Germany with Feldstein's for the United States reveals greater differences, above all, in terms of the intertemporal allocation of consumption. At 1.95 percent of GDP (according to our calculation), the direct welfare gain in this component is almost twice as large as Feldstein's, at 1.02 percent. In order to explain this difference, the direct benefit of price stability in consumption allocation has been broken down into the product of four factors in table 2.4: the relative price effect (RPE), the interest rate elasticity of consumption, the relative savings of the young generation, and the share of private saving in GDP. As this table shows, the differences in the first three of those effects are comparatively small and they mutually compensate each other. The greater benefit of price stability in our calculation hence ultimately rests on the fact that the saving ratio (as a percentage of GDP) is almost twice as high in Germany as it is in the United States.

The higher saving ratio in Germany also largely explains the greater (negative) indirect income effect in our calculation. Putting the saving ratio in our calculation at 5 percent for Germany, too, would produce a direct benefit in consumption allocation of 1.26 percent of GDP (compared with 1.02 percent for the United States) and an indirect income effect of −0.22 percent (−0.10

Table 2.4   **Comparison of Results with the United States**

Country	Relative Price Effect[a] (RPE)	Interest Rate Elasticity $(|\varepsilon_{C_p}|)$	Savings of Young Generation (S_y/S_N)	Saving Ratio (%) (S_N/GDP)	Direct Benefit (% of GDP) (G_{C_1})
Germany	0.109	0.854	2.251	9.30	1.95
United States	0.092	1.230	1.800	5.00	1.02
Ratio (Germany/U.S.)	1.19	0.69	1.25	1.86	1.91

[a]RPE $= [(p_1 - p_0)/p_2 + (p_2 - p_1)/(2p_2)] \, (p_2 - p_1)/p_2$.

percent). Despite all the other differences between the systems of taxation and the structural and behavioral parameters in the two economies, the overall benefit of a reduction of the inflation rate by 2 percentage points—given matching saving ratios—would be almost as large, at 0.94 percent of GDP, as for the United States (1.04 percent). Hence, it is the high saving rate in Germany, coupled with capital income taxes, that explains the large costs of even moderate rates of inflation.

2.3.6   The Risks: Some Sensitivity Calculations

Our calculations of the scale of the benefit due to price stability rely on a number of simplifying assumptions. Furthermore, some of the assumed quantitative values for the structural and behavioral parameters of the German economy are attended by considerable uncertainties. Appendix table 2D.2 contains an overview of all parametric assumptions (benchmark values) and a comparison with the coefficients assumed by Feldstein for the United States.

In order to obtain some initial points of reference for the sensitivity of the calculations to the assumptions that have been made, we have calculated each coefficient with alternative lower and upper values deviating from the benchmark. The range of these values was chosen to correspond to what we felt subjectively to be roughly two standard deviations.[55] As the results of these calculations show in appendix table 2D.3, varying the coefficients changes the overall benefit comparatively little; most results remain within the range of 1.41 ± 0.10 percent of GDP. The benefit of price stability that has been estimated thus appears to be quite robust in terms of the parametric assumptions that have been made.

An exception to this is the length of the *discounting period*. If the period is reduced (increased) from $T = 27$ to $T = 24$ (30) years, the benefit of price stability falls (rises) to 1.30 (1.51) percent of GDP. Another very important parameter is the *average rate of taxation* on distributed profits ($t = 60.7$ percent); a 3 percentage point reduction lowers the overall benefit to 1.31 percent of GDP, whereas an increase by the same amount raises the overall benefit of

55. For a normally distributed random variable, the stated interval includes the actual value with a probability of about .68.

Table 2.5   Benefits of Price Stability: Simulation (change as percent of GDP)

Item	Mean Value	Standard Deviation	Median	Skewness[a]
Consumption timing	1.44	0.490	1.39	0.30
Housing demand	0.10	0.065	0.09	0.62
Money demand	−0.03	0.023	−0.03	−0.22
Debt service	−0.12	0.044	−0.12	−0.28
Overall benefit	1.39	0.473	1.34	0.30

Note: Results are based on 10,000 stochastic simulations.

[a]Pearson's measure of skewness: 3*(arithmetic mean − median)/standard deviation.

disinflation to 1.52 percent. Besides this, the marginal rate of taxation ($\tau' = 37.6$ percent) has an appreciable influence.

In addition, the calculations react quite sensitively to the assumption concerning the *interest rate elasticity of savings,* for which a benchmark value of $\eta_{s_r} = 0.25$ was determined (see appendix B). Lowering this elasticity to 0.10 reduces the benefit to 1.11 percent of GDP, whereas increasing it to 0.40 (i.e., the benchmark value used by Feldstein) increases the benefit to 1.74 percent.[56]

The shadow price of taxation for calculating the indirect revenue effects was set by Feldstein at the benchmark value $\lambda = 0.4$ and the alternative value 1. As explained above, this parameter is not set exogenously in our calculations but is instead determined model-endogenously as the shadow price of capital income taxation with the value $\lambda = 0.34$.

Deterministic parameter variations, in which all the other input values are kept constant, can give only an incomplete description of the uncertainties contained in a model calculation of this kind. For that reason, we have also used a Monte Carlo simulation to assess the variability of the benefit of price stability. In doing this, we regard all 23 parameters as independently normally distributed random variables.[57] The mean values of this distribution are the benchmark values used in our calculation. The difference between the lower (or upper) parameter value shown in appendix table 2D.3 and the benchmark value was set as the (subjective) standard deviation in all cases. As mentioned above, we assume that there is a roughly .68 probability of the actual parameter value being within the stated interval. We have taken a random sample from each of the 23 distributions and recalculated the benefit of price stability. This operation was repeated 10,000 times.

Table 2.5 shows the results of these simulation exercises. At 1.39 percent of GDP, the arithmetic mean of the benefit of price stability is very close to the

56. This sensitivity to the interest rate elasticity of savings is likewise revealed in the calculations made by Feldstein, which show the overall benefit (0.65, 1.04, and 1.62) for alternative values of the interest rate elasticity (0, 0.4, and 1).

57. The assumption of independence is undoubtedly a great simplification. An empirically grounded estimation of the correlation structures between the structural parameters and the behavioral coefficients would go beyond the scope of this study, however.

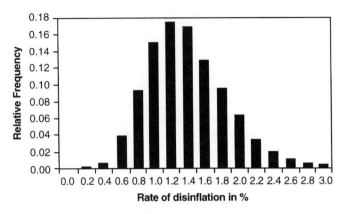

Fig. 2.2   Frequency distribution of benefits

deterministic value 1.41. The simulated standard deviation amounts to 0.47 percent of GDP. The median of the distribution of the overall benefit is 1.34 percent of GDP. This means (see also fig. 2.2) that the distribution of the benefit is positively skewed, which is likewise expressed in the positive Pearson measure of skewness of 0.30.

According to the simulation calculations, the probability of an overall benefit of less than 1 percent of GDP is 0.21. By contrast, the probability of the benefit being greater than the breakeven point of $G = 0.28$ percent of GDP (which was established in section 2.3) is 0.998.

2.3.7   On the Optimal Rate of Disinflation

We have assumed hitherto that the rate of inflation is reduced by 2 percentage points. In view of the determined costs and benefits, it remains questionable whether this is the optimal strategy, however. This requires an additional test criterion. Howitt, from a welfare-economic point of view, postulates the following rule in order to assess which (dis)inflation rate a central bank should aim for (Howitt's rule): "In order to estimate the optimal target rate of inflation, one must somehow balance the gains from reducing inflation against the costs of doing so. The reduction in inflation should continue as long as the present discounted value of the benefits to society from a further small reduction exceeds the present discounted value of the cost. The optimal target rate is the rate at which the benefit of further reduction just equals the cost of raising unemployment by the required amount above the natural rate."[58] As the preceding comments have shown, both the benefits (G) and the costs (C) are regarded as (nonlinear) functions of the rate of disinflation (π); see equations (11) and (51) and figure 2.3.

As a function of the constant discounting factor ρ (see subsection 2.2.3), the net benefit (g) of disinflation may be expressed as

---

58. Howitt (1990, 104). Howitt's rule is discussed in detail by Thornton (1996).

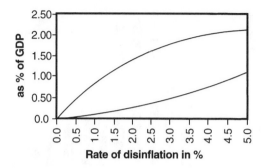

Fig. 2.3   Benefits and costs of price stability
Note: Upper curve shows benefits; lower curve, costs.

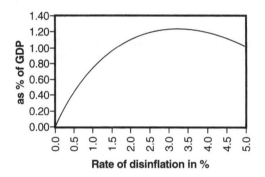

Fig. 2.4   "Optimal" rate of disinflation

$$(52) \qquad g(\pi) = G(\pi) - \rho C(\pi) = \pi^{\zeta} - \rho \sigma \pi^{1+\varphi}.$$

In accordance with Howitt's rule, the optimal disinflation rate (π^*) must fulfil the necessary condition $\partial g / \partial \pi = 0$, resulting in

$$(53) \qquad \pi^* = \left(\frac{1}{\rho\sigma} \cdot \frac{\zeta}{1 + \varphi} \right)^{1/(1+\varphi-\zeta)}.$$

The higher the discounting rate and the higher the sacrifice ratio, the lower the optimal disinflation rate. Assuming as before $\zeta = \varphi = 0.5$, $\rho = 2.5$ percent, and $\sigma = 4$, the *optimal disinflation rate is $\pi^* = 3.3$ percent* (see fig. 2.4). The empirical data used in the estimate reflect the average conditions in the period 1991–95 when the statistically measured average inflation rate was 3.3 percent. Bearing this in mind, the result achieved suggests the conclusion that it would be optimal to aim at a zero inflation rate or stability of the measured price level.[59] The result obtained for the optimal inflation rate in accordance with equation (53) depends to a considerable extent, however, on the choice of pa-

59. As Scarth (1990) has shown, a goal of this kind would be both transparent and credible.

rameters included in it and, for that reason, should not be overvalued. Additionally, there are uncertainties and risks both in quantifying the disinflation costs and (as the sensitivity analyses have shown) in quantifying the benefits, which suggest a cautious interpretation of the results.

> If there is anything in the world which ought to be stable it is money, the
> measure of everything which enters the channels of trade.
> —François Le Blanc, *Traité historique des monnayes de France* (1690;
> quoted in Einaudi 1953)

2.4   Summary and Conclusions

In the run-up to European monetary union and the discussion to be held on the monetary policy strategy of a future European Central Bank, Issing writes, "The current large measure of consensus is not a guarantee, however, that the pendulum will not swing back at some point in the future. . . . The risk of inflation is not dead simply because the statistics show price stability at present. It will have been really conquered only when it has disappeared once and for all from the range of attractive available policy options" (1996a, 309).

In that respect, this study has confirmed for Germany what Feldstein discovered for the United States: inflation is anything but an attractive option. The interaction of even moderate rates of inflation with the existing system of taxation results in a significant loss of welfare. The change from an equilibrium "true" inflation rate of 2 percent (which may correspond to a measured rate of 3 percent) to a rate of zero brings permanent welfare gains, equivalent to 1.4 percent of GDP year for year. The deadweight loss of 2 percent inflation is so great because Germany has a high saving rate, capital income is taxed heavily, and the tax system is not indexed. Inflation intensifies the distortions of taxation on capital income. For that reason the welfare gains of price stability should be measured not by a "Harberger triangle" but by a "Feldstein trapezoid." Even if we regard the output losses (in the form of a temporary Okun gap) during disinflation as far from negligible, there are, in our opinion, no convincing arguments that moderate inflation is superior to price stability.

In the years 1991–95, the base period of our calculations, the average measured rate of inflation turned out to be 3.3 percent per annum. In 1996 the rate of inflation was 1.5 percent. Considering the sustained economic problems of the new Länder in eastern Germany and the difficult labor market situation, one may ask whether this policy of disinflation by about 2 percentage points was justified or whether the Bundesbank should have executed a more expansionary monetary policy in order to stabilize the inflation rate at 3.3 percent.

According to our calculations, the disinflation by almost 2 percentage points was well justified, provided one is prepared to look not only at the short-lived costs of disinflation but also at the longer term gains of price stability. This is a powerful argument for putting monetary policy into the hands of an indepen-

Table 2.6   **Menu of Choices (costs and benefits as percent of GDP)**

Initial Measured Rate of Inflation[a]	3.3	3.3	3.3	3.3	3.3	3.3
Rate of Disinflation	0.0	1.0	2.0	3.3	4.0	5.0
Final Measured Rate of Inflation	3.3	2.3	1.3	0.0	−0.7	−1.7
Permanent benefits	0.00	0.85	1.41	1.86	2.01	2.24
Annualized costs	0.00	0.10	0.28	0.60	0.80	1.12
Benefits minus costs	0.00	0.75	1.13	1.26	1.21	1.12
Annual loss in welfare	−1.26	−0.51	−0.13	0.00	−0.05	−0.14

[a]Average rate of inflation between 1991 and 1995.

dent and forward-looking institution with a long time horizon. An independent central bank with the primary goal of price stability is able to invest in the public good called "price stability" even if the starting costs exceed the first-round benefits, as is usually the case for long-lived investments. Besides this, it should not be forgotten that the sacrifice ratio hinges on the degree of nominal rigidity, which can be influenced to some extent by carefully choosing the timing, speed, and policy mix of disinflation. The menu of choices in table 2.6 summarizes the main results of our study.

Stabilizing the rate of inflation at 3.3 percent would have avoided any costs of disinflation, but there would have been no gains either. Compared to the optimal strategy, the policy of preserving the status quo achieved at that time would have incurred a permanent annual welfare loss of roughly 1.3 percent of GDP. A modest disinflation by 1 percentage point already would have reduced the unexploited gains to 0.5 percent of GDP. The actual amount of disinflation by almost 2 percentage points exploits almost all potential gains, provided the present rate of inflation will be sustained. More disinflation (to bring the measured rate down to zero) would produce only small additional gains. On the other hand, as table 2.6 shows, overshooting the optimal rate of disinflation is associated with relatively small welfare losses. However, one should keep in mind that there are other costs and benefits of disinflation, not investigated in this paper. A too low (i.e., negative) inflation rate may, for example, destabilize international financial markets and cause a range of other adjustment problems.

Having made these caveats, we conclude our study as follows:

Importance: Inflation, even at moderate rates of 2 or 3 percent per annum, is a very costly economic policy option.

Asymmetry: The welfare loss of a too high inflation rate is large; the welfare loss of a too small inflation rate appears to be small.

Robustness: It does not matter much whether monetary policy aims at price stability in terms of the measured or the "true" rate of inflation. This decision should be based on such criteria as transparency, clarity, and— above all—credibility.

Price

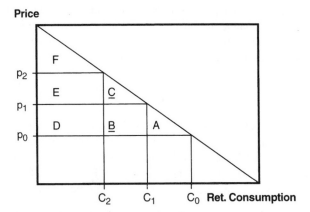

Fig. 2A.1   **Demand for retirement consumption**

At the outset we asked whether the benefits of price stability justify the costs of disinflation. To this we can now give a short, unequivocal answer: No inflation is better than low inflation! In fact, our results clearly indicate that the aim of price stability should receive priority. Tobin's often-quoted comment that "it takes a heap of Harberger Triangles to fill an Okun Gap" (1977, 467) therefore needs to be amended. In brief—and to extend the metaphor—it should continue "but it only takes one single Feldstein Trapezoid to do it."

Appendix A
The Welfare-Theoretical Approach

Consider the following three points (p_i, C_i) on the compensated demand function for retirement consumption, each corresponding to a specific type of regime (see fig. 2A.1):

No tax, no inflation	(p_0, C_0)
Tax, no inflation	(p_1, C_1)
Tax and inflation	(p_2, C_2)

Without taxes and inflation consumer surplus is the sum of areas A through F.[60] Introducing capital income taxes in an environment of price stability moves the equilibrium point from (p_0, C_0) to (p_1, C_1) with less retirement consump-

---

60. Problems with the concept of consumer surplus as a measure of welfare effects are discussed in detail by Silberberg (1978).

tion at a higher price. Consumer surplus is reduced to the area C + E + F and tax revenues corresponding to the area B + D are created. The difference, the triangle A, is a deadweight loss; it is the reduction of consumer surplus that is not compensated by higher tax revenues. The deadweight loss per deutsche mark of taxes raised is

(A1) $$\lambda_C = A/(B + D).$$

Introducing both taxes and inflation moves the equilibrium point to (p_2, C_2), with a reduced consumption level at a higher price. The remaining consumer surplus is the area F, whereas tax revenues correspond to the rectangle D + E. The deadweight loss increases to the triangle A + B + C. The following table summarizes the welfare accounting for the three regimes:

Regime	Consumer Surplus	Tax Revenues	Deadweight Loss
No tax, no inflation	A + B + C + D + E + F	–	–
Tax, no inflation	C + E + F	B + D	A
Tax and inflation	F	D + E	A + B + C

Hence, moving from the equilibrium with taxes and inflation to price stability increases consumer surplus by the area C + E and changes tax revenues by the amount (B + D) − (D + E) = B − E. The welfare difference between the two regimes is a reduction of deadweight loss, that is, a deadweight gain, measured by the *trapezoid* B + C.

Assuming that the government faces a strict budget constraint at the margin, the change in tax revenues needs to be compensated by increasing (if negative) or decreasing (if positive) other taxes. If the deadweight loss per deutsche mark of some compensating tax is denoted by λ, then

(A2) $$G_C = (B + C) + \lambda(B - E)$$

is the net deadweight gain of price stability.

Appendix B
An Overlapping Generations Model

Consider the following simple overlapping generations model with a constant relative risk aversion utility function:

(B1) $$\max \frac{C_{yt}^{1-\Psi}}{1 - \Psi} + s \frac{C_{ot+1}^{1-\Psi}}{1 - \Psi}; \qquad s = (1 + \rho)^{-T}, \quad \rho > -1, \quad \Psi > 0,$$

subject to

(B2)
$$C_{yt} + S_{yt} = W_t,$$

(B3)
$$C_{ot+1} = \frac{1}{p}S_{yt}, \qquad p = (1 + r)^{-T}.$$

C_y denotes consumption of the young generation and C_o is their retirement consumption; S_y represents savings of the young and W is their (exogenous) wage income. The parameter ρ represents the rate of time preference, and $1/\Psi$ measures the intertemporal elasticity of substitution.[61] Equation (B3) corresponds to equation (13) in the main text. The solution of this model is

(B4)
$$C_{yt}^* = W_t\Omega \qquad \text{with } \Omega = (1 + p^{1-1/\Psi}s^{1/\Psi})^{-1},$$

(B5)
$$S_{yt}^* = W_t(1 - \Omega),$$

(B6)
$$C_{ot+1}^* = \frac{1}{p}W_t(1 - \Omega).$$

The variable Ω is the young generation's propensity to consume out of wage income. Assuming that real wages grow with the rate $n + g$, from equation (B3) we can write consumption of the *presently old* as the sum of their previous period's savings and the accumulated interest income of these savings as

(B7)
$$C_{ot} = \frac{1}{p}S_{yt-1} = \frac{q}{p}S_{yt}, \qquad \text{where } q = (1 + n + g)^{-T}.$$

(Dis)saving of the presently old equals interest income minus consumption:

(B8)
$$S_{ot} = \frac{q}{p}(1 - p)S_{yt} - C_{ot} = -qS_{yt}.$$

Total savings (in period t) are equal to savings of the young plus savings of the *presently* old:

(B9)
$$S_{Nt} = S_{yt} + S_{ot} = (1 - q)S_{yt}.$$

In the period 1985–94 the average annual growth rate of real wages was $n + g = 2.2$ percent,[62] which discounted over a generation of $T = 27$ years yields $q = 0.556$, implying $S_N = 0.444S_y$. Private saving accounted for 9.3 percent of GDP on average between 1991 and 1995. Hence, from equation (B9) we get $S_y = 0.209$GDP.

---

61. See Blanchard and Fischer (1989) and Romer (1996). In the special case $\Psi \to 1$, the instantaneous utility function simplifies to the logarithmic utility function.

62. Due to German unification and other factors, the growth rate of real wages in West Germany in the period 1990–94 (1.4 percent) was exceptionally low and understates the long-term equilibrium growth rate. For this reason we use the average growth rate of the past 10 years.

Alternatively, equation (B5) can be used to calculate savings of the young. This requires estimating the intertemporal elasticity of substitution $(1/\Psi)$. Applying the Euler equation approach, Flaig (1990, 1994) obtains an intertemporal elasticity of substitution (IES) in the range 0.24–0.43 from aggregate consumption data for Germany. These low values imply a negative interest rate elasticity of saving. However, estimates of the IES by the Euler equation approach from aggregate data are likely to be biased downward. Attanasio and Weber show "that the bias introduced by using aggregate consumption data to estimate the elasticity of intertemporal substitution can be substantial" (1995, 569). In particular, aggregate data may imply an elasticity of substitution close to zero, even if it is one at the microlevel. This is confirmed in an empirical study by Beaudry and Wincoop (1996) for the United States based on a panel of state data. They find "that the IES for nondurables consumption is significantly different from 0, and probably close to 1." Hence, Flaig's results would seem to be consistent with $1/\Psi = 4/3$. Using the real interest rate calculated in the main text, that is, $r = r_2 = 4.24$ percent ($p = 0.326$) and assuming a rate of time preference of $\rho = 2.5$ percent ($s = 0.513$), yields $\Omega = 0.626$. Wages in West Germany accounted for $\alpha = 56$ percent of GDP on average over the period 1990–94. Hence, from equation (B5) we obtain $S_y = 0.209\text{GDP}$, which matches the result obtained via equation (B9).

Differentiating equation (B5) with respect to the interest rate yields the interest rate elasticity of the saving of the young:

$$(B10) \qquad \eta_{Sr} = \left(\frac{1}{\Psi} - 1\right)\Omega\frac{rT}{1 + r}.$$

This elasticity is positive if the elasticity of substitution $(1/\Psi)$ is greater than one. Using the same parameter values as before, we obtain an estimate of the interest rate elasticity of saving of the young of $\eta_{Sr} = 0.23$.

Appendix C
An Overlapping Generations Model with Transfers

The analysis so far has implicitly assumed that a fully funded system is in place for providing old-age pensions. The purpose of this appendix is to take into account the fact that many retirees actually receive a significant amount of exogenous income through an unfunded (pay as you go) system.

We retain the utility function (B1) of appendix B, that is,

$$(C1) \quad \max\frac{C_{yt}^{1-\Psi}}{1 - \Psi} + s\frac{C_{ot+1}^{1-\Psi}}{1 - \Psi}; \qquad s = (1 + \rho)^{-T}, \quad \rho > -1, \quad \Psi > 0,$$

but change the budget constraints for the young (B2) and the old (B3) generation to

(C2) $$C_{yt} + S_{yt} = W_t(1 - \tau - \gamma) + Z_t,$$

(C3) $$C_{ot+1} = \frac{S_{yt}}{p} + \frac{\gamma W_t}{q} - \frac{R_t}{q}.$$

We assume that the total wage income accrues to the young generation, as well as all government transfers, except pension payments. On the other hand, the old (retired) generation receives all nonwage income plus the pension payments. Hence, in equation (C2), W represents the (exogenous) gross wage income, including employers' contributions to social security (i.e., to the pension fund and to health and unemployment insurance); τ is an average "tax" rate that comprises employees' and employers' contributions to the social security system except for contributions to the pension fund; γ is the rate paid (by both employers and employees) to the pension fund; and Z is the amount of net government transfers received by the young generation. In equation (C3), $\gamma W/q$ is the amount of pensions received by the old generation; and R is the net amount of transfers left by the old generation. We assume that this amount is channeled through the government sector such that there is no direct link between the amount bequeathed by the old (R) and the amount of transfers received by the young (Z). Note that in contrast to the rate of return (r) of savings of the young, the implicit rate of return of contributions to the pay-as-you-go pension fund is the real growth rate $n + g$.[63]

Solving equation (C1) subject to the restrictions (C2) and (C3) yields the following optimal consumption and saving schedules:

(C4) $$C_{yt}^* = [W_t(1 - \tau - \gamma) + Z_t]\Omega + \frac{p}{q}[\gamma W_t - R_t]\Omega,$$

(C5) $$S_{yt}^* = [W_t(1 - \tau - \gamma) + Z_t](1 - \Omega) - \frac{p}{q}[\gamma W_t - R_t]\Omega,$$

(C6) $$C_{ot+1}^* = \frac{1}{p}[W_t(1 - \tau - \gamma) + Z_t](1 - \Omega) - \frac{1}{q}[\gamma W_t - R_t](1 - \Omega).$$

The parameter Ω is defined in equation (B4) of appendix B. Assuming, that the growth rate of real wages (W) and transfers (Z, R) is $n + g$, consumption of the presently old (eq. [B7]) becomes

(C7) $$C_{ot} = \frac{q}{p}S_{yt} + \gamma W_t - R_t.$$

<hr>

63. In a fully funded system we have $p = q$ and $\gamma W/p$ drops out of eq. (C3) when eq. (C2) is inserted. Hence, the optimal saving and consumption plan is independent of contributions to the pension fund (γ) in a fully funded system.

Table 2C.1   **Income and Expenditure of Private Sector**

Item	Young	Presently Old	Total
Saving	S_y	S_o	S_N
Consumption	C_y	C_o	C_N
Total	W_n	Q_n	Y_D

Table 2C.2   **Income and Expenditure of Private Sector under 2 Percent Inflation (percent of GDP)**

Item	Young	Presently Old	Total	Total (1991–95)
Saving	18.1	−10.1	8.1	9.3
Consumption	28.8	29.3	58.1	56.4
Total	46.9	19.2	66.2	
Total (1991–95)	46.2	19.5	65.7	

The equations for savings of the presently old (B8) and total private savings (B9) remain valid, however:

(C8)
$$S_{ot} = -qS_{yt},$$

(C9)
$$S_{Nt} = (1 - q)S_{yt}.$$

These relationships imply accounting table 2C.1 for period t.

In table 2C.1, $W_n = W(1 - \tau - \gamma) + Z$ denotes net wage income plus transfer payments (but excluding pensions), which is attributed to the young generation; Q_n is the sum of net income from capital ownership (profit plus interests) and pension payments, both attributed to the old generation; Y_D is disposable income of the private sector, which is broken down into private savings (S_N) and private consumption (C_N).

We use the same parameter values as in appendix B, that is, ρ = 2.5 percent, r_2 = 4.24 percent, $n + g$ = 2.2 percent ($\rightarrow \Omega$ = 0.626), and W = 0.56GDP, and additionally set

$$\gamma = 0.15, \quad \tau = 0.28, \quad Z = 0.15\text{GDP}, \quad R = 0.10\text{GDP}.$$

The parameter R was calibrated such that the model approximately reproduces the income and expenditure account of the private sector in Germany for the period 1991–95 (see the last row and last column of table 2C.2). Under conditions of price stability the net real interest rate rises from r_2 = 4.24 percent to r_1 = 4.87 percent (see subsection 2.3.1). A new equilibrium can be calculated, which is reported in table 2C.3.

The higher real interest rate increases saving of the young only by 0.5 percent of GDP and reduces consumption of the young accordingly (note that the

Table 2C.3   **Income and Expenditure of Private Sector under Price Stability (percent of GDP)**

Item	Young	Presently Old	Total
Saving	18.6	−10.4	8.3
Consumption	28.3	35.8	64.1
Total	46.9	25.4	72.4

net income of the young is given exogenously).[64] Because dissaving of the old rises by 0.3 percent of GDP, total private saving increases only by 0.2 percent of GDP. The biggest change occurs for *consumption of the old:* this aggregate increases from 29.3 to 35.8 percent of GDP.

What are the welfare consequences of this move from 2 percent inflation to price stability? To recalculate the benefits of price stability along the lines of section 2.3, we have to recognize that equation (13) ($S = pC$) changes to equation (C3), which is reproduced here for convenience, dropping subscripts, as

$$(C3'/13') \qquad S = pC - \frac{p}{q}(\gamma W - R).$$

From this equation we derive the following expression for the price elasticity of saving:

$$(C10) \quad \eta_{S_p} = -\left[\frac{W(1 - \tau - \gamma) + Z}{S} \eta_{\Omega_p} + \frac{p}{q} \frac{\gamma W - R}{S}(1 + \eta_{\Omega_p}) \right]\Omega,$$

where

$$\eta_{\Omega_p} = (1/\Psi - 1)(1 - \Omega).$$

The compensated price elasticity of retirement consumption becomes

$$(32') \qquad \varepsilon_{C_p} = -\left[\left(1 - \frac{\gamma W - R}{qC} \right)(1 - \eta_{S_p}) - \sigma_y \right],$$

with

$$\sigma_y = \frac{d(pC)}{dW} = (1 - \Omega)\left[1 - \tau - \gamma\left(1 - \frac{p}{q} \right) \right].$$

Introducing the parameter values used above produces $\eta_{\Omega_p} = 0.125$, $\eta_{S_p} = -0.170$ ($\eta_{S_r} = 0.186$), $\sigma_y = 0.246$, and $\varepsilon_{C_p} = -0.987$. This, in turn, yields $C_1 - C_2 = 7.82$ percent of GDP as the induced change of old-age consumption.

---

64. This suggests that the change of the marginal product of capital would be small, justifying our assumption of a constant pretax rate of return (r_0).

Using equations (15) through (19) we obtain the following areas under the compensated demand function:

A = 5.21 percent of GDP
B = 1.68 percent of GDP
C = 0.19 percent of GDP
D = 11.30 percent of GDP
E = 2.58 percent of GDP

The net benefit of price stability in this extended model incorporating intergenerational transfers turns out to be

$$G_c = 1.87 + 0.40*(-0.91) = 1.50\% \text{ of GDP.}$$

Hence, the gain from improved intertemporal allocation of consumption and saving is almost the same as that obtained on the basis of the simpler model in the body of the paper.

Appendix D

Table 2D.1   Taxation of Corporate Profit

	Rate[a] (%)	Distributed Profits of Domestically Incorporated Enterprise		Rate[a] (%)	Income of Partnership		Rate[a] (%)	Retained Profits of Domestically Incorporated Enterprise	
a. Gross rate of return (%)		10.80			10.80			10.80	
b. Trading capital (DM)		925.93			925.93			925.93	
c. Gross profit (DM)		100.00	101.00		100.00	101.00		100.00	101.00
d. Tax on trading capital (of b)	0.80	−7.41	−7.41		−7.41	−7.41		−7.41	−7.41
e. Trade earnings tax (of c + d)	16.67	−15.43	−15.60		−15.43	−15.60		−15.43	−15.60
f. Gross dividend/taxable income		77.16	77.99		77.16	77.99		77.16	77.99
g. Corporation tax (of f)	30.00	−23.15	−23.40				45.00	−34.72	−35.10
i. Trade earnings tax (of i + g)	25.00	−13.50	−13.65						
j. Solidarity surcharge (of g + i)	7.50	−2.75	−2.78					−2.60	−2.63
k. Corporation property tax (of b)	0.45	−4.17	−4.17					−4.17	−4.17
l. Income tax (of f)	35.00	−27.01	−27.30		−27.01	−27.30			
m. Solidarity surcharge (of l)	7.50	−2.03	−2.05		−2.03	−2.05			
n. Property tax (of b)	0.50	−4.63	−4.63	0.38	−3.47	−3.47			
o. Tax credit (g + i + j)		39.40	39.83						
p. Net profit (DM)		39.33	39.85		44.66	45.18		35.67	36.10
q. Net rate of return (%)		4.25							
r. Tax burden (DM)		60.67	61.15		55.34	55.82		64.33	64.90
s. Marginal tax burden (%)		48.02	48.02			48.02			56.98

[a]Effective calculated rates, relative to the respective basis for assessment.

Table 2D.2   **Assumptions for Calculating the Benefits**

Parameter	Germany	United States[a]
Effective inflation rate (%)	2.00	2.00
Fiscal policy parameters		
Average tax rate on distributed profits (%)	60.70	41.00
Marginal tax rate on distributed profits (%)	48.00	35.00
Marginal income tax rate (including solidarity surcharge; %)	37.60	25.00
Property tax rate (%)	–	2.50
Effective tax rate on capital gains (%)	–	10.00
Auerbach elasticity	–	0.57
Useful fiscal economic life of fixed assets (years)	10.00	–
Tax concession as percentage of acqusition costs of owner-occupied housing	2.00	–
Marginal excess burden of taxation	–	0.4, 1.5
Financial parameters		
Real gross rate of return (%)	10.80	9.20
Discounting period (years)	27.00	30.00
Ratio of corporate debt to capital (%)	45.00	40.00
Ratio of equity and bonds to net wealth of private households (%)	43.00	60.00
Depreciation and maintenance costs of housing (%)	4.00	4.00
Nominal mortgage rate (%)	8.50	7.20
Ratio of mortgage to value of owner-occupied houses (%)	60.00	20/50
Value of owner-occupied housing (% of GDP)	170.00	105.00
Debt service (% of public debt)	7.80	8.50
Public debt (% of GDP)	48.00	50.00
Macroeconomic relations		
Growth rate of real wages and of GDP (%)	2.20	2.60
Ratio of wages to GDP (%)	56.00	75.00
Ratio of saving to GDP (%)	9.30	5.00
Ratio of money stock (currency in circulation and minimum reserves; % of GDP)	9.00	17.00
Behavioral coefficients		
Interest rate elasticity of saving	0.25	0, 0.4, 1.0
Compensated interest elasticity of investment in housing capital	0.25	0.80
Interest rate elasticity of money demand	0.25	0.20

[a]From Feldstein (1997).

Table 2D.3   Sensitivity Calculations

Parameter	Benchmark	Assumptions A	Assumptions B	Results[a] A	Results[a] B
Effective inflation rate (%)	2.00	1.50	2.50	1.16	1.61
Fiscal policy parameters					
Average tax rate on distributed profits (%)	60.70	57.70	63.70	1.31	1.52
Marginal tax rate on distributed profits (%)	48.00	45.00	51.00	1.38	1.45
Marginal income tax rate (including solidarity surcharge; %)	37.60	32.60	42.60	1.35	1.47
Useful fiscal economic life of fixed assets (years)	10.00	13.00	7.00	1.32	1.51
Tax concession as percentage of acquisition costs of owner-occupied housing	2.00	1.00	3.00	1.40	1.42
Financial parameters					
Real gross rate of return (%)	10.80	9.80	11.80	1.40	1.42
Discounting period (years)	27.00	24.00	30.00	1.30	1.51
Ratio of corporate debt to capital (%)	45.00	50.00	40.00	1.32	1.50
Ratio of equity and bonds to net wealth of private households (%)	43.00	38.00	48.00	1.34	1.48
Depreciation and maintenance costs of housing (%)	4.00	5.00	3.00	1.40	1.42
Nominal mortgage rate (%)	8.50	9.50	7.50	1.40	1.43
Ratio of mortgage to value of owner-occupied houses (%)	60.00	65.00	55.00	1.40	1.43
Value of owner-occupied housing (% of GDP)	170.00	150.00	190.00	1.40	1.42
Debt service (% of public debt)	7.80	6.80	8.80	1.41	1.41
Public debt (% of GDP)	48.00	51.00	45.00	1.40	1.42
Macroeconomic relations					
Growth rate of real wages and of GDP (%)	2.20	2.70	1.70	1.32	1.51
Ratio of wages to GDP (%)	56.00	53.00	59.00	1.36	1.46
Ratio of savings to GDP (%)	9.30	8.30	10.30	1.34	1.47
Ratio of money stock (currency in circulation and minimum reserves; % of GDP)	9.00	10.00	8.00	1.41	1.42
Behavioral coefficients					
Interest rate elasticity of saving	0.25	0.10	0.40	1.11	1.74
Compensated interest rate elasticity of investment in housing capital	0.25	0.15	0.35	1.37	1.45
Interest rate elasticity of money demand	0.25	0.10	0.40	1.40	1.43

[a]Figures show the net benefit in comparison to the net benefit of 1.41 percent of GDP assuming the benchmark values.

References

Akerlof, G. A., W. T. Dickens, and G. L. Perry. 1996. The macroeconomics of low inflation. *Brookings Papers on Economic Activity,* no. 1: 1–59.

Attanasio, O. P., and G. Weber. 1995. On the aggregation of Euler equations for consumption in simple overlapping-generations models. *Economica* 62:565–76.

Auerbach, A. 1978. Appendix: The effect of inflation on the tax value of depreciation. In Inflation and taxes in a growing economy with debt and equity finance, by M. Feldstein, J. Green, and E. Sheshinski. *Journal of Political Economy* 86, no. 2, pt. 2 (April): S68–S70.

Bailey, M. 1956. The welfare costs of inflationary finance. *Journal of Political Economy* 64:93–110.

Ball, L. 1994. What determines the sacrifice ratio? In *Monetary policy,* ed. N. G. Mankiw, 155–93. Chicago: University of Chicago Press.

Barro, R. J. 1995. Inflation and economic growth. *Bank of England Quarterly Bulletin* 35 (2): 166–75.

Beaudry, T., and E. van Wincoop. 1996. The intertemporal elasticity of substitution: An exploration using a U.S. panel of state data. *Economica* 63:495–512.

Black, R., T. Macklem, and S. Poloz. 1994. Non-superneutralities and some benefits of disinflation: A quantitative general-equilibrium analysis. In *Economic behaviour and policy choice under price stability: Proceedings of a conference held at the Bank of Canada, October 1993,* ed. Bank of Canada. Ottawa: Bank of Canada.

Blanchard, O. J., and S. Fischer. 1989. *Lectures on macroeconomics.* Cambridge, Mass.: MIT Press.

Chari, V. V., L. J. Christiano, and P. J. Kehoe. 1991. Optimal fiscal and monetary policy: Some recent results. *Journal of Money, Credit, and Banking* 23 (3): 519–39.

Croushore, D. 1992. What are the costs of disinflation? *Federal Reserve Bank of Philadelphia Business Review,* May/June, 3–16.

Darby, M. 1975. The financial and tax effects of monetary policy on interest rates. *Economic Inquiry* 13:266–76.

Deutsche Bundesbank. 1994a. Macroeconometric model of the German economy. Frankfurt am Main: Deutsche Bundesbank.

———. 1994b. Verhältniszahlen aus Jahresabschlüssen westdeutscher Unternehmen für 1990. Frankfurt am Main: Deutsche Bundesbank.

———. 1996a. Ergebnisse der gesamtwirtschaftlichen Finanzierungsrechnung für Deutschland 1990–1995. Statistische Sonderveröffentlichung no. 4. Frankfurt am Main: Deutsche Bundesbank.

———. 1996b. Die gesamtwirtschaftlichen Finanzierungsströme in Deutschland in 1995. *Monatsbericht* 48 (May): 25–47.

———. 1996c. Makro-ökonometrisches Mehr-Länder-Modell. Sonderveröffentlichung. Frankfurt am Main: Deutsche Bundesbank.

Döpke, J. 1996. Zu den konjunkturellen Bestimmungsgründen von Wohnungsbauinvestitionen. *Die Weltwirtschaft* 132 (3): 300–17.

Edey, M. 1994. Costs and benefits of moving from low inflation to price stability. *OECD Economic Studies,* no. 23: 109–30.

Einaudi, L. 1953. The theory of imaginary money from Charlemagne to the French Revolution. In *Enterprise and secular change,* ed. F. C. Lane and J. S. Riemersma, 229–61. Homewood, Ill.: Irwin.

Expertenkommission Wohnungspolitik. 1994. Bericht der Expertenkommission Wohnungspolitik. Drucksache no. 13/159. Bonn: Deutscher Bundestag, 30 December.

Feldstein, M. 1976. Inflation, income taxes, and the rate of interest: A theoretical analysis. *American Economic Review* 66 (5): 809–20.

————. 1997. The costs and benefits of going from low inflation to price stability. In *Reducing inflation: Motivation and strategy,* ed. C. Romer and D. Romer, 123–56. Chicago: University of Chicago Press.

Feldstein, M., J. Green, and E. Sheshinski. 1978. Inflation and taxes in a growing economy with debt and equity finance. *Journal of Political Economy* 86, no. 2, pt. 2 (April): S53–S70.

Fischer, S. 1994a. The costs and benefits of disinflation. In *A framework for monetary stability,* ed. J. A. H. de Beaufort Wijnholds, S. C. W. Eijffinger, and L. H. Hoogduin, 31–42. Dordrecht: Kluwer.

————. 1994b. Modern central banking. In *The future of central banking,* ed. F. Capie, C. Goodhart, S. Fischer, and N. Schnadt. Cambridge: Cambridge University Press.

Flaig, G. 1990. Außenwirtschaftliche Impulse und privater Verbrauch. *Schriften des Vereins für Sozialpolitik,* n.s., 210: 565–78.

————. 1994. Die Modellierung des Einkommens- und Zinsrisikos in der Konsumfunktion: Ein empirischer Test verschiedener ARCH-M-Modelle. Volkswirtschaftliche Diskussionsreihe, no. 22. Augsburg: Institut für Volkswirtschaftslehre der Universität Augsburg.

Friedman, M. 1969. The optimum quantity of money. In *The optimum quantity of money and other essays.* Chicago: Aldine.

Goodhart, C. 1992. The objectives for, and conduct of, monetary policy in the 1990s. In *Inflation, disinflation and monetary policy,* ed. A. Blundell-Wignall, 314–39. Sydney: Ambassador.

Greenspan, A. 1989. Statement before House Committee on Banking, Finance and Urban Affairs. 101st Cong., 1st sess., 24 January.

Grimes, A. 1991. The effects of inflation on growth: Some international evidence. *Weltwirtschaftliches Archiv* 127:631–44.

Hagen, J. von, and M. J. M. Neumann. 1996. A framework for monetary policy under EMU. In *Monetary policy strategies in Europe,* ed. Deutsche Bundesbank, 141–65. Munich: Verlag Franz Vahlen.

Hallman, J. J., R. D. Porter, and D. H. Small. 1989. M2 per unit of potential GNP as an anchor for the price level. Staff Study no. 157. Washington, D.C.: Board of Governors of the Federal Reserve System.

Herrmann, H. 1996. Stabilisierungspolitik, sacrifice ratio und geldpolitische Koordination in Europa. Frankfurt am Main: Deutsche Bundesbank. Working paper.

Howitt, P. 1990. Zero inflation as a long-term target for monetary policy. In *Zero inflation: The goal of price stability,* ed. R. G. Lipsey. Toronto: C. D. Howe Institute.

Issing, O. 1992. Theoretical and empirical foundations of the Deutsche Bundesbank's monetary targeting. *Intereconomics* 27:289–300.

————. 1995. Die Geldmengenstrategie der Deutschen Bundesbank. In *Geldpolitik— Zwanzig Jahre Geldmengensteuerung in Deutschland,* ed. J. Siebke and J. Thieme, 9–34. Baden-Baden: Nomos Verlagsgesellschaft.

————. 1996a. Geldpolitik in einer Welt globalisierter Finanzmärkte. *Außenwirtschaft* 51 (3): 295–309.

————. 1996b. Staatsverschuldung als Generationenproblem. In *Festschrift für E.-J. Mestmäcker,* ed. U. Immenga, W. Möschel, and D. Reuter, 191–209. Baden-Baden: Nomos Verlagsgesellschaft.

Issing, O., and K.-H. Tödter. 1995. Geldmenge und Preise im vereinigten Deutschland. In *Neuere Entwicklungen in der Geldtheorie und Währungspolitik,* ed. D. Duwendag, 97–123. Berlin: Duncker and Humblot.

Jahnke, W. 1998. Probleme und Perspektiven in der Verwendung des makroökonometrischen Modells der Deutschen Bundesbank. In *Gesamtwirtschaftliche Modelle in der Bundesrepublik Deutschland: Erfahrungen und Perspektiven.* Schriftenreihe des Rheinisch-Westfälisches Institut für Wirtschaftsforschung, n.s., no. 61. Berlin: Duncker and Humblot.

King, M. 1996a. How should central banks reduce inflation? Conceptual issues. *Bank of England Quarterly Bulletin* 36 (4): 434–47.

———. 1996b. Monetary stability: Rhyme or reason? Speech at the Economic and Social Research Council's seventh annual lecture, Bank of England, London, 17 October.

King, M., and D. Fullerton. 1983. The taxation of income from capital: A comparative study of the U.S., U.K., Sweden, and West Germany—The theoretical framework. NBER Working Paper no. 1058. Cambridge, Mass.: National Bureau of Economic Research.

Konieczny, J. D. 1994. The optimal rate of inflation: Competing theories and their relevance to Canada. In *Economic behaviour and policy choice under price stability: Proceedings of a conference held at the Bank of Canada, October 1993,* ed. Bank of Canada, 1–46. Ottawa: Bank of Canada.

König, R. 1996. The Bundesbank's experience of monetary targeting. In *Monetary policy strategies in Europe,* ed. Deutsche Bundesbank, 107–40. Munich: Franz Vahlen.

Lucas, R. E., Jr. 1990. The case for stable, but not zero, inflation. In *Taking aim: The debate on zero inflation,* ed. R. C. York, 65–80. Ottawa: C. D. Howe Institute.

———. 1994. On the welfare cost of inflation. CEPR Publication no. 394. Stanford, Calif.: Center for Economic Policy Research, February.

Mishkin, F. S. 1992. Is the Fisher effect for real? *Journal of Monetary Economics* 30:195–215.

Phelps, E. S. 1973. Inflation in the theory of public finance. *Swedish Journal of Economics* 75:67–82.

Romer, D. 1996. *Advanced macroeconomics.* New York: McGraw-Hill.

Scarth, W. 1990. Fighting inflation: Are the costs of getting to zero too high? In *Taking aim: The debate on zero inflation,* ed. R. C. York, 65–80. Ottawa: C. D. Howe Institute.

———. 1994. Zero inflation versus price stability. In *Economic behaviour and policy choice under price stability: Proceedings of a conference held at the Bank of Canada, October 1993,* ed. Bank of Canada, 89–119. Ottawa: Bank of Canada.

Scharnagl, M. 1996a. Geldmengenaggregate unter Berücksichtigung struktureller Veränderungen an den Finanzmärkten. Discussion Paper no. 2/96. Frankfurt am Main: Volkswirtschaftliche Forschungsgruppe der Deutschen Bundesbank.

———. 1996b. Zur Stabilität der Geldnachfrage. Discussion paper for the symposium Zur Stabilität der Geldnachfrage, Frankfurt, October.

Schelde-Andersen, P. 1992. OECD country experiences with disinflation. In *Inflation, disinflation and monetary policy,* ed. A. Blundell-Wignall, 104–81. Sydney: Ambassador.

Sievert, O., H. Naust, D. Jochum, M. Peglow, and T. Glumann. 1989. Steuern und Investitionen, Teil 1 und Teil 2. Frankfurt am Main: Verlag Peter Lang.

Silberberg, E. 1978. *The structure of economics.* New York: McGraw-Hill.

Sinn, H.-W. 1987. Inflation, Scheingewinnbesteuerung und Kapitalallokation. *Schriften des Vereins für Socialpolitik,* n.s., 165:187–210.

Tanzi, V. 1980. *Inflation and the personal income tax: An international perspective.* Cambridge: Cambridge University Press.

Taylor, J. 1992. The great inflation, the great disinflation, and policies for future price stability. In *Inflation, disinflation and monetary policy,* ed. A. Blundell-Wignall, 9–35. Sydney: Ambassador.

Thornton, D. L. 1996. The costs and benefits of price stability: An assessment of Howitt's rule. *Federal Reserve Bank of St. Louis Review* 78 (March/April): 23–38.

Tobin, J. 1977. How dead is Keynes? *Economic Inquiry* 15:459–68.

Tödter, K.-H., and H.-E. Reimers. 1994. *P*-star as a link between money and prices in Germany. *Weltwirtschaftliches Archiv* 130 (2): 273–89.

Varian, H. R. 1984. *Microeconomic analysis,* 2d ed. New York: Norton.

3 A Cost-Benefit Analysis of Going from Low Inflation to Price Stability in Spain

Juan J. Dolado, José M. González-Páramo, and José Viñals

One of the most significant general economic developments of recent years in the industrialized countries has been the increasing orientation of macroeconomic policies—and of monetary policies in particular—to achieving lower inflation rates. In some countries, this trend has crystallized into legal reforms establishing price stability as the primary goal of monetary policy while at the same time granting extensive independence to central banks for achieving that goal. In other countries, even if there have been no specific legal changes, monetary policy has been pursuing direct inflation targets in order to enhance the transparency of the authorities' commitment to price stability. Finally, even in many of the countries that have maintained their earlier legal norms and monetary policy arrangements, there has been a de facto strengthening of the anti-inflationary orientation of monetary policy.

The above developments have been of particular importance in recent years within the European Union in the context of the preparations to establish a fully fledged Economic and Monetary Union (EMU) in 1999. Accordingly, the convergence criteria laid out in the Treaty of Maastricht to select future EMU participants specify that national inflation rates cannot be more than 1.5 percentage points higher than the average of the three lowest in the European Union. Furthermore, the statutes of the future European System of Central

Juan J. Dolado is professor of economics at Universidad Carlos III, Madrid, and program director of labor economics at the Centre for Economic Policy Research, London. José M. González-Páramo is professor of public finance at the Universidad Complutense de Madrid. José Viñals is head of Monetary and Financial Studies at the Banco de España and a research fellow of the Centre for Economic Policy Research, London.

The authors are very grateful to Andrew Abel, Rudiger Dornbusch, and Martin Feldstein for their valuable comments and suggestions; to Isabel Argimon, Angel Estrada, David López Salido, Antoni Manresa, and Ferran Sancho for helpful background calculations; and to José Félix Sanz for excellent research assistance. The views expressed are solely those of the authors and need not represent those of the Banco de España.

Banks establish price stability as the primary goal of European monetary policy.

At the end of 1996, when this paper was written, the annual inflation rate in the European Union stood at 2.5 percent, a significant improvement from the 6 to 7 percent registered in the previous decade. Nevertheless, since price stability is typically taken to mean an inflation rate of between 1 and 2 percent, and since almost all EU national central banks either already have price stability as the primary goal of monetary policy or will do under the Maastricht Treaty provisions, it is expected that further disinflation will be a major policy goal in Europe. For this reason, it is of the foremost importance that an attempt be made to properly estimate the costs and benefits of moving from low inflation to price stability.

The purpose of this paper is to conduct such a cost-benefit analysis for the Spanish economy. In Spain, in spite of the long-lasting disinflationary process that started in the second half of the seventies, the average annual inflation rate still stood around 3.5 percent at the end of 1996. If for the sake of simplicity we define price stability as the midpoint of the 1–2 percent inflation range (1.5 percent), then moving from low inflation to price stability implies further lowering inflation by about 2 percentage points.[1]

While we have followed the above route for the sake of comparability with the other country studies in this volume, there is admittedly some uncertainty about the inflation rate that exactly constitutes price stability in the case of Spain. If, for example, it were to be considered that an inflation rate of 2 percent—rather than 1.5 percent—more adequately represents price stability, then going from low inflation to price stability would mean further lowering inflation by 1.5 rather than 2 percentage points. In this case, the cost and benefit estimates presented in the paper could easily be rescaled.

Because the channels though which inflation affects the economy are multiple and highly complex (see Fischer and Modigliani 1978; Fischer 1994), any empirical analysis of the gains and losses to be made when lowering inflation is bound to be partial and highly speculative. The route taken in this paper—within the framework of the NBER project on the costs and benefits of achieving price stability—consists of making a macroeconomic estimate of the costs, and a microeconomic estimate of the benefits, of moving from low inflation to price stability in Spain. Regarding the costs, we evaluate the output losses through estimates of the well-known sacrifice ratios. Regarding the benefits, we follow Feldstein's (1997) approach and focus on the distortions resulting from the interaction between inflation and the Spanish tax system.

The main virtue of the approach followed in the paper is to make a compact and relatively homogeneous comparison between the costs and benefits of

---

1. An inflation rate of 1.5 percent probably comes close to being the upper bound of what we guess could be the measurement bias in the Spanish consumer price index (CPI). Unfortunately, no specific estimates of this bias are reported for Spain.

achieving price stability. Its main pitfall is that by focusing on the interactions between inflation and the tax system it ignores some of the channels through which lowering inflation might convey further economic benefits. All in all, however, the assessment provided in this paper is a useful starting point for ascertaining whether policies geared toward achieving price stability in Spain are justified from the standpoint of the general interests of society.

The rest of the paper is structured as follows. Section 3.1 assesses the likely economic costs of reducing inflation by 2 percentage points in Spain by estimating a simple two-equation macromodel of inflation and unemployment. Section 3.2 calculates the size of the likely economic benefits of reducing inflation by 2 percentage points, taking into account the main sources of interaction between inflation and the Spanish tax system. The concluding section compares costs and benefits and makes an overall assessment of the magnitude of the net benefits to be gained in achieving price stability.

3.1 Measuring the Costs of Disinflation

The purpose of this section is to estimate the "sacrifice ratio" for the Spanish economy, that is, how much output will be lost for each percentage point of permanent reduction in inflation. Because the relevant relationship that we seek to identify is what will be the real impact of a permanent reduction in inflation induced by a contraction in aggregate demand, it is important to have a model that can distinguish between supply and demand shocks. For this purpose, we adapt to the Spanish economy the general framework proposed by King and Watson (1994) with the modifications introduced by Dolado, López-Salido, and Vega (1996). While the model explores the dynamics of inflation and unemployment, its results regarding the sacrifice ratio can be easily translated into output losses through Okun's law.

As figure 3.1 shows, the evolution of inflation and unemployment in Spain is rather different before and after 1979. Before 1979, there were periods when inflation and unemployment moved in the same direction as a result of supply shocks. Thereafter, inflation and unemployment generally show an inverse relationship. For the sake of precision, table 3.1 reports means, standard deviations, and correlations for various subintervals in the 1964:1–95:4 period. The stagflationary episodes are clearly shown in the first three periods. In the rest, the correlations between inflation and unemployment are negative, with the exception of the 1986–91 period, where no correlation is present. However, because these simple correlations are dominated by both demand and supply shocks, they are not informative about the nature of the driving forces behind them. To disentangle the sources of these correlations and analyze the implicit Phillips curve trade-offs following a shock in aggregate demand we estimate a simple, but rather informative, empirical macromodel.

The basic model is that of King and Watson (1994) and consists of the following two structural relationships:

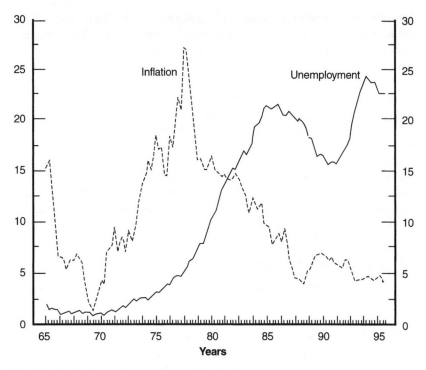

Fig. 3.1   Inflation and unemployment in Spain

$$(1) \qquad \Delta\pi_t = \delta\Delta u_t + \sum_{j=1}^{P} \alpha_{\pi\pi,j} \Delta\pi_{t-j} + \sum_{j=1}^{P} \alpha_{\pi u,j} \Delta u_{t-j} + \varepsilon_{st},$$

$$(2) \qquad \Delta u_t = \lambda\Delta\pi_t + \sum_{j=1}^{P} \alpha_{u\pi,j} \Delta\pi_{t-j} + \sum_{j=1}^{P} \alpha_{uu,j} \Delta u_{t-j} + \varepsilon_{dt}.$$

Equation (1) can be interpreted as an aggregate supply equation (Phillips curve) where inflation depends on unemployment—past and present—as well as lagged values of inflation. The error term ε_{st} is the "supply" shock. Equation (2) can be interpreted as an aggregate demand equation where unemployment depends on present and past inflation and past unemployment. The error term ε_{dt} is the "demand" shock.

The variables in the equations are expressed in first-difference form since u_t and π_t show clear signs of unit-root behavior and are non-cointegrated over the sample period. Under the present specification, the "long-run" effects of disturbances ε_{dt} and ε_{st} can be estimated. In particular, the sacrifice ratio stemming from a disinflationary process can be computed as

$$\sum_{k=0}^{\infty} \left(\frac{\Delta u_{t+k}/\Delta\varepsilon_{dt}}{\Delta\pi_{t+k}/\Delta\varepsilon_{dt}} \right) \qquad \text{when } \Delta\pi_{t+k} = -1 \quad \text{for } k \to \infty.$$

Table 3.1   **Summary Statistics**

	Unemployment		Inflation		Sample Correlation
Sample Period	$\bar{u}$	s_u	$\bar{\pi}$	s_π	
1964:1–70:1	1.23	0.25	6.20	3.65	0.71
1970:2–73:3	1.77	0.53	7.95	1.88	0.71
1973:4–79:2	4.70	1.79	16.90	3.13	0.32
1979:3–86:1	16.25	4.10	12.07	2.27	−0.90
1986:2–91:4	8.33	1.94	6.08	9.15	−0.04
1992:1–94:1	21.01	2.70	5.08	0.76	−0.80
1992:1–95:4	22.05	2.36	4.85	0.65	−0.79

Note: $\bar{x}$ denotes the sample mean, and s_x the sample standard deviation ($x = u, \pi$). The sample correlations correspond to the HP filtered series.

Naturally, a preliminary step to be discussed is how the primitive shocks are estimated since the previous structural system is not identified without further restrictions. Thus, as is standard in the vector autoregression (VAR) literature, we estimate the reduced-form VAR model

$$(3) \qquad \Delta\pi_t = a(L)\,\Delta u_{t-1} + b(L)\,\Delta\pi_{t-1} + e_{nt},$$

$$(4) \qquad \Delta u_t = c(L)\,\Delta u_{t-1} + d(L)\,\Delta\pi_{t-1} + e_{ut},$$

(where $a(L)$, $b(L)$, $c(L)$, and $d(L)$ are polynomials in the lag operator L) and recover the structural shocks from the residuals in equations (3) and (4). To do so, we assume, as is customary, that the demand and supply shocks are orthogonal plus the following restriction: in the long run, inflation is purely a monetary phenomenon; that is, the long-run stochastic trend of inflation is governed only by demand shocks.[2] Nevertheless, it should be noted that the latter restriction does not necessarily impose a fully vertical Phillips curve in the long run. Whether this is the case or not in reality will be revealed by the empirical estimates.[3]

The structural VAR model is estimated for Spain for the period 1964:1–95:4, yielding estimates regarding the unemployment costs of permanently bringing down inflation at different horizons.[4] In particular, after five years the long-run sacrifice ratio (in terms of higher unemployment per percentage point reduction in inflation) is estimated to be 1.3. Using Okun's law (around 2.0 for Spain)

2. While other identifying restrictions were considered that were closer in spirit to "Keynesian" or "real business cycle" models, the "monetarist" restrictions considered in the text seemed to be more reasonable. See Dolado et al. (1996) for a comparison of the three cases.

3. This is so because the long-run Phillips trade-off, i.e., $\lim (\Delta\mu_{t+k}/\Delta\varepsilon_{dt})/(\Delta\pi_{t+k}/\Delta\varepsilon_{nt})$ when $t \to \infty$, is equal to $[d + (1 - b)\theta]/[(1 - c) + a\theta]$, where a, b, c, and d are the gains of the lag polynomials $a(L)$, $b(L)$, $c(L)$, and $d(L)$ in eqs. (3) and (4), and $\theta = 1/\delta$. It is easy to check that the monetarist case corresponds to $\theta = 0$. Thus, even if $\theta = 0$, the trade-off differs from zero unless $d = 0$.

4. The VAR is estimated using first differences of EU12 inflation and unemployment rates as exogenous conditioning variables.

Table 3.2   **Output Costs of Moving to Price Stability**

Authors	Country	Output Loss (% of GDP per year)
Dolado, López-Salido, and Vega[a] 1996	Spain	1.0
Andrés, Vallés, and Mestre 1996	Spain	0.9
Ball 1997	Cross section of OECD countries	1.1–1.7
This paper	Spain	0.6–1.0

[a]Monetarist case.

to express the sacrifice ratio in terms of cumulative output losses (every five years) per percentage point of inflation reduction, it becomes 2.6 percent of GDP. This implies that the cost of reducing inflation by 2 percentage points in Spain is about 1 percent of GDP per year, its permanence being due to the existence of full hysteresis.[5]

In order to assess how reasonable our estimates are it is useful to look at the—unfortunately not very abundant—evidence obtained by other authors regarding the sacrifice ratio in Spain (see table 3.2). In a recent paper, Andrés, Vallés, and Mestre (1996) make use of a small quarterly macroeconometric model to compute the sacrifice ratio of permanently reducing inflation in Spain by 2 percentage points. They conclude that these costs are about 0.9 percent of GDP per year on a permanent basis, which is very similar to the 1 percent of GDP we find under our identification restriction. Other authors, however, obtain once-and-for-all (rather than permanent) output costs. For example, according to Ball (1994), reducing inflation by 2 percentage points would lead in Spain to a cumulative total output loss of slightly less than 2 percent of GDP. Nevertheless, as the author himself acknowledges, this estimate is based on the "a priori" assumption of no hysteresis, which seems to be at odds with much of the empirical evidence for Spain. Indeed, in another paper, Ball (1997) himself presents cross-sectional empirical evidence that suggests that hysteretic effects have been common in OECD countries during recent disinflationary episodes. His results suggest that a permanent reduction in inflation by 2 percentage points comes with a permanent annual output loss of about 1.1 percent of GDP—a number remarkably close to the 1 percent estimated with our small macromodel.

So far, we have relied on the sacrifice ratio computed from the bivariate VAR model for the Spanish economy that was presented in equations (3) and (4). Nevertheless, a controversial and somewhat discomforting implication of the model is that there seems to be a permanent Phillips curve trade-off even under the sensible assumption that inflation is a purely monetary phenomenon in the

5. In the Spanish case, there is ample evidence of full hysteresis nowadays, with the proportion of workers unemployed for spells longer than a year (two years) close to 60 (40) percent.

long run. Therefore, it is important to explore whether this result is robust to changes in the specification of the model.

As pointed out by Evans (1994), it may be the case that what this sort of model identifies as demand shocks are not necessarily (nominal) monetary shocks but a mixture of these and (preference) consumption shocks or fiscal policy shocks. Since our framework so far consists of a two-variable system we are just able to identify pooled demand shocks. Thus, to disentangle a pure "monetary" shock, one possibility is to add a third variable (x_t) to the system that contains information about "nonmonetary" shocks so that ε_{dt} can be interpreted appropriately. Empirically, this is done by adding lagged values of x_t to the system of equations (3) and (4), allowing x_t to be influenced by contemporaneous values of u_t and π_t in its own equation (technically the original demand and supply shocks are treated as Wold-causally prior to the third shock). We considered several candidates for x_t and found logged government current expenditure (in second differences) to be suitable. In this case we found that the long-run trade-off was marginally insignificant, giving rise to a cumulative transitory loss of output of 10 percent of GDP per 2 percentage points of inflation reduction. These numbers are about twice those taken by Feldstein (1997) as representative of the total output cost for the United States, which seems about right given the significantly larger increases in unemployment registered in Spain during past disinflationary episodes.

As shown, new results arising from attempting to distinguish between monetary and nonmonetary shocks yield very different implications regarding whether a long-run trade-off between inflation and unemployment exists (i.e., whether the output costs are transitory or permanent). Nevertheless, it is interesting to note that for the purposes of the exercise we want to perform in this paper, this very crucial conceptual difference can easily be taken into account from an empirical viewpoint. This can be seen once we express the total transitory output costs of moving to price stability (10 percent of GDP) in terms of an annual stream of costs with the same present value, which we can later compare to the annual stream of benefits to be estimated in section 3.3. As in Feldstein, the discount rate that we use to perform the above calculation is the difference between the average after-tax real rate of return that an individual investor received from investing in the stock market (9.5 percent in the Madrid Stock Exchange for the 1985–95 period) and the average real growth rate of the economy (2.5 percent in Spain).[6] This yields an equivalent permanent annual stream of costs of 0.6 percent of GDP, which is significantly below the permanent annual loss of 1 percent of GDP estimated with the original version of the model.

Thus, while there may be some controversy about whether the costs of mov-

---

6. See section 3.3 for the derivation of the discount rate. While the cumulated output loss is 10 percent of GDP, its present value is 9.1 percent of GDP. Thus $(0.07)(9.1) = 0.64$ percent of GDP.

ing from low inflation to price stability in Spain are transitory or permanent, and while recognizing that this as yet unsettled empirical issue has profound conceptual implications for one's view of how the economy works, for our purposes it amounts to taking an annual cost estimate of 0.6 percent of GDP in the transitory case and 1 percent of GDP in the permanent case. Taking a conservative stance, in what follows we will consider that going from low inflation to price stability in Spain will be worthwhile if the benefits from such a move are at least 0.6 to 1 percent of GDP per year on a permanent basis (see table 3.2).

It can be reasonably claimed that the estimates we and other researchers obtain for the sacrifice ratio in Spain may understate the true output costs of going from low inflation to price stability because these costs are likely to increase as the inflation rate gets lower (i.e., the Phillips curve gets flatter). On the other hand, there are also reasons to believe that historical estimates of the sacrifice ratio may overall significantly overstate the actual costs of disinflation to be faced by the Spanish authorities nowadays. First, our experience has been that with sufficiently low rates of inflation, indexation mechanisms are deactivated, which enhances relative price and real wage flexibility. And second, the disinflationary experiences of the past—on which econometric estimates are based—took place in a context characterized by a high degree of regulation in goods and factor markets, a lack of central bank independence, and an internally unbalanced macroeconomic policy mix. Very likely, this exacerbated the output costs of lowering inflation by reducing the credibility of the disinflationary strategies pursued and by increasing the degree of downward wage and price rigidity.

Nowadays the Spanish economy is considerably more open and flexible, mainly as a result of its integration into the European Union since 1986. In addition, the anti-inflationary reputation of the monetary authorities has been greatly enhanced, the Banco de España has been granted independent status, and the macroeconomic policy mix has become much more balanced as a result of progress in fiscal consolidation. Other things being equal, this makes it reasonable to expect that the actual cost of moving from low inflation to price stability will now be far lower than in the past given the strengthened anti-inflationary credibility of macropolicies and the greater flexibility of the overall economic structure.

That this may indeed be the case is reflected in the performance of the economy in the past few years, when progress on the inflationary front has been achieved with much better overall economic performance than normally experienced in previous similar cyclical situations. For all the above reasons, our impression is that the cost estimate of 0.6 to 1 percent of GDP per year that we use as a benchmark for comparison with benefits probably overestimates to some extent the true costs involved in moving toward price stability in Spain at present. If, as shown in the next section, the annual benefits do in fact exceed

even this conservative cost estimate, it could be claimed with some confidence that going toward price stability in Spain is a worthy enterprise.

3.2   Measuring the Benefits of Going to Price Stability

According to the analysis presented above, in Spain the benefits of achieving price stability outweigh the costs if the annual benefit of lower inflation is at least 0.6 to 1 percent of GDP. While an attempt to evaluate all the benefits associated with moving from low inflation to price stability would certainly be ideal (see Viñals, forthcoming), we follow the more modest—but more feasible—route of simply assessing the benefits stemming from the interrelationship between inflation and the tax system.[7] In what follows, we apply to the Spanish economy Feldstein's framework (chap. 1 in this volume), taking into account the peculiarities of the Spanish tax system. We consider those effects related to the lifetime allocation of consumption, to housing demand, to demand for money and to debt service. The total effects on each of these items will be decomposed into the direct effect of the reduced distortions and the associated welfare effects of the corresponding revenue changes.

3.2.1   Inflation and the Intertemporal Allocation of Consumption

A reduction in the rate of return that individuals earn on their saving, due to increases in effective tax rates at the corporate level and at the individual level, implies distortions in the allocation of consumption between the early years of working life and the age of retirement. Since the existence of tax laws creates such a distortion even in the presence of price stability, the extra distortion caused by inflation causes a first-order deadweight loss. In addition, associated effects on government revenue need to be taken into account since a loss (gain) of revenue would have to be offset by increases (reductions) in other distortionary taxes. In what follows, we evaluate first the traditional welfare gain and then turn to assess the additional welfare effect of changes in tax revenue.

Welfare Gain from Reduced Distortions in Intertemporal Consumption

Following Feldstein (1997), the direct welfare gain from reducing inflation is computed making use of a simple two-period model of individual consumption. In such a model individuals earn income when young and save a portion for retirement consumption by investing in a portfolio that earns a real net-of-tax return (r). Considering that individuals retire on average after T years, the price of retirement consumption (p) that is purchased through saving is inversely related to the real rate of return. As the negatively sloping compensated demand curve in figure 3.2 shows, the amount of retirement consumption (C)

---

7. Note that these benefits arise from lowering the rate of inflation even if it is perfectly anticipated.

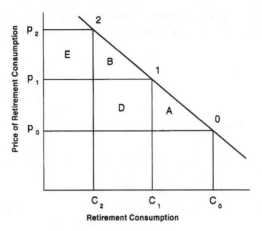

Fig. 3.2   Retirement consumption

purchased by individuals becomes lower when its price (p) rises. Because inflation interacts with the tax system to increase the effective tax rate on capital income, and thus to reduce the real net-of-tax return to individual savers, the higher the inflation rate, the higher the price of retirement consumption ($p_2 > p_1$) and the lower the demand for retirement consumption ($C_2 < C_1$) relative to the optimal situation of no inflation and no taxes (p_0, C_0).[8]

As explained in Feldstein's analysis, the welfare gain from inflation reduction to an individual who saves while working and retires and consumes the return on his savings after retirement can be expressed as the sum of triangle B and rectangle D under his compensated demand curve for retirement consumption, as depicted in figure 3.2.

Using the standard Slutsky decomposition of the uncompensated change between compensated and income effects, the welfare gain (with taxes but no inflation) can be expressed as

(5)   Deadweight gain $= G_1$

$$= \left(\frac{p_1 - p_0}{p_2} + \frac{1}{2} \frac{p_2 - p_1}{p_2} \right) \left(\frac{p_2 - p_1}{p_2} \right) S_2 (1 - \eta_{Sp} - \sigma),$$

where p_i is the price of retirement consumption: $p_i = (1 + r_i)^{-30}$ for $i = 0$ (no inflation, no taxes), 1 (taxes and no inflation), and 2 (taxes and inflation). S_2 is savings during preretirement years at the existing inflation rate; $\sigma = \partial S_2/\partial y$ is the marginal propensity to save out of exogenous income, and η_{Sp} is the uncompensated elasticity of saving with respect to the price of retirement consumption.

---

8. Throughout the text we refer to "no inflation" or "price stability" as a situation in which the actual inflation rate is 1.5 percent, as stated in section 3.1.

To evaluate the annual permanent welfare gain G_1 we must first measure the *price of retirement consumption* in the three situations described above (0, 1, and 2). First, to calculate the price of retirement consumption in the absence of inflation and taxes (p_0) we need an estimate of the real pretax return to capital. From 1985 to 1995, the median real return to capital in the Spanish manufacturing sector averaged 11.9 percent, according to company accounts of *Central de Balances* (Banco de España 1996a).[9] Thus $p_0 = (1.119)^{-30} = 0.0343$.

Second, to estimate the real net-of-tax return to savers in a world of taxes and inflation (p_2), we need to take into account the effects of the existence of corporate and personal taxes. Between 1988 and 1995, taxes (net of deductions) paid by corporations averaged 23 percent of pretax returns (including interest payments). Corporate income taxation operates under an imputation system that mitigates the double taxation of dividends at the shareholder level. Dividends carry a tax credit of 40 percent of the amount received by the shareholder. The tax credit is included in the income tax base, and it is deductible from the computed individual income tax. In the computation of the effective tax rate on company profits, we have netted out these deduction payments. From 1985 to 1995, dividends averaged 18 percent of pretax profits (Banco de España 1996a). Thus the after-tax rate of return is $11.9(1 - 0.23)(1 + 0.4 \times 0.18)$, where the second term in parentheses reflects the estimated amount of dividend tax credits that individuals can deduct against their tax liabilities. This leaves an after-corporate-tax return of 9.82 percent.

The after-tax rate of return to savers also depends on personal taxes. Spanish personal income taxation treats capital income differently, depending on how income is received. A taxpayer with average taxable income pays a statutory marginal tax rate of 30 percent, which is the rate falling on interest receipts. For dividends, we can use a marginal effective tax rate of 1.4 times 30 percent, or 42 percent, because the imputation tax credit is liable to taxes. Finally, the effective tax rate on capital gains can be calculated as in King (1977) and Bakhshi, Haldane, and Hatch (chap. 4 in this volume). Real capital gains are taxed at a fixed rate of 20 percent upon realization. The effective tax rate is 20 percent times $[\phi(1 + i)/(\phi + i)]$, where ϕ is the fraction of accrued capital gains realized every period and i is the investor's discount rate, which is the after-tax rate of return to stocks. From company accounts of *Central de Balances* (see Banco de España 1996a), the ratio of dividends to net assets between 1985 and 1995 averaged 2.1 percent. During the same years, stocks quoted on the Madrid Stock Exchange paid an average dividend of 5.8 percent. Here we use an intermediate figure of 4 percent. Over 1985–95, the Madrid Stock Exchange Index rose by 12.2 percent on average in nominal terms, or 8.1 percent times $(12.2 - (5.6 - 1.5))$ in real terms. Thus

---

9. We take the median since the average was severely distorted by huge outliers. This figure does not differ markedly from the real net return to business capital calculated by the OECD for Spain: 14.1 percent on average over the 1985–95 period.

$$i = (1 - 0.42) \times 4\% + [1 - 0.2 \times \phi(1 + i)/(\phi + i)] \times 8.1\%.$$

The solution for i is 9.5 percent for $\phi = 0.1$ or 9.2 percent for $\phi = 0.2$. In the absence of information on the "true" value of ϕ, we take $\phi = 0.1$, which yields an estimate of the effective marginal tax rate on real capital gains of around 11 percent.

In order to compute an aggregate marginal tax rate, we need weights for marginal tax rates falling on interest, dividends, and capital gains. From *Central de Balances*, the average debt-capital ratio for companies between 1985 and 1995 was close to 50 percent, a split we use also for individuals.[10] On the other hand, the above figures on average dividends and real capital gains imply a dividends/capital-gains split of 33/67. Therefore, the aggregate personal tax rate on corporate after-tax profits is

$$0.5 \times 30\% + 0.5(0.33 \times 42\% + 0.67 \times 11\%) = 25.6\%.$$

This tax rate implies a net real return to savers of $(1 - 0.256) \times 9.82$ percent, or 7.31 percent. Therefore, the associated price of retirement consumption is $p_2 = (1.0731)^{-30} = 0.1204$.

According to our calculations, the joint presence of inflation and taxes leads to a significant wedge between the before- and after-tax real rates of return to individual savers. In particular, this return drops from 11.9 to 7.3 percent, inducing an increase in the price of retirement consumption from 0.0343 to 0.1204.

Finally, we can now go on to calculate what the real rate of return would be in a world of taxes and no inflation (p_1). For this we need to specify some additional tax information (see Albi and Ariznavarreta 1995). Profit is taxed at a national tax rate of 35 percent. Interest payments are deductible. Capital gains are taxed at the corporation tax rate. Allowances for depreciation are available. Corporations may use the straight-line depreciation method (which is the only one available for buildings) and two variants of the declining-balance method ("sum of the years digits" and "constant percentage"); switchover is not allowed. From 1996 on, capital gains are partially indexed, and inventories can be valued using the LIFO method.

Consider thus a reduction in inflation of 2 percentage points. For corporations, this has two opposing effects. First, since nominal debt interest payments are tax deductible, a 2 percentage point decline in inflation raises the effective tax rate on profits. For a given real pretax cost of borrowing and a debt-capital ratio of 50 percent,[11] the effective tax rate would increase by $0.35(0.5)(0.02) = 0.0035$, or 0.35 percentage points. On the other hand, since depreciation allow-

---

10. An issue that deserves closer attention is the role of tax-privileged savings vehicles. In 1995, direct holdings of firms' bonds, loans, and stocks were less than 50 percent of total net financial assets held by households. On the other hand, the effective tax rate on other assets varies widely, a feature that is magnified when inflation increases (see González-Páramo 1991).

11. Data from *Central de Balances 1995* (Banco de España 1996a).

ances are not indexed, a 2 percentage point reduction in inflation lowers taxable profits by increasing the real value of the tax-deductible depreciation. We do not have an independent estimate of this effect comparable to that provided by Auerbach (1978) for the United States. However, available estimates of the overall effect of inflation on the effective tax rate on company profits broadly coincide: a 2 percentage point reduction in the rate of inflation leads to a fall in the effective tax rate of about 0.1 percentage points. In a comparative study of effective tax rates in developed countries, the Organization for Economic Cooperation and Development (OECD 1991) finds that a 5 percentage point reduction in inflation is associated with a 0.5 percentage point fall in taxable profits in the case of Spain. In a more detailed analysis, Sanz (1994), by evaluating effective tax rates in a sample of 883 private industrial companies,[12] finds that moving from 5 percent inflation to price stability causes the effective tax wedge to fall by approximately 1.1 percentage points. Given a fixed capital stock, this means that pretax profits fall by 0.22 percentage points for each percentage point decline in inflation. Thus a 2 percentage point reduction in inflation raises the net-of-tax corporate return by $0.35(0.22)(0.02) = 0.0015$, or 0.15 percentage points.[13] That is, the net effect of achieving price stability is to raise the rate of return after corporate taxes from 9.82 to 9.97 percent.

To calculate a real net-of-tax return to savers, we must consider the combined effect of taxes at the personal level. Applying the weighted personal tax rate to the 9.97 percent return after corporate taxes implies a net return to savers of 7.42 percent. In addition, there is an independent effect of inflation channeled through the tax treatment of interest income.[14] Taking the share of debt in individuals' portfolios to be the same as the debt-capital ratio of companies, a 2 percentage point fall in inflation reduces the effective tax rate by $0.3(0.5)(0.02) = 0.003$, or 0.3 percent. Adding to the new after-tax rate of return (7.42 percent) the gain to savers in the taxation of interest income (0.3 percent), we arrive at a net-of-tax return to individuals of 7.72 percent, up 0.41 percentage points from the return when inflation is 2 percentage points higher. Thus the associated price of retirement consumption is $p_1 = (1.0772)^{-30} = 0.1074$.

Substituting the values of p_0, p_1, and p_2 into the expression for the welfare gain (5), we have

$$(6) \qquad G_1 = 0.0714 S_2 (1 - \eta_{Sp} - \sigma).$$

Next we need to measure *savings* during preretirement years, the *marginal propensity to save* out of exogenous income, and the *uncompensated elasticity of saving* with respect to the price of retirement consumption to evaluate the welfare gain in equation (5).

---

12. Help from J. F. Sanz with these calculations is acknowledged.

13. Note that this estimate implies that the effect of inflation through depreciation allowances is a 0.71 percent reduction in the taxable profit rate per additional 1 percent reduction in inflation.

14. Since nominal capital gains are indexed, changes in the rate of inflation do not affect capital gains taxes.

To provide an estimate of savings of the young at the existing rate of inflation, S_2, Feldstein exploits the relationship between S_2 and net personal savings, S_N, in a steady state growth path:

$$(7) \qquad S_2 = \frac{1}{1 - (1 + n + g)^{-T}} \frac{S_N}{GDP} GDP,$$

where n is population growth, g is the growth rate of real per capita wages, and T is the length of the working period in years. Over the 1985–95 period, the growth of the wage bill in real terms was 2.8 percent, and the net personal saving rate averaged 5.0 percent of GDP (Banco de España 1996b). Taking $T = 30$, this implies that the saving of the young is 9 percent of GDP. However, recent evidence from the expenditure survey Encuesta de Presupuestos Familiares 1990–91 suggests that the foregoing figure is too low. Oliver, Raymond, and Pujolar (1996) find that population cohorts spanning the 35–65-year age range save around 20 percent of their income. Since the ratio of personal income to GDP has been quite stable around 0.7 over the 1985–95 period, the implied saving ratio for the young is $S_2 = 14$ percent of GDP, a figure that we will use in our calculations.[15]

In order to compute the welfare gain according to equation (5), we need estimates for the saving function parameters. Assuming that σ equals the sensitivity of saving to wage income, $\sigma = (S_2/GDP)/\alpha$, where α is the share of wages in GDP, which is around 0.66. Thus, for $S_2/GDP = 0.09$, σ is 0.135, and when $S_2/GDP = 0.14$, σ is 0.21,[16] our chosen estimate. On the other hand, the elasticity of saving with respect to the price of retirement consumption can be calculated as in Feldstein (1997): $\eta_{S_p} = -(1 + r)\eta_{S_r}/rT$, where η_{S_r} is the uncompensated saving elasticity with respect to after-tax real rate of return.

Argimón, González-Páramo, and Roldán (1993) estimate semielasticities of private consumption with respect to the real interest rate in the -0.2 to 0 range. For a given income, these elasticities are linked by the relationship: $\eta_{S_r} = -r(C/S)\eta_{C_r}$, where r is the real after-tax interest rate, C is personal consumption, S is private saving, and η_{C_r} is the semielasticity of consumption with respect to the real interest rate. Taking $r = 6$ percent and $C/S = 15.8$ from national accounts data, η_{S_r} ranges between 0 and 0.2. With $r = 4$ percent and $C/S = 5$, in line with expenditure surveys, the upper bound of these estimates would fall to 0.1. On the other hand, Estrada (forthcoming) suggests an even lower value for the saving elasticity (0.04). Thus we consider elasticities between 0 and 0.2 as reasonable estimates, and 0.4 for comparability with Feldstein's calculations.

15. Gross household saving over 1985–95 was 10.8 percent, 1.5 percent higher than the corresponding ratio in the United Kingdom. Since 11 percent is the lower bound of the saving ratio in the U.K. study, a 14 percent rate for Spain does not seem implausibly high.

16. These figures are within the range of the available econometric estimates. According to Marchante (1993), with an income elasticity of 0.85–0.90 and an average propensity to consume of 0.95, σ estimates fall in the 0.14–0.19 interval.

Once we substitute the values for the different variables and parameters into equation (5), the associated welfare gains are:

η_{Sr}	η_{Sp}	G_1 (% of GDP)
0	0	0.79
0.2	−0.12	0.91
0.4	−0.24	1.03

In spite of the differences between the economic parameters and tax systems of Spain and the United States, the estimated permanent annual welfare gains from achieving price stability are remarkably similar.

Welfare Revenue Effects of Lower Inflation

When inflation is lower, the tax revenue collected may be higher or lower than initially depending on the induced change in retirement consumption along the compensated demand curve. If we start from a situation such as that depicted by point 2 in figure 3.2, with consumption C_2 and price of retirement consumption p_2, a reduction in inflation lowers the effective tax rate on the return to savings, which implies a revenue loss corresponding to rectangle E. At the same time, a lower price of future consumption increases retirement consumption, which in turn generates additional revenues, reflected by rectangle D. Thus the overall net effect on revenue can be either positive or negative (D − E). Using again the uncompensated saving elasticity, since the young generally ignore the need to pay for future lost revenue (the compensated case), the aggregate revenue effect can be expressed as

$$(8) \qquad d\text{REV}_1 = \frac{S_2}{\text{GDP}} \left[\left(\frac{p_1 - p_0}{p_2} \right) \left(\frac{p_2 - p_1}{p_2} \right) (1 - \eta_{Sp}) - \left(\frac{p_2 - p_1}{p_2} \right) \right] \text{GDP}.$$

With the former parameter values computed in the previous subsection, the first effect dominates, generating the following revenue losses:

η_{Sr}	η_{Sp}	$d\text{REV}_1$ (% of GDP)
0	0	−0.59
0.2	−0.12	−0.48
0.4	−0.24	−0.37

These values are somewhat larger than those found for the United States, mainly reflecting differences in the saving ratio.

Now we can convert these revenue losses into welfare losses by scaling them using a deadweight loss coefficient λ. The value of λ measures the marginal deadweight loss per peseta of additional revenue, and it depends on the specific taxes used to make up for the revenue losses. Feldstein (1997) uses two benchmark values: 0.4 and 1.5. For the Spanish case, we can obtain estimates of λ

from the computable general equilibrium model calibrated by Kehoe et al. (1989). An across-the-board tax increase generating 100 pesetas of revenue produces a deadweight loss that is in the range of 29 to 47 pesetas.[17] These figures are very similar to those of Ballard, Shoven, and Whalley (1985) used by Feldstein. We take as our central estimate $\lambda = 0.4$. For the sake of comparability, however, we also use $\lambda = 1.5$, an estimate that seems too high to us.

With the two chosen values for λ, the welfare revenue losses are

		dREV$_1$ (% of GDP)	
η_{Sr}	η_{Sp}	$\lambda = 0.4$	$\lambda = 1.5$
0	0	−0.24	−0.88
0.2	−0.12	−0.19	−0.72
0.4	−0.24	−0.15	−0.56

As can be seen, the magnitude of the welfare revenue loss is quite sensitive to the assumed value of the marginal deadweight loss. All in all, however, in all cases but one the direct welfare gain is higher than the indirect welfare revenue loss.

The net welfare gain from reducing inflation by 2 percent is $NG_1 = G_1 + \lambda\, d$REV$_1$. This formula yields the following estimates (see first three rows of table 3.3 below):

		NG_1 (% of GDP)	
η_{Sr}	η_{Sp}	$\lambda = 0.4$	$\lambda = 1.5$
0	0	0.55	−0.09
0.2	−0.12	0.72	0.19
0.4	−0.24	0.88	0.47

It should be noted that for $\lambda = 0.4$, the range of estimates is around the size of U.S. calculations.

Pensions and Nonsavers

It must be noted that to the extent that individuals receive exogenous income during retirement (social security pensions), our annual estimates need to be adjusted downward. With exogenous income B, retirement consumption is $C = S/p + B$, whereby $\eta_{Cp} = (1 - k)(\eta_{Sp} - 1)$, where η_{Cp} is the uncompensated elasticity of retirement consumption with respect to its own price and $k = B/C$ is the benefit ratio for the relevant population (i.e., savers). This changes the welfare gain formula to $G_1 = 0.0714S_2 [(1 - k)(1 - \eta_{Sp}) - \sigma]$.

In 1990, the benefit ratio for households with heads aged 65 or older was

---

17. We are grateful to Antonio Manresa and Ferrán Sancho for providing us with calculations and guidance as to their interpretation.

around 30 percent.[18] However, 42 percent of them received the minimum pension because their contributions over their working years had been insufficient. Presumably, most of these retired individuals made no savings when young and depend solely on their pensions. Excluding this group reduces the implied estimate to $k = 20$ percent, on the assumption that all of the remaining pensioners were young-age savers as well. To see how taking B into account would alter our estimate of G_1, the following summarizes the results for $k = 0$ and 20 percent:

		G_1 (% of GDP)		
η_{Sr}	η_{Sp}	$k = 0$	$k = 0.2$	Change (%)
0	0	0.79	0.59	−25
0.2	−0.12	0.91	0.69	−24
0.4	−0.24	1.03	0.78	−24

Thus, while the existence of pensions reduces the welfare gains, the increase in the return to savings may cause some nonsavers to save, increasing both welfare and revenues. Nevertheless, though the magnitude of this "participation" decision is potentially important, reliable estimates are not readily available. Thus we have no way to assess the net effect of these two adjustments and we stick to the estimates provided in table 3.3, below.

3.2.2   Inflation and Demand for Housing

Welfare Gain from Reduced Distortions in Housing Demand

Inflation distorts all forms of private housing demand through two main channels. First, it reduces the net return of alternative assets, an effect that increases the demand for houses by potential users: owner-occupiers, non-owner-occupiers (mainly for second residences), and landlords in the private rented sector. In addition, the tax advantages given to a large number of owner-occupiers, and to a lesser extent to landlords, are magnified by inflation. In Spain, these tax privileges are quite generous by international standards, particularly in the case of owner-occupied housing, and the size of the housing stock is also relatively large. Therefore, a reduction in the rate of inflation is quite likely to produce sizable welfare gains through both a reduction of the distortions caused by housing overconsumption and a reduction in tax revenue losses.

The welfare gains discussed above can be readily illustrated with the help of figure 3.3, which shows the compensated demand curve relating the quantity

---

18. According to Oliver et al. (1996), average expenditure of the 4.2 million households with heads aged 65 or older was slightly below 1.9 million pesetas. From official statistics, the average pension of the 3,241,908 old-age pensioners was 717,626 pesetas. A minimum pension of about 47,000 pesetas a month was received by 1,368,142 pensioners (Albi et al. 1994).

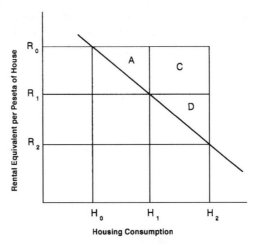

Fig. 3.3   Housing

of housing to its rental cost. In Spain, as in many other countries, the effective subsidies to housing demand arising from the combination of inflation and the tax system reduce the implied rental cost of housing and thus lead to overconsumption of housing (H_2) compared to a situation of taxes but no inflation (H_1) and of no taxes or inflation (H_0). Following Feldstein (1997), since the real pretax cost of providing housing capital is R_0, the existence of taxes with no inflation yields a welfare loss equivalent to triangle A. If, on top of taxes, there is also inflation, the welfare loss increases by the areas C and D in figure 3.3. In what follows, we estimate the deadweight gains obtained by reducing inflation (from H_2 to H_1) for owner-occupied housing, non-owner-occupied housing, and rental housing.

In the absence of taxes, the user cost of housing, R_0, net of maintenance costs (m) and depreciation (δ), must equal the real return to capital in the nonhousing sector (ρ); that is, $R_0 = m + \delta + \rho$. With $m = 2$ percent, $\delta = 2.2$ percent, and $\rho = 11.9$ percent (the real pretax return to capital in the manufacturing sector), we get $R_0 = 16.1$ percent.[19] Next we proceed to analyze the effect of taxes and inflation on the real rental cost, housing demand, and tax revenues.

One peseta of housing capital costs a home buyer $(1 - d)(1 + \tau_1)$ pesetas, where $\tau_1 = 7$ percent is the value-added tax (VAT) rate on house purchases and $d = 15$ percent is a tax credit given to owner-occupiers on the value of the house including taxes. Taxpayers may enjoy this advantage five years in advance of the purchase on the amounts invested in "housing savings accounts" and after the purchase on mortgage repayments. In order to qualify for the tax

19. Fundación BBV (1996) calculates that δ increased from 1.5 percent in 1970 to 2 percent in 1990, which implies an estimate of $\delta = 2.2$ percent for 1995.

credit, the house must be the main residence of the owner and cannot be sold in three years. Homeowners pay income tax on an "imputed rental": $\beta \tau_h z$ per peseta of housing cost, where $\beta = 2$ percent is the imputation rate, $\tau_h = 42.5$ percent is the weighted marginal tax rate of homeowners,[20] and $z = 33$ percent is the average ratio of the official tax value (*valor catastral*) to the market value of the house (see Gallego 1995). Local property taxes (*impuesto sobre bienes inmuebles*) are levied, with an average rate $\tau_p = 1$ percent, on the tax value of the house and are deductible from the income tax base. Maintenance costs and depreciation are not deductible, and real capital gains are taxed unless the proceeds of the sale are reinvested in a new main residence. In addition, interest expenses are deductible in nominal terms at the marginal tax rate, with a ceiling of 1.6 million pesetas for a two-earner household. Given a mortgage-to-value ratio of $\mu = 50$ percent,[21] an average price of a new house of 17 million pesetas (see Sociedad de Tasación SA 1996), and the 1995 average mortgage interest $i_m = 10.8$ percent, the interest deduction ceiling is not likely to be binding in most cases. Finally, it is worth noting that a large fraction of old houses do not benefit from tax-privileged treatment, either because they were bought before 1979 (when the tax credit was introduced) or because their mortgages have been paid off.

With this description of the tax rules relevant to *owner-occupiers with tax advantages,* the user cost of housing can be expressed as

$$RA_2 = (1 - d)(1 + \tau_i)$$

(9)
$$\times [\mu i_m(1 - \tau_h) + (1 - \mu)(r_n + \pi) + \delta + m - (1 - \tau_g)g - \pi]$$

$$+ (1 + \tau_i)[(1 - \tau_h)\tau_p z + \tau_h \beta z],$$

where $r_n = 7.31$ percent is the real after-tax rate of return on other investments, $\tau_g = 11$ percent is the effective tax rate on real capital gains, $g = 1.1$ percent is the average real capital gain on housing between 1988 and 1995 according to Sociedad de Tasación SA ($5.4 - 4.3$ percent), and $\pi = 3.2$ percent is the true rate of inflation in 1995. The computed rental is thus $RA_2 = 8.21$ percent. In order to evaluate the real return associated with a 2 percentage point reduction in the rate of inflation, RA_1, we have that

$$\frac{dRA}{d\pi} = (1 - d)(1 + \tau_i)\left[\mu(1 - \tau_h)\frac{di_m}{d\pi} + (1 - \mu)\frac{d(r_n + \pi)}{d\pi} - 1\right]$$

$$= -0.29\%,$$

---

20. Individual tax data suggest, according to Leal (1992), that 45 percent of the tax credit benefits taxpayers in the richest 10 percent of family income, 25 percent of the benefits are reaped by the following 20 percent, and the rest go to the remaining 70 percent of total taxpayers. Applying these weights to marginal tax rates of 56, 40, and 24.5 percent gives an average of 42.5 percent.

21. According to Banco de España's (1996b) data on financial liabilities of households, this ratio appears to be somewhat smaller. However, loans between individuals or between families and individual firms cancel each other out within the personal sector.

where it is assumed that $di_m/d\pi = 1$ and $dr_m/d\pi = 0.21$, the latter stemming from the fact that a 2 percentage point reduction in inflation raises the real after-tax return to savers from 7.31 to 7.72 percent. These calculations imply $RA_1 = 8.79$ percent. In the case of *owner-occupiers without tax advantages*, expression (9) simplifies to

$$(10) \quad RW_2 = (1 + \tau_i)[r_n + \delta + m - (1 - \tau_g)g + (1 - \tau_h)\tau_p z + \tau_h \beta z].$$

The resulting cost is $RW_2 = 11.77$ percent. On the other hand, since $dRW/d\pi = (1 + \tau_1)(dr_n/d\pi) = -0.23$, a 2 percentage point reduction in inflation raises the user cost to $RW_1 = 12.23$ percent.

Next, before evaluating the welfare effects, we need an estimate of the value of the housing stock and a value for the compensated elasticity of housing demand with respect to the rental price. Jaén and Molina (1994a, 1994b) provide econometric estimates that imply a compensated price elasticity of 0.9, with no significant differences between owner-occupied housing and rental housing. We assume that this elasticity applies to all forms of housing demand decisions. As to the value of the housing stock, Fundación BBV (1996) estimates a net stock of accumulated investment in housing of 117 percent of GDP. Given that land values represent on average 30 percent of total cost (see Sociedad de Tasación SA 1996), the former estimate must be raised to 170 percent of GDP. An alternative calculation, based on data of average square meters per house and number of houses (see Instituto Nacional de Estadistica, various years) and average market prices per square meter (see Ministerio de Obras Públicas y Urbanismo 1996; Sociedad de Tasación SA 1996), yields an estimate of 158.3 billion pesetas, or 227 percent of 1995 GDP.[22]

In order to decompose this figure among alternative house uses we can refer to the shares of owner-occupied, non-owner-occupied, and rental houses: 76.55, 10.45, and 13 percent, respectively. Assuming that non-owner-occupied houses (second residences and empty houses) have a price that is on average one-half of the value of owner-occupied and rental houses, the adjusted shares in the housing stock are owner-occupied housing, 80.77 percent; non-owner-occupied housing, 5.51 percent; and rental housing, 13.72 percent. On the other hand, in 1994 there were 8.5 million taxpayers who declared housing income, of which 3.2 million (38 percent) claimed tax credits (see Agencia Estatal de Administración Tributaria 1996). Since houses without tax advantages are old houses, with lower selling prices, a further adjustment is needed in order to disaggregate the value of owner-occupied housing according to tax status. From professional reports based on market valuations (seeq Tasaciones Inmobiliarias SA TINSA, 1997), the average value of a house 10 years old or older is 30 percent lower than the value of an equivalent house built more recently. Thus the value of the housing stock enjoying tax-privileged treatment can be scaled upward to 46.7 percent of owner-occupied housing. Following

22. Help with these calculations was kindly provided by Angel Estrada.

these adjustments, stock values of owner-occupied houses with and without tax advantages are $HA_2 = 85.6$ percent of 1995 GDP and $HW_2 = 97.8$ percent of GDP. The remaining stock values are $HN_2 = 12.5$ percent of GDP for non-owner-occupied housing and $HR_2 = 31.1$ percent of GDP for rental housing.

Let us return to owner-occupiers enjoying tax advantages. The welfare gain from a 2 percentage point reduction in the rate of inflation corresponds to the sum of rectangle C and triangle D under the compensated housing demand curve in figure 3.3 and can be expressed as

$$(11) \quad GA = \varepsilon_{HR} \left[\frac{R_0 - RA_1}{RA_2} \cdot \frac{RA_1 - RA_2}{RA_2} + \frac{1}{2} \left(\frac{RA_1 - RA_2}{RA_2} \right)^2 \right] RA_2 \frac{HA_2}{\text{GDP}} \cdot \text{GDP},$$

where ε_{HR} is the absolute value of the compensated elasticity of housing demand with respect to the rental cost and HA_2 is the 1995 market value of owner-occupied housing with tax advantages (59.7 billion pesetas). By substituting previous values and estimates into equation (11), we have $GA = 0.41$ percent of GDP. In the case of owner-occupied housing without tax advantages, we can use equation (11) with RW and HW, instead of RA and HA, to get $GW = 0.14$ percent of GDP. Adding up these figures, the resulting total welfare gain from the reduced distortion of owner-occupied housing demand is 0.55 percent of GDP. This estimate is five times Feldstein's calculation for the United States (chap. 1 in this volume), a sizable difference that reflects both the much higher ratio of housing values to GDP and the enormous implicit subsidy that tax rules and inflation give to the purchase of owner-occupied houses in Spain. With current taxes and inflation, the rental cost for owner-occupiers with tax advantages in 1995 was around 51 percent of the no-tax user cost (76 percent in the United States and 71 percent in the United Kingdom), and a 2 percentage point reduction in inflation would increase the rental cost of owner-occupied housing by nearly 7 percent (4.8 percent in the United States and 4.2 percent in the United Kingdom).

Inflation and taxes also distort the demand for *non-owner-occupied housing*. In this case, the rental cost can be written as

$$(12) \quad \begin{aligned} RN_2 = {} &(1 + \tau_i)[\mu i_m + (1 - \mu)(r_n + \pi) + \delta + m + \beta \tau_h z \\ &+ \tau_p z - g(1 - \tau_g) - \pi], \end{aligned}$$

where we assume a mortgage-to-value ratio of $\mu = 30$ percent. Note that here there are no tax credits or interest deductions, and that property taxes are not deductible. The resulting cost is $RN_2 = 12.1$ percent. Thus a 2 percentage point reduction in inflation raises the rental cost to $RN_1 = 12.42$ percent through its effect on the return of alternative investments. Computing the analog of expression (11) we obtain a welfare gain of $GN = 0.01$ percent of GDP.

Houses may be demanded as an investment: landlords buy residences and rent them out. When this is the case, interest, depreciation, property taxes, and

maintenance costs are deductible without limit. The user cost of *rental sector houses* is

(13)
$$RR_2 = (1 + \tau_i)[\mu i_m (1 - \tau_h) + (1 - \mu)(r_n + \pi)$$
$$+ (1 - \tau_h)(\delta + m + \tau_p z) - g(1 - \tau_g) - \pi].$$

With an assumed mortgage-to-value ratio of $\mu = 20$ percent, $RR_2 = 8.64$ percent. A 2 percentage point reduction in inflation increases the rental cost to $RR_1 = 9.18$ percent, which in turn implies a welfare gain of $GR = 0.13$ percent of GDP.

All in all, the value of the aggregate welfare gain from reduced distortions on housing implied by a 2 percentage point reduction in the rate of inflation is

$$G_2 = GA + GW + GN + GR = 0.69\% \text{ of GDP.}$$

Welfare Revenue Effects from Lower Inflation

Given the importance of the tax-inflation distortions and the composition of the housing stock, the revenue effects implied by a 2 percentage point reduction in the inflation rate are expected to be sizable and concentrated in the owner-occupied sector. Consider the effect of the inflation reduction on the stock of owner-occupied housing with tax advantages (from HA_2 to HA_1):

$$\frac{\Delta HA}{HA_2} = -\varepsilon_{HR} \frac{RA_1 - RA_2}{RA_1} = -5.9\%,$$

that is, a decline of 3.5 billion pesetas, from $HA_2 = 59.7$ billion pesetas to $HA_1 = 56.2$ billion pesetas.

On the assumption that housing capital shifts to the business sector, there are as many as six different channels through which the change in housing demand affects government revenues. First, net property tax payments are reduced by $\tau_p(1 - \tau_h)z \Delta HA = -0.0066$ billion pesetas. Second, as both mortgage interest rates and the housing stock decline, the amount of deductible interest payments falls, thus increasing net revenues by $\tau_h \mu[HA_2 i_m - HA_1(i_m - 0.02)] = 0.3192$ billion pesetas. Third, the tax credit on housing purchases declines. If the shift of capital out of the housing sector were instantaneous, the net revenue increase would be $d\Delta HA$, or in annuity terms $-i \, d\Delta HA = 0.0499$ billion pesetas, where i is the investor's discount rate ($i = 9.5$ percent). Fourth, taxes paid on imputed housing rentals fall by $\tau_h \beta \, \Delta HA = -0.0098$ billion pesetas. Fifth, as housing capital shifts to the business sector, revenues from taxes on capital income increase by $-(0.119 - 0.0772)\Delta HA = 0.1463$ billion pesetas, where the expression in parentheses is the difference between the pretax return to business investment and the after-tax return to savings when the rate of inflation is 2 percentage points lower. Finally, it should be noted that additional revenues arising from business investment must include

sales tax and VAT, an effect that can be estimated as $-0.361\tau_s \Delta HA = 0.2022$ billion pesetas, where $\tau_s = 16$ percent is the standard VAT rate.[23] The total revenue gain is thus $d\text{REV}_A = 0.7012$ billion pesetas $= 1.01$ percent of GDP.

In the case of owner-occupiers without tax advantages, the revenue gain is much smaller, given the absence of tax credits and mortgages outstanding. The reduction in the housing stock is 3.4 percent, or $\Delta HW = -2.3$ billion pesetas. Revenue losses from reduced imputation taxes and property taxes are 0.0064 and 0.0044 billion pesetas, respectively. Additional business taxes yield 0.0961 billion pesetas, and new VATs can be estimated at 0.1328 billion pesetas. The ensuing net revenue effect is $d\text{REV}_W = 0.2181$ billion pesetas $= 0.31$ percent of GDP.

The overall size of the revenue gain from the interaction of lower inflation and the tax treatment of owner-occupied housing is quite large: almost three times Feldstein's estimate for the United States and as much as five times the U.K. figure.[24] However, there should be little surprise once we recall the size of the tax-inflation subsidy to owner-occupied housing and the popularity of home ownership in Spain: the net per capita stock in 1992 was \$26,600, 27 percent higher than Germany's stock, 31 percent higher than the U.S. figure, and 67 percent higher than the per capita stock in the United Kingdom (see Tödter and Ziebarth, chap. 2 in this volume; Bakhshi et al., chap. 4 in this volume).

Turning to the non-owner-occupied sector (second residences and empty houses), the revenue effect is the result of two opposing changes: a transfer of capital to the business sector, which yields additional business taxes and VAT revenues, and a revenue loss from lower property taxes and imputation taxes. The reduction in the stock of houses is 2.3 percent, or $\Delta HN = -0.20$ billion pesetas. The additional revenues arising from the business sector are calculated as $-[(0.119 - 0.0772) + 0.361\tau_s]\Delta HN = 0.0199$ billion pesetas. The change in property taxes is $\tau_p z \,\Delta HN = -0.0007$ billion pesetas, and the loss of imputation taxes is $\tau_p \beta z \,\Delta HN = -0.0006$. Thus the resulting net revenue gain is $d\text{REV}_N = 0.0186$ billion pesetas $= 0.03$ percent of GDP.

Consider lastly the rental sector. Given an increase in the user cost of 0.54 percentage points, the implied decline in demand is -5.3 percent, or $\Delta HR = -1.15$ billion pesetas. The revenue impact is fivefold: (1) increased revenue from business investment, $-(0.119 - 0.0772)1.15 = 0.0481$ billion pesetas;

---

23. New business investment generates additional sales and value added, which in turn implies more revenues in an amount that could be nonnegligible. Note that value added, VA, equals capital income, ρK, plus wage income, W. Given a fixed labor income share $W/VA = 0.66$, we get $VA/K = 3.03$, implying 36.1 percent ($= 3.03 \times 0.119$) of the additional capital stock per year when $\rho = 11.9$ percent. New business capital of 3.5 billion pesetas arising from the owner-occupied sector would generate 1.2635 billion pesetas of value added per year. With a VAT rate of 16 percent this translates into 0.2022 billion pesetas per year of additional revenue, or 0.29 percent of GDP per year.

24. For homogeneity, this comparison does not include sales tax or VAT.

(2) additional revenue from VAT, $-0.361(0.16)(1.15) = 0.0664$ billion pesetas; (3) loss of interest deductions, $0.2[(0.108)(21.7) - (0.088)(20.55)] = 0.0455$ billion pesetas; (4) loss of maintenance and depreciation deductions, $-\tau_h(m + \delta)\Delta HR = 0.0215$ billion pesetas; (5) loss of property taxes, $z\tau_p(1 - \tau_h)\Delta HR = -0.0022$ billion pesetas. The revenue effect from all these sources is $d\text{REV}_R = 0.1793$ billion pesetas $= 0.26$ percent of GDP.

The overall revenue change through all sorts of housing demand is the sum of the previous effects, yielding

$$d\text{REV}_2 = d\text{REV}_A + d\text{REV}_W + d\text{REV}_N + d\text{REV}_R$$

$$= 1.1172 \text{ billion pesetas} = 1.60\% \text{ of GDP.}$$

It should be noted that 70 percent of this revenue gain comes from two sources: additional VAT (0.59 percent of GDP) and loss of interest deductions (0.52 percent of GDP).

In order to calculate the welfare effects of the above revenue gain we have to multiply it by λ. For $\lambda = 0.4$, it yields 0.64 percent of GDP; for $\lambda = 1.5$, 2.40 percent of GDP. As can be observed, the welfare revenue gains are quite significant. Relative to the direct welfare gains, they are roughly similar for low values of the marginal deadweight loss, and more than three times as high for high values (see row 4 in table 3.3).

Finally, the net welfare gain arising from the effects of a 2 percentage point reduction in inflation on the housing market is the sum of the direct gain from the reduced distortion and the indirect welfare gain associated with the resulting revenue gains, given by

$$NG_2 = G_2 + \lambda\, d\text{REV}_2 = (0.69 + \lambda 1.60)\% \text{ of GDP.}$$

The overall gains are 1.33 percent of GDP for $\lambda = 0.4$ and 3.09 percent of GDP for $\lambda = 1.5$ (see row 4 in table 3.3 below). Not surprisingly, given our previous discussion of the magnitude of the subsidy to owner-occupied housing and of the size of the housing stock in Spain, the net welfare gains are quite large: around six times the figures for the United States.

Needless to say, there are large margins of uncertainty in our calculations. In this respect, two key parameter values are the housing demand elasticity and the mortgage-to-value ratio in the owner-occupied tax-advantaged sector. Suppose that the mortgage-to-value ratio were $\mu = 25$ percent instead of the maintained $\mu = 50$ percent. The resulting overall direct gain would fall by 0.1 percent of GDP to 0.59 percent, still a sizable improvement. Revenue gains would decline to 1.29 percent of GDP from 1.6 percent, which in turn implies net welfare gains of 1.11 percent of GDP for $\lambda = 0.4$ and 2.52 percent of GDP for $\lambda = 1.5$. Assume, in addition to $\mu = 25$ percent, that the true value of ε_{HR} were 0.45 instead of 0.90. Then the net gains in this case would be 0.84 percent of GDP for $\lambda = 0.4$ and 2.00 percent of GDP for $\lambda = 1.5$. Therefore, although

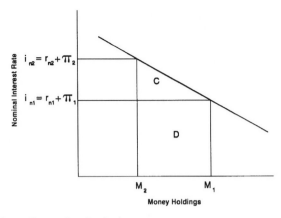

Fig. 3.4   Money demand and seigniorage

halving both μ and ε_{HR} reduces our reference estimates by about 35 percent, it still leaves welfare gains far larger than those found for the United States.

3.2.3   Inflation and the Demand for Money

Welfare Effects of Distorting Money Demand

Perhaps the best-known source of welfare loss resulting from inflation relates to distortions on money demand. As established in the seminal work of Bailey (1956), an increase in inflation increases the opportunity cost of holding money by raising interest rates and reduces the level of money holdings relative to the social optimum. This effect ("shoe leather costs") makes inflation socially costly because, as Friedman (1969) noted, money holdings are optimal only when the nominal interest rate is zero, thus equating the marginal utility and the (zero) social marginal cost of money. Consequently, any increase in an already positive nominal interest rate tends to lower the level of money holdings further below the optimum.

Assuming an initial situation characterized by inflation (π_2) and a positive nominal interest rate ($i_{n2} = r_{n2} + \pi_2$), reducing inflation entails a welfare gain. As shown in figure 3.4, which plots the demand for money as a function of the nominal interest rate, a reduction in inflation (from π_2 to π_1) leads to an increase in money demand (from M_2 to M_1) and to a welfare gain represented by area C plus area D between the money demand curve and the zero opportunity cost line. As can be seen, the size of the gain hinges on the interest elasticity of money demand.

To compute the welfare gain it is necessary to estimate the change in nominal interest rates induced by the reduction in inflation and the induced increase in money demand ($M_1 - M_2$). At a "true" initial inflation rate (π_2) of 2 percent

(3.5 − 1.5), the net-of-tax return on the debt-equity portfolio in Spain (r_{n2}) is 7.31 percent, thus leading to a nominal interest rate (i_{n2}) of 9.31 percent (7.31 + 2). When the "true" inflation rate (π_1) is zero (1.5 − 1.5), the real and nominal net-of-tax return $(r_{n1} = i_{n1})$ becomes 7.72 percent since $dr/d\pi = -0.21$. Thus the welfare gain corresponding to the area C + D in the figure is

(13)
$$G_3 = i_{n1}(M_1 - M_2) + \frac{1}{2}(i_{n2} - i_{n1})(M_1 - M_2)$$
$$= 0.0772[1 + 0.5(0.0931 - 0.0772)](M_1 - M_2)$$
$$= -0.08515\varepsilon_M M \frac{1}{r_n + \pi}(0.0159)\text{GDP}$$
$$= -0.00135\varepsilon_M \frac{M}{\text{GDP}}(r_n + \pi)^{-1}\text{GDP}.$$

In Spain, the long-run interest rate elasticity of money demand (ε_M) is estimated to be roughly 0.2, and in 1995 non-interest-bearing money balances amounted to 8.930 billion pesetas, or 12.8 percent of GDP (M). Substituting these values into equation (13) yields a total welfare gain of $G_3 = 0.04$ percent of GDP. Therefore, it follows that the size of the welfare gain associated with changes in money demand (Bailey effect) is rather small, although almost twice that for the United States. This is mainly due to the money-to-income ratio being twice as large in Spain.

Welfare Revenue Effects of Changes in Money Demand

Following Feldstein (1997), the reduction in inflation leads to changes in government revenue through several channels: (i) the loss of seigniorage associated with the lower "tax" on money holdings (the so-called Phelps effect), (ii) the loss due to the portfolio shift from other productive assets to money balances, (iii) and the gain related to the one-time replacement of interest-bearing government debt by higher money balances. These sources of revenue changes are examined in what follows.

The marginal change in seigniorage induced by a unit reduction in inflation is shown in Feldstein (1997) to be equal to

$$d\text{Seigniorage}/d\pi = M + \pi(dM/d\pi)$$
$$= M/\text{GDP}\{1 - \varepsilon_M[d(r_n + \pi)/d\pi](\pi/r_n + \pi)\}\text{GDP}$$
$$= 0.1236\text{GDP}.$$

Thus the loss of seigniorage will be $(0.02)(0.1236)\text{GDP} = 0.25$ percent of GDP. As in the United States, the "Phelps revenue effect" is higher than the "Bailey money demand effect."

As regards the revenue loss from shifting capital (taxed) to money balances

(nontaxed), since the reduction in productive capital is equal to the increase in money balances, we have that

$$M_1 - M_2 = \varepsilon_M M \frac{i_{n2} - i_{n1}}{i_{n2}} = 0.0044 \text{GDP}.$$

When these assets are invested in productive capital they earn a real pretax return of 11.9 percent but a net-of-tax return of only 7.72 percent. The difference between the two is the combined effective tax rate at the corporate and personal levels. Applying this difference to the reduction in productive capital yields a revenue loss of $(0.119 - 0.0772)0.0044\text{GDP} = 0.02$ percent of GDP.

Concerning the substitution of increased money balances for government debt, this implies a one-time reduction of the stock of government debt and thus a permanent reduction in debt service. Taking a value for the nominal interest on government debt (r_{ng}) of 8.5 percent in 1995, a value for the personal tax rate (θ_m) of 0.3, and a "true" inflation rate in 1995 of 2.8 percent, the real net-of-tax interest rate on government debt would be $(1 - 0.3)8.5 - 2.8$ percent $= 3.2$ percent, and the reduced debt service in perpetuity $r_{ng} (M_1 - M_2) = 0.01$ percent of GDP.

Combining the above three revenue effects yields a total revenue loss of

$$d\text{REV}_3 = -0.25 - 0.02 + 0.01 = -0.26\% \text{ of GDP}.$$

In welfare terms, the revenue loss depends on the assumed value of the marginal deadweight loss, amounting to 0.10 percent of GDP for $\lambda = 0.4$ and 0.39 percent of GDP for $\lambda = 1.5$.

On the basis of the above calculations, the *total welfare gain* (direct welfare plus indirect welfare revenue effects) can be estimated as

$$NG_3 = G_3 + \lambda \, d\text{REV}_3 = (0.037 - \lambda 0.26)\% \text{ of GDP}.$$

For $\lambda = 0.4$, this yields -0.07 percent of GDP; for $\lambda = 1.5$, -0.35 percent of GDP.

As can be seen, reducing inflation implies overall a welfare loss through the money demand channel. The reason is that the welfare losses arising from lost revenue more than outweigh the welfare gains resulting from reduced distortion of money holdings; that is, the Phelps effect dominates the Bailey effect (see row 5 of table 3.3 below).

Finally, it is important to point out that all of the above estimates hinge on the value taken for the interest elasticity of money demand. According to Lucas (1994), the money demand curve becomes infinitely elastic for sufficiently low nominal interest rates. Thus we would be seriously underestimating the direct welfare gain from reducing the distortion on money demand. On the contrary, according to Mulligan and Sala-i-Martin (1996), we would be seriously overestimating the direct welfare gain if it is the case—as these authors claim—that money demand becomes completely interest rate inelastic for sufficiently low

nominal interest rates. Unfortunately, the empirical work on money demand functions in Spain is based on linear specifications, and it is not yet possible to know whether we are under- or overestimating the direct welfare gain on money holdings.

3.2.4   Debt Service and the Government Budget Constraint

This final item relates to the higher cost of servicing the national debt that results from a reduction in inflation of 2 percentage points. This happens because inflation does not alter the real pretax interest rate on government debt while the inflation premium is taxed at the personal level. If the debt-GDP ratio is to be kept constant, an increase in taxes is required. This, in turn, implies welfare costs insofar as taxes are distortionary.

As shown in Feldstein (1997), in equilibrium the revenue loss resulting from lower inflation can be approximated as the product of the change in inflation ($d\pi$), the effective tax rate (θ_m), and the debt-GDP ratio (b): $d\text{REV}_4 = d\pi \, \theta_m b$. Considering that in Spain θ_m is 30 percent and the relevant[25] debt-GDP ratio is 40 percent (once we exclude debt in the hands of foreign investors and tax-favored institutional investors), the revenue change is

$$d\text{REV}_4 = -(0.02)(0.3)(0.4) = -0.24\% \text{ of GDP.}$$

In turn, the net welfare revenue is

$$NG_4 = -0.24\lambda,$$

which together yields -0.10 percent of GDP for $\lambda = 0.4$ and -0.36 percent of GDP for $\lambda = 1.5$ (see row 6 of table 3.3). These figures are in line with those obtained for the United States.

3.2.5   Total Benefits

Table 3.3 summarizes our estimates of the permanent annual benefits that can be obtained when moving from low inflation to price stability in Spain. As can be seen from the last three rows of the table, the total welfare effect is in all cases positive and sizable, ranging from 1.71 to 2.87 percent of GDP.[26]

The values reported in table 3.3 correspond to different assumptions regarding the marginal deadweight loss per peseta of additional revenue (λ) and the interest elasticity of saving (η), and some of these assumptions look more plausible than others. In particular, the empirical evidence available for Spain suggests that λ is very close to 0.4 and η is somewhere between 0 and 0.2. In this

---

25. If debt holders are tax exempt to begin with, there are no revenue losses.

26. It could be claimed that we are not taking into account the welfare losses resulting from the need to raise distortionary taxation to finance the revenue shortfall and higher unemployment compensation payments stemming from the lower output—transitorily or permanently—induced by the disinflation process and discussed in section 3.1 of the paper. In the case of Spain, our calculations show that this would amount, in welfare terms, to less than 0.1 percent of GDP in the more realistic scenario of $\lambda = 0.4$, and to 0.3 percent of GDP when $\lambda = 1.5$. These calculations are available on request.

Table 3.3   **Net Welfare Effect of Achieving Price Stability (percent of GDP)**

Source of Change	Direct Effect of Reduced Distortion (1)	Welfare Effect of Revenue Change		Total Effect	
		$\lambda = 0.4$ (2)	$\lambda = 1.5$ (3)	$\lambda = 0.4$ (4)	$\lambda = 1.5$ (5)
Consumption timing					
$\eta = 0$	**0.79**	**−0.24**	−0.88	**0.55**	−0.09
$\eta = 0.2$	**0.91**	**−0.19**	−0.72	**0.72**	0.19
$\eta = 0.4$	1.03	−0.15	−0.56	0.88	0.47
Housing demand	0.69	0.64	2.4	1.33	30.9
Money demand	0.04	−0.10	−0.39	−0.07	−0.35
Debt service		−0.10	−0.36	−0.10	−0.36
Total					
$\eta = 0$	**1.52**	**0.20**	0.77	**1.71**	2.29
$\eta = 0.2$	**1.64**	**0.25**	0.93	**1.88**	2.57
$\eta = 0.4$	1.76	0.29	1.09	2.04	2.87

Note: Table reports changes due to a 2 percentage point reduction in inflation. η is the uncompensated interest rate elasticity of saving. λ is the marginal deadweight loss per peseta of additional revenue. Numbers in boldface show what we consider to be more realistic figures for Spain given the available empirical evidence on λ and η.

more realistic scenario, the annual welfare benefits are estimated to be still quite significant, ranging from 1.71 to 1.88 percent of GDP.

As can be seen, the four types of effects considered in the table contribute quite differently toward the total net welfare effect. While the changes induced by lower inflation on retirement consumption and housing demand contribute favorably to the total welfare effect, the induced changes in money demand and in the cost of servicing the public debt make negative contributions. Under the most realistic scenario, the first two factors amount to 1.88 to 2.05 percent of GDP and the remaining two to −0.17 percent of GDP.

Another interesting feature is that both the direct welfare effect and the indirect welfare revenue effect are positive when we aggregate over the four economic categories in the table. Nevertheless, it should be observed that the traditional direct welfare effect is significantly higher than the indirect effect. For instance, in the more realistic scenario, the direct effect ranges from 1.52 to 1.64 percent of GDP, while the indirect effect ranges from 0.20 to 0.25 percent of GDP. So while the conceptual framework employed in the paper has clearly gained from the inclusion of indirect revenue effects, together with traditional direct welfare effects, in our more realistic scenario this does not seem empirically to make a big difference.

Finally, it is worth mentioning that the net welfare gains of achieving price stability increase with the marginal deadweight loss and with the interest elasticity of saving. One reason is that since a reduction of inflation increases total revenue, it allows other distortionary taxes to be reduced. Thus the larger the marginal deadweight loss per peseta of additional revenue, the higher the wel-

Table 3.4   Underlying Variables and Parameters in the Evaluation of the
                   Benefits of Going to Price Stability, Spain versus the United States

Variable or Parameter	Spain	United States
Fiscal		
Average tax on corporations (%)	23	41
Marginal corporate income tax (%)	35	35
Marginal capital income tax on individuals (%)	26	25
Effective marginal tax on capital gains (%)	11	10
Rate of property tax (%)	1	2.5
Tax credit on value of the house (%)	15	–
Marginal deadweight loss	0.4, 1.5	0.4, 1.5
Financial		
Pretax real return to capital in corporate sector (%)	11.9	9.2
Debt-capital ratio in corporations (%)	50	40
Share of equity in individuals' portfolios (%)	66	60
Interest paid on mortgage (%)	10.8	7.2
Value of owner-occupied housing (% of GDP)	184	105
Currency plus bank reserves (% of GDP)	12.8	6.1
Relevant government debt (% of GDP)	40	50
Mortgage as a proportion of the value of owner-occupied housing (%)	50	20–50
Maintenance cost (%)	2	2
Rate of depreciation (%)	2.2	2
Macroeconomic		
Rate of growth of the wage bill (%)	2.8	2.6
Inflation average[a] (%)	5.6	4.7
Current inflation[b] (%)	3.5	2.9
Inflation bias (%)	1.5	2.0
GDP growth[c] (%)	2.5	2.5
Share of wages in GDP (%)	66	75
Saving of the young (% of GDP)	14	9
Behavioral		
Elasticity of saving with respect to real net-of-tax return	0, 0.2, 0.4	0, 0.4, 1.0
Compensated elasticity of housing demand with respect to rental pricing	0.9	0.8
Elasticity of demand for money with respect to interest rate	0.2	0.2
Propensity to save	0.21	0.12

Sources: Feldstein (1997) and authors' elaboration.
[a]1985–95 for Spain; 1960–94 for the United States.
[b]1996 for Spain.
[c]1964–95 for Spain; 1970–94 for the United States.

fare revenue gain. The other reason is that the more interest elastic saving is, the larger the favorable effect of a reduction in inflation on the amount of retirement consumption purchased by individuals and the lower the revenue loss.

Table 3.4 presents the values of the underlying variables and parameters used in evaluating the benefits of going to price stability in Spain (and, for

Table 3.5   **Net Welfare Effects: Spain versus the United States (percent of GDP)**

	Direct		Revenue		Total		Difference
	Spain	U.S.	Spain	U.S.	Spain	U.S.	
Consumption timing	0.79	0.73	−0.24	−0.17	0.55	0.56	−0.01
Housing demand	0.69	0.1	0.64	0.12	1.33	0.22	+1.11
Money demand	0.04	0.02	−0.10	−0.05	−0.07	−0.03	−0.04
Debt service			−0.10	−0.10	−0.10	−0.10	0
Total	1.52	0.85	0.20	−0.21	1.71	0.65	+1.06

Source: U.S. figures from Feldstein (chap. 1 in this volume).

Note: Table reports changes due to a 2 percentage point reduction in inflation. $\eta = 0$ and $\lambda = 0.4$.

comparative purposes, in the United States), and table 3.5 presents a comparison of our results with those obtained by Feldstein for the United States within the same conceptual framework (chap. 1 of this volume). For the sake of comparability, we take $\lambda = 0.4$ and $\eta = 0$, which correspond to values for our more realistic scenario. As can be seen by looking at the last row of table 3.5, the total net welfare gain is almost three times larger in Spain (1.71 percent of GDP) than in the United States (0.65 percent of GDP). This is mostly due to the very different net gains associated with the effect of a reduction in inflation on the demand for housing (1.33 percent of GDP in Spain vs. 0.22 percent in the United States). For the other three economic categories, the gains are remarkably similar, as can be seen in the last column of the table. According to our analysis, the much larger effects of reduced inflation on housing demand in Spain mainly reflect the much higher ratio of housing values to GDP in this country and the huge implicit subsidy that tax rules and inflation give to the purchase of owner-occupied houses. Naturally, both factors are deeply interrelated from a general equilibrium viewpoint.

3.3   Costs and Benefits Compared

3.3.1   Benefits Minus Costs

The most important difficulty economists face when examining the costs and benefits of moving from low inflation to price stability is the absence of a fully satisfactory general equilibrium theory of money. In this paper, we have followed the more pragmatic route of combining a macroeconomic estimate of the costs and a microeconomic estimate of the benefits of achieving price stability in Spain within an admittedly partial equilibrium framework. Rather than trying to identify and quantify all of the various channels through which the inflationary process entails costs and benefits, we focus only on those channels that we consider most relevant.

Table 3.6 summarizes our estimates of both the costs and the benefits of achieving price stability in Spain. As regards the costs, we have relied on esti-

Table 3.6   Summary of Benefits and Costs of Achieving Price Stability
                   (percent of GDP)

	$\lambda = 0.4$	$\lambda = 1.5$
Benefits		
$\eta = 0$	**1.71**	2.29
$\eta = 0.2$	**1.88**	2.57
$\eta = 0.4$	2.04	2.87
Costs	0.60–1.00	0.60–1.00
Benefits minus costs		
$\eta = 0$	**0.71–1.11**	1.29–1.69
$\eta = 0.2$	**0.88–1.28**	1.57–1.97
$\eta = 0.4$	1.04–1.44	1.87–2.27

Note: Table reports permanent annual benefits and costs due to a 2 percentage point reduction in inflation. Numbers in boldface show what we consider to be more realistic figures for Spain given the available empirical evidence on λ and η.

mates of the sacrifice ratio to arrive at a rough figure for how costly it is to move to price stability in terms of lost output. We have concluded that in Spain such costs are in the range of 0.6 to 1 percent of GDP per year on a permanent basis. As regards the benefits, we have adopted Feldstein's (1997) approach and focused on the interactions between inflation and capital income taxation. Since inflation leads to increases in the effective rate of capital income taxation in non–fully indexed tax systems, it distorts consumption-saving decisions and asset allocation decisions, resulting in welfare losses. Our empirical estimates of the welfare gains to be obtained from achieving price stability in Spain—shown in table 3.3—are quite sizable by international standards, ranging from 1.7 to 2.9 percent of GDP per year on a permanent basis, depending on the assumptions made about the marginal deadweight loss of raising revenue and the interest elasticity of saving. In what we consider to be the more realistic scenario, the benefits are estimated to be in the range of 1.7 to 1.9 percent of GDP per year on a permanent basis. Consequently, the *net benefit* (benefit minus costs) of going from low inflation to price stability in Spain is estimated to be—in the more realistic scenario—*0.7 to 1.3 percent of GDP per year on a permanent basis.* Thus, according to our preliminary results, achieving price stability seems to be a worthwhile enterprise.

Given that our paper applies Feldstein's (1997) methodology to Spain, it is useful to compare our results to those he obtained for the United States. If we take Feldstein's more realistic scenario, then the estimated output costs of achieving price stability in the United States are equivalent to 0.16 percent of GDP per year on a permanent basis,[27] while the estimated benefits are 0.6 to 1 percent of GDP per year, again on a permanent basis. This yields an annual

27. While Feldstein finds the output costs of disinflation to be transitory in the United States, the figure mentioned in the text corresponds to an annuity that has the same present value as the cumulative transitory output costs.

net benefit of 0.5 to 0.8 percent of GDP, which is similar to, although somewhat smaller than, the 0.7 to 1.3 percent of GDP we find for Spain. Excluding the revenue effects from VAT, which does not exist in the United States, the annual net benefit for Spain would fall to 0.5 to 1.0 percent of GDP, a figure that is almost identical to the U.S. range of estimates.

The similarity between the estimated net benefits of achieving price stability in Spain and in the United States is rather striking considering the very significant differences between the two countries' economic structures and tax systems. Still, it happens to be the case that while the costs of achieving price stability are significantly higher in Spain so are the benefits, thus leading to net benefits of the same order of magnitude in both cases.

3.3.2   Some Caveats

As emphasized earlier, our calculations of the net benefits of going from low inflation to price stability are based on a relatively simple *partial* equilibrium framework. Still, even if we stick to the methodology that we have followed here, a number of factors should be mentioned to get some idea of the margin of uncertainty of our cost and benefit estimates.

Regarding the costs, since our simple macromodel is linear it does not take into account the possibility—often mentioned—that the Phillips curve becomes flatter as the inflation rate gets lower, thus making it costlier to achieve a given reduction in inflation.[28] While there is no empirical evidence on this issue in the Spanish case, if the above criticism were valid we would be underestimating the true output costs of further reducing inflation. This is, nevertheless, not the only—nor possibly the most important—source of bias in our estimate of the costs of reducing inflation. Indeed, it could seriously be claimed that we have overestimated the output costs of achieving further disinflation in Spain because anti-inflationary policies are now more credible and the degree of downward wage and price flexibility higher than in the past. While it is hard to assess which of the two biases is likely to be larger, the recent performance of the Spanish economy indicates that the disinflation process has tended to become easier in recent years, even as the inflation rate has been progressively lowered. This would suggest that, if anything, we may have empirically overestimated—rather than underestimated—on balance the true output costs of achieving price stability in Spain today.

As regards the benefits, by focusing on the interaction between inflation and capital income taxation, we have omitted other interactions with the tax system

---

28. As recently suggested by Akerlof, Dickens, and Perry (1996), reaching an inflation rate that is low enough to be consistent with price stability may deprive policymakers of the possibility of achieving the real wage cuts that are needed for the economy to perform adequately. Yet it is unclear to us why those real wage cuts may not also be obtained through nominal wage cuts in an environment where price stability prevails. Furthermore, it could be argued that in countries with wage indexation mechanisms—like Spain—going to a low enough rate of inflation leads to a deactivation of such mechanisms, thus improving real wage flexibility.

that could lower our estimated welfare gains from reducing inflation. In particular, as noted by Persson, Persson, and Svensson (1996), shifting to a lower rate of inflation has a permanent negative effect on tax revenues due to incomplete or delayed indexation of the transfer payment system and partial indexation of personal income tax brackets in progressive tax systems. Against this, it can be argued that with a lower inflation rate there is also a permanent increase in the real value of the tax revenues collected, insofar as tax collection lags behind the actual generation of income. While we have not attempted to make such estimates for Spain, the evidence presented by Persson et al. for Sweden suggests that, overall, our benefits could be overestimated.

On the other hand, a number of benefits also associated with lowering inflation are not related to the tax system and have not been considered in our analysis: for example, the saving from not having constantly to revise prices (menu costs), the more efficient allocation of resources that comes with lower—and thus generally more stable—inflation rates, and the redistribution of income and wealth in favor of those with fewer resources to protect themselves against inflation. While these benefits are quite hard to quantify reliably, they may nevertheless be significant (see, e.g., Andrés and Hernando, chap. 8 in this volume; Gylfason and Herbertsson 1996).

It is evident from the above that it is rather difficult at this stage to ascertain the net effect of the various factors mentioned regarding the net benefits of going from low inflation to price stability. Nevertheless, it is comforting to know that the sources of bias might to some extent cancel each other out.

Another word of caution concerns the time profiles of costs and benefits in our calculations. Regarding the costs, timing considerations have been taken fully into account when computing, in section 3.2, the "cost annuity" that is equivalent in present value to the transitory output losses resulting from disinflation. Nevertheless, regarding the benefits we have followed Feldstein (1997) in assuming that all the adjustments to the new equilibrium with price stability take place instantaneously and thus that the "steady state" benefits are obtained from year one. Thus, if it turned out to be the case that these adjustments take several years to be completed, this would reduce the estimated "benefit annuity." This effect might be particularly relevant in the case of demand for housing given the structural characteristics of the housing market. Since the reduced housing distortion accounts for three-quarters of the estimated total welfare gain of 1.7 to 1.9 percent of GDP per year in our more realistic scenario (see table 3.3), this downward revision might be nonnegligible.

In order to assess how important these time profile considerations are, we have considered how our net benefit calculations would be affected if, for example, the benefits stemming from housing demand were to occur, say, only after five or ten years rather than instantly. If we take, for simplicity, the more realistic scenario of $\lambda = 0.4$ and $\eta = 0.0$ or 0.2, our findings are that the benefits are always higher than the costs in the five-year case, while in the ten-year case annual benefits range from 1 to 1.1 percent of GDP relative to costs

Table 3.7   Sensitivity Analysis: Benefits Minus Costs (percent of GDP)

	$T = 0$	$T = 5$	$T = 10$
Mean value	0.62, 1.09	0.12, 0.53	−0.29, 0.14
Median	0.60, 1.14	0.09, 0.59	−0.22, 0.21
Percentage of cases when benefits are			
larger than costs	94.1, 100	64.7, 92.8	37.7, 53.6

Note: In each pair of numbers, the first refers to the case of permanent output costs (1 percent of GDP per year in annuity terms) and the second to the case of transitory output costs (0.6 percent of GDP per year in annuity terms).

of 0.6 to 1 percent of GDP.[29] Consequently, it seems that our conclusions would continue to hold even when considering significant delays in the benefits accruing from housing.

Next, to check how robust our results are, we have carried out a sensitivity analysis by allowing some of the parameters to take on a range of values containing those reference estimates considered above.[30] In particular, we have specified the following ranges for the key parameters: $\eta = 0.0, 0.1, \ldots, 0.4$; $\varepsilon_{HR} = 0.5, 0.6, \ldots, 0.9$; $\lambda = 0.4, 0.5, \ldots, 1.5$; and $\mu = 0.25$ and 0.50. These ranges give rise to 600 possible calculations of net benefits (benefits minus costs), which have been tabulated in table 3.7 for three alternative values of T (the number of years after which the housing benefits accrue). As can be seen from table 3.7, if the housing benefits start accruing within the first five years, it is very likely that the benefits of going to price stability will continue to exceed the costs.

A criticism that can be made regarding our conclusions is that since the welfare benefits from lower inflation could be obtained alternatively through first-best tax reform at an unchanged rate of inflation, it is fiscal policy rather than monetary policy that should be adjusted to reap the ensuing welfare gains. The problem is, however, that in practice it is very difficult to foresee such a radical tax reform, as a result of well-known political economy problems.

In the same vein, it could be argued that once disinflationary demand policies have been undertaken—and the output costs borne—if there were a tax reform of the sort described above, there would then be no more benefits to reap from having achieved price stability after the reform is in place, thus leading to an unfavorable "ex post" relationship between benefits and costs. A reply to this would be that as long as a fully comprehensive tax reform does not come very early in time, it will still be worthwhile to undertake demand poli-

29. In particular, the benefits (B) will be larger than the costs (C) in annuity terms if $B = x_R + x_H e^{-\rho t} > C$, where x_R is annual benefits other than housing and x_H is annual housing benefits starting to accrue after T years ($T = 5, 10$).

30. While, for the sake of comparability with the other country studies contained in this volume, we have omitted from our benefits calculations summarized in table 3.3 the impact of the net revenue losses arising from the output costs due to disinflation (i.e., payments for unemployment compensation), these nevertheless were taken into account when elaborating table 3.7.

cies oriented toward price stability. In fact, for Spain we have calculated that in the case of temporary output costs—which are borne mainly during the first five years—going to price stability would be justified on benefit-cost grounds as long as the tax reform does not happen during the first six years. For the case where the output costs are permanent, going to price stability would be justified as long as the tax reform does not take place during the first eleven years.

To conclude, it is evident from the above discussion that our cost-benefit analysis of achieving price stability in Spain is merely a rough and preliminary attempt to study a very complex phenomenon. Still, because it captures some of what are generally considered to be the most important costs and benefits, it is a useful starting point. According to our empirical results, going from low inflation to price stability in Spain seems to be a worthy enterprise, yielding a net beneficial effect of 0.7 to 1.3 percent of GDP per year in the more reasonable scenarios.

References

Agencia Estatal de Administración Tributaria. 1996. *Memoria de la Administracion Tributaria 1995*. Madrid: Ministerio de Economia y Hacienda.
Akerlof, G., W. Dickens, and G. Perry. 1996. The macroeconomics of low inflation. *Brookings Papers on Economic Activity*, no. 1: 1–59.
Albi, E., C. Contreras, J. M. González-Páramo, and I. Zubiri. 1994. *Teoría de la hacienda pública*, 2d ed. Barcelona: Ariel.
Albi, E., and J. L. García Ariznavarreta. 1995. *Sistema fiscal Español*. Barcelona: Ariel.
Andrés, J., J. Vallés, and R. Mestre. 1996. Inflation targeting and the transition to monetary union: The Spanish case. Madrid: Banco de España. Mimeograph.
Argimón, I., J. M. González-Páramo, and J. M. Roldán. 1993. Ahorro, riqueza y tipos de inters en España. *Investigaciones Económicas* 17 (2): 313–32.
Auerbach, A. 1978. Appendix: The effect of inflation on the tax value of depreciation. In Inflation and taxes in a growing economy with debt and equity finance, by M. Feldstein, J. Green, and E. Sheshinski. *Journal of Political Economy* 86, no. 2, pt. 2 (April): S68–S69.
Bailey, M. 1956. The welfare costs of inflationary finance. *Journal of Political Economy* 64:93–110.
Ball, L. 1994. What determines the sacrifice ratio? In *Monetary policy*, ed. N. G. Mankiw. Chicago: University of Chicago Press.
———. 1997. Disinflation and the NAIRU. In *Reducing inflation: Motivation and strategy*, ed. C. Romer and D. Romer, 167–85. Chicago: University of Chicago Press.
Ballard, C., J. Shoven, and J. Whalley. 1985. General equilibrium computations of the marginal welfare cost of taxes in the United States. *American Economic Review* 75: 128–38.
Banco de España. 1996a. *Central de balances 1995*. Madrid: Banco de España.
———. 1996b. *Cuentas financieras de la economía Española (1986–1995)*. Madrid: Banco de España.
Dolado, J., D. López-Salido, and J. L. Vega. 1996. Short and long-run Phillips curve

trade-offs and the cost of disinflationary policies. Madrid: Banco de España. Mimeograph.

Estrada, A. Forthcoming. *Análisis del gasto de las familias.* Estudios Económicos. Madrid: Banco de España.

Evans, C. L. 1994. The post-war U.S. Phillips curve: A comment. *Carnegie-Rochester Conference Series on Public Policy* 41:221–30.

Feldstein, M. 1997. The costs and benefits of going from low inflation to price stability. In *Reducing inflation: Motivation and strategy,* ed. C. Romer and D. Romer, 123–56. Chicago: University of Chicago Press.

Fischer, S. 1994. Modern central banking. In *The future of central banking,* ed. F. Capie, C. Goodhart, S. Fischer, and N. Schnadt. Cambridge: Cambridge University Press.

Fischer, S., and F. Modigliani. 1978. Towards an understanding of the real effects and costs of inflation. *Weltwirtschaftliches Archiv* 114:810–32.

Friedman, M. 1969. The optimal quantity of money. In *The optimal quantity of money and other essays.* Chicago: Aldine.

Fundación BBV. 1996. *El "stock" de capital en España y sus Comunidades Autónomas.* Bilbao: Fundación BBV.

Gallego, M. 1995. *Análisis y valoración del patrimonio inmobiliario en España.* Ministerio de Economia y Hacienda, Madrid: Centro de Gestión Catastral y Cooperación Tributaria.

González-Páramo, J. M. 1991. *Imposición personal e incentivos fiscales al ahorro en España.* Estudios Económicos, no. 46. Madrid: Banco de España.

Gylfason, T., and T. Thor Herbertsson. 1996. Does inflation matter for growth? CEPR Discussion Paper no. 1503. London: Centre for Economic Policy Research, December.

Instituto Nacional de Estadistica. Various years. *Censo de Población y Viviendas.* Madrid: Ministerio de Trabajo.

Jaén, M., and A. Molina. 1994a. Un análisis empirico de la tenencia y demanda de vivienda en Andalucía. *Investigaciones Económicas* 18:143–64.

———. 1994b. Un análisis estático de la demanda de vivienda. *Hacienda Publica Española* 128:101–7.

Kehoe, T., A. Manresa, C. Polo, and F. Sancho. 1989. Un análisis de equilibrio general de la reforma fiscal de 1986 en España. *Investigaciones Económicas* 13:337–85.

King, M. 1977. *Public policy and the corporation.* London: Chapman.

King, R., and M. Watson. 1994. The post-war U.S. Phillips curve: A revisionist econometric history. *Carnegie-Rochester Conference Series on Public Policy* 41:157–219.

Leal, J. 1992. Informe para una nueva politica de vivienda. Madrid: Ministerio de Obras Públicas y Urbanismo. Mimeograph.

Lucas, R. 1994. On the welfare costs of inflation. Chicago: University of Chicago.

Marchante, A. 1993. Consumo privado y gasto público. *Revista de Economía Aplicada* 1:125–49.

Ministerio de Obras Públicas y Urbanismo. 1996. *Informe anual.* Madrid: Ministerio de Obras Públicas y Urbanismo.

Mulligan, C., and X. Sala-i-Martin. 1996. Adoption of financial technologies: Implications for money demand and monetary policy. NBER Working Paper no. 5504. Cambridge, Mass.: National Bureau of Economic Research.

Oliver, J., J. L. Raymond, and D. Pujolar. 1996. El ahorro por grupos de edad de las familias españolas. *Cuadernos de Información Económica* (Fundación FIES-CECA) 115:113–24.

Organization for Economic Cooperation and Development (OECD). 1991. *Taxing profits in a global economy.* Paris: Organization for Economic Cooperation and Development.

Persson, M., T. Persson, and L. E. O. Svensson. 1996. Debt, cash flow and inflation incentives: A Swedish example. CEPR Discussion Paper no. 1488. London: Centre for Economic Policy Research, October.

Sanz, J. F. 1994. *Un análisis de las distorsiones impositivas sobre las rentas del capital en España.* Ph.D. thesis, Universidad Complutense, Madrid.

Sociedad de Tasación SA. 1996. Precios medios de la vivienda nueva en capitales de provincia. *Boletin ST.* Madrid.

Tasaciones Inmobiliarias SA. 1997. *Los precios de la vivienda crecen mas que la inflación.* Madrid: TINSAPRESS.

Viñals, J. Forthcoming. Monetary policy and inflation: From theory to practice. In *Monetary policy and inflation in Spain,* ed. J. L. Malo de Molina, J. Viñals, and F. Gutierrez. New York: Macmillan and St. Martin's Press.

4 Some Costs and Benefits of Price Stability in the United Kingdom

Hasan Bakhshi, Andrew G. Haldane, and Neal Hatch

4.1 Introduction

There is now widespread acceptance of price stability as a macroeconomic objective among policymakers. This price stability consensus appears to extend to the public at large and, to lesser extent, to professional economists too. That is the good news from Shiller's (1997) survey of these two sets of agents. The bad news from the survey is the reason the public gave for disliking inflation: it was thought to have eroded real wages over time, something that is patently at odds with the facts. There are two ways to interpret Shiller's results. The pessimistic interpretation would be to take Shiller's findings at face value and conclude that the costs of inflation are, literally, illusory—they derive from money illusion. The optimistic interpretation would be that policymakers and academics have, to date, done a poor job of identifying, quantifying, and ultimately advertising the costs of inflation to the public.

With the optimistic interpretation in mind, this paper aims to identify and quantify some such costs for the United Kingdom. Much has been written on the *theoretical* justification for stable prices (Fischer and Modigliani 1975 is a classic treatment; for surveys, see also Driffill, Mizon, and Ulph 1990; Fischer 1981; Briault 1995). But there is less *empirical* work quantifying the costs and benefits of price stability and, particularly, placing them in a welfare context.

One of the few previous attempts by the Bank of England to articulate con-

Hasan Bakhshi is an economist at the Bank of England. Andrew G. Haldane is an economist at the Bank of England. Neal Hatch is an economist at the Bank of England.

The authors are grateful to Clive Briault, Martin Feldstein, Max Fry, Nigel Jenkinson, Mervyn King, Peter Westaway, Tony Yates, and in particular to Andrew Dumble, Mark Robson, and Rupert Watson for valuable background calculations, comments, and suggestions. They also thank Kee Law and Lorna Hall for research assistance, and seminar participants at the Bank of England, the University of Cambridge, and the University of Strathclyde. Remaining errors are the responsibility of the authors. The views expressed within are not necessarily those of the Bank of England.

cretely some of the costs of inflation (Leigh-Pemberton 1992) listed the following costs of a *fully anticipated* inflation:

Cost of economizing on real money balances—so-called shoe-leather effects;

Costs of operating a less than perfectly indexed tax system;

Costs of "front-end loading" of nominal debt contracts;

Cost of constantly revising price lists—so-called menu costs.

Feldstein (1997b) seeks to quantify the first two of these costs when moving from 2 percent inflation to price stability in the United States. That is the primary aim of this paper too. It focuses on distortions to saving, (housing and business) investment, and money demand decision making brought about by a fully anticipated 2 percent inflation tax, operating either unilaterally or, more often, in tandem with the tax system in the United Kingdom.[1] The paper also explores the indirect effects on the government's period-by-period budget constraint of a shift to price stability. We end up with estimates of the costs of inflation in the United Kingdom that work through the channels identified by Feldstein in the United States. Exercises such as this inevitably require simplifying assumptions. So we also conduct some sensitivity analysis on our results. The analysis is clearly restrictive, as it ignores many of the other welfare costs of inflation—for example, those associated with *un*anticipated inflation. Because of this, the paper is best seen as quantifying a subset of the feasible range of welfare benefits that lower inflation might engender; it is strictly a lower bound. In other words, we calculate *some* of the benefits of lower inflation and then compare those with an estimate of the *total* cost of disinflating. This is rather a tough test.

Focusing on the effects of fully anticipated inflation means that the welfare costs we consider are the deadweight loss triangles familiar from public finance economics.[2] Until recently, many economists have believed that the costs of fully anticipated inflation are relatively unimportant, or at least that they are less important than the costs of unanticipated inflation. In a celebrated quote, Tobin summarized this view in "it takes a heap of Harberger triangles to fill an Okun gap." And on the face of it, there is little in the aggregate time-series or cross-sectional data to question this view at the levels of inflation currently prevailing within developed economies.

For example, in a cross-sectional study of over 100 countries, Barro (1995) finds little relationship between inflation and growth at rates of inflation below

---

1. Physical menu costs and front-end loading have generally been found to have small effects: E.g., survey evidence in Blinder (1992) for the United States and Hall, Walsh, and Yates (1996) for the United Kingdom does not support menu costs as an important influence on firms' price-setting behavior. Schwab (1982) finds that the welfare costs of front-end loading are not large for reasonably sized changes in inflation.

2. Bailey (1956) was one of the first exponents of such micro-to-macro welfare analysis in the context of money demand distortions.

10 percent—though at rates of inflation above this there is evidence that inflation is a significant drag on growth. Likewise, Sarel (1996) finds no evidence of inflation inhibiting growth at rates of inflation below 8 percent—but, again, that there are significantly adverse effects on growth at rates of inflation above this.[3] Looking at one level of disaggregation, Rudebusch and Wilcox (1994) find a significant inverse relationship between productivity growth and inflation in the United States over the period 1955–93. But even that relationship appears to disintegrate in the United Kingdom at levels of inflation below 5 percent (Bianchi and Smith 1995).[4] Taken together, there is little from this aggregate evidence to strongly support a move from single-digit inflation figures to price stability.

There are at least three reasons why these empirical studies are, by themselves, insufficient to close the case for price stability. First, even if lower inflation has little or no effect on an economy's *growth* rate, it can still generate a permanent boost to the *level* of GDP, with potentially infinitely lived effects on welfare (Feldstein 1979). The resulting welfare gain may well then have a large present value even if, at first blush, its first-round effect appears trivial. By contrast, in a world of policy neutrality, the welfare costs of disinflating are likely to be one-off and transient. So welfare analysis of the costs and benefits of inflation is inevitably a comparison between *static* costs and *dynamic* benefits—with the odds correspondingly weighted in favor of the latter (see King 1994). Importantly, such effects may well go undetected by empirical studies looking at secular growth rates over long runs of data.

Second, aggregate time series may simply be too crude a tool to pick up some of the distorting effects of inflation, especially as such distortions are likely to be smaller and more subtle at lower rates of inflation. One response to this mixed bag of macroempirical results would therefore be to look directly at the microlevel decisions that inflation is thought likely to be distorting. That has been the response most recently among general equilibrium real business cycle theorists (inter alia, Cooley and Hansen 1989; Dotsey and Ireland 1996). By viewing inflation as a tax on microlevel decisions, these authors have been able to identify explicitly, and quantify empirically, some sizable welfare costs of inflation at the macroeconomic level. This is broadly our approach too, though within a partial rather than general equilibrium setting.

Third, in a world of existing distortionary taxes, the consumer surplus forgone by the interaction of taxes and inflation is not just the conventional Harberger deadweight loss triangle, but a *trapezoid*.[5] Or, put differently, adding a distortion (inflation) to an existing distortion (taxes) is likely to lead to welfare

3. See also Fischer (1993), Smyth (1994), and Fry, Goodhart, and Almeida (1996) for cross-sectional evidence on inflation-growth correlations.
4. On the relationship between investment and growth in the cross section, see Barro (1995) and Fischer (1993).
5. This is the adjustment suggested by Tower (1971) to the original money demand welfare analysis presented by Bailey (1956).

losses that are first rather than second order in a world of unindexed tax systems. Because these first-order distortions derive inherently from the interaction between inflation and taxes, we cannot then uniquely ascribe these welfare costs to a failure of monetary policy. Fiscal policy could equally well step into the breach. But what we can identify is the welfare benefits monetary policy, acting via lower inflation, might bring. And in the absence of a response from fiscal policy, these effects will be first rather than second order, or trapezoids rather than triangles.

So what is the precise experiment we simulate? Much of the existing literature focuses on comparative static comparisons of low and moderate inflation—for example, the costs of moving from 10 percent to zero inflation. That type of experiment seems less apposite in today's low-inflation environment. For example, in the United Kingdom RPIX inflation—retail prices excluding mortgage interest payments, the government's targeted measure of consumer prices—averaged 12.7 percent in the 1970s, 7.0 percent in the 1980s, but has fallen to an average 4.4 percent in the 1990s so far. Feldstein's (1997b) study draws data from the period 1960–94 in the United States, during which time inflation averaged 4 to 5 percent. Making an allowance for the measurement bias in the U.S. CPI of 2 percent,[6] a shift to price stability would then be equivalent to a 2 percentage point fall in inflation from its historical levels in the United States. That is the policy experiment Feldstein simulates.

In the United Kingdom, RPIX inflation is currently around 3 percent. It is widely thought that available price indexes overstate inflation, but estimates of the extent of the overstatement are highly uncertain. Cunningham (1996) quotes a possible range of central estimates of 0.35 to 1.3 percent per year. It is possible that starting from its current position, a 2 percentage point reduction in inflation would deliver approximate price stability in the United Kingdom. So this is the experiment we consider for the United Kingdom: a 2 percentage point fall in inflation, as in Feldstein's U.S. study. Historically, of course, U.K. inflation has been rather higher than 3 percent, averaging 6 to 7 percent between 1970 and 1995.[7]

The paper is organized as follows. Section 4.2 quantifies the output costs of disinflationary transition, and it quantifies the discounted flow of future benefits needed to offset this cost. Section 4.3 calculates distortions to rates of return—and hence to the price of retirement consumption—resulting from

---

6. Recent estimates by Shapiro and Wilcox (1996) suggest that this adjustment may be on the high side. They estimate that there is a one-in-ten chance that the bias in the U.S. CPI is greater than 1.5 percent. The Shapiro-Wilcox estimates accord closely with Canadian evidence (Crawford 1994). But measurement biases remain an area of great uncertainty, in particular with regard to new goods and quality biases (see, e.g., Nordhaus 1997 and, indeed, Shapiro and Wilcox's 1996 Medicare example). See also Boskin (1996).

7. We select 1995 as the base year for our calculations because it is the most recent year for which a (near) full set of data is available. Because we are simulating the effect of a change in inflation from current levels, we use the effective marginal tax rates in operation during 1995, rather than historical averages.

Table 4.1   **U.K. Estimates: Welfare Effects of a 2 Percentage Point Reduction in Inflation (percent of GDP)**

Source of Change	Direct Effect of Reduced Distortion	Indirect Welfare Effect of Revenue Change		Net Welfare Effect	
		$\lambda = 0.4$	$\lambda = 1.5$	$\lambda = 0.4$	$\lambda = 1.5$
Consumption timing					
$\eta_{SR} = 0.2$	0.40	−0.12	−0.43	0.29	−0.03
$\eta_{SR} = 0.0$	0.35	−0.14	−0.51	0.21	−0.17
$\eta_{SR} = 0.4$	0.46	−0.09	−0.35	0.37	0.11
Housing demand	0.04	0.07	0.27	0.11	0.30
Money demand	0.02	−0.05	−0.17	−0.02	−0.15
Debt service	n.a.	−0.09	−0.33	−0.09	−0.33
Total					
$\eta_{SR} = 0.2$	0.47	−0.18	−0.67	0.29	−0.20
$\eta_{SR} = 0.0$	0.41	−0.20	−0.75	0.21	−0.34
$\eta_{SR} = 0.4$	0.52	−0.16	−0.59	0.37	−0.06

Note: λ is the marginal deadweight loss of an across-the-board tax increase that raises one extra pound of revenue. η_{SR} is elasticity of private saving with respect to the posttax real rate of return. n.a. = not applicable.

inflation. Sections 4.4 and 4.5 look at similar distortions affecting owner-occupied housing and money demand; while section 4.6 considers the impact on government debt servicing. Finally, the concluding section draws these estimates together and suggests some policy conclusions and extensions.[8] These estimates are summarized in table 4.1 for the United Kingdom; table 4.2 provides the equivalent estimates for the United States as a counterpoint.

4.2   Costs of Disinflation

4.2.1   Ball's Sacrifice Ratio for the United Kingdom

We begin by calculating some estimates of the output cost of a 2 percentage point reduction in inflation in the United Kingdom. Feldstein uses Ball's (1994) well-known work on the sacrifice ratio. Ball's approach is to estimate the cumulated loss in output required for each percentage point reduction in inflation. The resulting event-study sacrifice ratio estimates for the United Kingdom, based on two events in the 1960s, one in the 1970s, and a further two in the 1980s, are summarized in table 4.3. They suggest numbers that are typically smaller than those found by Ball for the United States, averaging less than 1 percent compared with 2 to 3 percent in the United States.

But just how robust are these estimates? One reason to be skeptical is that

---

8. An appendix provides some analysis of inflation effects on business investment.

Table 4.2   **U.S. Estimates: Welfare Effects of a 2 Percentage Point Reduction in Inflation (percent of GDP)**

Source of Change	Direct Effect of Reduced Distortion	Indirect Welfare Effect of Revenue Change		Net Welfare Effect	
		$\lambda = 0.4$	$\lambda = 1.5$	$\lambda = 0.4$	$\lambda = 1.5$
Consumption timing					
$\eta_{SR} = 0.4$	1.04	−0.07	−0.27	0.97	0.77
$\eta_{SR} = 0.0$	0.75	−0.18	−0.67	0.57	0.07
$\eta_{SR} = 1.0$	1.49	0.09	0.33	1.58	1.82
Housing demand	0.11	0.14	0.51	0.25	0.62
Money demand	0.016	−0.05	−0.19	−0.03	−0.17
Debt service	n.a.	−0.10	−0.38	−0.10	−0.38
Total					
$\eta_{SR} = 0.4$	1.17	−0.09	−0.33	1.09	0.84
$\eta_{SR} = 0.0$	0.87	−0.19	−0.73	0.68	0.14
$\eta_{SR} = 1.0$	1.61	0.07	0.27	1.69	1.89

Note: See note to table 4.1.

Table 4.3   **U.K. Sacrifice Ratios**

Period of Downturn	Ratio
1961:1–63:3	1.9[a]
1965:2–66:3	0.0[a]
1975:1–78:2	0.9[a]
1980:2–83:3	0.3[a], 0.8[b]
1984:2–86:3	0.9[a]
Average	0.8[a]
1990:3–94:4	2.8[b]

Note: Quarterly data. One reason for the difference between the two estimates for the 1980 downturn is that we use RPIX inflation rather than the RPI series used by Ball.
[a]From Ball (1994).
[b]Authors' estimates.

structural reforms in the United Kingdom in the 1980s—in particular in the labor market—may have led to a change in the short-run trade-off between inflation (wages) and output (unemployment).[9] Ball's last estimate for the United Kingdom relates to the period 1984–86 and is thus unlikely to capture these changes. Moreover, his latest estimates may be distorted by two supply shocks at either end of the sample: the 1984 miners' strike and the 1986 oil price shock. Further, the estimated trade-off might be different—less favor-

9. Other methodological questions are raised in Cecchetti (1994) and Mayes and Chapple (1995).

able—at the lower rates of inflation prevailing in the 1990s, compared to the 1970s and 1980s.[10] Recognizing this, we used Ball's approach to calculate an updated estimate of the sacrifice ratio for the most recent disinflationary episode in the United Kingdom, 1990:3–94:4. As shown in table 4.3, the ratio is considerably higher than earlier estimates, suggesting around a 3 percent output loss for each percentage point reduction in inflation. This is consistent with the notion of a flatter Phillips curve at lower rates of inflation and is more in line with the U.S. evidence.

4.2.2   Breakeven Benefits from Price Stability

If we take these estimates at face value, the cost of reducing inflation by 2 percentage points in the United Kingdom would be around 6 percent of annual output, close to Ball's U.S. estimates. With this cost estimate, we can then calculate the welfare gain (as a percentage of initial GDP) necessary to counterbalance this cost on the assumptions (a) that the welfare gain accrues indefinitely into the future, (b) that any future gains are discounted to give us a present value, and (c) that following Feldstein (1979) we make an allowance for growth effects—the fact that the level of the GDP base on which the welfare cost is being calculated grows over time. The net benefit (B, as a percentage of initial GDP) that ensures that disinflationary costs (C, also as a percentage of initial GDP) are exactly counterbalanced—the breakeven benefit—is given by

$$(1) \qquad\qquad B = C*(r - g),$$

where r is the discount rate and g is the steady state growth rate of the economy. Real growth in the U.K. economy over the past 25 years has averaged around 2 percent ($g = 0.02$).[11] For the discount rate, following Feldstein (1997b), we take the average net-of-tax real rate of return that an individual investor earned on a risky equity portfolio (the FT-SE All-Industrials Index) between 1970 and 1995.[12] Over this period, the FT-SE All-Industrials Index rose by 10.6 percent in nominal terms, with an average dividend yield of 4.9 percent. We need to adjust both dividend and capital gains income for taxes. For dividends, we assume an average marginal tax rate of 28.7 percent over the period.[13] For capital gains, we assume that realized gains are subject to the higher capital gains tax rate of 40 percent—that most capital gain investment income accrues

10. We discuss in greater detail below the evidence on such Phillips curve convexities.
11. Real growth should perhaps be defined on a per capita basis, but that would make little difference to our estimate here because the U.K. population has been steady over the period.
12. The choice of period over which to average is in some sense arbitrary.
13. To simplify calculations we use the 1995 tax system as a base. The marginal tax rate is calculated using Inland Revenue data for this year and the methodology in Robson (1988). It would have been costly to calculate an average of marginal tax rates operating in every year between 1970 and 1995. Our approach is likely to lead to a conservative estimate of the discount rate if, on average, tax rates in 1995 were lower than those over the period as a whole. However, this approach may provide a better estimate of the discount rate to apply when discounting *future* welfare gains.

to higher rate income tax payers. But we need to make two further adjustments to the marginal tax rate on capital gains to arrive at an *effective* marginal tax rate. First, capital gains tax is indexed in the United Kingdom, so it is only *real* capital gains that are subject to tax. Second, we need to make an adjustment for the £6,000 annual exemption limit on capital gains and for the fact that gains accrued but unrealized at death are exempt from capital gains tax.[14] The Inland Revenue publishes estimates of the tax revenue lost through the two exemptions and the indexation allowance. Adding these to actual capital gains tax revenue and using the 40 percent marginal tax rate allows us to derive an estimate of the underlying total capital gain. When combined with the actual figure for capital gains tax revenue, this provides an estimate of the effective capital gains tax rate. Using data for financial year 1994/95 gives an effective tax rate on capital gains of 14.1 percent, which is similar to Feldstein's estimate of 10 percent. Finally, note that RPIX inflation averaged 8.6 percent over the period 1970–95. Netting off the measurement bias thus gives a "true" inflation rate of 7.3 percent. Our estimate of the discount rate is then $r = 5.3$ percent $((1 - 0.141)10.6 + (1 - 0.287)4.9 - 7.3)$, again not too different from Feldstein's U.S. estimate.

From equation (1), this higher estimate of the discount rate, taken together with the United Kingdom's lower average real growth rate than the United States, raises the breakeven benefit, B, necessary to offset disinflationary costs. For the United Kingdom the breakeven benefit is 0.18 percent of GDP, compared with 0.16 percent in Feldstein's study.

4.2.3   Some Sensitivity Analysis

There are obviously risks to this present value calculus; it is sensitive to the underlying assumptions regarding r, g, and C. Particular risks attach to estimates of r and C. On discount rates, at one extreme Ramsey (1928) argued that any discounting of the utility of future generations was "ethically indefensible"—in which case the net benefits of moving to price stability would be infinite. At the other extreme, it is well known that firms in the United Kingdom often discount future income streams at much higher rates than would be implied by returns on the stock market (Wardlow 1994). Our discount rate estimate steers a—conservative—middle course between these extremes by taking a risky real return as a benchmark.

Just how conservative this discount rate estimate is can be gauged by looking at two alternatives. For example, it could be argued that the appropriate real return is one on a debt and equity, rather than a pure equity, portfolio. Over the period 1970–95, the real after-tax return to government bonds in the United Kingdom was only 0.2 percent.[15] That would drag down markedly the implied discount rate for any plausible personal sector asset-gearing ratio. Alternatively, following Feldstein (1995), we might derive a discount rate directly

---

14. Though not from inheritance tax; but this has a much higher exemption limit.
15. Calculated using redemption yields rather than holding period returns.

from the utility function. For example, assuming constant elasticity of substitution (CES) preferences and equating the discount rate with the marginal rate of substitution of consumption over time, it follows that

$$(2) \qquad 1 + r = (1 + w - n)^{\gamma},$$

where γ is the elasticity of marginal utility and w and n are steady state aggregate wage and population growth. Taking $\gamma = 2$ from Feldstein (1995) and plugging in values for w and n gives $r = 3.2$ percent, similar to Feldstein's U.S. estimate of 3.0 percent. This again would imply a much larger—and potentially infinite—present value of welfare gains. In sum, the risks to our welfare estimates from the discount rate appear clearly to lie on the upside.

Another area of particular uncertainty—most likely working in the opposite direction—is the cost estimate, C. There are theoretical arguments, and some empirical evidence, to suggest Ball's estimates may understate the costs of transitioning to price stability. There are at least two such transition costs. First, as illustrated in table 4.3, temporary disinflationary costs may be higher at lower rates of inflation. That would imply that even the 1990s sacrifice ratio for the United Kingdom may be an understatement of the true output costs of achieving price stability. Several strands of empirical evidence point in this direction. For example, Laxton, Meredith, and Rose (1995) find strong evidence of Phillips curve convexities among G-7 countries. And a similar result emerges from the work of Ball, Mankiw, and Romer (1988), looking at a cross section of 43 industrialized countries.[16] Indeed, Ball's (1994) own work finds some (albeit weak) evidence of the initial level of inflation affecting the size of the sacrifice ratio.

It is unclear, theoretically, why such asymmetries may exist, and hence whether they are likely to survive a shift in inflation regime. For example, rigidities in prices and wages—due, say, to psychological or legal impediments to nominal wage cuts—could explain Phillips curve convexities.[17] But these may well disappear if a shift to price stability is deemed credible. Other—real—rigidities may be more entrenched. One way of gauging possible Phillips curve convexities in a regime approximating price stability is to look at pre–World War II historical evidence. Figure 4.1, for example, is a simple scatterplot of inflation-growth outcomes over the period 1831–1938 in the United Kingdom, together with a second-order polynomial line of best fit.[18] While

---

16. E.g., table 8 of Ball et al. (1988) suggests that the output-inflation trade-off (and hence the implied sacrifice ratio) doubles between inflation rates of 5 percent—close to the historical mean for the United Kingdom over the sample—and zero. Yates and Chapple (1996) confirm this result using a more general formulation of the empirical output-inflation relationship.

17. Though North American and U.K. evidence on the distribution of prices and earnings finds mixed support for such a proposition: see Yates (1995) for a summary. Akerlof, Dickens, and Perry (1996) present evidence to suggest that the distribution of wage settlements in the United States is truncated below zero.

18. Higher order polynomial terms added nothing to the fit. Because we are attempting to fit an aggregate supply curve, we have crudely attempted to purge the data of supply shocks by removing observations where the changes in price level and output are oppositely signed.

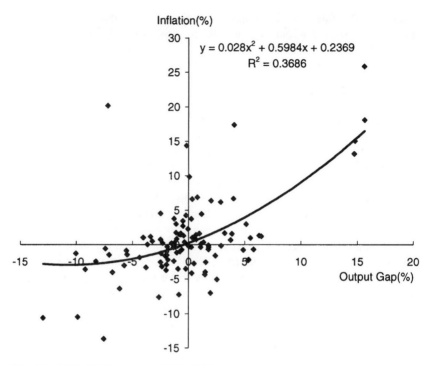

Fig. 4.1   U.K. Phillips curve, 1831–1938

there is some evidence of convexity, the degree of curvature is not great enough to suggest that our transitional cost estimates are a significant understatement.

A second potential cost of transitioning to price stability, which goes unquantified by Ball's (1994) analysis, is hysteresis—*permanent*—effects on output.[19] The empirical evidence on hysteresis effects has been equivocal. But a recent paper by Ball (1997) himself presents cross-sectional evidence to suggest that hysteretic effects on the NAIRU may have been both commonplace and large during recent disinflations among the OECD countries. On the assumption that any disinflation has a permanent effect on the *level* of output, the breakeven benefit becomes

(3) $B = C*(r - g) + D,$

where D is the effect of a disinflation on the natural level of output. If we take Ball's (1997) cross-sectional estimates at face value, each percentage point of disinflation is associated with a 0.42 percentage point rise in the NAIRU (Ball 1997, table 4.2). Taking a (conservative) estimate of Okun's law coefficient of 2, this would imply a 1.7 percent fall in the level of output for a 2 percentage

---

19. See, e.g., Layard, Nickell, and Jackman (1991) and more recently Akerlof et al. (1996).

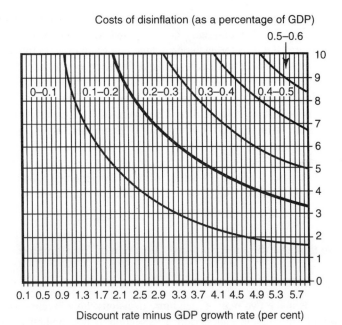

Costs of disinflation (as a percentage of GDP)

Discount rate minus GDP growth rate (per cent)

Fig. 4.2   Breakeven welfare benefits (percent of GDP)

point disinflation.[20] This then raises the breakeven benefit to around 1.9 percent, possibly exceeding the benefits Feldstein finds for the United States. This hysteresis estimate is no doubt an upper bound. Over the 1980s, Ball's estimate of the U.K. NAIRU rose by 1.1 percentage points, while inflation fell by 8.5 percentage points over the same period. This would imply a much lower hysteresis coefficient of maybe 0.1 in the United Kingdom, though even this would raise the breakeven benefit to just under 0.6 percent. Further, it could be that Ball is picking up highly persistent, rather than permanent effects from disinflation on the NAIRU.[21] The present value of these losses would then be overstated. But notwithstanding these caveats, it is clear that hysteresis effects, even if modest, have the potential to alter radically any cost-benefit evaluation of price stability.[22]

The above are indicative of the risks to the cost-benefit calculus. Figure 4.2

20. Ball (1997) also allows for multiplicative effects with the duration of unemployment benefits (table 4.4). Making an allowance for this effect raises the effect of disinflation on the level of output to 2 percentage points in the United Kingdom because of the greater duration of U.K. unemployment benefits.

21. E.g., because even discouraged and deskilled workers will exit the labor force at some stage, through death or retirement.

22. There may be costs to operating at, as well as transitioning to, price stability, such as the nonnegativity constraint imposed on real interest rates (Summers 1991). What little evidence there is suggests that the Summers constraint only rarely binds in a costly way (Fuhrer and Madigan 1994).

conducts some sensitivity analysis of the breakeven benefit under different assumptions about the disinflationary costs, C, and the discount rate, r. Intuitively, the more GDP lost for each percentage point reduction in inflation, the higher the welfare benefit required to make disinflation worthwhile. Similarly, the higher the discount rate, the higher the welfare benefit required. To take a specific example, assume welfare gains of 0.2 percent of GDP (as we calculate later in the paper). A welfare gain of 0.2 percent of GDP corresponds to the second thick line from the left. For any pair of parameter values lying in the two areas below the line, welfare benefits of 0.2 percent would suffice to offset disinflationary costs. So even with high estimates of the output costs of disinflation—say, 6 percent of a year's output lost for a 2 percentage point reduction in inflation—the welfare benefits of reducing inflation exceed the output costs of doing so.

4.3 Inflation and the Intertemporal Allocation of Consumption

4.3.1 Distortions to Saving Behavior

Households make two main expenditure decisions: how much to consume and how much to invest in each period. This section focuses on how household consumption decisions are affected by inflation; the next section considers the impact of inflation on housing investment decisions.

Feldstein (1997b) derives the welfare gain from reducing inflation in a two-period consumption model. Individuals are given an initial endowment and then decide how much to save in the first period in order to consume when they retire in the second period. Agents' first-period savings earn a real rate of return. So the period 1 price of retirement consumption (p) can be thought to be inversely related to this rate of return; the higher the return on savings, the cheaper the effective price of retirement consumption. It is here that inflation and the tax system come into play. Taxes drive a wedge between the pretax rate of return—which is assumed to be invariant under inflation—and the posttax return that households earn. Higher inflation raises the tax wedge and reduces the effective (real) posttax return to saving. This lowers retirement consumption from its (zero tax, zero inflation) optimum, with corresponding welfare implications. Rather than reproduce the basic arguments and calculations here, the gain to households from increased retirement consumption resulting from a reduction in inflation is simply stated here as equation (4) (see Feldstein 1997b, eq. [4] and fig. 3.1):

$$(4) \quad G_1 = C + D = [(p_1 - p_0)/p_2 + 0.5(p_2 - p_1)/p_2] \\ \times [(p_2 - p_1)/p_2]S_2(1 - \eta_{Sp} - \sigma),$$

where p_0 is the price of retirement consumption at zero inflation with no distortionary taxes, p_1 is the retirement price evaluated under the current tax regime

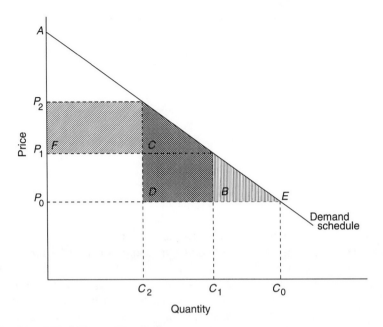

Fig. 4.3   Calculating welfare losses

with zero inflation, and p_2 is the price evaluated under the current tax regime with 2 percent inflation; S_2 represents the initial gross saving of individuals at the early stage of their life cycles; η_{Sp} is the uncompensated elasticity of saving with respect to the price of retirement consumption; and σ is the propensity to save out of exogenous income. The welfare gain associated with a reduction of inflation (and hence with a reduction in the retirement price $p_2 - p_1$) is the area under the compensated demand curve, the trapezoid C + D in figure 4.3. To evaluate equation (4), we first need a measure of the price of retirement consumption. Feldstein (1997b) calculates this as $(1 + r)^{-T}$, where r is the real posttax rate of return and T is the number of years that agents engage in saving for retirement. Following Feldstein, we take $T = 30$ years.[23]

To calculate p_0 we require a pretax rate of return to capital for U.K. industrial and commercial corporations. Such data are published by the U.K. Office for National Statistics. Between 1970 and 1995, this real rate of return averaged 8.2 percent. It is slightly below returns in the United States.[24] Using OECD data as a cross check confirms that returns to capital in the United Kingdom

23. All subsequent calculations are based on estimates up to and including 1995, the last year for which we have a full set of data. A number of changes to the tax system have been announced since 1995 but have not been taken into account.

24. As in Feldstein, the capital stock is defined net of depreciation; pretax profits are gross of interest payments, but unlike Feldstein, no attempt has yet been made to gross up for property taxes.

Table 4.4   **Advance Corporation Tax (ACT) and Mainstream Corporation Tax (MCT)**

Taxable profits	£100
Corporation tax (CT) rate	33%
Liability to CT	£33
ACT rate	25%
Dividend paid	£40
Payments of ACT	£10 (0.25*40)
Payments of MCT	£23 (33−10)

have on average been below those in the United States over the past 30 years. Translating the estimated pretax return into a price of retirement consumption in the absence of taxes, $p_0 = (1.082)^{-30} = 0.094$.

To estimate a real return to saving in a world of taxes and inflation, we need to adjust the above figures for both corporate and personal sector taxes. The United States operates a "classical" tax system under which dividends are taxed twice, once as profits at the corporate level and again as income at the personal level. By contrast, the United Kingdom operates an imputation tax system that provides protection against the double taxation of dividends through a system of advance corporation tax (ACT). When dividends are paid to individuals the companies pay ACT, currently 20 percent of gross dividends (25 percent of net dividends), but can use this payment to offset their later liability to mainstream corporation tax (MCT).[25] Individuals can then use this payment against their total tax liability at the end of the financial year. Individuals who have marginal tax rates above or below the ACT rate will incur a credit or debit accordingly. An example illustrates the imputation system (see table 4.4).

In our calculations we take payments of MCT having netted off ACT payments (to prevent double counting). We then deal with the taxation of dividends at the personal level. These MCT payments amounted to some 22 percent of firms' pretax profits in 1995. This tax ratio is not zero because not all profits are distributed and because corporate tax rates are on average generally higher than personal tax rates. Ceteris paribus, this leads to higher tax payments the lower the dividend payout ratio. But the effective tax rate is still much lower than the corresponding U.S. figure, reflecting the difference between the U.S. (classical) and U.K. (imputation) systems of dividend taxation. Netting off this ratio leaves a posttax rate of return of 6.38 percent. (For further details of the U.K. corporate tax system, see Kay and King 1990.)

To arrive at a real posttax return for savers, we also need to take account of personal taxes. What we need for our policy simulations are measures of the

25. This means that a number of firms each year have ACT credits outweighing their taxable income: they are "tax exhausted" (see, e.g., Devereux 1987). This tax credit typically gets carried forward. This gives rise to an asymmetry in the corporate tax system, but one that we ignore here.

currently effective marginal tax rates on capital income. But these effective marginal tax rates depend on how this income is received (dividends, capital gains, interest income) and the tax status of the individual. Feldstein proxies these effects by assuming an individual marginal tax rate of 25 percent across all sources of income. We look at one level of disaggregation, identifying separately average marginal tax rates on interest income, dividends, and capital gains and then weighting these to give an individual marginal tax rate. At this stage we make no allowance for tax-exempt savings, which are important in the United Kingdom. We assume, in effect, that marginal savings flow into taxable assets. But we return to this issue below, when we conduct some sensitivity analysis assuming a different—tax-exempt—margin.

For dividends we begin by calculating an average marginal tax rate on dividends using Inland Revenue individual data for financial year 1994/95 and the methodology in Robson (1988). This gives a headline tax rate of 28.7 percent. For interest income on corporate bonds we use a headline marginal tax rate of 31.1 percent, again based on Inland Revenue figures for 1994/95. The headline marginal tax rate on capital gains (on equity and bonds) is that used earlier when calculating the discount rate, 14.1 percent.

For the weights on dividends, capital gains, and bond interest income, Feldstein assumes the same debt-equity split for persons as for companies. That amounts to assuming that the corporate sector is owned directly by households. This assumption is, in turn, only valid under three conditions: first, when open economy considerations are unimportant; second, when there are no debt-equity transformations through financial intermediation; and third, when personal sector net banking assets are counterbalanced by their net banking liabilities, so that bank loans to companies are not backed by household saving. For the United States, a relatively closed economy where many debt and equity holdings are direct, these are reasonable approximations.

But the U.K. situation is rather different. Overseas holdings of U.K. company securities amounted to over 18 percent of these companies' balance sheets in 1995; while around 5 percent of the personal sector's equity holdings were with overseas companies. Further, the majority of households' equity and debt holdings are indirect—through pension funds, unit trusts, and the like— which may transform corporate debt to equity or vice versa. To overcome these problems, we take the debt-equity split directly from the personal sector's balance sheet by explicitly identifying their (direct and indirect) holdings of U.K. companies' capital using sectoral flow-of-funds data. That negates the problems of overseas holdings of company capital and possible debt-equity transformations of assets as they pass from the corporate to the personal sector. Doing this gives a 95/5 split of personal sector *nonbank* assets between equity and debt.[26] We then use this asset split when accounting for the incidence of

---

26. If we use instead the U.K. corporate sector's balance sheet to infer a equity-debt ratio for companies' nonbank liabilities, we get a ratio of around 8 percent in 1995.

personal taxation on corporate bonds and equity. For the split between dividends (interest) and capital gains of equity (bond) income, we assume that individuals receive income from dividends (interest) and capital gains in broadly the same ratio used in our discount rate calculation, roughly 60/40.

But to the extent that the personal sector's net *banking* assets are also indirectly financing U.K. companies' bank loans, we need to take account of these too.[27] Feldstein sidesteps this problem by assuming that household bank deposits and bank loans are offsetting. U.K. companies held net banking liabilities of around £60 billion in 1995. Because of the nature of banking, it is impossible to say which of these were financed from personal sector deposits and which from other sources; but if we assume that net bank loans to companies were effectively financed from personal deposits, we can calculate a marginal effective personal tax rate inclusive of the banking sector.[28] The weights in the personal sector's balance sheet are then 5/89/6 for corporate bonds, equity, and deposits, respectively.[29] For the average marginal tax rate on deposits we apply a rate of 23.6 percent, comprising a 26.2 percent tax rate on interest-bearing deposits and, trivially, a zero rate on non-interest-bearing deposits.

Using these weights and our adjusted average marginal tax rates gives us a total effective marginal individual tax rate of 23.0 percent. This implies a real net rate of return to savers in the United Kingdom of around 4.9 percent, which corresponds to a price of retirement consumption of 0.237 evaluated at 2 percent inflation. The wedge between pre- and posttax returns in the United Kingdom (3.3 percent) is around two-thirds that in the U.S. case (5.13 percent). This largely reflects the effects of ACT.

We now calculate the effect on the posttax real return to saving—and hence on the price of retirement consumption—of a reduction in inflation of 2 percentage points. Work in the United Kingdom, along similar lines to that in the United States, has shown that inflation tends to increase effective tax rates for both the personal and corporate sectors. For companies, this inflation nonneutrality in the U.K. tax system has three sources. First, since 1984 U.K. companies have received no stock relief; that is, any nominal capital gains made on inventories as a result of general price level rises are treated as taxable profit. Second, depreciation allowances are based on historic cost asset valuations and are thus reduced in real terms by inflation. And, third, acting against the first two effects is the fact that nominal debt interest payments are tax deductible.[30]

Bond, Devereux, and Freeman (1990) calibrate these inflation nonneutralities using microlevel data drawn from company accounts. They estimate that

27. We are only interested here in the savings channel running from households to companies, so personal sector assets that are backing non-U.K.-corporate liabilities are not included in the calculations—e.g., household holdings of government debt or foreign debt and equity.

28. We discuss variants on this assumption in the sensitivities section below.

29. There is an argument for basing the weights on gross rather than net banking liabilities. Using gross liabilities changes the weights to 4/81/15, but this does not appear to have a very significant effect on the estimates of the welfare gain.

30. In the United States, only the second and third of these effects is relevant.

moving from 10 percent inflation to price stability is associated with a decrease in companies' effective tax rate of over one-third. Making an assumption about the initial pretax rate of return and assuming a fixed capital stock, we can translate this ready-reckoner into an effect of inflation on companies' profit rates. The rule of thumb we use, based on Bond et al. (1990), is that a 1 percentage point fall in inflation is associated with a 0.37 percentage point rise in the taxable profit rate.[31] We take the average marginal corporation tax rate to be 32 percent, based on Inland Revenue data.[32] The effect of a 2 percentage point reduction in inflation is hence to raise the posttax return to savers by $0.32*0.37*0.02 = 0.0024$ (0.24 percentage points) as a result of corporation tax nonneutralities. That is, the rate of return after corporate taxes is raised from 6.38 to 6.62 percent.

The effect of inflation on households' effective tax rates depends on the debt-equity-deposit composition of their asset portfolios. We assume the same weights as earlier. For equity holdings, one key difference from the United States is that since 1985 capital gains in the United Kingdom have been indexed. This effectively neutralizes any effect from a change in inflation on equity income.[33] Taken alongside the higher proportion of equity in U.K. households' portfolios, this reduces substantially the fall in effective tax rates—and hence the rise in posttax saving rates—induced by a fall in inflation.

But a change in inflation *does* affect marginal tax rates on deposits and corporate debt because it is nominal interest income that is taxed. For deposits and for debt, we use our earlier average marginal effective tax rates of 23.6 and 31.1 percent, respectively. Taking these debt and deposit nonneutralities together, this gives a 0.06 percentage point reduction in the effective tax rate for a 2 percentage point fall in inflation. This then raises the posttax rate of return to individuals to 5.16 percent and implies that the price of retirement consumption falls to $p_1 = 0.22$ when inflation is zero. In the United Kingdom the move to price stability has less effect on the posttax saving rate (around 0.24 percentage points) than in the United States (around 0.49 percentage

31. If a 1 percentage point rise in inflation lowers tax liabilities by 3.7 percent, then, for fixed capital stock, this is equivalent to a 3.7 percent rise in the profit rate. The pretax return to capital in 1989—the year when Bond et al. (1990) do their analysis—was around 10 percent. Hence, a 1 percentage point rise in inflation implies an increase in the profit rate of 0.37 percentage points. This ready-reckoner takes account of all three tax nonneutralities simultaneously, whereas Feldstein looks at them separately. We can identify separately the debt interest deductibility effect to ensure our estimates are not too wayward. With debt 21 percent of Industrial Commercial Companies' capital and a marginal corporate tax rate of 32 percent, a 2 percentage point fall in inflation raises the effective corporate tax rate by $0.32*0.21*0.02 = 0.0013$ (or 0.13 percentage points). That would imply an effect on the effective tax rate from the lack of indexation of depreciation allowances and stock relief of 0.5 percentage points, not too dissimilar to the 0.57 percentage point depreciation nonneutrality used by Feldstein.

32. This is a weighted average of the 33 percent headline MCT rate and the 25 percent reduced rate for small firms.

33. Dividend income taxation is immune to inflation effects.

Table 4.5   **Saving Ratios in the United States and United Kingdom, 1990**

Age Cohort	United States	United Kingdom
31–35	7.1	8.0
36–40	9.4	12.0
41–45	9.8	12.0
46–50	11.2	11.0
51–55	13.9	10.0
56–60	16.6	13.0

Sources: Attanasio (1994) and Banks and Blundell (1994).

points). This is due largely to the indexation of capital gains and the greater importance of equity as a source of personal sector income in the United Kingdom.

The price of retirement consumption under the various tax and inflation assumptions (p_1, p_2, and p_0) can now be substituted into equation (4) to give

$$(5) \qquad\qquad G_1 = 0.038 S_2 (1 - \eta_{Sp} - \sigma).$$

To evaluate equation (5), we need an estimate of the saving of the young at an inflation rate of 2 percent (S_2). Feldstein derives an estimate from the steady state relationship between savers and dissavers implied by the two-period model. He shows that the saving of the young is $(1 + n + g)^T$ times the saving of the older generation, where n is the rate of population growth and g is the growth in per capita wages. If we follow that approach, real aggregate wage growth in the United Kingdom between 1970 and 1995 was 2 percent, somewhat lower than in the United States. Taking $n + g = 0.02$ and $T = 30$ implies that the saving of the young is around 2.23 times the *net* personal saving rate. Given an average U.K. personal saving rate of 9.2 percent of GDP between 1970 and 1995, this implies that S_2 is around 21 percent of GDP, more than double the U.S. figure.

This figure for gross saving seems high.[34] So we also considered some complementary microevidence from the U.S. Consumer Expenditure Survey and the U.K. Family Expenditure Survey (FES). Table 4.5 shows the saving ratios in 1990 of a set of population cohorts spanning the age range 30–60 in the United States (from Attanasio 1994) and the United Kingdom (Banks and Blundell 1994). This is the age range likely to match most closely with the theoretical notion of first-period savers because the very young are likely to be net borrowers and the very old gross dissavers.

---

34. Two possible reasons for this are, first, that our aggregate real wage growth assumption is too low—certainly, real wage growth is higher (around 2.5 percent) if we extend our data back to the 1960s—and, second, that our net saving ratio is too high. One cause of the latter is that our saving ratio is not inflation adjusted and average inflation over the sample has been higher than our 2 percent benchmark. An inflation-adjusted saving ratio would, over the 1980s, have been nearer to 4 percent.

Table 4.5 suggests two things.[35] First, there is little difference between saving ratios in the United Kingdom and the United States over the 30–60 age range; they both average around 11 percent. And, second, the U.K. saving ratio of the young is nearer to 10 percent than to the 21 percent implied by the macroestimates above. In what follows we use a lower implied estimate of gross saving ($S_2 = 0.11$), which seems more consistent with micro- and international evidence. Feldstein further assumes that the propensity to save out of exogenous income is the same as that out of earned income and that average and marginal saving propensities can be conflated. On these assumptions, given that earnings from employment are some 63 percent of GDP in the United Kingdom and $\sigma = S_2/0.63$, it follows that $\sigma = 0.17$.

The final piece in the jigsaw is the elasticity of saving with respect to real interest rates.[36] There is a good deal of academic controversy over this issue. Feldstein uses Boskin's (1978) work in the United States, which finds the elasticity to be around 0.4. Boskin's approach is to take the interest semielasticity from a standard consumption function and then infer from this the full interest elasticity of saving. On the assumption of fixed income, the full and semi-elasticities are linked by

$$(6) \qquad \eta_{SR} = -(\overline{R} * \overline{C})/\overline{S}\,\xi_{CR},$$

where C, S, and R denote consumption, saving, and the real interest rate, respectively, a bar denotes a mean value, and ξ_{CR} is the real interest rate semi-elasticity of consumption. To arrive at an estimate of η_{SR} for the United Kingdom, we take ξ_{CR} from a range of recently estimated consumption functions in the United Kingdom (Muellbauer and Murphy 1993; Bayoumi 1993; Fisher and Whitley, forthcoming)[37] and then convert them using equation (6) into saving elasticities. Most of the above studies imply saving elasticities fairly close to zero. So we take $\eta_{SR} = 0$ as our central guess but also consider $\eta_{SR} = 0.2$ and $\eta_{SR} = 0.4$ for comparability with Feldstein.

While our central assumption may seem extreme, there is a good deal of theoretical as well as empirical support for it. With CES preferences, a positive saving elasticity only obtains in a two-period model when the intertemporal elasticity of substitution exceeds unity.[38] And most empirical studies of the elasticity of substitution put it closer to zero than to unity (e.g., Hall 1988); certainly, there is little to suggest it is greater than unity. This implies that a zero saving elasticity—where income and substitution effects are broadly offsetting—is a reasonable central guess. Moreover, while a zero saving elasticity

35. One potential problem with the FES data set is that it is known to undersample high-income households. That, in turn, would depress the average saving ratio. But in 1990 the aggregate saving ratio in the United Kingdom was in line with the average reported by the FES.

36. It can be shown that $\eta_{SR} = -RT\eta_{Sp}/(1 + R)$.

37. Though only the first of these studies uses *post*tax real interest rates.

38. E.g., with Cobb-Douglas preferences in a two-period model, $\eta_{Sr} = 0.4$, and $r = 4$ percent, the implied elasticity of substitution is 1.7.

lowers the direct welfare costs calculated below, it certainly does not eliminate them. A larger part of the welfare gain is the result of a direct price effect of cheaper retirement consumption on the quantity of consumption purchased.

Using the above estimates of the saving elasticity, adjusted so that it is expressed as an elasticity of the price of retirement consumption,[39] together with our previous calculations, we can compute the overall gain from moving to price stability. Using equation (5), we estimate the gain to be $G_1 = 0.35$ percent of GDP with $\eta_{SR} = 0$ when $S_2 = 0.11$. At $\eta_{SR} = 0.2$, $G_1 = 0.40$ percent of GDP; at $\eta_{SR} = 0.4$, $G_1 = 0.46$ percent of GDP. All of these direct welfare costs are considerably smaller than in Feldstein. For example, if one makes the comparable assumption of $\eta_{SR} = 0$ for the United States, the gain would be some 0.75 percent of GDP. In large part this is due to the lesser susceptibility of the U.K. tax system to inflation-induced distortions.

4.3.2 Indirect Revenue Effects

Next we consider the effect on government revenue of the above experiment. The working assumption here, as in Feldstein (1997b), is that any effect of a move to price stability on government revenues cannot be made good by a rise in lump-sum taxes. Instead, distortionary taxes are required to fill any financing gap, with corresponding welfare implications.

Assume we start from a price of retirement income p_2 and consumption level C_2 (see fig. 4.3) with inflation at 2 percent and the current tax system in place. Now consider lowering the inflation rate to zero. There are two offsetting effects on revenue. First, lower inflation raises the real return to saving and hence lowers the price of retirement consumption to p_1. This results in a loss of revenue equal to $(p_2 - p_1)C_2$. Against this, the lower price of retirement consumption stimulates higher consumption $(C_1 - C_2)$ that is in turn revenue generating by an amount $(p_1 - p_0)(C_1 - C_2)$. The aggregate change in revenue is

$$(7) \qquad d\text{REV} = S_2\{[(p_1 - p_0)/p_2][(p_2 - p_1)/p_2](1 - \eta_{Sp}) - (p_2 - p_1)/p_2\}.$$

This expression can in principle be either positive or negative. But with $\eta_{SR} = 0$, and substituting in earlier parameter values, we get a net revenue *loss*, $d\text{REV} = 0.34$ percent of GDP. The corresponding net revenue losses at $\eta_{SR} = 0.2$ and $\eta_{SR} = 0.4$ are 0.29 and 0.23 percent of GDP, respectively. These are typically much larger than Feldstein's U.S. numbers, in part owing to the United Kingdom's higher gross saving ratio and in part the result of our lower assumed interest elasticity of saving.

We can map this change in revenue into a change in welfare by scaling it using a deadweight loss coefficient, λ. This measures the marginal deadweight loss of an across-the-board tax increase that raises one extra pound of revenue. Feldstein bases his estimate of λ on Ballard, Shoven, and Whalley's (BSW

---

39. This involves scaling by $-(1 + R)/RT$, where R is some benchmark saving rate. We take R to be the posttax saving rate at 2 percent inflation, 4.9 percent.

1985) computable general equilibrium model of the United States. BSW concluded, "The welfare loss from a 1 per cent increase in all distortionary taxes is in the range of 17 to 56 cents per dollar of extra revenue." There are many reasons why such a λ-range might be inaccurate for our exercise. For example, the BSW estimates refer to the United States and are based on a model that is calibrated on data drawn from 1973. More generally, λ can only really be pinned down by simulating the effects of a specific tax experiment in a general equilibrium model in which the existing configuration of distortionary taxes is fully set down (see Ballard and Fullerton 1992): λ is not a fixed, policy-invariant parameter. But in the absence of such estimates for the United Kingdom, we take as our benchmark two values of λ (λ = 0.4, 1.5) as in Feldstein. This broadly covers the range of estimates found in other recent studies of specific tax simulations (inter alia, Stuart 1984; Hansson and Stuart 1985; Fullerton and Henderson 1989).

We can go a little further toward justifying these values. Abel (1997) uses Sidrauski's (1967) general equilibrium model to compute the welfare effects of eliminating inflation in the United States. He extends the model to include both housing and nonhousing capital, includes a government budget constraint, and endogenizes labor supply. We take Abel's model and recalibrate it for U.K. data. It is then possible to arrive at an estimate of the deadweight loss parameter by simulating the effects of a tax change on utility, subject to the government budget constraint being satisfied. We conduct two experiments. In the first experiment, all three tax rates (on labor income, housing capital, and nonhousing capital) are raised by 10 percent. There is a rise in overall tax revenue and a fall in consumption. Using the utility function, we then calculate the change in consumption necessary to maintain the new level of utility, with money and labor income (the other two arguments in the utility function) held at their base values. This yields an estimate of around £0.40 of welfare loss for every pound in revenue gained—a λ of around 0.4. As a second experiment, we raise all three taxes by 1 percentage point. The resulting estimate of the deadweight loss parameter is 0.37. Although the general equilibrium model we use is small and the calibrated results depend on a number of key parameters, there appears to be some support for a λ estimate of around 0.4. This is taken as our central estimate below.

The total welfare gain from the reduced distortion to consumption timing resulting from a 2 percentage point reduction in inflation is then

(8) $G_2 = G_1 + \lambda\, d\text{REV}.$

As table 4.1 illustrates, assuming λ = 0.4 the net welfare gain from price stability operating through saving distortions is bounded between 0.21 and 0.37 percent of GDP. This is around a quarter the size of Feldstein's U.S. estimates. Much of the difference is due to offsetting revenue effects. This is shown up clearly when we raise the deadweight loss coefficient to λ = 1.5. All net welfare gains are then sacrificed.

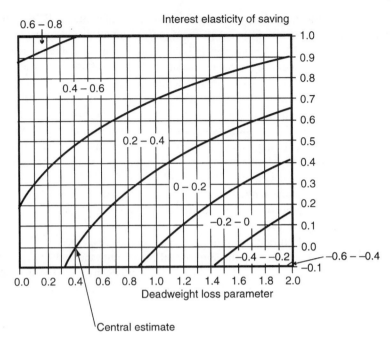

Fig. 4.4   **Net welfare benefits from consumption (percent of GDP)**

4.3.3   Some Sensitivity Analysis

Figure 4.4 illustrates more generally the sensitivity of the welfare calculations to different assumptions about the saving elasticity and deadweight loss parameter. For any given pair of parameter values, there is a point on the contour map that shows the size of the net welfare gain from a 2 percentage point reduction in inflation. It is evident that relatively small adjustments to the central assumptions—in particular regarding the deadweight loss parameter—can markedly alter the estimated net welfare gain. But the net welfare benefit in the central case is still nontrivial, at around 0.2 percent of GDP, even when the saving elasticity is assumed to be low.

There are further extensions and risks we might consider. First, Feldstein (1997b) points out that his calculations exclude current nonsavers. This is a potentially important omission if, first, nonsavers are a significant proportion of the population and, second, they are responsive to changes in real interest rates. Were both conditions to be satisfied, the estimated welfare costs above could be a significant understatement, as they would miss the effect of higher real interest rates in inducing previous nonsavers to save.

Using data from the 1991/92 Financial Research Survey of 6,600 households in the United Kingdom, Banks, Dilnot, and Low (1994) found that over half of the households in the survey held gross financial assets of less than £455 (net assets of less than £180) while around 10 percent had no gross savings

whatsoever. These results suggest that as in the United Savers, nonsavers are nontrivial in number. How responsive these agents might be to changes in real interest rates is less clear. That depends on whether nonsaving is a voluntary decision (e.g., among young "life cycle" savers) or an involuntary one (e.g., among credit-constrained "Keynesian" consumers). The former set are likely to be interest sensitive; the latter set much less so. In fact, the saving elasticity we derived from the aggregate consumption functions already implicitly embodies the average effect of real interest rates on both savers and nonsavers. And since our central case has $\eta_{SR} = 0$, this nonsaver effect is in any case likely to be quantitatively small.

Second, the above calculations take no account of the depressing effect of increased saving on the marginal product of capital. This would tend to reduce estimated welfare gains; but the effect is small. For example, assuming Cobb-Douglas technology, the implied fall in the marginal product of capital is only 0.06 percentage points when $\eta_{SR} = 0.2$ and 0.1 percentage points when $\eta_{SR} = 0.4$. Of course, when $\eta_{SR} = 0$, our central case, the marginal product of capital is unchanged. These effects in turn translate into small welfare changes: for example, a fall of 0.0027GDP when $\eta_{SR} = 0.2$. Moreover, these losses are almost exactly counterbalanced by the rise in the marginal product of labor resulting from the rise in the capital stock. For example, this leads to an offsetting welfare gain of 0.0025GDP when $\eta_{SR} = 0.2$. So the net welfare effect of these production mix adjustments seems likely to be negligible.

Third, more substantively, the stylized life cycle model makes no allowance for social security income received during retirement. Recognizing this exogenous source of second-period income lowers the implied interest elasticity of saving by an amount $(C - B)/C$ (see Feldstein 1997a), where C is retirement consumption and B social security benefits. Taking $B/C = 0.25$, as in Feldstein, lowers the direct welfare gain by around 30 percent: for example, with $\eta_{SR} = 0$ direct welfare gains fall from 0.35 to 0.25 percent of GDP.

Fourth, our central case assumes that all net company bank loans are effectively financed from personal sector deposits. Assuming instead that company bank loans are financed from elsewhere—that is, stripping out the banking system from our calculations—lowers the welfare gain from around 0.21 to 0.19 percent with $\eta_{SR} = 0$.

Finally, the analysis so far has assumed that all marginal saving flows into taxable assets. In practice, a relatively high proportion of U.K. personal sector saving is held in tax-exempt forms. We estimate that around 38 percent of personal sector equities are tax exempt (including pensions funds, pension business of life assurers, and personal equity plans—PEPs).[40] Direct holdings of equity that are taxed account for 37 percent. The remainder are equities held

---

40. The tax treatment of PEPs and pensions is not the same: in the former case, final receipts are tax deductible, whereas in the latter, initial contributions are tax deductible. We ignore that complication here.

indirectly via non-tax-exempt unit trusts and the nonpension business of life assurers (25 percent). Direct shareholdings are assumed to be taxed at the headline rate of 28.7 percent, and the remaining 25 percent of taxable holdings are taxed at 20 percent. Tax-exempt equity holdings are obviously taxed at a zero rate. So assuming that the marginal tax rate on equity holdings is the same as its average, this would give an adjusted average marginal tax rate of dividend income of 15.7 percent (0.38*0 − 0.37*28.7 + 0.25*0.20).

Doing the same thing for deposits, we need to make an adjustment for tax-exempt special savings accounts (TESSAs). These made up 6 percent of total personal sector bank deposits in 1995. So the marginal tax rate on deposits, inclusive of tax-exempt funds, would fall to 22 percent. Finally, for interest income on corporate bonds, we estimate that around 26 percent of personal sector holdings of corporate bonds are held in tax-exempt vehicles (pension funds, corporate bond PEPs, etc.). A further 68 percent are held by taxed institutions, and 6 percent are held directly. Direct bondholdings are taxed at the 31.1 percent headline rate, and non-tax-exempt unit trusts and the nonpension business of life assurers are assumed to be taxed at the basic rate of income tax.[41] This gives an adjusted average marginal tax rate on bond interest of 19.0 percent (0.26*0 + 0.06*0.311 + 0.68*0.25).

The headline marginal tax rate on capital gains (on equity and bonds) is that used earlier when calculating the discount rate, 14.1 percent. But again, these capital gains will be earned on securities held in a range of saving outlets, and we assume the same distribution of holdings across these outlets as for dividends and bonds. Direct holdings are taxed at 14 percent, indirect holdings via non-tax-exempt unit trusts and the nonpension business of life assurers at the basic rate (25 percent in 1994/95), and tax-exempt holdings are tax free. This gives an adjusted marginal effective capital gains tax rate of 11.6 percent on equities and 17.9 percent on bonds.

The effects of the tax-exempt saving adjustments are significant. For example, the effective marginal individual tax rate after weighting dividends, bond interest, deposit income, and capital gains was 23.0 percent before adjustment for tax-exempt saving. This falls to 14.8 percent after adjusting for tax-exempt saving. At $\eta_{SR} = 0.2$ and $\lambda = 0.4$, the effect of tax-exempt saving is to reduce the net welfare gains by 0.07 percent of GDP to 0.14 percent; at $\eta_{SR} = 0.2$ and $\eta_{SR} = 0.4$, the reductions are 0.08 percent (to 0.21 percent) and 0.13 percent (to 0.27 percent) of GDP, respectively. So the choice of destination for marginal saving is clearly crucial to the welfare calculus. Indeed, if all saving flowed into tax-exempt vehicles, the welfare gain arising from the effects of lower inflation on saving behavior would be zero.

---

41. Policyholder and shareholder funds actually have different tax treatments in the United Kingdom: bond interest and capital gains on the former are taxed at the basic rate of income tax (and at a lower rate of 20 percent from April 1996), whereas the latter are taxed at the higher corporation tax rate of 33 percent. In the absence of disaggregated data, our calculation assumes that all bondholdings are taxed as policyholder funds.

But this would almost certainly overestimate the effects of tax-exempt savings vehicles. For example, there are restrictions on the quantity of marginal saving that is allowed to flow into tax-exempt assets. And there are ceilings on the amount that can be invested in a TESSA and restrictions on the additional voluntary contributions (AVCs) that can flow into personal pensions. Further, ACT credits to pension funds were abolished with immediate effect in the July 1997 budget. These institutional features help to justify the main case, under which saving flows into taxable assets.

4.4   Inflation and Residential Investment

4.4.1   Distortions to Housing Investment

House prices in the United Kingdom have been around 25 percent more volatile than the general level of prices since 1970. And U.K. house price inflation has outstripped general price inflation by 2 percent per year on average over this period. Without question, the tax environment has played a role in this. The availability of mortgage interest relief—which in the United Kingdom is normally implemented through "mortgage interest relief at source" (MIRAS)—has meant that the tax system has consistently favored housing over alternative real and financial assets. More recently, there has been a progressive scaling back of the tax benefits available for owner-occupiers. The nominal ceiling on which relief is available has been raised only once since it was first introduced in 1974, while the effective rate of tax relief has also come down progressively over this period to its current rate of 15 percent (table 4.6). Indeed, one irony is that much of the reduction in the effective impact of mortgage tax relief in the 1980s was achieved through the rise in house prices itself. This took the average value of a mortgage well above the £30,000 ceiling for mortgage relief.

While it is widely perceived that distortionary tax benefits have led to a switch of resources toward housing, investment in dwellings is actually lower as a percentage of GDP, and the capital stock lower, in the United Kingdom

Table 4.6   **Changes in Mortgage Interest Relief**

Pre-1974/75	Mortgage interest relief given on the full amount of any loan
1974/75	Limit introduced of £25,000
1983/84	Limit raised to £30,000, and relief given at source (MIRAS)
1988/89	Tax relief on new loans for home improvement withdrawn; limit of one claim on each property (home sharers were previously able to claim double tax relief)
1991/92	Higher rate relief abolished; relief restricted to basic rate (25%)
1994/95	Rate of tax relief reduced to 20%
1995/96	Rate of tax relief reduced to 15%

Table 4.7   Value of Housing Stock, 1992

	Gross[a] (billion $)	Net[a] (billion $)	Net Stock per Capita ($)
United Kingdom	1,425	919	15,845
Australia	361	252	14,376
United States	8,086	5,190	20,314
Germany[b]	3,280	2,252	36,286

Sources: Organization for Economic Cooperation and Development, *Flows and Stocks of Fixed Capital* and *Main Economic Indicators.*
[a]Calculations based on market exchange rates: £1.512 per U.S. dollar, $1.6139 per deutsche mark, and $1.4513 per Australian dollar.
[b]Estimate for Western Germany.

than in many other countries (table 4.7). That perhaps suggests that tax-induced distortions to housing investment are not obviously more serious in the United Kingdom than elsewhere—a conclusion borne out by the welfare analysis that follows.

The tax incentives offered by the MIRAS system in the United Kingdom lower the effective user cost of housing to owner-occupiers. Moreover, because relief is given on nominal interest payments, the effective extent of this tax relief rises with inflation, further lowering the user cost. This is identical to the situation in the United States. Its effect is to induce an overinvestment in housing compared to a situation of zero inflation—where tax distortions would be minimized—or one where tax distortions were eliminated entirely. Figure 4.5 illustrates these three situations. A "0" subscript denotes the no-tax outcome, a "1" subscript the zero-inflation outcome, and a "2" subscript the current (2 percent inflation) outcome. As in the previous section, the deadweight distortion is equal to the area C + D. And the resulting gain from a reduction in inflation is (see Feldstein 1997b, eq. [19])

$$(9) \quad G_2 = \varepsilon_{HR}\{[(R_0 - R_1)/R_2][(R_1 - R_2)/R_2] + 0.5(R_1 - R_2)^2 R_2^{-2}\}R_2 H_2,$$

where the elasticity of housing with respect to the user cost, $\varepsilon_{HR} = -(R_2/H_2)$ (dH/dR).

To evaluate this expression we need to determine the three user costs, R_0, R_1, and R_2. In a zero-tax world, the implied rental cost of housing per pound of housing capital is reduced to $R_0 = \rho + m + \delta + t$, where ρ is the pretax rate of return (8.2 percent), m is the maintenance cost per pound of housing capital, t are transactions costs, and δ is the rate of housing depreciation.

For depreciation and maintenance costs, we assume 0.8 percent per annum.[42] We assume transactions costs are around 0.6 percent per annum (Rob-

42. This is based on the figure of 1.4 percent contained in the 1995 report of the Retail Prices Index Advisory Committee, representing the average annual expenditure on renovation—ex-

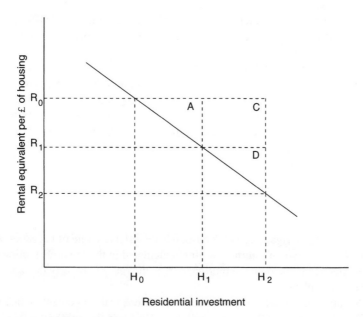

Fig. 4.5   Residential investment

inson and Skinner 1989; Woolwich Building Society 1996). This takes account of stamp duty, legal and estate agent fees, and removal costs, written off over the lifetime of a mortgage. So in sum we arrive at a figure of 1.4 percent, covering miscellaneous housing costs. This estimate is in line with those used by Henry and Pain (1994), Miles (1994), and Pain and Westaway (1996) for the United Kingdom. Using these values gives $R_0 = 0.096$ for the United Kingdom, a user cost of 9.6 pence per pound of housing investment. This is somewhat lower than calculated by Feldstein for the United States.

Turning to a world with taxes, Feldstein uses an itemizer/nonitemizer classification of owner-occupiers in the United States. The situation in the United Kingdom is somewhat different, but it is useful (as we demonstrate below) to make a similar distinction—between that part of the mortgage stock subject to MIRAS below the £30,000 ceiling and that proportion not.[43] The non-MIRAS mortgage stock will largely reflect the value of the outstanding mortgage stock that falls above the £30,000 MIRAS ceiling. But it will also include mortgages

---

pressed as a percentage of the value of the dwelling *excluding* land—needed to make good deterioration and obsolescence. But the value of land may be as much as half of the total price of a dwelling. This would tend to lower the percentage cost of maintenance and depreciation by around half, to around 0.7 percent. There is also some expenditure necessary to maintain the value of the land for each dwelling of, say, 0.1 percent per annum.

43. The U.S. and U.K. distinctions are different. In the United States, nonitemizers get a lump sum of interest relief, whereas in the United Kingdom the non-MIRAS component gets no relief of any kind. Feldstein is able to ignore the lump-sum benefit to nonitemizers because it has no effect at the margin.

on second properties, which are not eligible for tax relief. The MIRAS/non-MIRAS distinction we make is clearly artificial but is nonetheless useful analytically.[44]

The average price of a house in the United Kingdom is £55,000 according to Halifax Building Society figures. Even assuming a low mortgage-to-value ratio, this means that the majority of new mortgages in the United Kingdom will exceed the ceiling. But it takes some time for the mortgage stock to turn over. So mortgages that do not exhaust the tax relief fully are still nontrivial in number and an important factor in the calculations below. For loans subject to MIRAS, the user cost of housing is

$$
(10) \quad \begin{aligned} R_{\text{MIRAS}} &= \mu(1 - \theta)i_m + (1 - \mu)(r_n + \pi) + (1 - \varphi)\tau_p \\ &\quad + m + \delta + t - \pi, \end{aligned}
$$

where μ is the mortgage-to-value ratio, θ is the effective rate of tax relief, r_n is the real posttax rate of return on saving (calculated in the previous section), i_m is the interest rate paid on the mortgage, τ_p is the rate of property tax, and π is house price inflation.

The rate of tax relief (θ) used in the calculations was 16 percent, which was the marginal rate of MIRAS prevailing in 1995 for the value of mortgages under the £30,000 ceiling.[45] The interest rate paid on building society mortgages (i_m) averaged 7.5 percent in 1995, when the (bias-adjusted) inflation rate was 1.6 percent. Thus the mortgage rates that would apply under zero and 2 percent inflation would be 5.9 and 7.9 percent, respectively, on the assumption that the Fisher effect holds exactly. On property taxes (τ_p), the ratio of council tax payments to the value of the housing stock was around 0.8 percent per annum in 1995. There is no tax relief on these payments, so $\varphi = 0$.

Finally, on the expected house price inflation term (π), Feldstein assumes that house prices grow in line with the general price level. We do the same for consistency. It could be that a premium should be added to the inflation term, to reflect the fact that U.K. house prices have tended historically to grow faster than retail prices. But adding a constant to the user cost would have little impact on our calculations at the margin.

In order to calculate the implicit rental rate, we need an estimate of the mortgage-to-value ratio. For new business, this is around 70 percent. But

44. There are various alternative ways of capturing the MIRAS limit. E.g., presentationally it might appear preferable to make a distinction between those households who claim MIRAS and those who do not. E.g., Hills (1991) calculates that 90 percent of the mortgage stock and some 22 percent of all mortgages were above the £30,000 ceiling at the end of 1988. These figures will of course have increased since 1988, since when the MIRAS ceiling has been fixed in nominal terms. It is possible to use these as weights to calculate an effective rate of tax relief for all those who claim MIRAS, but the effective rate of tax relief would then vary systematically with the mortgage stock in response to any change in the rental price.

45. I.e., one-fourth of the tax rate in financial year 1994/95 (20 percent) and three-fourths of the rate in 1995/96 (15 percent).

the average mortgage-to-value ratio for the *outstanding* mortgage stock will clearly be lower as, for example, loans are repaid through time. Aggregate mortgage and housing stock data suggest that the ratio is 35 percent. For loans qualifying for MIRAS, the ratio is likely to be higher than this average. We make a somewhat arbitrary assumption that the ratio is 60 percent. And using equation (10), this then suggests that a combination of 2 percent inflation and the current tax regime would reduce the rental cost of housing from around 9.6 pence to around 6.9 pence ($R_2 = 0.069$) per pound of housing capital.

Next we consider the effect of inflation on the user cost. From equation (10) we can see that the change in rental cost for a given change in inflation is

(11) $dR_{MIRAS}/d\pi = \mu(1 - \theta)(di_m/d\pi) + (1 - \mu)[d(r_n + \pi)/d\pi] - 1.$

Assuming $di_m/d\pi = 1$,[46] we calculate that $dR_{MIRAS}/d\pi = -0.15$. A 1 percentage point rise in inflation reduces the implicit rental rate on housing by 0.15 pence per pound of housing capital. This occurs through two channels: a direct channel, whereby higher inflation increases the real value of MIRAS, and an indirect channel, as the fall in the real savings rate reduces the opportunity cost of the owner-occupier's equity stake in the house. Hence, the rental rate of 6.9 pence per pound of housing capital at 2 percent inflation rises to 7.2 pence ($R_1 = 0.072$) at zero inflation.

The implicit rental rate on the non-MIRAS part of the owner-occupied mortgage stock is given by

(12)
$$R_{NON-MIRAS} = \mu_{NON-MIRAS}i_m + (1 - \mu_{NON-MIRAS})(r_n + \pi)$$
$$+ \tau_p + m + \delta - \pi.$$

The only differences are that we drop the tax relief terms and assume a different mortgage-to-value ratio. Despite the disappearance of the direct tax wedge, inflation still affects the user cost because of its impact on the opportunity cost of housing equity. We would expect the mortgage-to-value ratio to be lower for non-MIRAS mortgages and set it to be 35 percent. Using this estimate in equation (8), we calculate the rental price to be 7.5 pence ($R_{NON-MIRAS_2} = 0.075$) at 2 percent inflation and 7.6 pence ($R_{NON-MIRAS_1} = 0.076$) at zero inflation. Not surprisingly, both are higher than the MIRAS user costs.

Finally, we consider the private rented sector.[47] A significant proportion of the value of the private rented sector housing stock is likely to be owned outright and rented out. But there are also some landlords who let their properties

---

46. It is unclear whether we would expect the pretax Fisher effect to hold exactly.

47. We exclude any effects from the public or housing association sectors and concentrate on the private rented sector. Together, public sector housing (19 percent) and housing associations (4 percent) account for 23 percent of the housing stock by tenure. Given an owner-occupied rate of 67 percent, the residual of 10 percent reflects the proportion of households in the private rented sector. We assume that the value of the housing stock is divided in the same proportion as tenure rates. This is likely to underestimate the value of the owner-occupied sector.

but who have mortgages outstanding. Further, there is tax relief available on these loans at the rate of income tax; and there is no ceiling on this relief. Hence, inflation and the tax system again introduce wedges into the rental user cost. The user cost for the rental sector, equation (13), is similar to the MIRAS user cost, equation (10):

$$
\begin{aligned}
R_{\text{RENTAL}} = \ &\mu_{\text{RENTAL}}(1 - \theta_{\text{RENTAL}})i_m + (1 - \mu_{\text{RENTAL}})(r_n + \pi) \\
&+ (1 - \varphi)\tau_p + m + \delta + \tau - \pi.
\end{aligned}
$$

(13)

There is likely to be a different mortgage-to-value ratio (μ_{RENTAL}) for the rental sector than for MIRAS owner-occupiers. We can deduce this by residual. This gives us a 25 percent mortgage-to-value ratio for the rental sector, which, as we would expect, is low. The second difference from the MIRAS calculation is that the rate of tax relief (θ_{RENTAL}) is levied at the individuals' rate of income tax. We calculate this to be 32 percent. This reflects the average effective rate of relief claimed by taxpayers in the three income tax bands (20, 25, and 40 percent).[48] Not surprisingly, this is higher than the basic rate because of the preponderance of landlords in the higher rate tax bracket. So despite the smallness of the rental sector in stock terms and its low mortgage-to-value ratio, the sector is still important because of the size of the tax wedge. From equation (13), the implied user cost is 7.1 pence with inflation at zero and 6.7 pence with inflation at 2 percent. Not surprisingly, these figures differ little from those obtained for MIRAS mortgages.

We next identify the outstanding stock of loans for each sector and the corresponding value of their housing stocks. Inland Revenue figures show that the value of MIRAS tax deductions in 1995 was £2.9 billion. Given a 16 percent average rate of tax relief, this implies total mortgage interest payments of around £18 billion. Using the average building society mortgage rate of 7.5 percent in 1995 implies that the value of the mortgage stock on which these MIRAS deductions were made was around £239 billion. If the mortgage-to-value ratio is around 60 percent, as we assumed earlier, this makes the value of the housing stock on which MIRAS deductions are claimed worth around £398 billion. For the rental sector, the current market value of their housing stock was around £113 billion in 1995. With a 25 percent mortgage-to-value ratio, this implies an outstanding stock of mortgages of around £28 billion held by the rental sector. We also know that the total stock of lending secured on dwellings in 1995 was some £390 billion. So we can determine the non-MIRAS mortgage stock by residual. This was around £124 billion (£390 − £239 − £28 billion) in 1995. The value of the non-MIRAS housing stock also drops out by residual at £356 billion (£753 − £398 billion).[49]

---

48. Inland Revenue figures suggest that 8 percent of individuals' rental income is taxed at 20 percent, 44 percent at 25 percent, and 48 percent at 40 percent.
49. Hence, the aggregate mortgage-to-value ratio is 35 percent (123/345∗100), as above.

We can now evaluate equation (9). See figure 4.5. With no taxes, the rental price is R_0 and the housing stock is H_0. With existing tax rules and zero inflation the rental price drops to R_1 and the housing stock increases to H_1. Finally, with inflation at 2 percent the rental cost drops further to R_2 and the housing stock increases to H_2. The additional deadweight loss of 2 percent inflation is the area C + D. By substituting values for the user cost into equation (9) and adding subscripts to distinguish MIRAS, non-MIRAS, and rental variables, we have

$$(14) \qquad G_{\text{MIRAS}} = 0.0154\varepsilon_{HR}R_{\text{MIRAS}_2}H_{\text{MIRAS}_2},$$

$$(15) \qquad G_{\text{NON-MIRAS}} = 0.0059\varepsilon_{HR}R_{\text{NON-MIRAS}_2}H_{\text{NON-MIRAS}_2},$$

$$(16) \qquad G_{\text{RENTAL}} = 0.0205\varepsilon_{HR}R_{\text{RENTAL}_2}H_{\text{RENTAL}_2}.$$

Adding these terms together gives us our estimate of the aggregate welfare gain G_3.

To evaluate equations (14), (15), and (16) we now only need an estimate of the compensated elasticity of housing demand with respect to the user cost. Feldstein (1997b) assumes $\varepsilon_{HR} = 0.8$. We take an estimate of the uncompensated elasticity of 0.53 from King (1980), a unit income elasticity, and a budget share of housing of 13.5 percent.[50] This gives an estimated compensated elasticity of around 0.4.

But the assumption that this elasticity holds for all three categories of housing seems implausible. In practice, changes in the user cost are more likely to affect the fraction of housing investment that lies above the £30,000 MIRAS ceiling. To account for this, we assume that the elasticity of MIRAS housing investment is closer to zero—say, around 0.1—while the elasticity of non-MIRAS investment is correspondingly higher at around 1.0.[51] This leaves the average aggregate elasticity unchanged at 0.4. Substituting these values into equations (14), (15), and (16) and summing gives an estimated total welfare gain of around 0.038 percent of GDP. This is around a quarter the size of Feldstein's U.S. estimate. This difference reflects the somewhat smaller mortgage interest relief distortions under the current U.K. tax system.

4.4.2   Indirect Revenue Effects

The fall in the housing capital stock associated with a move to price stability totals around £12 billion. There are four main channels through which this change in housing demand affects government revenues. First, there is a flow effect as the reduction in inflation lowers the value of the tax relief subsidy to MIRAS holders and to those claiming relief outside of MIRAS (the rental sector). This translates into increased revenues of £0.96 billion. Second, there are

50. Which is the average share of housing costs in the RPI in the 1990s.
51. The elasticity of the private rental sector is still set equal to 0.4.

direct stock effects on tax revenue. The reduction in the stock of mortgages reduces mortgage payments, thus reducing the value of tax relief and increasing net tax revenues. This is worth £0.03 billion. It is small because we have assumed a low elasticity for the MIRAS mortgage stock. Third, there will also be a loss of revenue from property taxes, estimated at £0.09 billion. Finally, the transfer of capital to the business sector affects tax revenue. The extra business investment yields a return—which is subject to tax—and this is worth around £0.36 billion.[52] The overall change in revenue is

(17) $d\text{REV}_2 = £0.96 + £0.03 + £0.36 - £0.09 = £1.25$ billion.

The overall gain from lower inflation on housing investment is the sum of these effects:

(18) $$G_4 = G_3 + \lambda\, d\text{REV}_2.$$

With these adjustments and $\lambda = 0.4$, the overall gain is around 0.11 percent of GDP. This estimate is less than half Feldstein's U.S. estimate (table 4.2). That is not too surprising given the gradual erosion in the real value of MIRAS over the past 20 years in the United Kingdom. For example, the cost of mortgage relief was reduced from a peak of over £6 billion per annum at the end of the 1980s to under £3 billion in 1995.

4.4.3   Sensitivity Analysis

Figure 4.6 offers some sensitivity analysis on the results, plotting net welfare gains against ε_{HR} and λ. Here the risks to net benefits are more clearly on the upside, searching across the two parameters. The plane is everywhere positive and is increasing in both parameters. The gains themselves are never that large over reasonable parameter ranges: they are very unlikely to exceed 0.3 to 0.4 percent of GDP. But they are nonetheless tangible. Indeed, given the risks that attach to achieving such gains via monetary policy, it might plausibly be argued that a strong case can be made for fiscal reform. Unlike monetary policy, the abolition of MIRAS could be targeted explicitly at extracting the welfare gains in figure 4.6; it would have few downside (potentially negative welfare) risks, unlike monetary policy, and it could be achieved without incurring transient output costs, again, unlike monetary policy.

Counterbalancing these upside risks, however, is the fact that our compara-

---

52. However, this calculation only includes the revenue gained from the existence of the wedge between the rate of return earned by companies and the posttax real rate of interest earned by households. Following Dolado, González-Páramo, and Viñals (chap. 3 in this volume), there is also a value-added tax (VAT) effect. With a capital share of value added assumed fixed at 37 percent in 1995 and a pretax return of 8.2 percent, value added will be around 22 percent of the capital stock per year. Given our estimated £10.4 billion rise in the business capital stock, this generates an additional £2.3 billion of value added, which in turn generates £0.4 billion (0.06 percent of GDP) of VAT receipts with VAT at 17.5 percent. To maintain consistency with other countries' calculations this additional revenue effect has not been added to the results in the main table.

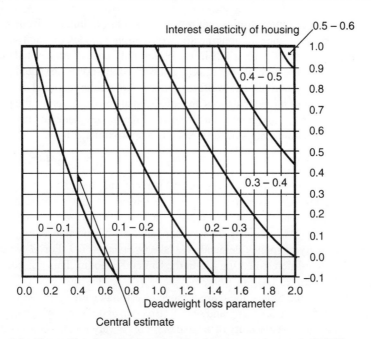

Fig. 4.6   Net welfare benefits from housing investment (percent of GDP)

tive static analysis implicitly assumes that the MIRAS/non-MIRAS split of mortgages would remain constant if 2 percent inflation were to persist indefinitely. That is clearly implausible if the MIRAS ceiling were to remain unchanged in nominal terms, as historically it largely has. Inflation then increases over time the stock of mortgages ineligible for MIRAS; it denudes the real value of MIRAS relief. This dynamic effect is not taken into account in the above calculus and would act to reduce net welfare benefits over time.[53]

4.5   Inflation and the Demand for Money

4.5.1   "Shoe Leather" Costs

Following Bailey (1956), the most widely studied deadweight losses of a fully anticipated inflation derive from distortions to money demand, so-called shoe leather costs. In essence, these costs capture the transactions time agents expend in replenishing money balances, the stock of which is held at a suboptimally low level at any positive nominal interest rate.[54]

---

53. We can gauge its size—and put a lower bound on welfare gains—by assuming all of the mortgage stock is effectively ineligible for MIRAS. The welfare gain would then fall to 0.04 percent of GDP.
54. On the assumption that the marginal cost of money creation is close to zero.

The gain in consumer surplus that results from a fall in inflation from π_2 to π_1 is given by the trapezoid underneath a conventional money demand schedule. This is associated with a fall in the opportunity cost of money balances (proxied here by the nominal net return on a debt-equity portfolio) equal to $(r_n + \pi_2) - (r_n + \pi_1)$. Friedman's welfare optimum, where the marginal cost and marginal benefit of money balances are equalized at zero, is given by the point $r_n + \pi_0 = 0$. On the assumption of linearity of the money demand curve, the trapezoid of lost consumer surplus (G_5) can be approximated by

(19) $G_5 = 0.5[(r_n + \pi_2) - (r_n + \pi_1)](M_2 - M_1) + (r_n + \pi_1)(M_2 - M_1).$

From earlier we have $r_n = 4.9$ percent at 2 percent inflation and $r_n = 5.1$ percent at zero inflation, given $dr_n/d\pi = -0.12$. Observing that, again under the linearity assumption, $M_2 - M_1 = -\varepsilon_M[(r_n + \pi_2) - (r_n + \pi_1)][M/(r_n + \pi)]$, then $G_5 = 0.00109\, \varepsilon_M[\overline{M/(r_n + \pi)}]$, where a bar denotes a mean value and ε_M is the interest elasticity of money demand. We take $\overline{(r_n + \pi)} = 6.9$. For M we take the stock of non-interest-bearing M1 in the United Kingdom. This was equivalent to 4.9 percent of GDP in 1995.[55]

As in the United States, there are a range of estimates for ε_M in the United Kingdom. But the Bank of England's work (Breedon and Fisher 1993) suggests a steady state interest elasticity of around 0.3. This is very much a conservative estimate. Others have arrived at higher elasticities looking at longer and more recent runs of data.[56] But on these conservative assumptions, $G_5 = 0.023$ percent of GDP. This is similar to Feldstein's estimate of 0.016 percent of GDP. Moving to the Friedman optimum—of deflation equal to the real rate of interest—yields a welfare gain of $G_5 = 0.051$ percent of GDP. The gains are larger here than in Feldstein (0.02 percent of GDP) but remain small quantitatively. And although small, these estimates are of the same order of magnitude as those found in previous partial equilibrium studies, when measured over the same interest rate interval. For example, Fischer (1981) and McCallum (1989) both arrive at a figure of around 0.3 percent of GDP when transitioning from 10 percent to zero inflation. Linearly interpolating, this would deliver a gain of around 0.06 percent of GDP when moving from 2 percent to zero inflation, which is in the same ballpark as the estimates here.[57]

---

55. Most authors use an M1 measure of the money stock. This will lead to an *over*statement of money demand distortions because much of the M1 stock is interest bearing. Feldstein (1995) takes the stock of currency and reserves, which will be an *under*statement because it omits non-interest-bearing bank deposits.

56. Chadha, Haldane, and Janssen (1998) look at narrow money demand relationships between 1870 and 1994 and find an interest elasticity of around 0.8. Janssen (1996) looks at the behavior of M0 during the 1990s and finds that its interest elasticity has risen markedly compared with the 1980s.

57. Neither of these studies takes account of tax effects that mean that the interest rate opportunity cost falls less than proportionately with inflation. They also use a broader (M1) measure of the money stock. This largely accounts for the differences. See also Feldstein (1979) and, more recently, Dotsey and Ireland (1996).

4.5.2   Indirect Revenue Effects

Feldstein (1997b) considers three government revenue implications of the higher real money balances held by agents at lower rates of inflation: (a) the reduction in direct seigniorage revenues as the (inflation) tax rate falls (the Phelps 1972 effect), (b) the revenue loss as assets are switched from (taxed) capital assets to (nontaxed) money balances (a kind of Mundell-Tobin effect), and (c) the reduction in debt service costs as money balances substitute for interest-bearing debt.

On (a), Feldstein shows that the marginal response of seigniorage to a change in inflation is

$$(20) \quad d\text{SEIG}/d\pi = M_2\{1 - \varepsilon_M[d(r_n + \pi_2)/d\pi_2]\pi_2/(r_n + \pi_2)\}.$$

The term $\varepsilon_M[d(r_n + \pi_2)/d\pi_2]$ captures the direct price effect of the fall in the tax rate (inflation); and the term $\pi_2/(r_n + \pi_2)$, the offsetting effect on revenues of the rise in the tax base as money balances increase. Using the assumptions from earlier gives a net revenue loss equal to 0.09 percent of GDP.

On (b), the fall in business capital is equal to the rise in money balances $(M_2 - M_1)$. The gross real rate of return to capital in the United Kingdom between 1970 and 1995 averaged 8.2 percent with a net return of 4.9 percent, giving a tax wedge of 3.3 percent points. The revenue loss is 0.012 percent of GDP.

Finally on (c), we calculate the reduction in government debt service costs as $r_{ng}*(M_2 - M_1)$, where r_{ng} is the real return on government debt, net of the tax the government receives on those interest payments. Proxying gross *nominal* interest payments by the ratio of debt interest payments to national debt in 1995 (6.8 percent), a 1995 inflation rate of 1.6 percent (netting off the measurement bias), and assuming a marginal tax rate of 31.1 percent gives $r_{ng} = (1 - 0.31)*(0.068) - 0.016 = 0.031$. The reduction in debt servicing is 0.012 percent of GDP.

Bringing these estimates together, we have a shoe leather gain of 0.023 percent of GDP and revenue losses totaling 0.11λ percent of GDP. So at $\lambda = 0.4$ we have a net welfare loss of around 0.022 percent of GDP. These net welfare losses are smaller than in Feldstein but are still negative. In all of our cases, the Phelps effect dominates the Bailey effect.

4.5.3   Risks to the Calculus

Figure 4.7 conducts some sensitivity analysis, plotting net shoe leather gains against ε_M and λ. From this it is clear that it is quite difficult to make a case for a positive net welfare contribution from money demand distortions. The net welfare gains are also everywhere small. This reflects the smallness of the aggregate currency stock compared with the housing stock.

But there may also be some upside risks—in particular to the assumed interest elasticity—that are not captured by figure 4.7. We have assumed throughout linearity of the money demand function. But Lucas (1994) has recently argued,

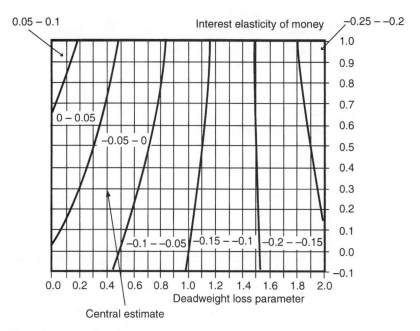

Fig. 4.7   Net welfare benefits from money demand (percent of GDP)

on theoretical and empirical grounds, that money demand functions are best viewed as a *log*-linear representation. Such an assumption can have a dramatic impact on welfare cost calculus. As we approach nominal interest rates of zero, money demand asymptotes on the zero axis, raising the size of the welfare triangle. Lucas (1994) suggests that deadweight losses could then amount to as much as 1 percent of GDP when moving to zero nominal interest rates; and Chadha et al. (1998) arrive at similar numbers for the United Kingdom also using a logarithmic specification.

Against this, the Lucas specification does imply that the largest welfare gains accrue—the interest elasticity is largest—near the Friedman optimum. That is not our experiment here. Moreover, neither the United Kingdom nor the United States has very much time-series evidence on money demand at near-zero interest rates to shed light on the plausibility of Lucas's thesis. Indeed, Mulligan and Sala-i-Martin (1996) argue, contrarily, that money demand is likely to be largely interest *in*elastic at low nominal interest rates. This follows from the fact that at low interest rates, the incentive to shift into interest-bearing assets is reduced for a large fraction of the population. They present some cross-sectional evidence to support their thesis. And Chadha et al. (1998) ultimately reject a log specification over a conventional semilog form as a description of steady state (if not dynamic) money demand behavior in the United Kingdom.

Another uncertainty concerns the use of a partial rather than general equilibrium framework. The latter approach often appears to have yielded larger welfare benefits (Cooley and Hansen 1989; Dotsey and Ireland 1996). The source of these higher costs is the explicit recognition of labor/leisure choices. So, for example, if—as in Cooley and Hansen (1989)—lower inflation lowers the tax on consumption goods and leads agents to supply extra labor, income will rise. The money demand schedule will then shift outward. And welfare gains will be correspondingly greater than when income is held fixed, as under the partial equilibrium approach. Likewise, the conventional Mundell-Tobin effect of moving to price stability—a fall in capital accumulation as agents switch into money balances—need not arise in a general equilibrium setting. Because investment is simply deferred consumption and since inflation acts as a consumption tax, lower inflation may actually increase investment and the capital stock. That would, in turn, reduce some of the revenue losses described above.[58]

But even after allowing for these effects, Cooley and Hansen (1989) and Dotsey and Ireland (1996) still arrive at welfare costs that are similar to those here over the same inflation rate range. For example, a fall in inflation from 4 to 2 percent in Dotsey and Ireland (1996) still yields a welfare benefit of only around 0.045 percent of GDP.[59] Moreover, and perhaps most important, neither of the above papers recognizes distortionary taxes. Cooley and Hansen (1991) do explicitly introduce labor and capital taxes into their earlier equilibrium framework. They conclude that while adding in taxes doubles the gross welfare costs of inflation, these gains are more than counterbalanced by the need to raise distortionary taxes elsewhere to satisfy the government's budget constraint. So the upshot is a net welfare loss—as here and in Feldstein (1997b)—and for the same reasons. So the risks to the above analysis seem to be broadly counterbalancing; and they do not clearly imply that the net distortions to money demand are anything other than negligible and quite possibly negative.

4.6 Debt Service and the Government Budget Constraint

Lower inflation lowers tax receipts on the nominal interest payments made by the government when servicing its debt. Using the government's cash-flow identity and a steady state condition of a stable debt-GDP ratio, Feldstein (1997b) shows that the increase in taxes necessary to maintain a stable debt-GDP ratio in the light of this higher debt servicing cost is[60]

---

58. Other effects might be introduced into a general equilibrium setup that would aggravate inflation's distortions. E.g., Dotsey and Ireland (1996) have a model where higher inflation leads to an employment redistribution from production toward financial intermediation, where the returns to the latter are smaller.

59. Using a currency specification—as in Feldstein—and switching off the endogenous growth channel. The benefits are, however, much greater as we approach the Friedman optimum.

60. Assuming no change in the inflation risk premium on government debt.

(21) $$dT = d\pi \, \theta_i H,$$

where T denotes taxes (as a percentage of GDP), θ_i is the effective tax rate on interest payments, and H denotes government debt (again as a percentage of GDP).

The calculus is complicated slightly in the United Kingdom because, first, some large-scale holders of U.K. government debt are tax exempt—in particular pension funds and charities—and, second, some domestic debt is also held by overseas residents, on most of which the U.K. government levies no tax.[61] At the end of 1995, pension funds held 21 percent of the stock of government debt and the overseas sector around 14.5 percent. Deducting these tax-exempt holdings from the stock of debt gives $H = 0.355$ (as a percentage of GDP in 1995, using Maastricht definitions). We take $\theta_i = 0.31$, the marginal personal tax rate on debt interest income used earlier, and $d\pi = 0.02$. So the welfare costs associated with higher net debt-servicing costs—and hence higher taxes—when moving to price stability are 0.221λ. Hence, at $\lambda = 0.4$ the welfare cost is 0.088 percent of GDP, and at $\lambda = 1.5$ it is 0.33 percent of GDP. Both of these welfare losses are slightly lower than in Feldstein (1997b), though not by much.

4.7 Conclusions

Adding together the net welfare gains arising from consumption, housing investment, money demand, and debt-servicing distortions gives an aggregate welfare benefit of 0.21 percent of GDP, using central estimates of the key parameters (see table 4.1). This annual net welfare gain is translated into a present value using formula (1). Given an estimated discount rate of 5.3 percent and growth rate of 2 percent, the net present value of an annual welfare gain of 0.21 percent of GDP is equivalent to around 6.5 percent of GDP.

There are of course uncertainties on both sides of this central estimate, not least about the magnitude of the key parameters, and in particular the parameters measuring the welfare loss resulting from an extra pound of taxation and the saving elasticity. Figure 4.8 considers the sensitivity of the aggregate net welfare benefit to both of these parameters.

Any combination of the two parameters is associated with a point on the contour map indicating the size of the net welfare gain. High values of the deadweight loss parameters, such as 1.5, eliminate the aggregate benefits entirely. But a higher saving elasticity increases the estimated welfare benefits.

The welfare benefits of lowering inflation must be set against any potential disinflationary costs. In section 4.2 it was shown that the breakeven benefit is

---

61. A third complication comes in the tax treatment of index-linked debt. Coupons are taxed in nominal terms and so changes in inflation do have revenue implications, but this is not true generally of the capital gains component. We ignore this effect here.

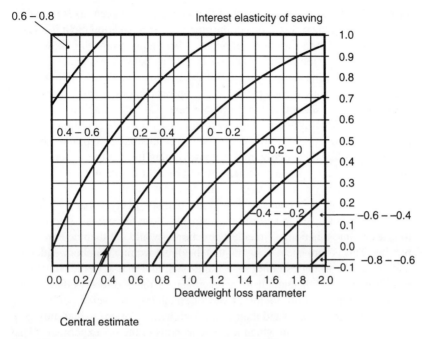

Fig. 4.8   Aggregate welfare benefits (percent of GDP)

0.18 percent of GDP. So on our central estimates of the key parameters, the benefits of reducing inflation exceed the costs.

A major uncertainty concerns the marginal tax rates used in the study. For example, when discussing saving, the crucial question is whether marginal funds are invested in proportion to their existing share of households' saving (average and marginal tax rates are equal), or whether instead they flow exclusively into either taxable or tax-exempt vehicles.

Notwithstanding this caveat, we would make the following observations on the basis of our welfare comparisons: First, it is clear that aggregate welfare gains in the United Kingdom are much smaller than those of Feldstein for the United States—perhaps around one-quarter the size. Idiosyncrasies in the two countries' tax systems largely account for these differences. Tax wedges tend to be smaller in the United Kingdom than the United States. And the sensitivity of tax rates to inflation is likewise less in the United Kingdom than in the United States—for example, because of indexation of capital gains. The gradual erosion of MIRAS and the indexation of capital gains, to take two examples, mean that some of the welfare benefits identified by Feldstein for the United States have already been realized in the United Kingdom.

This leads on to the second point: can we say whether the welfare benefits we have identified are best secured through monetary or fiscal policy? The

identified distortions are the result of the interaction between taxes and inflation, rather than the result of one or the other acting in isolation. So it is unclear a priori whether monetary or fiscal policy is best suited to reaping these benefits. A full discussion of that issue would take us beyond this paper and into the realms of optimal fiscal policy. But the Institute for Fiscal Studies in the United Kingdom has already put forward proposals that would all but eliminate inflation-induced distortions to corporate taxes, at little administrative cost (Institute for Fiscal Studies 1995). Likewise, the complete abolition of mortgage interest relief would not be a difficult administrative step, though there are clearly political economy implications. Upping the limit, or extending the range, of tax-exempt savings vehicles would be a third option.

Third, our analysis takes as given the fact that we are currently operating at a second best. It is conceivable—if not perhaps likely—that the existing configuration of taxes and subsidies is already close to optimal. Adjustments to taxes around this point—in either direction—would not then be Pareto improving. This is equivalent to saying that the direct welfare benefits we identify may in fact be triangles rather than trapezoids, and that λ would, in general equilibrium, be high enough to counterbalance these direct welfare gains. More generally, the only foolproof way of simulating the welfare effects of a specific change in taxes (and their interaction with inflation) is in a fully general equilibrium model in which λ is endogenous to the tax experiment. That is the task of another—and very different—paper.

Finally, the welfare costs we identify are only a subset of the total costs of inflation, and there are a variety of possible extensions to the existing analysis. A complete treatment of business investment is one. An initial attempt has been made in the appendix. A formal treatment of front-end loading, as it relates to household and corporate debt, is another. And capital flow effects may be considered, as in Desai and Hines (chap. 6 in this volume). A fourth is an analysis of inflation's effect on the financing and investment mix of firms. A fifth is an analysis of distortions to that part of household savings that is not financing U.K. companies—for example, holdings of government bonds. Hence, the calculations in the paper clearly understate the benefits of reducing inflation. A subset of the benefits of reducing inflation is being compared with all of the costs of achieving price stability. Other benefits of price stability, such as those associated with the—possibly much larger—welfare costs of unanticipated inflation, are not quantified. Because these costs are positive, they would increase the permissible breakeven range of discount rates and output costs. All in all, the costs of inflation quantified here go some distance toward justifying and explaining the aversion to inflation that is shared by the public, economists, and policymakers alike.

Appendix
Inflation and Business Investment

Distortions to Business Investment

In the main text we considered the effects of a reduction in inflation on household consumption and saving, on residential investment, on money demand, and on government financing. One area that remains is business investment. But because households do not consume—at least directly—the capital stock, it is more difficult to conduct welfare analysis on business investment. Capital services are not strictly speaking demanded by individual households. So the estimates below have a less direct mapping into welfare than those from previous sections. That said, it is plausible to think that the physical capital stock could enter into agents' utility functions *in*directly, for much the same reasons as might the money stock or the human capital stock. Physical capital, like human capital and money, is time saving and is thereby leisure and utility enhancing. That is one way to interpret the thought experiment below.

There are a variety of channels through which inflation, operating in tandem with the tax system, might affect investment and the capital stock. The most widely studied effect of inflation on investment is through the cost of capital (in a U.K. context see, inter alia, King 1974, 1977; King and Fullerton 1984; Devereux 1989). With no taxes, the return on a hypothetical investment project and the return on the savings used to finance this project will be equalized. There is no "tax wedge" between the returns to saving and investment. But once distortionary taxes are admitted, the returns to saving and investment will differ. There is a tax wedge. The effect of the wedge, for a given saving rate, is to increase the effective pretax rate of return that a project must earn to make it worthwhile to undertake: it raises the effective cost of capital. This tax wedge depends on both the corporate and personal tax systems and their interaction with inflation, as well as on the nature of the investment project and its method of finance. Higher (personal and corporate) taxes increase the tax wedge and hence the cost of capital. So too does higher inflation as it raises effective personal and corporate tax rates. Both taxes and inflation will hence lower the capital stock below its no-tax equilibrium.

The distorting effects of taxes and inflation, acting through business investment, can be analyzed using the residential investment framework described earlier. Let r_0 be the cost of capital in the absence of taxes (a zero-tax wedge), with corresponding capital stock K_0. With taxes and zero inflation, the cost of capital rises to r_1 (a wedge of $r_1 - r_0$) and the capital stock falls to K_1. With taxes and 2 percent inflation the corresponding cost of finance and capital stock are subscripted with a "2": the cost of capital is suboptimally high and the capital stock suboptimally low. The resulting distortion from inflation is the conventional trapezoid, approximated by

(A1) $G_6 = \varepsilon_K\{[(r_1 - r_0)/r_2][(r_2 - r_1)/r_2] + 0.5(r_2 - r_1)^2 r_2^{-2}\}r_2 K_2,$

where ε_K is the elasticity of the capital stock with respect to the cost of capital.

Calculating the cost of capital at different tax and inflation rates requires a detailed breakdown of the components of the existing capital stock and its sources of financing, as well as knowledge of the tax system itself (see, e.g., Cohen, Hassett, and Hubbard, chap. 5 in this volume). But our earlier calculations, based on the saving-investment nexus, contain most of the basic ingredients. For example, the Hall and Jorgenson (1967) tax-adjusted formula for the real cost of capital is

(A2) $r = (\rho + \delta - dq/q)(1 - \tau_c z)/(1 - \tau_c),$

where ρ is the cost of (debt and equity) financing, δ is the depreciation rate, q is the relative price of capital goods, τ_c is the rate of corporation tax, and z is the present value of depreciation allowances. We devise a proxy for this cost of capital at 2 percent inflation (r_2) by adding $\delta[(1 - \tau_c z)/(1 - \tau_c)]$ to the pretax real rate of return to capital among U.K. companies between 1970 and 1995. This proxy can be reconciled with equation (A2) as follows.

As is conventional (King and Fullerton 1984), we assume that providers of capital—savers—demand a fixed posttax return. We set this posttax return equal to its historic value at 2 percent inflation, 4.9 percent.[62] But the cost of this capital to firms is affected by taxation at both the personal and corporate levels. This is embodied in the tax wedge calculated earlier, which explicitly takes account of the historical debt-equity split of investment financing and the personal and corporate tax rates attaching to returns as they are passed down from firms to households. This tax wedge is equal to 3.3 percent. Adding this to the posttax return demanded by providers of capital gives us the cost of funds for firms (ρ); it tells us the pretax returns available for distribution to holders of debt and equity. Our measure of pretax returns already embodies the direct effect of depreciation allowances (z) on the cost of funds; these are captured directly in the corporation tax wedge. We assume throughout that $dq/q = 0$ and is invariant under inflation.

But the pretax real return to capital is insufficient by itself to capture fully the cost of capital for firms. This is because both the numerator (profits plus interest payments) and the denominator (the capital stock) are defined net of depreciation. So this measure of the pretax return makes no adjustment for the cost of depreciation. We take the average depreciation rate, $\delta = 5.5$ percent, from Bond, Denny, and Devereux (1993). We then need to make a further adjustment for the interaction between depreciation and z.[63] This gives $r_2 = 14.3$

---

62. The assumption here is that the supply of international capital is perfectly elastic at this rate, which is not unreasonable in an open economy setting. To prevent double counting of the capital stock effects from section 4.3, we are also effectively assuming $\eta_{SR} = 0$, i.e., that private saving is interest inelastic at the domestic level.

63. Investment in vehicles and plant and machinery made up around 75 percent of gross domestic fixed capital formation in 1995, with buildings making up the further 25 percent. Applying

percent. This constructed measure captures quite accurately the cost of capital in equation (A2). We arrive at a rate of return that takes full account of tax distortions at the corporate and personal level, of depreciation and depreciation allowances, and of the debt-equity financing split of firms.[64]

We can now simulate the effects of moving to zero inflation. This has the effect of narrowing the tax wedge between the returns to saving and investment because of the nonneutralities associated with both personal taxation (of bond interest) and corporate taxation (bond interest deductibility and the nominal value of depreciation allowances). Our earlier estimates provided ready-reckoners for these nonneutralities. To these we add a further adjustment to reflect the depreciation allowance nonneutrality embodied in the extra depreciation term. Their combined effect is to narrow the tax wedge—and hence lower the effective user cost of capital—by 0.18 percent points for every percentage point fall in inflation. This gives $r_1 = 13.9$ percent. Note also that with no taxes, the cost of capital equals the return on saving plus depreciation, $r_0 = 10.4$ percent—the minimum posttax return that savers are willing to accept to finance a project. Thus we have values for the three costs of capital necessary to evaluate equation (A1).

For the elasticity of the capital stock with respect to the cost of capital, we take $\varepsilon_K = 0.5$. This is in line with the estimates set out in Mayes and Young (1993) for the United Kingdom and is consistent with the international evidence in Cummins, Hassett, and Hubbard (1996). The net stock of capital held by firms at the end of 1995 (K_2) was around £664 billion. Plugging in these estimates, the fall in the cost of capital from r_2 to r_1 as we move to price stability raises the capital stock by around £17.5 billion. Evaluating equation (A1), this then gives a direct "welfare" gain of $G_6 = 0.05$ percent of GDP.

Indirect Revenue Effects

Again, there are revenue effects associated with this rise in the capital stock. In particular, extra tax receipts accrue on the additional investment income generated by the higher equilibrium capital stock. These have further positive effects on welfare as distortionary taxes elsewhere are lowered, though these effects are relatively small, equal to 0.03 percent of GDP with $\lambda = 0.4$. This gives a total net "welfare" gain from the removal of distortions to business investment of around 0.08 percent of GDP with $\varepsilon_K = 0.5$ and $\lambda = 0.4$.

---

these weights to capital allowance rates of 25 percent for vehicles and plant and machinery and 4 percent for buildings gives a weighted average capital allowance rate of 19.7 percent. Assuming a declining balance method of depreciation and discounting at the rate of return demanded by investors plus the inflation rate provides a measure of z.

64. One restriction that the analysis imposes is that the market value of a company's capital and its capital stock are equal, that Tobin's q is unity.

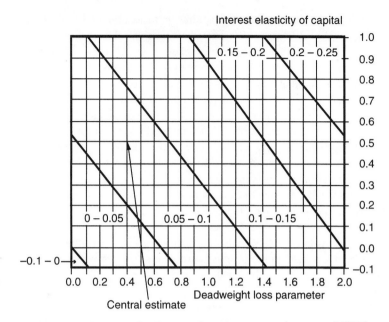

Fig. 4A.1   Net welfare benefits from business investment (percent of GDP)

Sensitivity Analysis

Figure 4A.1 plots net benefits arising from reduced distortions to business investment against ε_K and λ. As with residential investment, the net gains are almost everywhere positive, though they are generally smaller than with residential investment. But as well as the cost of capital there are other channels through which inflation might affect investment. Information asymmetries may mean that corporate cash flow has a direct impact on investment, over and above cost-of-capital effects (Fazzari, Hubbard, and Petersen 1988). Since corporate cash flow is affected by inflation through higher effective tax rates, inflation may have further direct effects on investment spending. Blundell et al. (1992) report evidence of just this in a study of U.K. manufacturing companies, as do Cummins et al. (1996) in an international context. Because of this, the above calculations probably underestimate the benefits of price stability arising from business investment distortions.

References

Abel, A. 1997. Comment on "The costs and benefits of going from low inflation to price stability," by M. Feldstein. In *Reducing inflation: Motivation and strategy,* ed. C. Romer and D. Romer, 156–66. Chicago: University of Chicago Press.

Akerlof, G. A., W. T. Dickens, and G. L. Perry. 1996. The macroeconomics of low inflation. *Brookings Papers on Economic Activity,* no. 1: 1–56.

Attanasio, O. P. 1994. Personal saving in the United States. In *International comparisons of household saving,* ed. J. M. Poterba. Chicago: University of Chicago Press.

Bailey, M. 1956. The welfare cost of inflationary finance. *Journal of Political Economy* 64:93–110.

Ball, L. 1994. What determines the sacrifice ratio? In *Monetary policy,* ed. N. G. Mankiw. Chicago: University of Chicago Press.

———. 1997. Disinflation and the NAIRU. In *Reducing inflation: Motivation and strategy,* ed. C. Romer and D. Romer, 167–85. Chicago: University of Chicago Press.

Ball, L., N. G. Mankiw, and D. Romer. 1988. New Keynesian economics and the output-inflation trade-off. *Brookings Papers on Economic Activity,* no. 1: 1–65.

Ballard, C. L., and D. Fullerton. 1992. Distortionary taxes and the provision of public goods. *Journal of Economic Perspectives* 6:117–31.

Ballard, C., J. Shoven, and J. Whalley. 1985. General equilibrium computations of the marginal welfare cost of taxes in the United States. *American Economic Review* 75:128–38.

Banks, J., and R. Blundell. 1994. Household saving behavior in the United States. In *International comparisons of household saving,* ed. J. M. Poterba. Chicago: University of Chicago Press.

Banks, J. W., A. Dilnot, and H. Low. 1994. The distribution of wealth in the U.K. Commentary no. 45. London: Institute for Fiscal Studies.

Barro, R. 1995. Inflation and economic growth. *Bank of England Quarterly Bulletin* 35 (May): 166–75.

Bayoumi, T. 1993. Financial deregulation and household saving. *Economic Journal* 103:1432–43.

Bianchi, M., and J. Smith. 1995. Inflation and productivity growth: An empirical investigation. London: Bank of England. Mimeograph.

Blinder, A. S. 1992. Why are prices sticky? Preliminary results from an interview survey. *American Economic Review* 81:89–96.

Blundell, R., S. Bond, M. Devereux, and F. Schianterelli. 1992. Investment and Tobin's *Q. Journal of Econometrics* 51:233–57.

Bond, S., K. Denny, and M. Devereux. 1993. Capital allowances and the impact of corporate tax on investment in the U.K. *Fiscal Studies* 14 (2): 1–14.

Bond, S., M. Devereux, and H. Freeman. 1990. Inflation non-neutralities in the U.K. corporation tax. *Fiscal Studies* 11, no. 4 (November): 21–28.

Boskin, M. 1978. Taxation, saving and the rate of interest. *Journal of Political Economy* 83 (3): 447–75.

———. 1996. *Toward a more accurate measure of the cost of living.* Final report to the Senate Finance Committee. 104th Cong., 2d sess.

Breedon, F. J., and P. G. Fisher. 1993. M0: Causes and consequences. Bank of England Working Paper no. 20. London: Bank of England.

Briault, C. B. 1995. The costs of inflation. *Bank of England Quarterly Bulletin* 35 (1): 33–45.

Cecchetti, S. G. 1994. Comment on "What determines the sacrifice ratio?" by L. Ball. In *Monetary policy,* ed. N. G. Mankiw. Chicago: University of Chicago Press.

Chadha, J., A. G. Haldane, and N. Janssen. 1998. Shoe-leather costs reconsidered. *Economic Journal* 108:363–82.

Cooley, T. F., and G. D. Hansen. 1989. The inflation tax in a real business cycle model. *American Economic Review* 79:733–48.

———. 1991. The welfare costs of moderate inflations. *Journal of Money, Credit and Banking* 23 (August): 483–503.

Crawford, A. 1994. Measurement biases in the Canadian CPI: A technical note. Bank of Canada Technical Report no. 64. Ottawa: Bank of Canada.

Cummins, J. G., K. A. Hassett, and R. G. Hubbard. 1996. Tax reforms and investment: A cross-country comparison. *Journal of Public Economics* 62:237–73.

Cunningham, A. W. F. 1996. Measurement bias in price indices: An application to the U.K.'s RPI. Bank of England Working Paper no. 47. London: Bank of England.

Devereux, M. 1987. Taxation and the cost of capital: The U.K. experience. *Oxford Review of Economic Policy* 3 (4): 17–32.

———. 1989. Tax asymmetries, the cost of capital and investment: Some United Kingdom evidence. *Economic Journal* 99 (Supp.): 103–12.

Dotsey, M., and P. Ireland. 1996. The welfare cost of inflation in general equilibrium. *Journal of Monetary Economics* 37:29–47.

Driffill, J. J., G. E. Mizon, and A. Ulph. 1990. Costs of inflation. In *Handbook of monetary economics,* ed. B. M. Friedman and F. H. Hahn. Amsterdam: North Holland.

Fazzari, S. M., R. G. Hubbard, and B. C. Petersen. 1988. Financing constraints and corporate investment. *Brookings Papers on Economic Activity,* no. 1:141–95.

Feldstein, M. 1979. The welfare cost of permanent inflation and optimal short-run economic policy. *Journal of Political Economy* 87 (4): 749–68.

———. 1995. Would privatising social security raise economic welfare? NBER Working Paper no. 5281. Cambridge, Mass.: National Bureau of Economic Research.

———. 1997a. Adjustments to the calculations in Working Paper no. 5469. Cambridge, Mass.: Harvard University. Mimeograph.

———. 1997b. The costs and benefits of going from low inflation to price stability. In *Reducing inflation: Motivation and strategy,* ed. C. Romer and D. Romer, 123–56. Chicago: University of Chicago Press.

Fischer, S. 1981. Toward an understanding of the costs of inflation, II. *Carnegie-Rochester Conference Series on Public Policy* 15:15–42.

———. 1993. The role of macroeconomic factors in growth. *Journal of Monetary Economics* 32:485–512.

Fischer, S., and F. Modigliani. 1975. Towards an understanding of the real effects and costs of inflation. *Weltwirtschaftliches Archiv* 114:810–33.

Fisher, P. G., and J. D. Whitley. Forthcoming. The Bank of England suite of models. Bank of England Working Paper.

Fry, M. J., C. A. E. Goodhart, and A. Almeida. 1996. *Central banking in developing countries: Objectives, activities and independence.* London: Routledge.

Fuhrer, J., and B. Madigan. 1994. Monetary policy when interest rates are bounded at zero. Working Paper no. 94-1. Boston: Federal Reserve Bank of Boston.

Fullerton, D., and Y. K. Henderson. 1989. The marginal excess burden of different capital tax instruments. *Review of Economics and Statistics* 71:435–42.

Hall, R. E. 1988. Intertemporal substitution in consumption. *Journal of Political Economy* 96:339–57.

Hall, R. E., and D. W. Jorgenson. 1967. Tax policy and investment behaviour. *American Economic Review* 57:391–414.

Hall, S., M. Walsh, and A. Yates. 1996. How do U.K. companies set prices? *Bank of England Quarterly Bulletin* 36 (2): 180–92.

Hansson, I., and C. E. Stuart. 1985. Tax revenue and the marginal cost of public funds in Sweden. *Journal of Public Economics* 27:331–53.

Henry, S. G. B., and D. L. Pain. 1994. The user cost approach to housing costs in the RPI. Bank of England submission to the RPI Advisory Committee, June–July 1992.

Hills, J. 1991. *Unravelling housing finance: Subsidies, benefits and taxation.* Oxford: Oxford University Press.

Institute for Fiscal Studies. 1995. Options for 1996: The Green Budget. London: Institute for Fiscal Studies.

Janssen, N. J. 1996. Can we explain the shift in M0 velocity? Some time-series and cross-section evidence. *Bank of England Quarterly Bulletin* 36 (1): 39–48.

Kay, J. A., and M. A. King. 1990. *The British tax system,* 5th ed. Oxford: Oxford University Press.

King, M. A. 1974. Taxation and the cost of capital. *Review of Economic Studies* 41: 21–35.

———. 1977. *Public policy and the corporation.* London: Chapman and Hall.

———. 1980. An econometric model of tenure choice and demand for housing as a joint decision. *Journal of Public Economics* 14:137–59.

———. 1994. Monetary policy in the U.K. *Fiscal Studies* 15 (3): 109–28.

King, M. A., and D. Fullerton, eds. 1984. *The taxation of income from capital: A comparative study of the United States, the United Kingdom, Sweden and West Germany.* Chicago: University of Chicago Press.

Laxton, D., G. Meredith, and D. Rose. 1995. Asymmetric effects of economic activity on inflation. *IMF Staff Papers* 42 (2): 344–74.

Layard, R., S. Nickell, and R. Jackman. 1991. *Unemployment: Macroeconomic performance and the labour market.* Oxford: Oxford University Press.

Leigh-Pemberton, R. 1992. The case for price stability. *Bank of England Quarterly Bulletin* 32:441–48.

Lucas, R. E., Jr. 1994. On the welfare costs of inflation. Chicago: University of Chicago. Mimeograph.

Mayes, D., and B. Chapple. 1995. The costs and benefits of disinflation: A critique of the sacrifice ratio. *New Zealand Reserve Bank Bulletin* 58 (1): 9–22.

Mayes, D., and G. Young. 1993. Industrial investment and economic policy. National Institute Discussion Paper no. 56. London.

McCallum, B. T. 1989. *Monetary economics: Theory and policy.* New York: Macmillan.

Miles, D. 1994. *Housing, financial markets and the wider economy.* New York: Wiley.

Muellbauer, J., and A. Murphy. 1993. Income expectations, wealth and demography in the aggregate U.K. consumption function. Paper presented at HM Treasury's academic panel.

Mulligan, C. B., and X. Sala-i-Martin. 1996. Adoption of financial technologies: Implications for money demand and monetary policy. NBER Working Paper no. 5504. Cambridge, Mass.: National Bureau of Economic Research.

Nordhaus, W. 1997. Do real-output and real-wage measures capture reality? The history of lighting suggests not. In *The economics of new goods,* ed. T. Bresnahan and R. J. Gordon, 29–66. Chicago: University of Chicago Press.

Pain, N., and P. Westaway. 1996. Modelling structural change in the U.K. housing market: A comparison of alternative house price equations. Paper presented at Society of Housing and Property Economists 1996 conference, London Business School.

Phelps, E. S. 1972. Inflation in a theory of public finance. *Swedish Journal of Economics* 75:67–82.

Ramsey, F. P. 1928. A mathematical theory of saving. *Economic Journal* 38:543–59.

Retail Prices Index Advisory Committee. 1995. Treatment of owner occupiers' housing costs in the Retail Prices Index. London: Central Statistical Office, January.

Robinson, W., and T. Skinner. 1989. Reforming the RPI: A better treatment of housing costs? Commentary no. 15. London: Institute for Fiscal Studies.

Robson, M. 1988. Estimating tax rates on income from capital in the U.K. from official statistics. LSE Financial Markets Group Discussion Paper no. 28. London: London School of Economics.

Rudebusch, G. D., and D. W. Wilcox. 1994. Productivity and inflation: Evidence and interpretations. Washington, D.C.: Board of Governors of the Federal Reserve, May. Mimeograph.

Sarel, M. 1996. Nonlinear effects of inflation on economic growth. *IMF Staff Papers* 43 (1): 199–215.

Schwab, R. M. 1982. Inflation expectations and the demand for housing. *American Economic Review* 72 (1): 143–53.

Shapiro, M. D., and D. W. Wilcox. 1996. Mismeasurement in the consumer price index: An evaluation. NBER Working Paper no. 5590. Cambridge, Mass.: National Bureau of Economic Research.

Shiller, R. 1997. Why do people dislike inflation? In *Reducing inflation: Motivation and strategy,* ed. C. Romer and D. Romer, 13–65. Chicago: University of Chicago Press.

Sidrauski, M. 1967. Rational choice and patterns of growth in a monetary economy. *American Economic Review* 57 (2): 534–44.

Smyth, D. J. 1994. Inflation and growth. *Journal of Macroeconomics* 16:261–70.

Stuart, C. E. 1984. Welfare costs per dollar of additional tax revenue in the United States. *American Economic Review* 74:352–62.

Summers, L. H. 1991. How should long-term monetary policy be determined? *Journal of Money, Credit and Banking* 23:625–31.

Tower, E. 1971. More on the welfare costs of inflationary finance. *Journal of Money, Credit and Banking* 3:850–60.

Wardlow, A. 1994. Investment appraisal criteria and the impact of low inflation. *Bank of England Quarterly Bulletin* 34 (3): 250–54.

Woolwich Building Society. 1996. Cost of moving survey. Greenwich, U.K.: University of Greenwich/Woolwich Building Society.

Yates, A. 1995. On the design of inflation targets. In *Targeting Inflation,* ed. A. G. Haldane. London: Bank of England.

Yates, A., and B. Chapple. 1996. What determines the short-run output-inflation trade-off? Bank of England Discussion Paper no. 53. London: Bank of England.

Comment on Chapters 2, 3, and 4   Andrew B. Abel

The case studies of Germany, Spain, and the United Kingdom—chapters 2, 3, and 4—calculate the costs and benefits of moving from a low rate of inflation to a zero rate of inflation using the framework developed by Feldstein (1997). This framework emphasizes fiscal channels, both direct and indirect. The direct fiscal channels arise because the tax codes in these countries are not neutral with respect to inflation. In particular the taxation of capital income is sensitive to the rate of inflation. The indirect fiscal channels arise through the government's budget constraint, which requires that any changes in seigniorage associated with a reduction in inflation be offset by changes in other taxes or government expenditures.

All three case studies adhere to the framework developed in Feldstein (1997), though the details of tax codes and differences in institutions require some modification of the framework for each country. The adherence to a common framework simplifies comparisons among these three countries and with

Andrew B. Abel is the Robert Morris Professor of Banking in the Finance Department at the Wharton School of the University of Pennsylvania and a research associate of the National Bureau of Economic Research.

the United States, which was studied by Feldstein (1997). In addition, it simplifies my task as a discussant of three papers because I have already published a comment on Feldstein (1997). In that comment (Abel 1997) I developed and calibrated a suitably modified version of the Sidrauski (1967) model to provide an alternative set of calculations of the welfare effects of eliminating inflation in the United States. Here I will apply this modified Sidrauski model to Germany, Spain, and the United Kingdom. The presentation of the model is taken largely from Abel (1997). I will present the basic model so that all of the notation and definitions are contained in this comment, and I will present the first-order conditions to give a flavor of the analytic results. However, I will not include the details of the solution procedure but instead refer interested readers to Abel (1997).

An Extension of the Sidrauski Model

The fiscal channels analyzed in the case studies can be incorporated into the Sidrauski model with three modifications. First, the model will include two types of capital, which are to be interpreted as housing capital and nonhousing capital. Second, the model will include a government budget constraint that integrates monetary and fiscal policy. This budget constraint will capture the effects of various distortionary taxes and will take account of changes in distortionary tax rates needed to offset any change in seigniorage when inflation is eliminated. Third, labor supply will be endogenized so that taxes on labor income are distortionary. In the standard version of the Sidrauski model with exogenous labor supply, taxes on labor income do not distort labor supply and thus are lump sum. The presence of lump-sum taxes would provide a nondistortionary way of offsetting changes in seigniorage revenue, which would violate the spirit of Feldstein's (1997) analysis and the analyses in the case studies.

Consider a closed economy with N_t identical consumers in period t. The population grows at rate n so that $1 + n \equiv N_t/N_{t-1}$. There are two types of capital: nonhousing capital (type 1) and housing capital (type 2). Let $K_{i,t}$ be the aggregate capital stock of type $i(i = 1, 2)$ at the beginning of period t, L_t be the aggregate labor input in period t, p_t be the price of goods in terms of money, M_t be the aggregate nominal money supply at the beginning of period t, and B_t be the aggregate nominal stock of government bonds at the beginning of period t. The real per capita values of these variables are $k_{i,t} \equiv K_{i,t}/N_t$, $l_t \equiv L_t/N_t$, $m_t \equiv M_t/(p_t N_t)$, and $b_t \equiv B_t/(p_t N_t)$.

The Consumer's Problem

Asset accumulation of an individual consumer is described by

(C1)
$$c_t + (1 + n)(k_{1,t+1} + k_{2,t+1}) + (1 + n)\pi_{t+1}m_{t+1} + (1 + n)\pi_{t+1}b_{t+1}$$
$$= (1 - \tau_w)w_t\ell_t + R_{1,t}k_{1,t} + R_{2,t}k_{2,t} + (1 + i_t^b)b_t + m_t.$$

The right-hand side of equation (C1) represents the consumer's real disposable resources in period t, which consist of (a) after-tax wage income, where w_t is the real wage rate and τ_w is the tax rate on wages; (b) the value of capital held at the beginning of period t plus any earnings on the capital, where $R_{i,t}$ represents the real after-tax gross return (i.e., principal plus income, after tax) on capital of type i; (c) the value of government bonds held at the beginning of period t plus after-tax interest earnings on the bonds, where i_t^b is the after-tax interest rate on bonds; and (d) the real value of money balances held at the beginning of period t. The left-hand side of equation (C1) represents the consumer's spending in period t, which consists of (a) consumption c_t; (b) capital to carry into period $t + 1$; (c) real money balances to carry into period $t + 1$, where $\pi_{t+1} \equiv p_{t+1}/p_t$ is the gross rate of inflation; and (d) bonds to carry into period $t + 1$.

The utility function of the consumer is

$$\text{(C2)} \qquad \sum_{t=0}^{\infty} \beta^t u(c_t, m_t, \ell_t) \equiv \sum_{t=0}^{\infty} \beta^t \left(\frac{c_t^{1-\rho}}{1 - \rho} + \phi \frac{m_t^{1-\delta}}{1 - \delta} - \psi \frac{\ell_t^{1+\eta}}{1 + \eta} \right),$$

where ρ, δ, η, ϕ, and ψ are positive constants. The consumer chooses consumption, each type of capital, real money balances, bonds, and labor supply to maximize utility in equation (C2) subject to the budget constraint in equation (C1). Letting $\beta^t \lambda_t$ be the Lagrange multiplier on the constraint in equation (C1), the first-order conditions are

(C3a) (c_t): $c_t^{-\rho} = \lambda_t$,

(C3b) $(k_{i,t})$: $\beta \lambda_t R_{i,t} = \lambda_{t-1}(1 + n)$, $i = 1, 2$,

(C3c) (m_t): $\beta \phi m_t^{-\delta} + \beta \lambda_t = \lambda_{t-1}(1 + n)\pi_t$,

(C3d) (b_t): $\beta \lambda_t (1 + i_t^b) = \lambda_{t-1}(1 + n)\pi_t$,

(C3e) (ℓ_t): $-\psi \ell_t^\eta + \lambda_t(1 - \tau_w)w_t = 0$.

I will focus on the steady state in which all of the time-subscripted variables in equations (C3a) through (C3e) are constant. Solving these equations yields the following steady state relations

(C4a) $$R_i = \frac{1 + n}{\beta}, \qquad i = 1, 2,$$

(C4b) $$1 + i^b = \frac{1 + n}{\beta} \pi,$$

(C4c) $$\frac{\phi m^{-\delta}}{c^{-\rho}} = i^b,$$

(C4d)
$$\frac{\psi \ell^{\eta}}{c^{-\rho}} = (1 - \tau_w)w.$$

In the steady state, the real after-tax gross return on all nonmonetary assets is $(1 + n)/\beta$. According to equation (C4a), the real after-tax return on both types of capital is $(1 + n)/\beta$.[1] The real after-tax return on bonds is $(1 + i^b)/\pi$, which, according to equation (C4b), is also equal to $(1 + n)/\beta$. Money offers a lower pecuniary rate of return than bonds (if $i^b > 0$), but consumers willingly hold money because money offers a nonpecuniary return $\phi m^{-\delta}$. The optimal holding of money is reflected in equation (C4c). Finally, equation (C4d) shows that the consumer supplies labor to the point that the disutility of working an additional unit is just offset by the additional utility made possible by earning additional after-tax wage income.

The debt service channel analyzed by Feldstein (1997) and the case studies is absent in the Sidrauski model. As noted above, equation (C4b) implies that the steady state real after-tax rate of return on bonds is invariant to the rate of inflation. Thus the real cost of financing debt, net of taxes levied on interest income, is invariant under changes in the rate of inflation. Therefore, no debt service channel is reported for the results of the Sidrauski model (summarized in table 4C.4, below).

The Production Function

The production function is a Cobb-Douglas function of labor and each type of capital. Under the assumption of constant returns to scale, the production function can be written (omitting time subscripts) in intensive form as

(C5)
$$y = A k_1^{\alpha_1} k_2^{\alpha_2} \ell^{1-\alpha_1-\alpha_2},$$

where $y \equiv Y/N$ is output per capita and the factor shares α_1, α_2, and $1 - \alpha_1 - \alpha_2$ are all positive. In a competitive economy, factors are paid the value of their marginal product. Thus the wage rate equals the marginal product of labor

(C6)
$$w = (1 - \alpha_1 - \alpha_2)y/\ell.$$

The marginal product of type i capital is $\alpha_i y/k_i$. Thus, assuming that capital does not depreciate, the after-tax gross rate of return on type i capital is

(C7)
$$R_i = (1 - \tau_i)\alpha_i \frac{y}{k_i} + 1,$$

where τ_i is the tax rate on the (net) return to capital of type i.

---

1. The rate of return on each type of capital is determined endogenously by eq. (C7) below. In the absence of any taxes, the condition that the gross rate of return on capital equals $(1 + n)/\beta$ is simply the "modified golden rule."

Government Budget Constraint

Monetary and fiscal policy are integrated by the government budget constraint. In the steady state the government budget constraint is

(C8)
$$\tau_w(1 - \alpha_1 - \alpha_2)y + \tau_1\alpha_1 y + \tau_2\alpha_2 y + [(1 + n)\pi - 1]m$$
$$= g + [1 + i^b - (1 + n)\pi]b.$$

The four terms on the left-hand side of equation (C8) are the sources of government revenue: (a) wage tax revenue, (b) tax on income accruing to k_1, (c) tax on income accruing to k_2, and (d) seigniorage revenue. The right-hand side of equation (C8) contains two types of government spending: (a) real purchases of goods and services in the amount of g per capita and (b) interest payments on government debt, net of taxes on interest and rollover of debt. Now divide both sides of equation (C8) by y, and use equation (C4b) to obtain

(C9)
$$\tau_w(1 - \alpha_1 - \alpha_2) + \tau_1\alpha_1 + \tau_2\alpha_2 + [(1 + n)\pi - 1]\frac{m}{y}$$
$$= \frac{g}{y} + (\beta^{-1} - 1)(1 + n)\pi\frac{b}{y}.$$

The government chooses the values of inflation π, the tax rates on capital τ_1 and τ_2, the ratio of government purchases to output g/y, and the ratio of government bonds to output b/y. The tax rate on wages τ_w is determined endogenously by equation (C9).

Steady State Equilibrium

The steady state is characterized by equations (C4a) through (C4d), (C5), (C6), (C7), (C9), and the goods-market-clearing condition

(C10)
$$c + n(k_1 + k_2) = (1 - g/y)y.$$

It is straightforward to derive closed-form expressions for the steady state values of k_1, k_2, c, m, and l. These expressions are presented in equations (11a) through (11e) in Abel (1997).

Calibration of the Model

The values of parameters used in the initial calibrations of the model for Germany, Spain, and the United Kingdom are presented in table 4C.1. Many of the parameter values are the same as in the baseline calibration for the United States in Abel (1997). The sensitivity analysis in table 3C.4 in Abel (1997) indicates that the general results are fairly robust to variations in parameter values.

Of the six preference parameters, four are set exogenously. In the absence

Table 4C.1   **Initial Calibration of the Model**

	Germany	Spain	United Kingdom	Source
Preference parameters				
β	0.95	0.95	0.95	Exogenous
ρ	4	4	4	Exogenous
η	10	10	10	Exogenous
δ	4	4	4	Exogenous
ϕ	3.08E-5	1.04E-4	2.84E-6	Chosen to match m below
ψ	7.44E-11	8.18E-15	8.67E-9	Chosen to make $\ell = 1$
Production parameters				
A	235.855	1722.52	71.662	Chosen to match y below
α_1	0.233	0.233	0.233	Exogenous
α_2	0.067	0.067	0.067	Exogenous
n	0.01	0.01	0.01	Exogenous
Government policy variables				
g/y	0.22	0.19	0.24	Exogenous
b/y	0.60	0.65	0.50	Exogenous
π	1.02	1.02	1.02	Exogenous
τ_1	0.6074	0.3866	0.4024	Exogenous
τ_2	−0.4020	−0.3778	−0.2583	Exogenous
τ_w	0.1926	0.2230	0.2700	Residual: government budget constraint
Empirical aggregates to be matched				
y	2,881	57,138	598	GDP minus depreciation
m	299	8,271	33	Noninterest money

of compelling evidence to the contrary, and to facilitate comparisons across countries, the values of these four exogenously chosen preference parameters do not vary across countries. The time preference discount factor β is 0.95, which implies a rate of time preference of about 5 percent per year. Calibration studies typically choose values of ρ greater than one but generally not much larger than 5, though there are examples of much larger values of ρ in the asset-pricing literature. Here I choose $\rho = 4$. The value of η is even less well established. Here I set $\eta = 10$. The interest elasticity of money demand equals $-1/\delta$. Estimates of this elasticity are small, so I choose $\delta = 4$, which implies an interest elasticity of money demand equal to -0.25. The value of ϕ is chosen so that the value of the money supply m produced by the model equals the value shown at the bottom of table 4C.1. The value of ψ is chosen so that the model produces a value of $l = 1$ in its initial calibration.

The values of the parameters α_1 and α_2 in the production function are the same as those used in the calibration for the United States in Abel (1997). The total factor productivity parameter A is chosen so that y matches the value of actual output. The assumption that capital does not depreciate can be interpreted to mean that all depreciation is a reduction in output, and thus the production function can be viewed as a function that yields gross domestic prod-

Table 4C.2   Tax Rates on Capital

	Germany	Spain	United Kingdom
Nonhousing			
$\tau_1 \ (\pi = 1.02)$	0.6074	0.3866	0.4024
$\tau_1 \ (\pi = 1.0)$	0.5491	0.3513	0.3707
Δ_1	-0.0583	-0.0353	-0.0317
Housing			
Category 1 (share)		(0.3771)	(0.4591)
$\tau_2 \ (\pi = 1.02)$	-0.4020	-0.4901	-0.2813
$\tau_2 \ (\pi = 1.0)$	-0.3858	-0.4540	-0.2500
Δ_2	0.0162	0.0360	0.0312
Category 2 (share)		(0.4308)	(0.4106)
$\tau_2 \ (\pi = 1.02)$		-0.2689	-0.2188
$\tau_2 \ (\pi = 1.0)$		-0.2404	-0.2083
Δ_2		0.0286	0.0104
Category 3 (share)		(0.0551)	(0.1303)
$\tau_2 \ (\pi = 1.02)$		-0.2484	-0.3021
$\tau_2 \ (\pi = 1.0)$		-0.2286	-0.2604
Δ_2		0.0199	0.0417
Category 4 (share)		(0.1370)	
$\tau_2 \ (\pi = 1.02)$		-0.4634	
$\tau_2 \ (\pi = 1.0)$		-0.4298	
Δ_2		0.0335	
Weighted average			
$\tau_2 \ (\pi = 1.02)$	-0.4020	-0.3778	-0.2583
$\tau_2 \ (\pi = 1.0)$	-0.3858	-0.3462	-0.2342
Δ_2	0.0162	0.0316	0.0241

Note: Categories of housing capital for Spain are owner occupied with tax advantages (1), owner occupied without tax advantages (2), non–owner occupied (3), and rental (4). Categories for the United Kingdom are owner occupied, MIRAS (1), owner occupied non-MIRAS (2), and rental (3).

uct less depreciation. The model is calibrated to match GDP less depreciation in each country (shown as y in table 4C.1).

Of the six variables representing government policy in table 4C.1, three are chosen to match the data directly: the ratio of government purchases to output (g/y), the ratio of government debt to output (b/y), and the gross rate of inflation (π). The tax rates on the two types of capital are based on the calculations in the case studies as shown in table 4C.2. Consider, for example, nonhousing capital in Germany. The pretax rate of return, $R_1 - 1$, on this capital is 10.8 percent per year, and the after-tax rate of return is 4.24 percent per year, when the rate of inflation is 2 percent per year. Thus the tax rate on nonhousing capital when inflation is 2 percent is $\tau_1^{\pi=1.02} = 0.6074$. The case study of Germany calculates that at zero inflation the after-tax rate of return on nonhousing capital is 4.87 percent so that the tax rate on type 1 capital is $\tau_1^{\pi=1} = 0.5491$. Thus the change in the tax rate that results directly from a reduction in inflation is $\Delta_1 = -0.0583$. Similar calculations yield the tax rates on housing capital in table 4C.2. For Spain and the United Kingdom there are multiple categories of

housing capital, and I have computed tax rates for each type of housing capital and then computed a weighted average tax rate using the shares reported in table 4C.2. Finally, the tax rate on wage income, τ_w, is a residual that makes the government's steady state budget constraint in equation (C9) hold.

Effect of Eliminating Inflation

The effective tax rates on both types of capital depend on the rate of inflation. Therefore, the elimination of inflation changes these effective tax rates. Let Δ_i be the direct effect on the tax rate τ_i of reducing the rate of inflation from 2 percent per year to zero (i.e., reducing π from 1.02 to 1.00). In addition, there are indirect effects on the tax rates that are needed to satisfy the government's budget constraint. The new set of tax rates, incorporating both the direct effect of inflation (including the possibility of a direct effect, Δ_w, of inflation on the labor income tax rate) and the indirect effect of the government's budget constraint, are

(C11a)
$$\tau_w = (\tau_w^0 + \Delta_w)\theta,$$

(C11b)
$$\tau_1 = (\tau_1^0 + \Delta_1)\theta,$$

(C11c)
$$\tau_2 = (\tau_2^0 + \Delta_2)\theta,$$

where the superscript 0 denotes the initial values of the tax rates and θ is the amount by which all three tax rates must be multiplied in order to satisfy the government's steady state budget constraint. The direct effects, Δ_i, are exogenous, but the indirect effect, captured by θ, is endogenous.[2]

To measure the welfare effects of eliminating inflation, I compare the initial equilibrium in which the steady state value of the triplet (c, m, l) equals $(c^0, m^0, 1)$ and the new steady state equilibrium in which the triplet equals $(c^{new}, m^{new}, l^{new})$. To express the change in welfare in terms of a change in consumption, define c^* to be the level of consumption, combined with the initial values of real money balances and labor, that yields the same level of utility in the steady state as the zero-inflation steady state equilibrium. That is,

(C12)
$$u(c^*, m^0, 1) \equiv u(c^{new}, m^{new}, l^{new}).$$

I will use $(c^* - c^0)/c^0$ as a measure of the benefit of eliminating inflation.

Tables 4C.3A, 4C.3B, and 4C.3C present the effects of reducing the inflation rate from 2 percent per year ($\pi = 1.02$) to zero ($\pi = 1$) in Germany, Spain, and the United Kingdom, respectively. Column (1) in each table ignores the direct effect of inflation on the effective tax rates on the two types of capital and takes account only of the indirect effects on tax rates arising as a result of the change in seigniorage revenue when inflation is reduced. This channel corresponds most closely to the "money demand" channel. Column (2) focuses

---

2. In all policies examined here, the values of g/y and b/y are held constant.

Table 4C.3A   **Effects of Policy Changes: Germany**

	(1)	(2)	(3)	(4)
Government policy variables: exogenous				
Δ_w	0	0	0	0
Δ_1	0	−0.0583	0	−0.0583
Δ_2	0	0	0.0162	0.0162
π	1	1.02	1.02	1
Government policy variables: endogenous				
θ	1.0055	1.0576	0.9957	1.0586
τ_w	0.1936	0.2037	0.1917	0.2039
τ_1	0.6108	0.5807	0.6048	0.5813
τ_2	−0.4042	−0.4252	−0.3841	−0.4084
Steady state effects (%) Change in				
k_1	−1.08	8.72	0.75	8.44
k_2	−0.07	3.49	−1.19	2.14
y	−0.23	1.81	0.08	1.67
c	−0.21	1.64	0.09	1.53
m	7.30	1.64	0.09	9.17
l	0.04	−0.55	−0.02	−0.53
$(c^* - c^0)/c^0$	−0.17	2.09	0.11	2.04

Table 4C.3B   **Effects of Policy Changes: Spain**

	(1)	(2)	(3)	(4)
Government policy variables: exogenous				
Δ_w	0	0	0	0
Δ_1	0	−0.0353	0	−0.0353
Δ_2	0	0	0.0316	0.0316
π	1	1.02	1.02	1
Government policy variables: endogenous				
θ	1.0096	1.0387	0.9905	1.0383
τ_w	0.2252	0.2316	0.2209	0.2316
τ_1	0.3903	0.3649	0.3829	0.3648
τ_2	−0.3814	−0.3924	−0.3429	−0.3595
Steady state effects (%) Change in				
k_1	−0.77	4.52	0.57	4.35
k_2	0.10	2.02	−2.56	−0.58
y	−0.16	0.95	−0.03	0.76
c	−0.15	0.82	0.00	0.68
m	7.36	0.82	0.00	8.26
l	0.01	−0.31	0.02	−0.28
$(c^* - c^0)/c^0$	−0.06	1.06	−0.01	1.00

Table 4C.3C   **Effects of Policy Changes: United Kingdom**

	(1)	(2)	(3)	(4)
Government policy variables: exogenous				
Δ_w	0	0	0	0
Δ_1	0	−0.0317	0	−0.0317
Δ_2	0	0	0.0241	0.0241
π	1	1.02	1.02	1
Government policy variables: endogenous				
θ	1.0020	1.0286	0.9940	1.0243
τ_w	0.2705	0.2777	0.2684	0.2766
τ_1	0.4032	0.3813	0.4000	0.3797
τ_2	−0.2588	−0.2657	−0.2328	−0.2399
Steady state effects (%) Change in				
k_1	−0.18	4.47	0.37	4.66
k_2	0.00	1.51	−2.07	−0.65
y	−0.04	0.91	−0.04	0.83
c	−0.04	0.79	−0.01	0.74
m	7.49	0.79	−0.01	8.32
l	0.00	−0.30	0.02	−0.27
$(c^* - c^0)/c^0$	0.00	1.02	−0.03	0.98

on the direct effect of inflation on the effective tax rate on nonhousing capital, which corresponds most closely to the "consumption timing"—that is, "non-housing capital"—channel. Column (3) focuses on the direct effect of inflation on the effective tax rate on housing capital, which corresponds most closely to the "housing" channel. Column (4) considers all three effects together.

Table 4C.4 summarizes the results of the various calculations for all three countries using the modified Sidrauski model and compares these results with those reported in the case studies. It is important to keep in mind that the welfare costs calculated using the Sidrauski model are expressed as a percentage of steady state consumption, whereas the welfare costs reported in the case studies are expressed as a percentage of GDP. Since consumption is roughly two-thirds of GDP, the overall welfare cost of 2.04 percent of consumption resulting from the application of the Sidrauski model to Germany is remarkably close to the overall welfare cost of 1.41 percent of GDP reported in the case study of Germany. The results of the Sidrauski model for Germany are close to those of the case study in three additional ways: First, the benefits arising through the money demand channel are very small and slightly negative. Second, the benefits arising through the housing channel are also very small but are positive. Third, the largest benefits arise as a result of reducing the distortions in the effective tax rate on nonhousing capital.

The Sidrauski model and case study for Spain produce very similar results

Table 4C.4   Summary

	Germany	Spain	United Kingdom
Parameter			
τ_1 ($\pi = 1.02$)	0.6074	0.3866	0.4024
Δ_1	−0.0583	−0.0353	−0.0317
τ_2 ($\pi = 1.02$)	−0.4020	−0.3778	−0.2583
Δ_2	0.0162	0.0316	0.0241
m/y	0.104	0.145	0.055
Effect on consumption			
Nonhousing capital channel	2.09	1.06	1.02
Housing channel	0.11	−0.01	−0.03
Money demand channel	−0.17	−0.06	0.00
Overall	2.04	1.00	0.98
	Findings of Case Studies[a]		
Effect as a percentage of GDP			
Nonhousing capital channel	1.48	0.55–0.88	0.21–0.37
Housing channel	0.09	1.33	0.11
Money demand channel	−0.04	−0.07	−0.02
Overall[b]	1.41	1.71–2.04	0.21–0.37

[a]$\lambda = 0.4$ for Spain and the United Kingdom.
[b]Includes debt service.

for the effects operating through the nonhousing capital channel (1.06 percent of consumption computed by the Sidrauski model is comparable to the 0.55 to 0.88 percent of GDP reported by the case study) and through the money demand channel (both the Sidrauski model and the case study report a tiny negative effect). The major difference between the Sidrauski model and the case study concerns the effect operating through the housing channel. According to the calculations using the Sidrauski model, this effect is negligible, whereas the case study reports this effect to be 1.33 percent of GDP. Not only is the value of 1.33 percent reported by the case study much higher than that calculated using the Sidrauski model, it is also an order of magnitude higher than the effects reported for the housing channel in the case studies of Germany and the United Kingdom. One might expect the housing channel effect to be larger in Spain than in Germany and the United Kingdom because elimination of inflation changes the tax rate on housing capital by more in Spain than in either of the other two countries. However, Δ_2, the change in the tax rate on housing capital, is only about a third larger in Spain than in the United Kingdom, so it is surprising that the effect operating through the housing channel is 12 times as large in Spain as in the United Kingdom.

For the United Kingdom the results of the Sidrauski model and the case study are somewhat closer than for Spain, though not as close as for Germany. Both the Sidrauski model and the case study report very small effects for the housing channel and for the money demand channel. Although the Sidrauski model and the case study disagree about the signs of these effects, the effects

are all so small as to be essentially zero anyway. As in the case of Germany, the largest effect for the United Kingdom operates through the nonhousing capital channel according to both the Sidrauski model and the case study. However, the effect reported for the Sidrauski model is about two or three times the size of the effect reported in the case study. The nonhousing channel in the case study of the United Kingdom is also smaller than in the case studies of Germany and Spain. One might expect a smaller effect in the United Kingdom because Δ_1, the change in the tax rate on nonhousing capital, is smaller in the United Kingdom than in Germany or Spain. However, Δ_1 is only 10 percent smaller in the United Kingdom than in Spain, so one might not expect the calculated effect operating through the nonhousing channel to be only half as large in the United Kingdom as in Spain.

The Sidrauski model used here has served as a helpful diagnostic tool for examining the calculations reported in the case studies. When the Sidrauski model and a case study produce different results, there is no presumption that one set of results is more reliable than the other. However, in the instances in which the Sidrauski model and a case study have produced different results for a particular country, the case study results for that country also differ from the case study results for the other countries. Thus we are left having to explain why, for example, the housing channel effect in the case study of Spain is so much larger than in the case studies of Germany and the United Kingdom as well as being larger than in the Sidrauski model. Further investigation is needed to resolve these differences.

References

Abel, Andrew B. 1997. Comment on "The costs and benefits of going from low inflation to price stability," by Martin Feldstein. In *Reducing inflation: Motivation and strategy*, ed. Christina D. Romer and David H. Romer, 156–66. Chicago: University of Chicago Press.

Feldstein, Martin. 1997. The costs and benefits of going from low inflation to price stability. In *Reducing inflation: Motivation and strategy*, ed. Christina D. Romer and David H. Romer, 123–56. Chicago: University of Chicago Press.

Sidrauski, Miguel. 1967. Rational choice and patterns of growth in a monetary economy. *American Economic Review* 57:534–44.

Comment on Chapters 2, 3, and 4   Rudiger Dornbusch

The comparative evaluation of the case for reducing inflation invites two kinds of comments. First, here is an outstanding, and successful, effort, which provides a new kind of public finance research effort. Second, the case for reduc-

Rudiger Dornbusch is the Ford Professor of Economics and International Management at the Massachusetts Institute of Technology and a research associate of the National Bureau of Economic Research.

Table 4C.5   International Cost-Benefit Comparison of 2 Percent Inflation Cut
             (percent of GDP)

	Spain	Germany	United Kingdom	United States
Consumption timing	0.6	1.4	0.2	0.6
Housing	1.3	0.1	0.1	0.2
Money	−0.1	−0.0	−0.0	−0.0
Debt	−0.1	−0.1	−0.1	−0.1
Benefit per annum	1.7	1.4	0.2	0.7
Annual cost	0.6–1.0	0.3	0.2	
Sacrifice ratio	0.6–1.0	4.0	3.0	2.0–3.0

Sources: Chapters 1 through 4 in this volume.
Note: All numbers rounded to the next decimal.

ing inflation is intriguing but far from made: the painstaking detail in the public finance research is matched by the coarsest summing of evidence from macroeconomics. The two do not mix well.

The cross-country evaluation is refreshing in highlighting differences in tax structures, interacting with differences in the environment, and thus fertilizes our thinking about the welfare costs of distortions. The benefits of such cross-country comparisons, within the discipline of a unified framework, come in a number of ways. First, they are missionary work. They spread their practice of rigorous public finance analysis of distortions to countries where little or no work may have been done in the past. Not in the least, they create the benefit of public finance networks, which are an important ingredient for research.

The cross-country comparisons are also immediately useful in highlighting instances where a particular country's estimates are far out of line with what is reported elsewhere. Table 4C.5 summarizes from the various papers the cost-benefit analyses of disinflation using the Feldstein setup. The point about the great merit of cross-country research is immediately made by the very fact that such a table can be created, including sensitivity tests and the resulting ranges of estimates.

Such a comparison will highlight immediately that in Spain, for example, the welfare cost of inflation in the housing sector is unusually large relative to the other countries. Similarly, in Germany inflation has a relatively large welfare cost in affecting consumption timing.

For the question at hand—do public finance considerations warrant disinflating by 2 percentage points to alleviate the welfare cost arising from the interaction of the tax system and inflation?—the answer is 3:1. The central banks of Germany and Spain come out strongly in support of low inflation—no surprise here. The U.S. analysis, in Feldstein's hands, yields the same result. Interestingly, the preferred estimate of the Bank of England passes the test only by a hair's breadth. Across the wider range of estimates reported in chapter 4, the net benefit of moving to price stability may be positive or negative. The reason for the difference resides in the relatively small distortion of consump-

tion choices. But 3:1 is a victory. So let us assume that the public finance case for reducing inflation in countries with U.S.-style tax distortions in interaction with inflation is made. Does that mean the public policy debate is finished and we should just move ahead, make the necessary recession, get it over with, and enjoy the better allocation of resources forever after?

The issue, of course, is to take more seriously two problems. The first is whether there is some benefit from moderate inflation in making markets function better. The second is whether disinflation sacrifice ratios are a good public finance tool.

It is common sense that extreme inflation, if only because of its instability, is destructive to productive activity. Beyond that, it is deeply destructive of social relations more generally, from property to peace. No more need be said on that. But when it comes to the distinction between 2 and zero percent inflation per year—fully anticipated and stable—does the professional bias against inflation still apply and does it go all the way to zero? There is very little modeling of this issue, but a few ideas have been around. One strand, coming from the 1950s, argues that relative price adjustment needs to happen in a dynamic economy and that it is more easily done when there is an ever so slight upward trend in the general price level. The idea is that it is easier to raise some prices than to cut some wages. The idea has been picked up again by Akerlof, Dickens, and Perry (1996) in their influential case against deflation. The analysis remains crude, but a more careful micromodeling of the productivity issues in the workplace (à la Solow) that arise from wage policy is surely possible. If it is easier not to give a wage increase in an environment of rising prices than to administer a wage cut in an environment of stable prices, the case is made. The evidence of Shiller (1997) powerfully supports the contention that people do have illusions, and there is every reason to believe that their productivity is linked to their perception of what is happening to them and how "just" they think it is. All of this remains mushy, but it is worth exploring even if it is far away from public finance and dangerously close to "human resource management."

A second strand is the interaction between inflation and search in monopolistic markets. Some modeling suggests that via signal extraction problems, inflation has an impact on the intensity of search effort and hence on the elasticity of demand facing an oligopolist. More search is better—though it comes at a resource cost too—because oligopoly represents a welfare cost. Hence, what is the optimal rate of inflation? Not zero! If these considerations are valid, the presumption for price stability that comes from the interaction of distortionary taxcs and inflation is incomplete and there may be reasons pushing in the direction that a bit of inflation is a good idea.

Even more important is the whole discussion of a short recession to harvest the lasting benefits of better resource allocation. True, the authors do not belittle the fact that there will be an output loss to disinflation, and there is no attempt to lick the lowest sacrifice ratios. But there is nevertheless a temptation

to claim that credibility might just come into play and make the entire disinflation effort far less costly. It is worth pointing out that there is no evidence to support this notion. Argentina is a case in point. Interest differentials on peso and dollar assets show that there is no expectation of a regime change; yet in the face of 18 percent unemployment, disinflation proceeds at a minimal pace. We may not understand why wages and prices do not fall more rapidly, but we surely have no right to believe that a credible strategy (whatever that means) may not be far more costly than historical experience suggests.

But there is more important criticism. The sacrifice ratio does a very poor job of measuring the costs of disinflation. Not only are the numbers extraordinarily crude to serve as a benchmark, with, possibly minor, extra questions of revenue lost during a recession that needs to be made up by distortionary taxes and of capital accumulation not having taken place while the recession lasted. There is also the much more important question of whether loss in output is a good measure of the cost. The most obvious reason for doubt is that the incidence of a recession is borne very unequally across individuals. The cohort that enters the labor market during a recession is very unlikely to have the same lifetime performance as other cohorts. There is obviously no compensation for this since nobody imagines that we use neutral lump-sum taxes to make compensation payments (beyond unemployment insurance) to the losers. For something as important as a recession, glossing over the distribution issue is bad public economics.

Consider the case of Germany. Unemployment is high and has been rising for a decade. It is proposed to make a recession at the cost of a 11.8 percent loss in output to reach the benefits of better resource allocation. It is difficult to believe that this is a priority project compared to restructuring, which is at least as controversial as recession but presumably carries far larger benefits. In the United States, likewise, there is surely little enthusiasm for ending the exploration of just where full employment is in favor of a program of recession and the inevitable social fallout it brings. And if one puts the two together, and all the other countries, the idea of making a world recession to cure the welfare cost of tax distortions interacting with inflation seems outright preposterous. There are simply more pressing economic agendas with more clearly identified benefits.

The setup in the comparative exercise is to assume that tax distortions cannot be changed—just take it for granted as an accepted fact of public finance—and if that is so, let us at least reduce some of the welfare costs of these distortions by eliminating inflation. I would submit that making a world recession to get at these costs meets just the same opposition. There is just no enthusiasm for recessions, perhaps even less than for tax reform. Economists should concentrate on first-best policies rather than create a dubious backdoor case and a crude one at that.

References

Akerlof, G., W. Dickens, and G. Perry. 1996. The macroeconomics of low inflation. *Brookings Papers on Economic Activity*, no. 1: 1–59.

Shiller, R. 1997. Why do people dislike inflation? In *Reducing inflation: Motivation and strategy*, ed. C. Romer and D. Romer, 13–65. Chicago: University of Chicago Press.

Discussion Summary for Chapters 2, 3, and 4

In response to Dornbusch's discussion, *Gerhard Ziebarth* noted that the policy implications of his paper can be interpreted in two ways: both as an argument for disinflation and as an argument against more inflation. *Rudi Dornbusch* replied that he would applaud the paper as support for an explicit inflation target but that the argument made in the paper is really an argument for disinflation, not just an argument against more inflation.

José González-Páramo conjectured that a reason for the discrepancy between Andrew Abel's estimate of the housing distortion in Spain and his own estimate may be that housing capital does not directly enter into the utility function in Abel's model whereas it does in his own model.

Abel concurred but also noted that Spain looks very different from Germany and the United Kingdom when Feldstein's partial equilibrium framework is used. *Mervyn King* added that it is striking that Abel's calculations do match the other authors' calculations for Germany and the United Kingdom.

Neal Hatch remarked that the consumption distortion effect in the different country case studies are not fully comparable because the U.K. case study assumes that tax-exempt savings vehicles affect the marginal returns to saving whereas the other studies assume that tax-exempt savings is mainly inframarginal.

José Viñals agreed with Rudi Dornbusch that one should pay more attention to the microeconomics of the labor market and to how inflation affects search behavior. He also noted that the benefits of going to price stability may still outweigh the costs even if the capital income tax is lowered in the future, as the payback time for price stability is short. He noted further that Spain recently experienced disinflation, apparently without an increase in unemployment, indicating that the sacrifice ratio may be lower for Spain than was assumed in the paper. Viñals then acknowledged the importance of political economy considerations. It seems politically very difficult to remove the underlying distortions in the housing market, so disinflation may be the best way to effectively reduce these distortions. The same point may not apply to the labor market because there are now so many unemployed that there may be enough political support to change labor market institutions.

Stephen Cecchetti remarked that the sacrifice ratio estimates do not seem to be very reliable but are rather like glorified back-of-the-envelope calculations.

In particular, the estimates have three main problems. First, they do not take into account that some component of a recession may permanently decrease output. Second, one has to be careful about the underlying source of shocks, which seems unlikely. Third, standard econometric techniques are ill suited to dealing with policy shifts to new regimes, leading to estimates of sacrifice ratios that are very imprecise. He concluded that there is still a long way to go before we obtain useful estimates of the costs of disinflation.

James Hines noted that the nature of the model is important for the estimated housing distortion. In a one-good model the only possible distortion is to the total quantity consumed, but in a multigood model there are also possible distortions in the allocation of consumption.

Rudi Dornbusch wondered how the housing distortion in Spain as calculated by Dolado et al. can be five times as large as the housing distortions in the other country studies. *Martin Feldstein,* while agreeing that the difference seems very large, suggested that the tax rules and other subsidies for housing in Spain may be different enough to explain the greater distorting effect of inflation. *Andrew Abel* agreed with Rudi Dornbusch and stated that he does not want to argue whether or not his estimates for Spain are more accurate than those of Dolado et al. but remarked that the real puzzle is why Spain differs so much from the other countries. *José González-Páramo* suggested that a nonlinearity may account for Spain's apparent anomaly. *Abel* acknowledged that a nonlinearity may explain something but said that he remains unconvinced and surprised by the difference of an order of magnitude.

Edmund Phelps inquired how disinflationary costs, as measured by the sacrifice ratio, are compared to the infinite stream of welfare benefits. In particular, does the calculation take into account that the marginal utility of consumption declines as per capita GDP rises. Why is the discount rate $r - g$ instead of r? *Martin Feldstein* responded that the discounting by the real net-of-tax return that individuals receive has the effect of taking into account the decline in the marginal utility of consumption (since individuals equate the ratio of the marginal utilities to $1 + r$). He noted further that g, the growth rate of GDP, is subtracted from r, the real net-of-tax return on risky assets, in order to take into account the growth of the welfare gains, which increase in proportion to GDP.

Mervyn King asserted that the virtue of the four case studies is that they all use the same framework, which focuses on interactions between inflation and taxes. This make the studies comparable and very interesting. The real contribution of the papers is the analysis of the tax-inflation interaction, not their analysis of the costs of disinflation. Sacrifice ratios are endogenous policy choices, and hence, it is not obvious that past experiences are relevant for the future. The estimates of the sacrifice ratio could be over- or underestimates. Estimation of sacrifice ratios is a fruitful area for future research. Another key question raised by the papers is which margin for savings should be examined. How should one take forced savings, pension benefits, and other tax-preferred

savings vehicles into account? What are marginal savings and what are inframarginal savings? This is a very hard issue to determine.

Martin Feldstein emphasized the great potential gains from the interaction of macroeconomics and public economics of the type provided by this conference. He expressed his delight with Andrew Abel's contribution and agreed with Abel's assessment of his paper as a useful start at analyzing the issue from a general equilibrium macroeconomic perspective.

Feldstein said that he was puzzled that Abel's calculation for the United Kingdom shows that the increase in nonhousing capital causes a steady state consumption gain of 0.75 percent of GDP, which is much larger than the gain calculated in chapter 4. This difference might be traced to the different ways of calculating the welfare costs of the revenue effect. In principle, it is good to derive λ, the marginal cost of public funds, endogenously, but we really need to use marginal tax rates to derive λ rather than the average tax rates that Andrew Abel chose in order to calibrate the government budget constraint. The implicit marginal cost of public funds may therefore be too low in his comment, which would mean that revenue effects are undervalued.

In response to Rudi Dornbusch's point about the possibility of a future capital income tax reduction, Feldstein noted that he is more pessimistic about this prospect. He agreed with the earlier remarks about the importance of correctly incorporating tax-favored savings but said that he thinks that many of these tax-favored savings are inframarginal. He agreed with the authors of the British case study that the effects of inflation on business investment should not be part of the main welfare calculation. Finally, he emphasized that the role of VAT can be important: If housing consumption falls and nonhousing consumption rises, VAT revenues increase which increases welfare.

Rudi Dornbusch argued that the fiscal effects of the recession caused by the reduction in inflation should be part of the welfare calculation. *Martin Feldstein* responded that these fiscal effects can be seen as a perpetual increase in the national debt and that a simple calculation shows that the welfare costs of this increase are small enough to ignore.

Philip Cagan noted that the estimates of sacrifice ratios used in the conference papers lie significantly below Arthur Okun's U.S. estimates of 6 to 18. An often-used methodology involved interpolating GDP between peaks and measuring the cumulative difference between actual GDP and interpolated GDP. The problem with this method was that GDP at the peaks was not sustainable because it was too high. Could the method used here to calculate sacrifice ratios suffer from the same problem?

Benjamin Friedman offered a clarification of Okun's original methodology. Arthur Okun estimated an increase in unemployment of 2 to 6 percentage points (with a median of 3 percentage points) per percentage point of disinflation. He and others then multiplied these figures by 3, from Okun's law, to convert them into percentage points of forgone output. However, present estimates of Okun's law are lower, so our estimates of sacrifice ratios are lower as

well, but in terms of unemployment our estimates are similar to estimates from Okun's time.

Frederic Mishkin observed that policymakers often think about the uncertainty that is created by high levels of inflation. It is an open question whether inflation uncertainty would indeed go down if inflation levels were lower. In the past five years, there has been very little variability with a level of inflation around 3 percent. Would inflation variability decrease if we went to price stability, or would variability increase because there would be less political support to combat inflationary shocks if the level of inflation is close to zero anyway?

Stephen Cecchetti asserted that more work is needed to determine the frontier relating inflation variability to output variability. One could also measure whether this frontier depends on the level of inflation. Variability is ultimately an issue of how policies respond to shocks. The stability of the past couple of years may simply be due to the absence of significant shocks.

5   Inflation and the User Cost of Capital: Does Inflation Still Matter?

Darrel Cohen, Kevin A. Hassett, and R. Glenn Hubbard

5.1 Introduction

High and rising rates of inflation in the United States during the 1970s stimulated economists to examine the effects of inflation on household and business decisions about household saving and business investment (see, e.g., Darby 1975; Feldstein 1976; Feldstein, Green, and Sheshinski 1978; Auerbach 1981; Gordon 1984). Indeed, a substantial body of research has concluded that one of the most important channels through which a change in the anticipated rate of price inflation can affect real economic activity is a nominal-based capital income tax structure (see Feldstein 1983).[1] In the United States, for example, nominal interest payments are treated as tax deductions by businesses and taxable income by investors, capital gains are taxed without an adjustment for inflation, and depreciation is written off on a historical cost basis. While these features of the tax code have not changed in the past 20 years, other features—such as the corporate income tax rate and depreciation schedules—have changed considerably. In addition to these tax changes, the period has experienced a dramatic increase in the flow of capital across national boundaries. While the United States may not face a perfectly elastic supply of foreign

Darrel Cohen is an economist in the Division of Research and Statistics of the Federal Reserve Board. Kevin A. Hassett is a resident scholar at the American Enterprise Institute. R. Glenn Hubbard is the Russell L. Carson Professor of Economics and Finance at Columbia University and a research associate of the National Bureau of Economic Research.

The authors are grateful to Alan Auerbach, Martin Feldstein, Laurence Meyer, Edmund Phelps, and participants in the Columbia Macro Lunch Group and the NBER conference for helpful comments and suggestions. This paper does not necessarily reflect the views or opinions of the Board of Governors of the Federal Reserve System.

1. Other distortions include those in the demand for money (see, e.g., Bailey 1956; Feldstein 1979) and in investment in housing (see, e.g., Poterba 1994). For general overviews of the costs of inflation, see, e.g., Fischer (1981), Feldstein (1997), and Hubbard (1997b, chap. 28).

capital, rates of return in U.S. capital markets have become more closely linked to foreign returns.

Most of the existing studies of the effect of anticipated inflation on the effective tax on business investment were written during periods of significant—at least by U.S. standards—inflation. In recent papers, Feldstein (1997) and Abel (1997), using different methodological approaches, estimate significant welfare gains from greater business capital accumulation from reducing even modest rates of inflation.[2] Indeed, the present value of gains from reducing inflation substantially exceeds the costs of disinflation estimated by Ball (1994).

In this paper, we extend prior approaches to estimating the impact of domestic inflation on business investment—based on subsequent modifications to the tax code, the increasing openness of world capital markets, and recent developments in the theoretical modeling of investment decisions. In particular, we quantify the impact of an immediate and permanent change in the rate of inflation on the user cost of capital for different types of assets in a partial equilibrium framework.[3] In addition, we show the relationship between the resulting inflation sensitivity of the user cost and the choice of capital durability. We also present estimates of the sensitivity of current investment incentives to anticipated changes in future rates of inflation and explore the effects of inflation on steady state consumption. Finally, we present estimates of the impact of inflation on intratemporal distortions in the allocation of capital.

In brief, we conclude that for the United States (1) inflation, even at its relatively low current rates, continues to increase the user cost of capital significantly; (2) the marginal percentage reduction in the user cost of capital per percentage point reduction in inflation is higher the lower the level of inflation; (3) the beneficial effects of lowering inflation even further than has been achieved to date would be notable; and (4) inflation has almost no impact on intratemporal distortions in the allocation of capital within the domestic business sector. These conclusions support the arguments by Feldstein (1997) that there are potentially significant economic benefits for the U.S. economy of reducing even modest levels of inflation. However, we also show that there is a great deal of uncertainty concerning the relevance of these conclusions for small open economies.

---

2. In both sets of estimates, the gains from a reduced distortion in the allocation of lifetime consumption between early years and later years account for the vast majority of total welfare gains from disinflation.

3. In our analysis of the effects of inflation on the effective tax rate on investment, we assume that there is no correlation between changes in capital income tax rates and changes in inflation; i.e., we do not allow for the possibility that the legislative process takes into account the effect of inflation on the effective tax burden when deciding on individual and corporate tax rates. It might be the case, e.g., that the Congress introduces more generous depreciation allowances or lower statutory tax rates on capital gains when inflation is higher. While there is some discussion of this connection in the context of the Economic Recovery Tax Act of 1981 (see Joint Committee on Taxation 1981), we could find no record of such discussion in the debate over the Tax Reform Act of 1986 and the Omnibus Budget Reconciliation Act of 1993 (the tax acts governing the current period we analyze).

By focusing on the effects of disinflation on the user cost of capital and the capital stock, we are abstracting from two general questions. First, we do not present estimates of the welfare gains from the higher capital stock made possible by lower inflation.[4] Second, we do not attempt to estimate the optimal rate of inflation. Such a calculation requires a more comprehensive model of the costs and benefits of inflation.

The remainder of the paper is organized as follows. In section 5.2 we analyze the theoretical linkages between inflation and the user cost of capital. In section 5.3 we present empirical estimates of the effects of an immediate and permanent change in the rate of inflation on the user cost for different types of capital, taking into account the details of current U.S. corporate tax law. Section 5.4 extends these results by analyzing the impact on the user cost of anticipated future changes in the rate of inflation. In section 5.5 we examine the effects of lower inflation on steady state consumption. Section 5.6 examines the effects of inflation on the welfare losses associated with differential taxation of capital. In the final section, we offer some concluding thoughts and directions for future research.

5.2 Inflation and the User Cost of Capital

5.2.1 Inflation and the Cost of Funds

Firms can obtain their financing from three sources: they can issue debt, they can issue equity, or they can use internal funds. In this section, we discuss the effects of the interaction of inflation and tax variables on the marginal cost of finance for U.S. firms from these different sources. The effects depend importantly on open economy issues, in particular the degree of openness of international capital markets. For simplicity, however, we begin with a discussion of effects of inflation on the cost of funds in a closed U.S. capital market; then we expand the analysis to incorporate an open capital market and the international tax regime.

Debt Financing

In a closed economy, U.S. holders of corporate debt are assumed to require a fixed real after-tax rate of return, r,[5] where

---

4. To do so would require separating transition gains and losses from steady state efficiency gains, which is beyond the scope of this paper. As we argue in section 5.7, however, under the assumption that the United States is a closed economy, one can use golden rule calculations to argue that the level of the fixed nonresidential capital stock is too low.

5. The assumption of a constant real rate of interest represents the traditional Fisher hypothesis (see Fisher 1930). The Fisher hypothesis need not hold in the presence of the inflation-tax interactions that we analyze here. Indeed, if the only nonneutrality of interest were the deductibility and taxability of nominal interest payments for debt-financed investments, nominal interest rates would rise more than one for one with anticipated inflation (see Feldstein 1976). Offsetting this consideration, as we note below, are other tax nonneutralities, the presence of equity finance, and interna-

(1) $r = R(1 - \tau_p) - \pi,$

and R is the nominal interest rate on corporate debt, τ_p is the marginal personal tax rate on interest income, and π is the expected rate of inflation. This expression for the real return on funds loaned reflects the fact that under current U.S. tax law, nominal interest income—which includes both the real and the inflation premium components of market interest rates—is taxable to bondholders. For a given r and π, a reduction in the marginal tax rate of the holder of debt lowers the nominal interest rates that firms pay, and for a given r and τ_p, a 1 percentage point reduction in the rate of inflation lowers the interest rates that firms pay by more than 1 percentage point. In addition to the tax-adjusted Fisher effect, we also examine the case in which the real before-tax interest rate is held constant, which is especially relevant for a small open economy; with this assumption, a 1 percentage point reduction in the rate of inflation raises the real after-tax interest rate, r, by τ_p percentage points.

The firm's real cost of debt, ρ_d, depends on its own marginal income tax rate, τ_c:

(2) $\rho_d = R(1 - \tau_c) - \pi.$

Expression (2) reflects the deductibility of nominal interest payments on corporate debt under current law. Combining equations (1) and (2) yields the firm's real cost of debt from the perspective of the ultimate supplier of debt capital rather than from that of the firm's manager:

$$\rho_d = (r + \pi)\frac{(1 - \tau_c)}{(1 - \tau_p)} - \pi$$

(3)

$$= \frac{r(1 - \tau_c)}{(1 - \tau_p)} + \pi\frac{(\tau_p - \tau_c)}{(1 - \tau_p)}.$$

Note that for a given real required return r, inflation has very little effect on the cost of debt finance if τ_c is approximately equal to τ_p. In this case, while lower inflation reduces the nominal interest deduction, thereby raising the firm's tax liability, it also lowers the tax liability of bondholders by about the same amount. In addition, the effects of inflation on the cost of debt finance

---

tional capital mobility (see also Hartman 1979; Feldstein 1983; Hansson and Stuart 1986; Bayoumi and Gagnon 1996). Empirical evidence presented by Mishkin (1992) and by Bayoumi and Gagnon (1996) argues that the real pretax rate of interest is not affected by a change in expected inflation.

We investigated these empirical estimates: Using the nominal one-year Treasury bill rate, the Livingston measure of expected (one-year-ahead) inflation, and a time series of the effective marginal tax rate on interest income of Prakken, Varvares, and Meyer (1991), we find that both the nominal before-tax rate and the after-tax rate are cointegrated with the expected inflation measure and that both the real before-tax rate and the real after-tax rate are stationary. We view this as providing ambiguous evidence of whether the tax-adjusted or non-tax-adjusted Fisher effect holds. In any case, the fact that results of Prakken et al. show that taxes are in fact paid on interest income at a rate between zero and the maximum statutory rate suggests that the marginal investor may well be taxable and that the tax-adjusted Fisher effect is a reasonable case to examine.

will vanish for a given required real after-tax return if firms are required to deduct only real, rather than nominal, interest payments and if bondholders are allowed to include only real interest income in taxable income. Such would be the case with a fully indexed tax structure.[6] Note also that the effects of inflation on the cost of debt finance depend crucially on the assumption that the marginal debt holder is taxable at the statutory rate τ_p. If the marginal debt holder is a financial intermediary such as a pension plan (whose income is nontaxable under current law), then lower inflation can *increase* the cost of debt finance. Firms receive smaller interest deductions, and pension funds do not accrue an offsetting decrease in tax liability. Although convincing evidence of the tax rate of the marginal debt holder in the United States probably is not available, the observation made above that taxes appear to be paid on interest income at a fairly high effective rate lends some support for the proposition that the effects of inflation on the user cost through the debt channel will be relatively small.

The results differ somewhat in the case of integration of the U.S. capital market with an open international capital market. In particular, the results depend on the degree to which the United States exerts market power and on the extremely complicated details of international tax law. At one extreme, one could assume that the United States is so large that it determines all relevant market and tax conditions; this assumption essentially reduces to the prior closed economy case. By contrast, if the United States participates as a price taker in a world with perfect international capital mobility, the real cost of debt is determined in world capital markets and is exogenously given to U.S. firms.[7] Moreover, under a pure residence-based income tax structure, which is likely to be the most relevant modeling assumption in the case of international taxes on interest income, the interest rate that U.S. corporations must pay on their debt obligations may be independent both of domestic and foreign tax rates on interest income.[8]

With perfectly integrated capital markets (and no transactions or information costs), uncovered or open interest parity holds. That is, for a marginal risk-

6. With the tax structure indexed for inflation, bondholders' real after-tax rate of return becomes $r = (R - \pi)(1 - \tau_p)$, while firms' real cost of debt becomes $\rho_d = (R - \pi)(1 - \tau_c)$. Combining these two expressions yields $\rho_d = r(1 - \tau_c)/(1 - \tau_p)$, which is independent of the rate of inflation for a given r.

7. Hartman argues that when taxes are taken into consideration, domestic inflation in a small open economy raises the desired capital stock and reduces domestic saving, thereby increasing capital inflows from the rest of the world. Empirical support for this proposition is provided by Bayoumi and Gagnon (1996).

8. A residence-based tax system can be summarized briefly as follows. If country A has a residence-based tax system applicable to interest income, the residents of country A are taxed uniformly on their worldwide interest income, whether the source of that income is country A or the rest of the world; nonresidents are not taxed by country A on their income originating in that country. In fact, residence-based taxation of interest income holds approximately in the United States and many other countries (for a more complete discussion of international tax law, see Hubbard 1995; Hines and Hubbard 1995). Such a tax structure generates a particular form of international arbitrage or parity relationships.

neutral investor, the nominal after-tax rate of return on U.S. debt instruments equals the exogenous after-tax rate of return on a foreign debt instrument plus the expected percentage rate of depreciation of the dollar relative to foreign currencies. With residence-based taxation, the applicable tax rate for a U.S. investor is the U.S. tax rate, while the applicable tax rate for the foreign investor is the foreign tax rate. This implies two separate parity conditions. For the U.S. investor we have $R(1 - \tau_p) = R^*(1 - \tau_p) + \Delta s^e(1 - \tau_g)$, where s^e denotes the expected log future spot dollar value of foreign exchange, R^* denotes the exogenous foreign nominal interest rate, and τ_g represents the U.S. tax rate on foreign exchange gains; this condition implies that U.S. investors are indifferent between investing at home or abroad. Similarly, for the foreign investor, the parity condition is $R(1 - \tau_p^*) = R^*(1 - \tau_p^*) + \Delta s^e(1 - \tau_g^*)$, where τ_p^* denotes the foreign tax rate on interest income, and τ_g^* represents the foreign tax rate on foreign exchange gains.[9] If $\tau_p \approx \tau_g$ and $\tau_p^* \approx \tau_g^*$, then the international arbitrage relationships imply the equality of pretax interest rates (adjusted for expected exchange rate changes). In this case, the interest rate that U.S. corporations must pay on their debt is not influenced by either the U.S. or the foreign tax rate on interest income.[10] In a small open economy setting in which purchasing power parity holds (which implies that $\Delta s^e = \pi - \pi^*$, where π^* denotes the foreign inflation rate), then, the traditional Fisher hypothesis obtains: $dR/d\pi = dR^*/d\pi^* = 1$.[11] Thus in our work below we will consider two cases. In the "closed economy case," the tax-adjusted Fisher effect holds. In the "open economy case," the traditional Fisher effect holds.

Equity Financing

An analogous distinction between open and closed economy effects holds in the case of equity financing; we focus again initially on the closed economy case. The firm's real cost of equity finance, ρ_e, is defined as

$$(4) \qquad \rho_e = D + E - \pi,$$

where D is the dividend per dollar invested and E is the ex-dividend nominal return per dollar invested. In contrast to interest payments, dividends and retained earnings are not deductible for corporations. In what follows, we adopt the tax capitalization view of equity taxation (see Auerbach 1979; Bradford

9. Desai and Hines (chap. 6 in this volume) discuss complications arising from differences in the taxation of interest income and foreign exchange gains and losses and illustrate the effects of changes in inflation on international capital flows.

10. In most OECD countries, tax authorities treat gains and losses on foreign currency for tax purposes as interest receipts or interest payments (see, e.g., Organization for Economic Cooperation and Development 1992).

11. Levi (1977) and Hansson and Stuart (1986) discuss complications arising when interest income and foreign exchange capital gains and losses are taxed at different rates.

Both equalities implicitly assume that domestic and foreign inflation rates move independently. More generally, one could model the expected exchange rate change making assumptions about the relative importance of traded and nontraded goods. Such a modification would produce a different "Fisher effect" result.

1981; King 1977), which suggests that the relevant equity tax rate is the effective capital gains tax rate, regardless of dividend policy.[12] This view is premised on the assumptions that equity funds come primarily from retained earnings (i.e., lower dividends paid out of current earnings) rather than from new share issues and that earnings distributions to shareholders are primarily through dividends rather than share repurchases. The idea is that taxes on dividend distributions are capitalized into the value of the equity rather than imposing a burden on the returns to new investment, as would be the case if new investment were financed by the issue of new shares.

Under the tax capitalization view, marginal equity funds for a dividend-paying firm come through retained earnings. Hence, the opportunity cost to the shareholder of a dollar of new investment is reduced by the dividend taxes forgone (evaluated at the dividend tax rate τ_d), net of the increased tax burden on the capital gains induced by the accrual (evaluated at the accrual-equivalent tax rate on capital gains, c). Because the value of new investment per dollar invested, q, equals its cost to the shareholder, the equilibrium cost of retaining a dollar is $q = 1 - \tau_d + cq$, which implies that $q = (1 - \tau_d)/(1 - c)$.

Capital market equilibrium requires additionally that the after-tax rate of return on the firm's investment in (nominal terms) equals the investor's required rate of return, $\tilde{\rho}_i$. Following Auerbach (1983), for a given value of q:

(5a) $$\tilde{\rho}_i = (1 - \tau_d)D/q + (1 + c)E.$$

Substituting for q and converting to real terms:

(5b) $$\rho_i = \tilde{\rho}_i - \pi = (1 - c)(D + E) - \pi.$$

Combining terms in equation (4) and (5b), we can express the firm's real cost of equity financing as

(6) $$\rho_e = \frac{\rho_i}{1 - c} + \frac{c}{1 - c}\pi,$$

where i refers to the marginal investor.

Further, in equilibrium, investors' after-tax real returns on debt and equity, adjusted for a risk premium, X, must be equal; that is, $r = \rho_i - X$. Solving for ρ_i and substituting the resulting expression into equation (6), using equation (1), we get

(7) $$\rho_e = X/(1 - c) + [(1 - \tau_p)/(1 - c)]R - \pi.$$

Differentiation of this expression, assuming that the risk premium is unaffected by inflation and deferring consideration of open economy effects to below, we find that for a given r (i.e., in the tax-adjusted Fisher effect case), lower

12. Recent evidence in support of the tax capitalization view is presented in Auerbach and Hassett (1997) and Harris, Hubbard, and Kemsley (1997). For a more general discussion of alternative views of dividend taxation, see Poterba and Summers (1985).

inflation unambiguously reduces the cost of equity finance by the factor $c/(1 - c)$. This term captures the "inflation tax" paid by shareholders who receive purely nominal gains; taxation of real capital gains would eliminate this effect. There is another, offsetting effect, however, if the traditional Fisher effect holds (in which the nominal bond rate rises point for point with inflation). In this case, lower inflation also raises r by τ_p times the change in inflation and, hence, ρ_i by the same amount. As a result, the total impact on the firm's real cost of equity financing in this case depends on the difference between the personal tax rate on interest and the effective capital gains tax rate.

Turning to equity-financing issues that arise in an open economy setting, the degree of U.S. market power and complexity of the international taxation of equity returns are once again central to the analysis. If the United States is very large relative to the rest of the world, then the analysis essentially reduces to the closed economy case. However, to the extent that the United States is a price taker, the details of international taxation of equity returns become important. In this case, the residence-based taxation discussed above in the case of debt finance no longer applies. Instead, source-based taxation is more applicable. In its pure form, source-based country taxation implies that income originating in country A is taxed uniformly, regardless of the residency of the recipient of the income; in addition, residents of country A are not taxed by country A on the residents' foreign-source income. For either a risk-neutral U.S. investor or a foreign investor, the same parity relationship holds (assuming no expected change in the exchange rate). In this case, a viable equilibrium exists in which the U.S. equity rate of return is related to the corresponding exogenous foreign equity rate of return as well as to the domestic and foreign tax rates.

In practice, however, tax law is much more complicated; to simplify, it is roughly the case that the United States taxes the foreign-source equity income of its residents but allows a tax credit against the taxes paid to foreign governments. The credit is limited to the product of the U.S. tax rate and the amount of foreign-source income (with carryforward and carrybackward provisions for excess credits). Thus U.S. residents generally end up paying taxes on their foreign-source income at the higher of the foreign and U.S. tax rate but pay at the U.S. rate on their U.S.-source income. A special provision applies to multinational firms. Foreign subsidiaries of U.S. parents are allowed to defer U.S. taxes on foreign earnings until they are repatriated, at which time taxes paid to foreign governments are credited against the U.S. tax liability (see Hines and Hubbard 1995); deferral makes sense in periods in which foreign tax rates are lower than U.S. tax rates (see, e.g., Hines and Hubbard 1990; Altshuler, Newlon, and Randolph 1995).

Assuming symmetrical treatment by foreign governments of their residents' foreign-source income, the parity conditions now depend on the difference between tax rates; if the U.S. rate is smaller than the foreign rate (i.e., if $\tau^* > \tau$) the parity relationship facing a U.S. investor compares the real after-U.S.-tax return on a U.S. equity investment with a real after-foreign-tax return on a

foreign equity investment; however, the relationship facing a foreign investor is given by a comparison of the real after-foreign-tax return on a U.S. equity investment and the real after-foreign-tax return on a foreign equity investment.[13] An equilibrium exists in the case of tax harmonization (i.e., identical tax rates, credits, etc.). In this case, the arbitrage conditions suggest equality between pretax equity rates of return. For the firm in a small open economy the world pretax rate of financing ρ_e^* is taken as given. Thus, for the firm using both debt and equity financing, $\rho_e^* = R^*(1 - \tau_c) - \pi$, which holds only by accident given the absence of any equilibrating mechanism. (In general, domestic and international capital market equilibrium will hold simultaneously only if the risk premium and capital structure adjust.) For simplicity, we focus only on the all-debt or all-equity firm in the open economy examples below.

Cost of Funds

The total real cost of investment funds equals the weighted average of the cost of equity and the cost of debt:

$$(8) \qquad \rho = w_d \rho_d + w_e \rho_e,$$

where w_d and w_e are, respectively, the shares of debt and equity in total finance. For the closed economy simulations presented below, these weights will be treated as empirical constants, although in general they would vary with changes in tax law and inflation. For our open economy simulations, we do not explicitly impose assumptions about the weights. Rather than make arbitrary assumptions about the effect of inflation on the equilibrium risk premiums and capital structure, we provide the estimates for the all-debt and all-equity cases. Of course, it is relatively easy to consider intermediate cases once one knows the values at the corners, and we do not mean to imply that all foreign companies are at financing corners. Rather, it is likely the case that the risk premium increases with indebtedness, and this serves as an equilibrating factor in explaining the observed behavior of firms in open economies.

5.2.2 Corporate After-Tax Cash Flow

We assume that managers of corporations make production and input decisions in a manner that maximizes the wealth of shareholders. In particular, firms acquire new capital so as to maximize the present discounted value of the generated after-corporate-tax cash flow. Before-tax cash flow is equal to revenues (net of optimal variable input costs) less the total cost of the new capital goods; in addition, taxes are paid at rate τ_c on revenues, with deductions allowed for depreciation and interest paid on corporate debt. Each of the terms making up after-tax cash flow requires some explanation.

The expected before-tax revenue stream generated by an investment is not

---

13. Cummins and Hubbard (1995) describe the effect of international tax rules and parent company foreign tax credit provisions on the cost of capital.

constant over time. It declines because the economic service flow of the capital good is assumed to decay exponentially at rate δ (where this decay rate does not vary with time but does vary with the durability of the capital good) and rises because the general level of prices is assumed to increase exponentially at rate π. Moreover, the choice of asset durability—short lived versus long lived—is endogenous, a point to which we will return below. The total cost of new capital goods includes the purchase price, as well as installation or adjustment costs that possibly rise at an increasing rate with the quantity of investment. The cash outlays associated with financing, either through corporate debt obligations or payments to equity holders, are not included as part of cash flow; rather these financing costs are included as part of the firm's discount rate, discussed above.

Taxes also are part of cash flow. In the United States, the tax treatment of capital investments has changed substantially over time (see the description in Cummins, Hassett, and Hubbard 1994). The last major change occurred with the Tax Reform Act of 1986, which eliminated the investment tax credit and reduced the top federal statutory corporate income tax rate from 46 to 34 percent (which was increased to 35 percent in 1993). In addition, depreciation allowances were changed significantly.

Currently, only the historical or original cost of a capital asset, HC, may be written off even if the cost of replacing the asset is rising over time, and this is the most important channel through which inflation interacts with the tax code to lower investment. Further, assets are depreciated over a fixed period of time—the service life, T—depending on the type of asset. Most machinery and equipment, so-called personal property, has a service life of seven years, although computers and light vehicles have five-year service lives and small tools three-year service lives. Commercial real property can be written off over 39 years. The dollar amount that can be written off in any year also depends on the type of asset. Personal property is allowed to be depreciated at a rate greater than that using the method of straight-line depreciation ($= HC/T$ per year), and in this sense the depreciation on personal property is said to be accelerated. More precisely, personal property can employ the 200 percent (or double declining balance) method with a half-year convention in the first year and switch to straight line when optimal. We explain this method of accelerated depreciation in detail in the appendix. Put simply, the dollar magnitude of depreciation allowed is equivalent to that of straight-line depreciation in the first year that depreciation is taken (because of the half-year convention), greater than straight-line depreciation for the next few years, and less than straight-line depreciation for the final few years.[14] Nevertheless, with a positive

---

14. The part of the accelerated depreciation scheme that allows a switch to straight-line depreciation when such a switch is optimal means that the undepreciated balance remaining at the time of the switch is written off in equal increments over the remaining service life; it does not imply that a full HC/T is allowed in each remaining year.

discount rate, the present value of depreciation allowances using this method of accelerated depreciation exceeds that using straight line. In contrast to the tax treatment of personal property, real property must be written off using the straight-line method under current law. The present value of depreciation allowances per dollar invested will be denoted by z.

5.2.3   Taxes and the User Cost of Capital

The nominal marginal cost of funds, $\rho + \pi$, where ρ is given above as the total real cost of investment funds, is the discount rate that the firm applies to each component of its after-corporate-tax cash flows related to investment. Maximization of the present discounted value of these cash flows over an infinite horizon, under the assumptions of no adjustment or installation costs for new capital and no change in the relative price of capital goods, q, implies that the pretax marginal product of capital today equals today's user cost of capital, C_t, where

$$(9) \qquad C_t = q_t(\rho + \delta)(1 - \tau_c z)/(1 - \tau_c).$$

This is the familiar formula derived by Hall and Jorgenson (1967), which itself draws on the seminal work of Jorgenson(1963).[15] If the instantaneous expected rate of change of the relative price of new capital goods, $\dot{q}/q$, is not zero, the user cost becomes

$$(10) \qquad C_t = q_t(\rho + \delta - \dot{q}/q)(1 - \tau_c z)/(1 - \tau_c).$$

Introduction of corporate taxes affects the user cost of capital in three ways. First, in the absence of tax deductions for depreciation and interest costs, an increase in the corporate income tax rate, τ_u, increases the before tax marginal

15. Switching for a moment to discrete time and assuming no corporate taxes ($\tau_c = 0$) or change in the price of output ($\pi = 0$), the economic logic underlying the user cost concept becomes readily apparent for the firm that finds it desirable to buy a new capital good at the beginning of period t at price q_t^* and sell it at the beginning of the next period at a different price q_{t+1}^*; there are no costs of installing the new capital and no transactions costs in its purchase or sale. Assume that the resulting increment to production, MPK, takes place at the beginning of period t, is stored costlessly during the period, and is sold at the beginning of period $t + 1$ for $(p\text{MPK})_{t+1}$, where p denotes the constant price of output. Also assume that like production, depreciation of the capital takes place at the beginning of the period and assume that the firm spends δq_t^* at the beginning of the period to replace the worn-out δ units of capital. If ρ is the required rate of return for investors, then the present value of the net cash flow is given by $-q_t^* - \delta q_t^* + [(p\text{MPK})_{t+1} + q_{t+1}^*]/(1 + \rho)$, which equals zero for a marginal investment. Rearranging this expression yields $(p\text{MPK})_{t+1} = q_t^* [\rho + \delta + \rho\delta - (\Delta q_{t+1}^* / q_t^*)]$, where $\Delta q_{t+1}^* / q_t^*$ denotes the capital gain or loss on the asset due to a change in its market price; in our simple example, the capital gain or loss is realized, but in general it may be accrued rather than realized. The expression arising in the one-period problem approximates the continuous-time version of the user cost (with no corporate taxes or change in output prices); indeed, the interaction term, $\rho\delta$, vanishes in continuous time.

Put another way, with no corporate taxes the firm's cost of capital in use has three components: the first is the combined real cost of debt and equity financing, ρq_t, which incorporates the required real rate of return of bondholders and shareholders, each on an after-personal-tax basis; the second is the economic rate of decay of capital with an unchanging relative price of new capital δq_t; and the third is an offset due to an instantaneous real capital gain on the capital, $(\dot{q}/q) q_t$.

product of capital necessary to yield an acceptable after-tax rate of return to investors, thereby increasing the user cost. Second, a higher corporate income tax rate increases the value of depreciation deductions and hence reduces the user cost. The multiplicative factor, $(1 - \tau_c z)/(1 - \tau_c)$, in equation (10) captures the combination of these two effects; on balance, the user cost is increased under current U.S. tax law because expensing—or the immediate write-off—of plant and equipment expenditures is not permitted (i.e., $z < 1$). Third, a higher corporate tax rate increases the value of interest deductions and hence, all else being equal, reduces the real cost of debt financing, ρ_d. Given realistic parameter values, however, the first effect dominates: on balance, corporate taxes increase the user cost or the minimum pretax marginal product of capital necessary to yield an acceptable real rate of return to investors.[16] As a consequence, corporate taxes in the United States diminish the incentive to invest.

5.2.4   Inflation, Taxes, and the User Cost of Capital with No Adjustment Costs

For given values of ρ and δ, the user cost varies directly with the rate of price inflation because the present value of depreciation—which uses the nominal rate $\rho + \pi$ for discounting—varies inversely with inflation as a result of historical cost depreciation. Although not examined here, other treatments of this issue, such as the comparative study edited by King and Fullerton (1984), emphasize that inflation increases the "effective tax rate" on capital (the pretax real rate of return on a marginal investment project, net of depreciation less the posttax real rate of return to savers, as a fraction of the former). Thus, for given values of ρ and δ, a reduction in the general rate of inflation creates an incentive on the margin for a higher level of capital accumulation.

In addition, the sensitivity of the user cost to expected inflation depends on the amount by which the total real corporate cost of funds, ρ, responds to changes in the inflation rate. As we noted above, the real cost of debt financing, ρ_d, is subject to offsetting influences in the closed economy case. On the one hand, the tax deductibility of nominal interest payments, for a given required real after-tax return, r, by corporate debt holders, implies that a reduction in the general rate of inflation increases the cost of debt financing in proportion

---

16. To obtain a sense of the magnitudes involved for the first effect, suppose that new capital received no depreciation allowances ($z = 0$) and that the corporate income tax rate were 0.5; in this case, the pretax marginal product of capital would have to double in value relative to the no-tax case. Under current law, the federal corporate income tax rate is 0.35, while depreciation allowances for equipment investment imply that z is roughly 0.75 (with an inflation rate of 3 percent per year); together these imply that corporate taxes raise the minimum pretax marginal product of equipment capital by about 15 percent. For investment in structures, depreciation allowances imply that z is about 0.40, and corporate taxation raises the minimum pretax marginal product of structures by about 30 percent. The final effect of corporate taxation is to reduce the real cost of debt financing, ρ_d; given reasonable parameter values and an assumed constancy of the debt-equity ratio, this effect cuts the former effect roughly in half.

to the marginal corporate income tax rate. On the other hand, bondholders must pay taxes on their nominal interest income at the marginal personal tax rate on interest income, implying that lower inflation reduces the cost of debt financing. On balance, the effect of inflation on the cost of debt financing is proportional to the difference between the marginal personal and corporate income tax rates, $\tau_p - \tau_c$, and the effect vanishes if the tax rates are equal. In our open economy case, however, only the former effect holds, and thus lower inflation raises the cost of debt financing. In the closed economy, a lower inflation rate unambiguously reduces the real cost of equity financing, ρ_e, for a given required real after-tax rate of return by bondholders and, hence, shareholders (i.e., if the tax-adjusted Fisher effect holds) because of the taxation of nominal capital gains on corporate assets. By contrast, in a small open economy, the real cost of equity financing will not depend on inflation.

5.2.5   Inflation, the User Cost, and the Durability of Capital

The sensitivity of the user cost of capital to inflation also varies with the durability of capital. In the special case in which the rate at which historical costs can be written off for tax purposes equals the rate of economic depreciation (assumed above to be constant over time for a given type of capital)— approximately a declining-balance method in discrete time—Auerbach (1981) establishes the result that the inflation sensitivity of the user cost declines with asset durability, for a given ρ;[17] this implies that inflation weighs more heavily on short-lived than long-lived assets, an effect that is confirmed by our simulations for personal property reported below (which also allow for ρ to change with inflation). As a result, lower inflation promotes a substitution of short-lived for long-lived assets, with a consequent increase in an aggregate δ; while we do not allow for this effect in our simulations, its inclusion would only diminish the sensitivity of the user cost to inflation for personal property such as equipment. However, for different types of real property, we find that the inflation sensitivity of the user cost is virtually independent of asset durability; indeed, one can show analytically that the general relationship between the two is no longer unambiguously negative with straight-line depreciation allowances. In section 5.6 we attempt to quantify the interasset distortions arising from inflation.

5.2.6   Inflation, Taxes, and the User Cost of Capital with Adjustment Costs

While our analysis to this point captures effects of current changes in the tax code and inflation on current incentives to invest, it omits other relevant features that might allow current incentives to depend on future changes in the tax code and inflation. For example, our assumption of no adjustment costs

---

17. Auerbach actually demonstrates the equivalent proposition that the inflation sensitivity of the required internal rate of return before taxes, $v = (c/q) - \delta$, declines with asset durability; he also shows that the inflation sensitivity of the effective corporate tax rate, $(v - \rho)/v$, declines with asset durability.

implies that investment decisions made today can be implemented immediately and in no way depend on either expected future financial or tax conditions. The potentially large instantaneous increment to a firm's capital stock implied by this view has long been recognized to contrast with an empirical investment process at the firm level that appears to be much smoother. This suggests that firms cannot adjust their capital stocks quickly without incurring substantial adjustment costs. If these costs rise nonlinearly with the level of capital expenditures and, perhaps, are themselves of an investment nature—such as workforce training—then firms find it desirable to spread capital expenditures over time in a manner that depends on expected future financial and tax conditions.

Jorgenson and various collaborators in the development of the neoclassical model derive an expression for the desired and actual capital stock as a function of the user cost of capital and net revenue. The gap between the desired and actual capital stock was closed by an ad hoc mechanism (such as delivery lags). A more contemporary application is offered by Auerbach (1989b). Auerbach begins with the Euler equation for investment and assumes a production function, productivity shocks, and convex adjustment costs. He approximates the optimal solution for perturbations by solving a linearized version of the Euler equation.

The above discussion assumes a one-time permanent change in the rate of inflation. One might also be interested in the effects of a gradual reduction in inflation. For this purpose, we can use Auerbach's result that the optimal level of investment at date t varies inversely with the weighted average of the current and all expected future user costs of capital

$$C_t^* = E_t \sum_{s \geq t} w_{s-t} C_s,$$

where the weights, w_i, sum to unity; because the weights decline exponentially, expected changes in the distant future will have relatively small effects on the current value of the user cost. In contrast to the conventional (Hall-Jorgenson) user cost formulation, the user cost also incorporates expected changes in tax parameters. Specifically, the user cost of capital at date s is

$$C_s = q_s(1 - \Gamma_s)[\rho + \delta + \Delta\Gamma_{s+1}/(1 - \Gamma_s)]/(1 - \tau_{cs}).$$

In this expression, Γ denotes the present value of the tax savings from depreciation allowances per dollar of investment, D; that is,

$$\Gamma_s = \sum_t (1 + i)^{-(t-s)} \tau_t D_{t-s};$$

note that depreciation allowances are discounted at the default risk-free nominal interest rate, i, in recognition of the fact that historically in the postwar United States legislated changes in depreciation schedules have never been applied to capital already in place nor has the corporate income tax rate varied substantially (with the exception of the changes legislated in the Tax Reform Act of 1986). This formulation simplifies to the conventional Hall-Jorgenson

formulation only if today's rate of general price inflation, the relative price of capital goods, and the tax code are expected to remain unchanged into the indefinite future (in which case Γ does not change over time).

Such conditions are unlikely to hold in practice, of course. Indeed, we are particularly interested in the effects on current investment incentives of a future reduction in the inflation rate, anticipated, perhaps, as a result of a credible long-term policy goal by the Federal Reserve to achieve a stable price level. We expand on the analysis presented earlier of the effect of a decline in inflation on investment using the forward-looking formulation of the user cost of capital in section 5.4. Intuitively, if expectations of lower inflation in the future reduce future user costs and hence increase firms' long-run desired capital stock, then, in order to minimize adjustment costs, firms begin to increase investment in the current period.

5.3   Estimating Effects of Inflation on the User Cost of Capital

In this section, we present empirical estimates of the effects of the rate of inflation on the user cost of capital under current U.S. tax law. For purposes of this exercise, we assume that firms take inflation as given; in particular, inflation is not affected by the investment policies of firms. In addition, inflation is assumed not to affect the rate of economic depreciation, δ, and tax parameters such as the corporate income tax rate and nominal depreciation allowances per dollar invested. In one set of simulations, inflation also does not affect bondholders' required real after-tax rate of return, r, and local taxes affect the cost of equity as well. In another set, inflation does not affect the real before-tax rate of interest, $R - \pi$, or real before-tax cost of equity. Finally, our results are partial equilibrium estimates of the effect of inflation on the user cost of capital; none of our results in this section allow for the general equilibrium effects of inflation on capital formation and, hence, on the real before-tax rate of return.

Table 5.1 presents the user cost of three types of equipment at various inflation rates, in the closed economy case, assuming that 30 percent of inventories

Table 5.1   **User Cost, Equipment Investment: Closed Economy Case, $\eta = .3$**

Inflation Rate	7-Year Life	5-Year Life	3-Year Life
0	0.209	0.266	0.401
0.02	0.218	0.276	0.412
0.04	0.227	0.286	0.422
0.06	0.235	0.295	0.432
0.08	0.244	0.303	0.442
0.10	0.251	0.311	0.451
0.12	0.259	0.320	0.461

Source: Authors' calculations.

Note: η represents the fraction of inventories subject to FIFO accounting.

Table 5.2   **User Cost, Equipment Investment: Closed Economy Case, $\eta = 0$**

Inflation Rate	7-Year Life	5-Year Life	3-Year Life
0	0.209	0.266	0.401
0.02	0.218	0.276	0.412
0.04	0.227	0.285	0.422
0.06	0.235	0.294	0.432
0.08	0.243	0.302	0.441
0.10	0.251	0.311	0.450
0.12	0.258	0.318	0.459

Source: Authors' calculations.

Note: η represents the fraction of inventories subject to FIFO accounting.

are subject to FIFO accounting;[18] table 5.2 assumes that no firms use FIFO accounting. Tables 5.3 and 5.4 present the same calculations for the open economy case. Tables 5.5 through 5.8 present summary results for two types of structures. The first column of each table gives the rate of price inflation, which varies from 0 to 12 percent per annum. The remaining columns show the user cost of capital for a one-dollar investment. The "debt financing" columns assume that r is 2 percent per year, ρ_i is 6 percent per year, τ_c is 0.35, τ_p is 0.45, and c is 0.10.[19]

The results in tables 5.1 and 5.2 show that for each of the three types of personal property, the marginal effect of inflation on the user cost of capital is approximately independent of the rate of inflation when the economy is closed. Of course, this conclusion reflects variation in modest rates of inflation. For very high inflation, the cost of an extra percentage point of inflation may be small because the present value of real depreciation deductions is already very low. For each type of capital asset, a 1 percentage point decline in the annual rate of inflation lowers the user cost by slightly less than 0.5 percentage points, no matter which assumption we make about inventory accounting. The relative unimportance of the inventory accounting method also holds in the remainder of our results and reflects the relatively low levels of inflation explored here.

18. In the empirical work below, we assume that output is produced and held as finished goods inventories for one year; we allow for inflation's impact on inventory profits to increase the corporate tax rate by $\eta\tau\pi$, where η is the fraction of inventories subject to FIFO accounting. This is not a fully satisfactory treatment of inventories because it treats them as entirely finished goods rather than as raw materials or work in progress.

19. Results for the closed economy case are sensitive to the choice of τ_p; the impact of inflation on the user cost of capital is independent of τ_p in the open economy case. Our assumed value for τ_p of 0.45 corresponds to the (combined federal and average state) rate paid by the top-bracket investor. If, alternatively, we assume that $\tau_p = 0.21$ (based on an update of the average marginal tax rate in Prakken et al. 1991), the effects of inflation on the user cost of capital are somewhat smaller than those reported in tables 5.1, 5.2, 5.5, and 5.6. For equipment investment, e.g., each percentage point decline in inflation reduces the user cost by about 0.25 percentage points when $\tau_p = 0.21$, as opposed to 0.5 percentage points when $\tau_p = 0.45$.

The rough constancy of the relationship between the user cost and inflation implies that a reduction in the rate of inflation from a low initial level has a larger positive *percentage* impact on the user cost than a reduction from a high level, for any given durability of capital. Thus, if the elasticity of firm investment demand with respect to the user cost is constant, as is the case with a Cobb-Douglas production technology, the beneficial impact on the incentive to invest of lowering the rate of inflation from its current level of about 3 percent per year to zero may be greater than the beneficial effect of lowering it by 3 percentage points from the higher levels that prevailed in the United States during the late 1970s and early 1980s.

Tables 5.3 and 5.4 indicate how our results change for a small open economy. When the marginal source of financing is new equity issuance, the results are comparable to the closed economy case, but when the marginal source of financing is debt, the deductibility of interest payments is important enough to reverse the results. The results for structures are qualitatively similar to those for equipment, although there are quantitative differences. Clearly, the choice of marginal financing source is the dominant factor in the open economy case.

Another interesting finding follows from the fact that the response of the user cost to small changes in inflation is not constant across either types of capital or levels of inflation. A large change in the inflation rate, say 10 percentage points, has a differential effect on the user cost depending on the durability of capital. In particular, a large increase in the inflation rate raises the user cost of assets (or limits the decline in the open economy debt-financing case) with a three-year service life more than those with a five-year or a seven-year life, but variation across real property assets is essentially nonexistent. These findings are consistent with the discussion in subsection 5.2.5, in which we argued on analytic grounds that the inflation sensitivity of the user cost declines unambiguously with asset durability in the case of assets, such as equipment, that can be written off using a declining-balance method of depreciation, but that the relationship is ambiguous in the case of assets, such as structures, that are subject to the straight-line method.

5.4   Estimating Effects of a Gradual Reduction in Inflation on the User Cost

In this section, we present estimates of the effects of inflation on the user cost of equipment capital (seven-year life) and on the growth rate of the capital stock using the formulation we described earlier. The estimates are summarized in figures 5.1, 5.2, and 5.3. The top panel of each figure presents the time path of inflation, the middle panel shows the time path of the user cost, and the bottom panel shows the growth rate of the capital stock. The key assumptions are that the tax-adjusted Fisher effect holds; that the elasticity of investment with respect to the user cost is -0.75; and that the decay rate used to calculate the weights, w_s in C_t^*, which embed adjustment costs, is 0.5, the preferred

Table 5.3   User Cost, Equipment Investment: Open Economy Case, $\eta = .3$

Inflation Rate	Equity Financing			Debt Financing		
	7-Year Life	5-Year Life	3-Year Life	7-Year Life	5-Year Life	3-Year Life
0	0.223	0.281	0.416	0.195	0.252	0.387
0.02	0.229	0.287	0.423	0.190	0.248	0.384
0.04	0.234	0.293	0.430	0.186	0.244	0.380
0.06	0.239	0.298	0.436	0.181	0.240	0.377
0.08	0.244	0.303	0.442	0.175	0.234	0.372
0.10	0.248	0.308	0.448	0.169	0.229	0.368
0.12	0.252	0.313	0.454	0.162	0.223	0.363

Source: Authors' calculations.

Note: η represents the fraction of inventories subject to FIFO accounting.

Table 5.4   User Cost, Equipment Investment: Open Economy Case, $\eta = 0$

Inflation Rate	Equity Financing			Debt Financing		
	7-Year Life	5-Year Life	3-Year Life	7-Year Life	5-Year Life	3-Year Life
0	0.223	0.281	0.416	0.195	0.252	0.387
0.02	0.229	0.287	0.423	0.191	0.248	0.384
0.04	0.234	0.292	0.429	0.186	0.244	0.381
0.06	0.238	0.297	0.435	0.181	0.240	0.377
0.08	0.242	0.302	0.440	0.176	0.235	0.373
0.10	0.246	0.306	0.446	0.170	0.230	0.369
0.12	0.249	0.310	0.451	0.164	0.225	0.364

Source: Authors' calculations.

Note: η represents the fraction of inventories subject to FIFO accounting.

Table 5.5   User Cost, Structures Investment: Closed Economy Case, η = .3

Inflation Rate	39-Year Life	27-Year Life
0	0.091	0.102
0.02	0.100	0.111
0.04	0.107	0.119
0.06	0.114	0.127
0.08	0.119	0.133
0.10	0.125	0.139
0.12	0.130	0.144

Source: Authors' calculations.

Note: η represents the fraction of inventories subject to FIFO accounting.

Table 5.6   User Cost, Structures Investment: Closed Economy Case, η = 0

Inflation Rate	39-Year Life	27-Year Life
0	0.091	0.102
0.02	0.100	0.111
0.04	0.107	0.119
0.06	0.113	0.127
0.08	0.119	0.133
0.10	0.125	0.139
0.12	0.130	0.144

Source: Authors' calculations.

Note: η represents the fraction of inventories subject to FIFO accounting.

Table 5.7   User Cost, Structures Investment: Open Economy Case, η = .3

	Equity Financing		Debt Financing	
Inflation Rate	39-Year Life	27-Year Life	39-Year Life	27-Year Life
0	0.115	0.124	0.082	0.092
0.02	0.118	0.130	0.076	0.087
0.04	0.121	0.134	0.068	0.079
0.06	0.124	0.138	0.059	0.071
0.08	0.125	0.142	0.050	0.061
0.10	0.127	0.145	0.040	0.050
0.12	0.128	0.148	0.030	0.038

Source: Authors' calculations.

Note: η represents the fraction of inventories subject to FIFO accounting.

estimate in Auerbach and Hassett (1991). The figures indicate that changes in inflation can generate large effects on capital stock growth.

Figure 5.1 simulates a likely path investment might take if a credible commitment were announced to gradually move toward price stability. The simulation indicates that a fully anticipated decline in the inflation rate from 4 percent in year t to zero four years later (in equal increments) begins to affect the

Table 5.8   **User Cost, Structures Investment: Open Economy Case, $\eta = 0$**

	Equity Financing		Debt Financing	
Inflation Rate	39-Year Life	27-Year Life	39-Year Life	27-Year Life
0	0.115	0.124	0.082	0.092
0.02	0.118	0.130	0.076	0.087
0.04	0.121	0.134	0.068	0.079
0.06	0.122	0.138	0.060	0.071
0.08	0.124	0.142	0.051	0.061
0.10	0.125	0.145	0.042	0.050
0.12	0.126	0.148	0.032	0.038

Source: Authors' calculations.

Note: η represents the fraction of inventories subject to FIFO accounting.

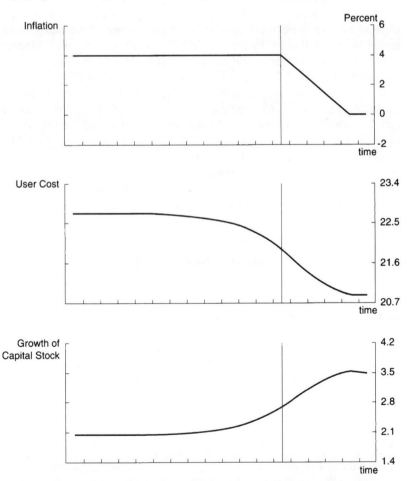

Fig. 5.1   Effects of anticipated decline in inflation on user cost and capital stock (seven-year life; tax-adjusted Fisher effect)

user cost before the inflation rate actually declines because of the changes to investors' expectations when the commitment is announced. Indeed, the user cost has completed about 40 percent of its total adjustment by time t; the full adjustment—which from table 5.1 is 180 basis points—is completed exactly four years after time t. The capital stock growth rate also increases in advance of the completed disinflation, rising nearly 0.5 percentage points by time t; the growth rate increases by nearly 1.5 percentage points when inflation equals zero and subsequently begins its decline back to the initial steady state value. If the shock occurs while the capital stock is growing at about its historical trend rate, then this reduction in inflation will increase capital stock growth over the period by roughly 50 percent.

Figure 5.2 shows the effects of an even larger anticipated decline in the inflation rate from 12 percent per year, the level that obtained in the early 1980s, to 4 percent over an eight-year period. Again, a sizable part of the complete adjustment in the user cost and in the growth rate of the capital stock occurs by time t. Further, by the time inflation reaches 4 percent, the capital stock growth rate over the period has more than doubled from its initial steady state level. In figure 5.3, we consider a slightly different experiment. In this case, we consider the impact on the user cost of an unanticipated increase in the inflation rate of 1 percentage point (from a 4 percent level) that occurs at time t. After time t, we simulate the subsequent response of the level of inflation to the shock reflecting the estimated time-series properties of the Livingston expected inflation series mentioned above. These suggest that a 1 percentage point current shock to inflation would ultimately increase the level of inflation by 1.5 percentage points. The latter effect magnifies the increase in the user cost that would otherwise occur by about 20 basis points (or 50 percent).

5.5   Effects of Lower Inflation on Consumption

Auerbach and Hassett (1991) and Cummins, Hassett, and Hubbard (1994, 1995, 1996) demonstrate that estimates of the effect of the user cost of capital (or tax-adjusted Q) on investment during major tax reforms are more likely to reflect the true underlying effect than conventional panel data estimates.[20] They estimate the elasticity of the equipment investment rate with respect to its user cost in the United States to be about -0.75 and the corresponding elasticity for structures at about -0.5. If the annual inflation rate were reduced from 4

20. They argue that major tax reforms offer periods in which there is substantial exogenous cross-sectional variation in the change in the user cost of capital or tax-adjusted Q. During reform periods, an unusually large portion of the variation in the user cost or tax-adjusted Q is observable, and the signal-to-noise ratio may be much higher. Using firm-level data, an estimate using tax reforms to isolate observable variation in the user cost or Q may significantly decrease the bias in the estimate of the effect on investment of the user cost or Q. Cummins et al. (1996) show that this is the case for the United States and 11 other OECD countries.

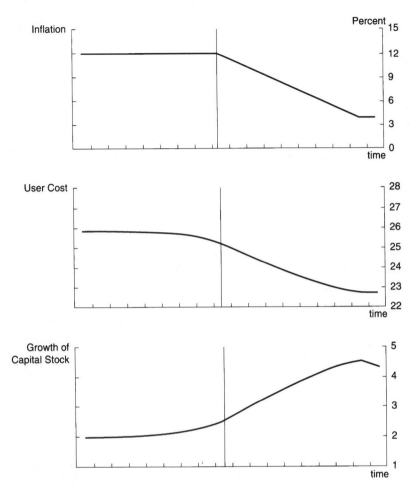

Fig. 5.2   Effects of anticipated decline in inflation on user cost and capital stock (seven-year life; tax-adjusted Fisher effect)

percent to zero, the user cost of equipment capital, as shown above, would decline by about 2 percentage points, proportionally about 8 percent when the tax-adjusted Fisher effect holds. Such a permanent decline in inflation would increase the equipment investment rate by about 6 percent; a similar calculation implies that the nonresidential structures investment rate would increase 7.5 percent. This implies that total business fixed investment rises about 6.5 percent and the ratio of business fixed investment to private GDP rises about 5.5 percent.

In principle, one can calculate the long-run gains in sustainable per capita real private consumption that would result from the permanent reduction in

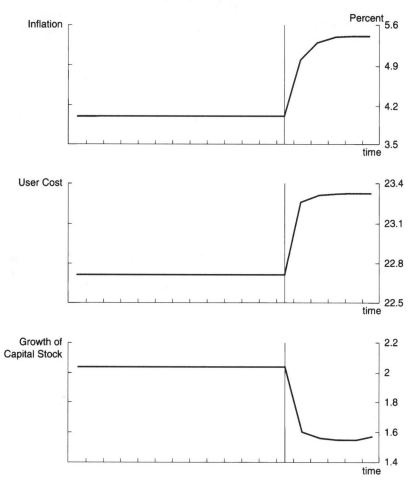

Fig. 5.3   Effects of unanticipated increase in inflation on user cost and capital stock (seven-year life; tax-adjusted Fisher effect)

inflation.[21] In the steady state, investment is proportional to the capital stock, and hence, the investment-output and capital-output ratios are proportional. Thus, eventually, the 5.5 percent increase in the investment-output ratio boosts the capital-output ratio by the same percentage amount. This implies that eventually output per worker rises 2.2 percent, assuming a Cobb-Douglas production technology with capital's share equal to 0.3 and, hence, an elasticity of output per worker with respect to the capital-output ratio equal to 0.4. Thus

21. This calculation assumes, of course, that the supply of funds to the U.S. business sector is highly elastic. This high elasticity does not require high interest elasticity of private saving per se; funds could flow to the business sector from previously tax-favored domestic sectors (e.g., housing) or from foreign investors.

investment per worker (equal to output per worker times the investment-output ratio) rises 7.7 percent. It follows that private consumption per worker, whose increase equals the weighted percentage growth of output per worker less the weighted percentage growth of investment per worker, eventually rises 1.3 percent permanently.

Our estimate of the effect of inflation-induced changes in the user cost of capital on investment is determined in a partial equilibrium setting. This is because we implicitly assume that the supply of funds to the domestic business sector is perfectly elastic. To the extent that household saving and portfolio decisions (e.g., housing capital vs. business fixed capital) are insensitive to changes in net returns, the increase in investment and the capital stock in response to reductions in the user cost of capital will be attenuated.

5.6   Inflation, Differential Taxation, and Capital Allocation

In addition to its effect on the overall level of capital formation, inflation can affect the allocation of capital, leading to distortions in the composition of the nation's capital stock. Such distortions are likely to be large when effective tax rates on capital income vary widely across assets and sectors (as, e.g., in response to the Economic Recovery Tax Act of 1981 in the United States). Measuring the deadweight loss from nonneutral capital taxation requires a model with explicit decisions about saving, capital accumulation, production, and allocation of consumption. In our analysis of the intratemporal efficiency consequences for the allocation of the capital stock of a decline in inflation, we employ a simplified version of the model developed by Auerbach (1989a). Because other papers in this volume deal with intertemporal distortions in detail, we chose to simplify Auerbach's model to the static case. This is especially important in our application because critics of low-inflation policies have often argued that while low inflation can generate steady state efficiency gains, it may exacerbate intratemporal distortions by increasing the importance of differences in depreciation allowances. An assessment of the accuracy of this claim is an important component of any evaluation of the impact of inflation on investment.

The model contains a three-factor production technology (labor, capital, and land) and nine production sectors (agriculture; mining; construction; durable goods manufacturing; nondurable goods manufacturing; transportation, communication, and utilities; wholesale and retail trade; finance, insurance, and real estate; and other services). Each industry potentially uses three fixed capital goods (equipment, nonresidential structures, and residential structures).

Solving the model requires a set of assumptions about technology and preferences. On the technology side, the production function for each sector is of the nested constant elasticity of substitution (CES) form, requiring assumptions about the elasticity of substitution among land and capital goods and the elasticity between each of these and labor. On the preferences side, the house-

Table 5.9   Change in Deadweight Loss from Reducing Inflation

	Change in Deadweight Loss (% of steady state consumption)
Key Parameters	
$\sigma = \omega = e = 1$	−0.01
$\sigma = \omega = 1; e = .25$	−0.03
$\sigma = \omega = 1; e = 2$	0
$\sigma = \omega = .25; e = 1$	0
$\sigma = 2; \omega = .25;$	
$e = 1$	0.02

Source: Authors' calculations.

Note: σ is elasticity of substitution between capital and labor. ω is elasticity of substitution among capital goods (and land). e is intratemporal elasticity of substitution in consumption.

hold utility function is of the nested CES form, with leisure in the first-period nest, requiring assumptions about the intratemporal elasticity of substitution in each period, the intertemporal elasticity of substitution, and the fraction of hours worked in the initial equilibrium. For the baseline case, we adopt the set of parameters adopted by Auerbach (1989a).

Table 5.9 contains our estimates of the change in intratemporal distortion attributable to a permanent reduction of inflation from 4 percent to zero. We assume that the tax on residential structures is zero and the tax on labor is 0.5. Prior to the inflation reduction, the effective tax rate on nonresidential structures is assumed to be 0.425, and the effective tax rate on equipment is assumed to be 0.37 (both values taken from Fullerton and Karayannis 1993). After the reduction, we estimate that the effective tax rate on structures drops to 0.39 while that on equipment drops to 0.31. The table contains our estimates of the effect of this drop on the intratemporal distortion. For base-case values of the elasticity of substitution between capital goods, and between capital and labor, the change in the distortion is almost zero. The relative insensitivity of the intratemporal distortion likely reflects the overwhelming impact of the low tax on residential capital. Thus it seems unlikely that sizable intratemporal distortions can offset the intertemporal gains estimated by Feldstein (1997).

While Auerbach's model accounts for the distortion arising from inflation nonneutralities in the tax system because of differences in capital intensity across different consumption-goods-producing sectors, for tradable goods such distortions are unimportant because goods prices are set in an international market. For nontraded goods, however, a reduction in the user cost of capital accompanying a decline in inflation reduces the price of relatively capital-intensive goods, so that the Auerbach model applies. Many of the most capital-intensive sectors (measured by capital-labor ratios) identified by Fullerton and Rogers (1997) produce nontraded goods (e.g., real estate and transpor-

tation, communications, and utilities). Moreover, efficiency gains from reducing capital taxes actually benefit (relatively) low-income households because of the capital intensity of the weighted average of goods consumed by those households (see Fullerton and Rogers 1997). Thus there may well be distributional benefits to lowering inflation as well. This is an important topic for future research.

5.7   Conclusions and Directions for Future Research

The inflation nonneutralities we have identified in the taxation of household and business capital income indicate that given the current tax code, a reduction in inflation, all else being equal, would stimulate physical capital accumulation in the United States (unless the United States is best modeled as a small open economy in which a typical firm finances investment exclusively with debt). The equilibrium effects on capital formation depend in part on the responsiveness of saving and portfolio allocation to rates of return, making desirable more complete analytic integration of saving and portfolio investment decisions. While such an endeavor is beyond the scope of this paper, more research along these lines is likely to be fruitful.

Would additional physical capital accumulation made possible by lower inflation be socially valuable? Available evidence for the United States indicates that it would be, at least in the case in which the United States is assumed to be a closed economy. Reviewing predictions of several tests of dynamic efficiency, Hassett and Hubbard (1997) conclude that incentives for equipment investment have positive social returns. Cohen, Hassett, and Kennedy (1995) estimate that for the United States, golden rule capital stocks for producers' durable equipment significantly exceed their actual levels over the past two decades. The welfare analyses in Feldstein (1997) and Abel (1997) also suggest significant welfare gains from the increased investment in response to a lower rate of inflation.

An alternative means of reaping such a gain would, of course, be to remove the inflation nonneutralities from the tax codes by, say, indexing the tax code. As long as the tax code attempts to distinguish between debt and equity, however, indexing poses significant practical difficulties (see the discussion in Feldstein 1997). Fundamental reform of the income tax or the replacement of the income tax with a broad-based consumption tax would be required to eliminate inflation distortions arising from the taxation of capital income.[22]

22. Under the Comprehensive Business Income Tax (see Department of the Treasury 1992) or a consumption tax administered as the combination of a wage tax and a business cash-flow tax, the user cost of capital is independent of inflation as long as real depreciation allowances are inflation neutral and the Fisher hypothesis holds approximately; see Hubbard (1997a).

Appendix
Tax Depreciation Allowances in the United States

The amount of depreciation allowed for tax purposes on a capital investment depends on whether the asset is personal property, such as machines and tools, or real property, such as a commercial building, and on the asset's service life or cost recovery period, T, stated in years. Service lives, method of depreciation (straight line vs. declining balance), and first-year conventions currently in use were established in the Tax Reform Act of 1986.

Real Property

Consider a $1 investment in real nonresidential property (excluding land). The service life of real nonresidential property placed in service after May 1993 is 39 years. The straight-line method is used; in its simplest form this implies that in each of the 39 years, $1/39 can be written off. However, expenditure on real property is subject to a midmonth convention in the first year. For example, if the property is initially placed in service any day in January, then for tax purposes it is treated as if the starting date were in the middle of January, and hence the first-year write-off is only $(11.5/12)(\$1/39)$. In general, for an initial investment in month m—where $m = 1$ corresponds to January, $m = 2$ to February, and so on—the first-year write-off is $[(12 - m + 0.5)/12](\$1/39)$. In years 2 through 39, straight-line depreciation is allowed; in year 40, the remaining undepreciated balance is written off.

With a nominal discount rate of d percent per year, the present value of depreciation allowances for a $1 investment in real property is given by

$$z = [1/(1 + d)][(12 - m + 0.5)/12](1/T) + \sum_{l=2}^{T} [1/(1 + d)]^l (1/T)$$
$$+ [1/(1 + d)]^{T+1}(1/T)[1 - ((12 - m + 0.5)/12)].$$

Personal Property

There are several cost recovery periods applicable to personal property. The three-year class includes small tools; the five-year class includes light motor vehicles and computer equipment; the seven-year class includes most machinery and equipment; the ten-year, fifteen-year, and twenty-year classes include a limited number of other assets, such as land improvements. In addition, investment in personal property is subject to a midyear convention in the first year that depreciation is taken; this convention assumes that the property is depreciable for half of the taxable year in which it is placed in service, regardless of the date it actually began to be used.

Further, personal property can be written off using the 200 percent declining-balance (or double declining balance) method of accelerated depreciation. This method results in depreciation that is twice the straight-line

amount in the first year that depreciation is taken (i.e., it is $2/T$ for an investment of $1); because of the half-year convention though, depreciation allowances in the first year are equal to the straight-line amount. In each subsequent year the acceleration factor, $2/T$, is applied only to the remaining undepreciated balance. In the year S that depreciation using the double-declining-balance method falls below that allowed under the straight-line method (as applied only to the remaining $T - S + 1.5$ years), firms are allowed to switch to the straight-line method. For example, the optimal year to switch is the fourth year for assets in the five-year recovery class and the fifth year for assets in the seven-year recovery class.

With a nominal discount rate of d percent per annum, the present value of depreciation allowances for a $1 investment in personal property with service life T is given by

$$z = \sum_{k=1}^{S-1} [1/(1 + d)]^k D_k + \sum_{k=S}^{T} [1/(1 + d)]^k [1 - \sum_{i=1}^{S-1} D_i]/(T - S + 1.5)$$

$$+ [1/(1 + d)]^{T+1} (1/2)[1 - \sum_{i=1}^{S-1} D_i]/(T - S + 1.5), \qquad \text{where}$$

$$D_1 = (1/2)(2/T) = 1/T,$$

$$D_2 = (1 - D_1)(2/T),$$

$$D_3 = (1 - D_1 - D_2)(2/T),\ldots,$$

$$D_{S-1} = (1 - \sum_{i=1}^{S-2} D_i)(2/T).$$

References

Abel, Andrew B. 1997. Comment on "The costs and benefits of going from low inflation to price stability," by Martin Feldstein. In *Reducing inflation: Motivation and strategy,* ed. Christina Romer and David Romer, 156–66. Chicago: University of Chicago Press.

Altshuler, Rosanne, T. Scott Newlon, and William C. Randolph. 1995. Do repatriation taxes matter? Evidence from the tax returns of multinationals. In *The effects of taxation on multinational corporations,* ed. Martin Feldstein, James R. Hines, Jr., and R. Glenn Hubbard. Chicago: University of Chicago Press.

Auerbach, Alan J. 1979. Wealth maximization and the cost of capital. *Quarterly Journal of Economics* 93:433–46.

———. 1981. Inflation and the tax treatment of firm behavior. *American Economic Review* 71 (May): 419–23.

———. 1983. Taxation, corporate financial policy, and the cost of capital. *Journal of Economic Literature* 21 (September): 905–40.

———. 1989a. The deadweight loss from "non-neutral" capital income taxation. *Journal of Public Economics* 40:1–36.

————. 1989b. Tax reform and adjustment costs: The impact on investment and market value. *International Economic Review* 30:939–62.

Auerbach, Alan J., and Kevin Hassett. 1991. Recent U.S. investment behavior and the Tax Reform Act of 1986: A disaggregate view. *Carnegie-Rochester Conference Series on Public Policy* 35 (autumn): 185–215.

————. 1997. On the marginal source of investment funds. Berkeley: University of California, April. Mimeograph.

Bailey, Martin. 1956. The welfare cost of inflationary finance. *Journal of Political Economy* 64 (February): 93–110.

Ball, Laurence. 1994. What determines the sacrifice ratio? In *Monetary policy,* ed. N. Gregory Mankiw. Chicago: University of Chicago Press.

Bayoumi, Tamim, and Joseph Gagnon. 1996. Taxation and inflation: A new explanation for international capital flows. *Journal of Monetary Economics* 38:303–30.

Bradford, David F. 1981. The incidence and allocation effects of a tax on corporate distributions. *Journal of Public Economics* 15:1–22.

Cohen, Darrel, Kevin Hassett, and Jim Kennedy. 1995. Are U.S. investment and capital stocks at optimal levels? Finance and Economics Discussion Series, no. 95-32. Washington, D.C.: Board of Governors of the Federal Reserve System, July.

Cummins, Jason G., Kevin A. Hassett, and R. Glenn Hubbard. 1994. A reconsideration of investment behavior using tax reform as national experiments. *Brookings Papers on Economic Activity,* no. 2: 1–74.

————. 1995. Have tax reforms affected investment? In *Tax policy and the economy,* vol. 9, ed. James M. Poterba. Cambridge, Mass.: MIT Press.

————. 1996. Tax reforms and investment: A cross-country comparison. *Journal of Public Economics* 62:237–73.

Cummins, Jason G., and R. Glenn Hubbard. 1995. The tax sensitivity of foreign direct investment: Evidence from firm-level panel data. In *The effects of taxation on multinational corporations,* ed. Martin Feldstein, James R. Hines, Jr., and R. Glenn Hubbard. Chicago: University of Chicago Press.

Darby, Michael. 1975. The financial and tax effects of monetary policy on interest rates. *Economic Inquiry* 13 (June): 266–76.

Department of the Treasury. 1992. *Integrating the corporate and individual tax systems: Taxing business income once.* Washington, D.C.: Government Printing Office.

Feldstein, Martin. 1976. Inflation, tax rules, and the rate of interest: A theoretical analysis. *American Economic Review* 66 (June): 809–20.

————. 1979. The welfare cost of permanent inflation and optimal short-run economic policy. *Journal of Political Economy* 87 (August): 749–68.

————. 1983. *Inflation, tax rules and capital formation.* Chicago: University of Chicago Press.

————. 1987. Inflation, tax rules, and investment: Some econometric evidence. *Econometrica* 50 (July): 825–62.

————. 1997. The costs and benefits of going from low inflation to price stability. In *Reducing inflation: Motivation and strategy,* ed. Christina Romer and David Romer, 123–56. Chicago: University of Chicago Press.

Feldstein, Martin, Jerry Green, and Eytan Sheshinski. 1978. Inflation and taxes in a growing economy with debt and equity finance. *Journal of Political Economy* 86, no. 2, pt. 2 (April): S53–S70.

Feldstein, Martin, and Lawrence H. Summers. 1979. Inflation and the taxation of capital income in the corporate sector. *National Tax Journal* 32 (December): 445–70.

Fischer, Stanley. 1981. Towards an understanding of the costs of inflation, II. *Carnegie-Rochester Conference Series on Public Policy* 15:15–42.

Fisher, Irving. 1930. *The theory of interest.* New York: Macmillan.

Fullerton, Don, and Marios Karayannis. 1993. United States. In *Tax reform and the cost of capital*, ed. Dale W. Jorgenson and Ralph Landau. Washington, D.C.: Brookings Institution.

Fullerton, Don, and Diane Lim Rogers. 1997. Neglected effects on the uses side: Even a uniform tax would change relative goods prices. *American Economic Review* 87 (May): 120–25.

Gordon, Roger H. 1984. Inflation, taxation, and corporate behavior. *Quarterly Journal of Economics* 94 (May): 313–27.

Hall, Robert E., and Dale W. Jorgenson. 1967. Tax policy and investment behavior. *American Economic Review* 57 (June): 391–414.

Hansson, Ingemar, and Charles Stuart. 1986. The Fisher hypothesis and international capital markets. *Journal of Political Economy* 94 (December): 1330–37.

Harris, Trevor S., R. Glenn Hubbard, and Deen Kemsley. 1997. Are dividend taxes and imputation credits capitalized in share values? New York: Columbia University. Mimeograph.

Hartman, David. 1979. Taxation and the effects of inflation on the real capital stock in an open economy. *International Economic Review* 20 (June): 417–25.

Hassett, Kevin A., and R. Glenn Hubbard. 1997. Tax policy and investment. In *Fiscal policy: Lessons from economic research*, ed. Alan J. Auerbach. Cambridge, Mass.: MIT Press.

———. 1998. Are investment incentives blunted by changes in prices of capital goods? *International Finance* 1 (October): 103–26.

Hines, James R., Jr., and R. Glenn Hubbard. 1990. Coming home to America: Dividend repatriation decisions of U.S. multinationals. In *Taxation and the global economy*, ed. Assaf Razin and Joel Slemrod. Chicago: University of Chicago Press.

———. 1995. Appendix. In *Taxing multinational corporations*, ed. Martin Feldstein, James R. Hines Jr., and R. Glenn Hubbard. Chicago: University of Chicago Press.

Hubbard, R. Glenn. 1995. U.S. tax policy and foreign direct investment: Incentives, problems, and reform. In *Tax policy and economic growth*. Washington, D.C.: American Council for Capital Formation.

———. 1997a. How different are income and consumption taxes? *American Economic Review* 87 (May): 138–42.

———. 1997b. *Money, the financial system, and the economy*, 2d ed. Reading, Mass.: Addison-Wesley.

Joint Committee on Taxation. 1981. *General explanation of the Economic Recovery Tax Act of 1981 (H.R. 4242)*, 97th Cong., 1st sess. Washington, D.C.: Government Printing Office, 29 December.

Jorgenson, Dale W. 1963. Capital theory and investment behavior. *American Economic Review* 53 (May): 247–59.

King, Mervyn A. 1977. *Public policy and the corporation*. London: Chapman and Hall.

King, Mervyn A., and Don Fullerton, eds. 1984. *The taxation of income from capital: A comparative study of the United States, United Kingdom, Sweden, and West Germany*. Chicago: University of Chicago Press.

Levi, Maurice D. 1977. Taxation and "abnormal" international capital flows. *Journal of Political Economy* 85 (June): 635–46.

Mishkin, Frederic S. 1992. Is the Fisher effect for real? *Journal of Monetary Economics* 30:195–215.

Organization for Economic Cooperation and Development. 1992. *Taxing profits in a global economy: Domestic and international issues*. Paris: Organization for Economic Cooperation and Development.

Poterba, James M. 1994. Tax subsidies to owner-occupied housing: An asset market approach. *Quarterly Journal of Economics* 99 (November): 729–45.

Poterba, James M., and Lawrence H. Summers. 1985. The economic effects of dividend taxation. In *Recent advances in corporate finance,* ed. Edward Altman and Marti Subrahmanyam. Homewood, Ill.: Irwin.

Prakken, Joel L., Chris P. Varvares, and Laurence H. Meyer. 1991. Tax reform and potential output: A retrospective analysis of the Tax Reform Act of 1986. *Carnegie-Rochester Conference Series on Public Policy* 35:113–80.

Comment   Alan J. Auerbach

This is an interesting paper that focuses on an important distortion deriving from the interaction of inflation and the tax system, the impact on business fixed investment. It also gives attention to interasset distortions and implicitly raises the issue of the distortion between debt and equity, although not addressing this issue directly.

The authors' basic conclusion is that a reduction in inflation would lower the cost of capital—more so in a closed than an open economy—and lead to more capital accumulation, which, in the current environment, would increase steady state consumption per capita. They find that lowering inflation has a very small welfare effect through its impact on interasset distortions. I am in basic agreement with these results and so will concentrate on the authors' interpretation and on certain questions of methodology.

Before going into details, it is useful to stand back and evaluate these findings. First, a higher steady state level of consumption is not the same as a reduction in deadweight loss. To construct a welfare measure, we need to take transition generations into account. Indeed, the observed outcome could represent a reduction in welfare, depending on the state of other distortions in a second-best situation.

Second, why not calculate such a welfare measure? It would be quite straightforward to do so, using the same model the paper uses to estimate the intratemporal distortions considered in table 5.9. Indeed, this model was originally developed precisely for the purpose of measuring the impact of interasset and intertemporal distortions simultaneously. Even though the intertemporal issue has been considered in other papers, assumptions may differ, leaving us comparing interasset apples to intertemporal oranges. Such a comparison in the same units might be quite enlightening. For example, in the paper where this model was introduced, I found that the reduction in interasset distortions due to the Tax Reform Act of 1986, though small in absolute terms, had roughly same (and offsetting) impact as the rise of several percentage points in the effective tax rate on capital income overall that occurred at same time.

Alan J. Auerbach is the Robert D. Burch Professor of Economics and Law and director of the Burch Center for Tax Policy and Public Finance at the University of California, Berkeley, and a research associate of the National Bureau of Economic Research.

Third, let us consider a fundamental question: why should we attribute to inflation these welfare costs of a higher tax on capital and greater interasset distortions? Perhaps it is plausible for interasset distortions, as it may be tough to adjust specific schedules to keep balance at different rates of inflation. But if inflation causes taxes to rise, why is it so hard to reduce tax rates? There may be frictions, but the possibility that nominal tax rates can change should not be ignored in our discussion. Indeed, changes over time suggest that tax policy does respond. The Accelerated Cost Recovery System was introduced in 1981, in part to compensate for the erosion of depreciation allowances being induced by the high inflation of that period; the depreciation schedules of the Tax Reform Act of 1986 were constructed to deliver roughly the same present value as indexed economic depreciation allowances would have, given the inflation rate prevailing at the time.

Now let us turn to the paper's more specific results, primarily about impact of the tax system on the user cost of capital. To review the theory, inflation raises the effective tax rate due to (1) taxation of the inflation component of nominal capital gains, (2) taxation of the inflation component of interest receipts, and (3) the use of historic cost depreciation allowances; and it lowers the effective tax rate through the deductibility of the inflation component of interest payments. (The paper also considers the impact of FIFO inventory accounting. FIFO accounting certainly raises the cost of holding inventories when inflation is present, but it is unclear from the paper how this effect is being modeled. In any event, the effect as measured in the tables is very small.) Thus a key question is the relative magnitude of tax rates τ_p (at which interest receipts are taxed) and τ_c (at which interest receipts are deducted).

The paper relates the choice of τ_p to the question of whether the economy is open or closed. It imposes the standard Fisher equation for the open economy, consistent with the assumption that marginal debt holders do not face any U.S. tax on interest income. At the other extreme, for the closed economy case, it assumes a value of 0.45 for τ_p compared to 0.35 for the corporate tax. This is a key parameter, and it is not clear where it comes from. My last information from TAXSIM (for 1993) had the value $\tau_p = 0.22$ for individuals; for tax exempts, it is zero, and these two groups make up a large share of debt holdings. Adding foreigners, also at zero, leaves a lot of high marginal tax payments to be made up by the residual holders of debt, such as insurance companies. It seems, then, that the closed economy assumption with respect to τ_p is extreme. Given that the closed and open economy cases are polar ones, it might have been more helpful to present results for a variety of values of τ_p, rather than these two cases.

Before concluding, let me raise one final point. I have trouble with the use of all-equity or all-debt extremes for the open economy case. The paper takes this route because, it argues, an interior solution to the optimal financial ratio is unlikely. But this is true for the closed economy case, too, and simply indicates that our model of financial policy is too simple. Given that we do observe

debt and equity finance in coexistence, it would be helpful to consider intermediate cases.

To conclude, one may ask what else this paper might have considered that would influence its results. One thing in particular comes to mind, the presence of various limitations on the use of tax losses and tax credits. With an increase in inflation, interest expenses increase in real value. On the other hand, inflation reduces the real value of depreciation allowances. If the net impact is to increase the real value of deductions, then inflation lessens the probability of full deduction and, conversely, a decline in the inflation rate would lead to a larger reduction in the cost of capital than the paper estimates. It is not clear which way the net effect goes, but it could be important, given that historically a large number of firms have not been fully taxable.

Discussion Summary

In response to the discussant's remarks, *Glenn Hubbard* said that the paper deliberately focuses on the effects of inflation on steady state consumption because welfare calculations would require controversial assumptions about transition issues and compensating policies. To study the effect of inflation on the allocation of capital, the authors deliberately did not include other distorting margins, such as the intertemporal margin, in order not to confound effects.

Hubbard acknowledged that the endogeneity of political decisions to set taxes is potentially important, although, in practice, the Congress does not appear to have taken this link into account in its discussion of tax bills. Hubbard said that extending the closed economy analysis to the open economy case is harder than dealing with debt and equity because in the open economy case a greater variety of capital allocations is possible.

Benjamin Friedman asked for an intuitive explanation of the authors' conclusion that the marginal gain to a percentage point reduction in inflation is larger at lower levels of inflation. *Hubbard* responded that the effect of inflation is approximately linear on the user cost of capital in terms of levels, and hence, the relative effect is larger at low levels of inflation.

Friedman then asked how the authors' results compare to the results in Martin Feldstein's paper. *Feldstein* responded that it is hard to make a comparison because his results are expressed as welfare gains whereas the results here are in terms of percentage changes in the steady state capital stock.

Finally, *Friedman* inquired about the optimal inflation rate implied by the paper. *Hubbard* responded that they are not suggesting an optimal inflation rate because the paper does not put forth a specific welfare criterion. However, if one simply wanted to maximize steady state capital, a negative inflation rate could be optimal.

Edmund Phelps noted that the golden rule capital stock is problematic in an open economy and suggested that a way around this problem may be found by introducing a variable real exchange rate in the analysis. Otherwise, the capital stock adjustment would be very fast. *Hubbard* agreed that in an open economy there is no golden rule capital stock per se and that all capital adjustments take place instantaneously. *Alan Auerbach* suggested that the welfare adjustment nevertheless may be slow, but *Phelps* argued that the welfare adjustment may be instantaneous because there must be an optimal capital stock on each day.

Laurence Meyer remarked that lower inflation works like an investment incentive in the sense that it lowers the real cost of capital. However, it is crucial that savings increase to finance the investment. If savings do not increase, the interest rate will simply rise, and the capital stock cannot increase. This is why the open economy issue is so important—it implies that there is a very elastic savings supply from abroad.

Martin Feldstein noted that there exists a big puzzle concerning international capital flows. On a daily basis there seem to be huge international capital flows, but when the dust settles, the net flows are relatively small. This may indicate that the large net capital flows predicted by the open economy model may not happen after all.

Matthew Shapiro inquired about the appropriate average marginal tax rate for the calculations, noting that the tax rate of the marginal holder of debt generally differs from the marginal rate faced by the average holder. *Hubbard* responded that they weighted marginal tax rates faced by debt holders by the taxable interest income of each holder, assuming that all debt holders have the same saving elasticity. *Martin Feldstein* noted that this procedure still may not be quite right because some untaxed inframarginal income (e.g., the income of pension funds) should also be part of the weighting. Another participant stressed that it is important to take into account that different people may have different saving elasticities.

Martin Feldstein emphasized the important contribution made by this paper, namely, that the "intratemporal dog did not bark." In other words, the effect of inflation on intratemporal asset misallocations is very small compared to the intertemporal distortions caused by inflation. This important conclusion contradicts the argument that is sometimes made that interasset distortions would be made worse at lower inflation, offsetting the intertemporal efficiency gain. *Hubbard* agreed but added the caveat that they assumed that the same debt-equity ratio was used to finance different assets.

6   Excess Capital Flows and the Burden of Inflation in Open Economies

Mihir A. Desai and James R. Hines Jr.

6.1   Introduction

Access to the world capital market provides economies with valuable borrowing and lending opportunities that are unavailable to closed economies. At the same time, openness to the rest of the world has the potential to exacerbate, or to attenuate, domestic economic distortions such as those introduced by taxation and inflation. This paper analyzes the efficiency costs of inflation-tax interactions in open economies. The results indicate that inflation's contribution to deadweight loss is typically far greater in open economies than it is in otherwise similar closed economies. This much higher deadweight burden of inflation is caused by the international capital flows that accompany inflation in open economies.

Small percentage changes in international capital flows now represent large resource reallocations given two decades of rapid growth of net and gross capital flows in both developed and developing economies. For example, the net capital inflow into the United States grew from an average of 0.1 percent of GNP in 1970–72 to 3.0 percent of GNP in 1985–88. Gross capital flows have also expanded rapidly, as indicated by the growth of international loans from a stock of 5 percent of GNP in industrial countries in 1973 to 17 percent of GNP in 1989 (International Monetary Fund [IMF] 1991). Similarly, the ratio of the stock of foreign direct investment in the United States to U.S. GNP grew from 1.2 percent in 1972 to 7.4 percent in 1990 (Graham and Krugman 1991).

Mihir A. Desai is assistant professor of business administration at Harvard Business School. James R. Hines Jr. is professor of business economics at the University of Michigan Business School and a research associate of the National Bureau of Economic Research.

The authors thank Kathryn Dominguez, Martin Feldstein, Jeffrey Frankel, Erzo Luttmer, James Poterba, and Shang-Jin Wei for helpful comments on an earlier draft.

Inflation rate differences have the potential to reroute much of this international capital because prices inflate at widely different rates around the world. For example, average inflation rates from 1973 to 1989 among OECD countries range from 3.8 percent for Germany to 10.6 percent for the United Kingdom. Variation in inflation experiences is even greater in the developing world, with Malaysia averaging 4.6 percent and Bolivia 206.7 percent during the same period.[1]

The analysis in this paper starts by considering the effects of inflation on saving and investment when governments provide nominal depreciation accounting for tax purposes, firms are able to deduct nominal interest payments, and individual savers are taxed on their nominal interest receipts and capital gains. The model then incorporates open economy considerations, including the taxation of foreign exchange gains and losses, international portfolio capital mobility, and foreign direct investment. The welfare effects of inflation in open domestic and foreign economies are then compared to those in closed economies.

The main finding of this analysis is that inflation in an open economy can generate worldwide reallocations of capital with large associated efficiency consequences. As such, the international dimensions of the effects of inflation are properly considered together with effects that are well known from conventional closed economy analyses. Furthermore, the international effects of inflation-tax interactions suggest that there may be possibilities for efficiency gains through international coordination of monetary and fiscal policies.

Section 6.2 of the paper reviews the effects of inflation in closed and open economies with nominal-based tax systems. Section 6.3 develops an open economy model incorporating inflation-tax interactions and uses the model to analyze the effect of domestic inflation on domestic and foreign interest rates, saving, and investment. Section 6.4 translates the real effects of inflation into efficiency terms in order to contrast its welfare consequences in open and closed economies. Sections 6.5 and 6.6 generalize the model to include consideration of imperfect international capital mobility and foreign direct investment, respectively. Section 6.7 is the conclusion.

6.2 Inflation and Taxation in Closed and Open Economies

Irving Fisher's (1930) hypothesis that nominal interest rates rise by exactly the rate of inflation ($dr/d\pi = 1$, in which r is the nominal rate of interest and π the inflation rate) was once thought to carry the strong implication that inflation does not influence the size of the capital stock because real interest rates and therefore real borrowing costs would not change with inflation. Mundell

---

1. Data drawn from Romer (1993). These figures represent average annual changes in log GDP, or GNP deflators, from 1973 to 1989.

(1963) and Tobin (1965) dispute this conclusion, noting that inflation could raise the capital intensity of an economy through its effect on the demand for liquidity. As nominal interest rates increase, the cost of holding nominal money balances rises, thereby shifting portfolio demand from money to real capital and putting downward pressure on interest rates ($dr/d\pi < 1$). Subsequent work by Darby (1975) and Feldstein (1976) argues that inflation is likely to have the opposite effect on interest rates ($dr/d\pi > 1$) in realistic settings in which savers pay taxes on interest receipts and borrowers deduct interest payments.

Darby and Feldstein observe that the tax structure is based on nominal values. In particular, nominal interest payments are deductible and nominal interest receipts are taxed. As a consequence, inflation has two countervailing effects. Since lenders are taxed on the pure inflation component of interest rates, higher rates of inflation reduce their after-tax returns. At the same time, borrowers deduct their nominal interest payments, and therefore, higher rates of inflation reduce their after-tax borrowing costs. The net effect of inflation on the real rate of interest depends on the difference between tax rates applicable to savers and borrowers. Darby and Feldstein conclude that nominal rates rise by more than the rate of inflation (the modified Fisher hypothesis, or $dr/d\pi > 1$) and that inflation may influence the size of the capital stock in a closed economy. Even after incorporating liquidity effects, Feldstein concludes that, for plausible parameter values, inflation is likely to depress the capital stock of a closed economy through its interaction with the tax structure. While these initial models are limited by their exclusive consideration of investments that are fully debt financed and tax systems that permit assets to be depreciated at economic rates, the results have been extended to consider alternative means of financing and historic cost depreciation (see Feldstein, Green, and Sheshinski 1978; Feldstein 1983).

Hartman (1979) extends this analysis to open economy settings. In particular, he reconsiders the implication that nominal interest rates rise by more than the rate of inflation. In an open economy with flexible exchange rates and purchasing power parity, Hartman concludes that capital flows will remove any real interest rate differentials caused by interactions between tax systems and inflation. In Hartman's model, inflating countries receive capital inflows that prevent interest rates from rising more than one-for-one with inflation. Howard and Johnson (1982) extend this logic to suggest that the interaction of inflation and taxation could result in *either* a worldwide reallocation of capital as suggested by Hartman *or* a violation of purchasing power parity. More recent investigations focus on ways in which details of tax structure may imply something other than the Hartman result. Sorenson (1986) notes that the differential taxation of exchange gains and losses can generate an outcome in which the inflating country does not receive capital inflows, while Sinn (1991) shows that inflation in countries with tax systems that use historic cost depreciation may also have effects other than those Hartman posits. Bayoumi and Gagnon (1996)

suggest that inflation-taxation interactions can explain observed patterns in capital flows between developed countries.

International evidence of the relationship between nominal interest rates and inflation provides tests of these theories. Hansson and Stuart (1986) survey empirical work suggesting that $dr/d\pi$ is close to or less than unity, thereby rejecting the modified Fisher hypothesis. More recent empirical work closely examines certain aspects of this evidence. In particular, Mishkin (1992) analyzes the stochastic trends underlying inflation and interest rates to distinguish between the absence of a short-run Fisher effect and the presence of a long-run Fisher effect.

6.3   A Model of a Small Open Economy with Taxation

In order to assess the effect of interactions between inflation and taxation in open economies, it is helpful to review the reasoning that underlies Hartman's (1979) analysis. This framework is then applied to a more general model of saving and investment in a small open economy.

6.3.1   The Fisher Effect in a Small Open Economy with Taxation

Consider the case of a small open (home) economy. In the notation that follows, foreign variables bear asterisks and domestic variables do not. The expected after-tax net return to foreign lenders ($r_{n,w}$) investing in the small open economy is

$$(1) \qquad r_{n,w} = (1 - \theta^*)r + (1 - g^*)\dot{e}^*,$$

in which θ^* is the foreign tax rate on interest receipts from abroad (inclusive of any withholding taxes), r is the home country nominal interest rate, g^* is the foreign tax rate on exchange-rate-related gains and losses, and $\dot{e}^*$ is the anticipated appreciation (in foreign currency) of domestic assets held by foreign lenders. We assume exchange rates to be determined by purchasing power parity (PPP) in the goods market, which implies $\dot{e}^* = \pi^* - \pi$ (in which π^* is the foreign inflation rate).[2] A small open economy must offer foreign lenders an after-tax rate of return equal to returns available elsewhere.[3] Consequently, capital market equilibrium implies that $dr_{n,w}/d\pi = 0$, and differentiating equation (1) with respect to π implies

$$(2) \qquad \frac{dr}{d\pi} = \frac{1 - g^*}{1 - \theta^*},$$

2. While this assumption is fairly standard, it is important to note that the literature suggests that PPP is best understood as a long-run phenomenon. See, e.g., Abuaf and Jorion (1990), Johnson (1990), Frankel (1991), Wei and Parsley (1995), and Froot, Kim, and Rogoff (1995).

3. Strictly speaking, capital market equilibrium requires that risk-adjusted after-tax returns be equalized. In the certainty framework used here, risk considerations are absent and capital market equilibrium requires only that after-tax returns be equalized. Explicit considerations of risk would greatly complicate the model without significantly changing its implications. See, e.g., Gordon and Varian (1989).

in which it is implicit that $d\pi^*/d\pi = 0$. If foreign tax systems treat exchange-rate-related gains and losses in the same way as ordinary income, $g^* = \theta^*$, and the modified Fisher effect fails to hold because $dr/d\pi = 1$.[4]

This mirrors Hartman's (1979) argument and is consistent with much of the empirical work on the relationship between interest rates and inflation. Hartman infers from this analysis that capital is drawn toward inflating economies. The following analysis indicates that Hartman's result is a special case of a broader set of possible outcomes in which inflation alters the worldwide allocation of capital.

Why does the modified Fisher effect fail to appear in an open economy? The result stems from the fact that inflation does not penalize foreign savers in the same way that it does domestic savers. If PPP holds and foreign-exchange-related gains and losses are taxed in the same way as ordinary income, foreign lenders are able to deduct foreign exchange losses created by home country inflation. By contrast, domestic savers are unable to deduct from their taxable incomes the real losses they incur as a result of domestic inflation. As a consequence, the modified Fisher effect fails to appear, and instead interest rates obey the traditional Fisher relationship $dr/d\pi = 1$.

6.3.2 The Impact of Domestic Inflation on Worldwide Saving and Investment

In order to understand the interaction of inflation and taxation in open economies, it is necessary to specify the way that inflation and taxation affect investment and saving. First, consider the role of perfectly anticipated, permanent changes in domestic inflation in altering the incentives to invest domestically and abroad. Inflation affects domestic investment incentives through the use of historic cost depreciation, the taxation of nominal capital gains, and the ability to deduct interest payments. The incentives to invest abroad may also be affected if domestic inflation changes exchange rates or foreign interest rates. In equilibrium, worldwide inflation-induced changes in investment must equal worldwide inflation-induced changes in saving.

Firms invest up to the point at which after-tax marginal returns equal the after-tax marginal cost of funds:[5]

$$(3) \qquad (1 - \tau)f' - \delta\pi + b\pi = b(1 - \tau)r + (1 - b)s,$$

in which τ is the statutory corporate tax rate, f' is the marginal product of capital (net of depreciation), δ reflects the nominal nature of depreciation allow-

---

4. In practice, the capital-exporting countries whose tax systems are described by Commission of the European Communities (1992, 235–303) generally set $g^* = \theta^*$. For the issues that arise when these tax rates differ, see Levi (1977) and Wahl (1989).

Note that the condition $dr/d\pi = 1$ is also consistent with financial arbitrage for domestic savers. If $g = \theta$ and $dr/d\pi = 1$, then domestic inflation reduces equally after-tax returns to investing at home and abroad.

5. This notation follows that of Feldstein et al. (1978).

ances ($\delta = 0$ implies that the tax system uses economic depreciation),[6] and $b\pi$ is the effect of inflation in reducing the value of nominal debt. The right-hand side of equation (3) consists of two terms, the first of which is the after-tax cost of debt, and the second of which is the after-tax cost of equity (in which s is the required payment to shareholders). The firm is assumed to finance a fraction b of marginal investments with debt and a fraction $1 - b$ with equity.

Differentiating both sides of equation (3) with respect to inflation, and taking b to be unaffected by inflation,[7] yields

$$(4) \qquad (1 - \tau)\frac{df'}{d\pi} = (\delta - b) + b(1 - \tau)\frac{dr}{d\pi} + (1 - b)\frac{ds}{d\pi}.$$

In order to simplify this expression, it is useful to impose the condition that equilibrium net after-tax returns to holding debt and equity are equal:

$$(5) \qquad (1 - \theta)s - c\pi = (1 - \theta)r - \pi,$$

in which c is the tax rate on inflation-induced capital gains. The left-hand side of equation (5) consists of after-tax real returns to equity holders, whose share values appreciate at the rate of inflation but who incur tax obligations at rate c on such appreciation; the right-hand side of equation (5) is the after-tax real return to holding a one-period bond.[8] This specification yields a value of s high enough to imply that firms should generally prefer debt to equity finance because interest payments are deductible and shareholders care only about net returns. Hence, the assumption that b takes a fixed value less than unity is based on considerations, such as bankruptcy, that are omitted from the model.

The shape of the production function determines the extent to which changes in f' translate into changes in investment, K. This relationship is defined locally as $dK \equiv -\gamma\, df'$ (with $\gamma > 0$ for concave functions). Similarly, $dK^* \equiv -\gamma^*\, df'^*$. Differentiating equation (5) to obtain an expression for $ds/d\pi$, substituting the result into equation (4), and using the result that $dr/d\pi = 1$ generates expressions for changes in domestic and foreign investment:

$$(6) \qquad \frac{dK}{d\pi} = -\gamma\left[\frac{\delta - b}{1 - \tau} + b + \frac{(1 - b)(c - \theta)}{(1 - \tau)(1 - \theta)}\right],$$

6. In this formulation, the tax system provides economic depreciation allowances in the absence of inflation, but after-tax values of these allowances erode at rate δ with inflation. Actual depreciation schedules tend to be fixed in nominal terms, generating positive short-run values of δ. Over long periods of time, however, governments may adjust depreciation schedules in response to prevailing inflation rates, thereby reducing δ. Auerbach and Hines (1988) offer evidence of such long-run adjustment for the United States in the postwar period.

7. Optimal choices of b are generally functions of π (and other parameters) rather than fixed values. From the envelope theorem, however, it is appropriate to take b as fixed in calculating the effect of small changes in π on the cost of capital.

8. Eq. (5) is an arbitrage condition for domestic savers, implicitly ruling out the possibility that foreigners are marginal investors in domestic equities (and that domestic savers invest marginal funds in foreign equities). The model assumes that international investment takes the form of debt rather than equity contracts. This assumption, which is consistent with available evidence, is discussed further in sections 6.5 and 6.6.

(7)
$$\frac{dK^*}{d\pi} = -\frac{\gamma^*}{1 - \tau^*}\frac{dr^*}{d\pi}(1 - b^*\tau^*).$$

Equations (6) and (7) express the inflation-induced changes in capital demand to which it is then possible to match inflation-induced changes in the supply of capital.

Domestic saving is a function of the after-tax real rate of return to domestic savers:

(8)
$$r_n = (1 - \theta)r - \pi,$$

in which θ is the personal tax rate on interest receipts. The after-tax real rate of return to foreign savers is

(9)
$$r_n^* = (1 - \theta^*)r^* - \pi^*,$$

in which θ^* is the foreign tax rate on interest receipts. Using equations (8) and (9), it is possible to translate changes in inflation into changes in domestic and foreign saving:

(10)
$$\frac{dS}{d\pi} = -\theta\frac{dS}{dr_n},$$

(11)
$$\frac{dS^*}{d\pi} = \frac{dS^*}{dr_n^*}\frac{dr^*}{d\pi}(1 - \theta^*),$$

in which dS/dr_n denotes the responsiveness of domestic saving to the after-tax rate of return. It is then possible to use the world capital account identity $dK/d\pi + dK^*/d\pi \equiv dS/d\pi + dS^*/d\pi$ to determine $dr^*/d\pi$ and the worldwide capital reallocations that accompany inflation.[9]

Consider first the case in which domestic and foreign firms finance marginal investments exclusively with debt. Suppose in addition that domestic and foreign personal and corporate tax rates are all equal ($\theta = \tau = \tau^* = \theta^*$) and that depreciation allowances reflect economic depreciation ($\delta = \delta^* = 0$). Define the parameter ψ to equal the ratio of the size of the rest of the world's economy to the size of the home economy. Taking behavioral responses to be proportional to economic size, it follows that $\gamma^* = \psi\gamma$ and $dS^*/dr_n^* = \psi\ dS/dr_n$. Equating inflation-induced changes in world capital demand to inflation-induced changes in world capital supply yields

(12)
$$\frac{dr^*}{d\pi} = \frac{1}{\psi}\left(\frac{\tau}{1 - \tau}\right),$$

(13)
$$\frac{dK}{d\pi} = \gamma\frac{\tau}{1 - \tau} = -\frac{dK^*}{d\pi},$$

9. In imposing this identity, the domestic and foreign economies are taken to have single sectors. This formulation abstracts from distortions created by inflation-induced subsidies to certain assets, such as owner-occupied housing.

(14)
$$\frac{dS}{d\pi} = -\tau \frac{dS}{dr} = -\frac{dS^*}{d\pi}.$$

In this special case of 100 percent debt finance, economic depreciation, and all tax rates equal, there is a reallocation of capital but no worldwide reduction in saving and investment. Equation (13) implies that domestic investment increases with inflation and is offset exactly by reduced foreign investment. Similarly, equation (14) indicates that domestic saving is reduced by an amount exactly equal to that by which foreign saving increases. Capital flows to the inflating country from the noninflating rest of the world, which confirms the basic Hartman (1979) result. Note that the mechanism by which this takes place is one in which domestic inflation raises the foreign nominal interest rate, thereby generating capital exports from the noninflating rest of the world to the inflating domestic economy. Moreover, the degree to which domestic inflation affects the foreign nominal interest rate is determined by the relative sizes of the domestic and world economies.

It is useful to consider the effect of alternative tax regimes in which depreciation allowances decline in value as inflation rises ($\delta > 0$), those in which tax rates differ ($\theta \neq \theta^*$), and cases in which firms are financed at least in part by equity ($b < 1$ and $b^* < 1$). In these more general cases, the inflating home economy is described by equations (6) and (10). Note that equation (10) indicates that domestic saving declines with inflation because the behavior of domestic savers is influenced by inflation-induced reductions in real after-tax interest rates. Equation (6) suggests that investment can increase with inflation, as in the special case above, but might alternatively fall with inflation if governments offer historic cost depreciation allowances and if marginal investments are financed in part by equity. Equation (6) further implies that $d^2K/d\pi\, db < 0$ and $d^2K/d\pi\, d\delta < 0$. These inequalities suggest that both the extent to which firms rely on equity finance and the extent to which inflation erodes the present value of depreciation allowances are responsible for reduced domestic investment at higher rates of inflation.

Equations (7) and (11) present results for the rest of the world. Changes in foreign saving and investment depend on the impact of domestic inflation on foreign interest rates. Equating world inflation-induced supply and demand changes, and imposing $dr/d\pi = 1$, produces a modified expression for $dr^*/d\pi$:

(15)
$$\frac{dr^*}{d\pi} = \frac{1}{\psi}\left[\frac{\theta \dfrac{dS}{dr} - \gamma\left(\dfrac{\delta - b}{1 - \tau} + b + \dfrac{(1 - b)(c - \theta)}{(1 - \tau)(1 - \theta)}\right)}{\dfrac{dS}{dr}(1 - \theta^*) + \dfrac{\gamma}{1 - \tau^*}(1 - b^*\tau^*)} \right].$$

The sign of $dr^*/d\pi$ in equation (15) is indeterminate but can be easily evaluated in the case in which capital gains are taxed at ordinary income rates ($c = \theta$) and saving and investment elasticities are equal ($\gamma = dS/dr$). In this case, there are two alternatives, which are summarized in table 6.1.

Table 6.1   Summary of Influence of Domestic Inflation on Worldwide Interest Rates, Saving, and Investment

	A $\delta < b\tau$		B $\delta > b\tau$		
	Domestic	Foreign	Domestic	Foreign	
				$\theta > (\delta - b\tau)/(1-\tau)$	$\theta < (\delta - b\tau)/(1-\tau)$
Interest rate	$\dfrac{dr}{d\pi} = 1$	$\dfrac{dr^*}{d\pi} > 0$	$\dfrac{dr}{d\pi} = 1$	$\dfrac{dr^*}{d\pi} > 0$	$\dfrac{dr^*}{d\pi} < 0$
Saving	$\dfrac{dS}{d\pi} < 0$	$\dfrac{dS^*}{d\pi} > 0$	$\dfrac{dS}{d\pi} < 0$	$\dfrac{dS^*}{d\pi} > 0$	$\dfrac{dS^*}{d\pi} < 0$
Investment	$\dfrac{dK}{d\pi} > 0$	$\dfrac{dK^*}{d\pi} < 0$	$\dfrac{dK}{d\pi} < 0$	$\dfrac{dK^*}{d\pi} < 0$	$\dfrac{dK^*}{d\pi} > 0$

Note: Interest rates, inflation, saving levels, and investment are denoted by r, π, S, and K, respectively. Foreign variables are denoted with an asterisk, τ denotes the domestic corporate tax rate, θ denotes the domestic personal tax rate on interest income, b denotes the fraction of investment financed by debt domestically, and δ denotes the degree of historic depreciation accounting for tax purposes (where $\delta = 0$ corresponds to economic depreciation). The above calculations assume that the domestic tax rate on interest income equals the domestic tax rate on capital gains ($\theta = c$) and a nonnegative elasticity of saving with respect to the real rate of return ($\eta_{sr} > 0$).

Panel A of table 6.1 outlines the results when $\delta < b\tau$. If $\delta < b\tau$, foreign nominal interest rates rise with domestic inflation, foreign investment declines, and foreign saving rises. Inflation reduces domestic saving by lowering the after-tax domestic real interest rate and increases domestic investment because the benefits of nominal interest deductibility outweigh the tax costs imposed by historic cost depreciation. Consequently, capital flows from the noninflating rest of the world to the inflating country. The case in which $\delta > b\tau$ is outlined in panel B and is somewhat more complex. If $\delta > b\tau$, domestic saving *and* domestic investment decline with inflation because the tax penalties associated with historic cost depreciation exceed the benefits of nominal interest deductibility. Signs of the effects of inflation on foreign nominal interest rates, saving, and investment then depend on more detailed parameter values.

The intuition for the effects of τ, δ, and b is fairly straightforward. As firms use more debt or pay taxes at higher statutory rates, they benefit from the ability to deduct nominal interest payments—so inflation can stimulate domestic investment. On the other hand, to the degree that the tax system provides something other than economic depreciation allowances, higher rates of inflation raise the cost of capital and discourage investment. In cases in which $c \neq \theta$, the sign of $dr*/d\pi$ depends as well on elasticities of capital supply and demand.

The magnitude of the effect of domestic inflation on foreign nominal interest rates, expressed in equation (15), can be illustrated by reference to specific parameter values. Table 6.2 presents values of $dr*/d\pi$ for a range of home country parameters. For purposes of the calculations presented in table 6.2, the home country's economy is taken to represent 9 percent of the world economy ($\psi = 10$).[10] Foreign parameters are fixed at $b* = 0.5$, $\theta* = 0.35$, $\delta* = 0.1$, and $\tau* = 0.35$. For the base case in the center of table 6.2, a 1 percentage point rise in domestic inflation increases the world interest rate by 0.0091 percent. For the range of home country parameter values considered in table 6.2, the magnitude of the change in the world interest rate accompanying a 1 percentage point change in domestic inflation ranges from -0.0158 to 0.0788 percent for a 1 percentage point change in domestic inflation.[11]

The sensitivity of $dr*/d\pi$ to home country parameters is evident from the pattern within table 6.2. For example, the greatest values of $dr*/d\pi$ appear in cases in which corporate tax rates are highest and debt financing most perva-

10. The relevant value of ψ depends on country size. Using the 1993 share of world output as a measure of the relative size of an economy, ψ is 2.8 for the United States, 4.6 for Japan, 11.7 for Germany, 24.0 for the United Kingdom, and 51.4 for Spain. These measures are based on data from World Bank (1995) and IMF (1997). Measures of ψ based on saving or investment differ from these based on GDP. For example, the values of ψ for the United States and Japan are reversed, 4.6 and 2.8, respectively, when ψ is measured on the basis of saving.

11. Strictly speaking, arbitrage in world capital markets implies that $dr/d\pi = 1 + dr*/d\pi$. While the approximation that $dr/d\pi = 1$ is valid for small open economies, a precise analysis of inflation in a large open economy should incorporate this more accurate value. From a practical standpoint, however, this adjustment is unlikely to make a major difference to estimated welfare costs of inflation, even for large economies such as those of the United States and Japan.

Table 6.2   **Sensitivity of $dr*/d\pi$ to Home Country Parameters**

	$\tau = 0.20$ (1)	$\tau = 0.35$ (2)	$\tau = 0.50$ (3)
$b = 1.0$			
$\delta = 0.0$	0.0197	0.0424	0.0788
$\delta = 0.1$	0.0098	0.0303	0.0630
$\delta = 0.2$	0.0000	0.0182	0.0473
$b = 0.5$			
$\delta = 0.0$	0.0098	0.0212	0.0394
$\delta = 0.1$	0.0000	**0.0091**	0.0236
$\delta = 0.2$	−0.0099	−0.0030	0.0079
$b = 0.2$			
$\delta = 0.0$	0.0039	0.0085	0.0158
$\delta = 0.1$	−0.0059	−0.0036	0.0000
$\delta = 0.2$	−0.0158	−0.0158	−0.0158

Notes: Col. (1) presents inflation-induced changes in foreign interest rates when the domestic corporate tax rate, τ, is 20 percent. Cols. (2) and (3) report results for the same calculation when the domestic corporate tax rates are 35 and 50 percent, respectively.

The parameter b denotes the fraction of domestic investment financed at the margin by debt, and δ is a measure of the degree to which depreciation accounting for tax purposes is sensitive to inflation ($\delta = 0$ corresponds to zero sensitivity, or economic depreciation). The calculations take the domestic tax rate on interest income to be equal to the domestic tax rate on capital gains ($\theta = c$). The fraction of foreign investment financed at the margin by debt, $b*$, is taken to equal 0.5, and the foreign corporate tax rate, $\tau*$, is taken to equal 35 percent. The calculations also assume a zero elasticity of saving with respect to the real rate of return ($\eta_{sr} = 0$) and that the domestic economy is one-tenth the size of the world economy ($\psi = 10$, which roughly characterizes Germany).

The base case is shown in boldface.

sive (inflation thereby generating the largest subsidies to domestic corporate borrowers) and departures from economic depreciation the smallest (inflation thereby imposing the smallest costs of lost real depreciation allowances). By encouraging domestic investment, inflation is responsible for capital movement from the rest of the world to the inflating country—thereby raising foreign interest rates.

The cases in which $dr*/d\pi < 0$ are those for which inflation reduces domestic saving and domestic investment. If $dr*/d\pi < 0$, then domestic investment falls by *more* than does domestic saving due to erosion of depreciation allowances by inflation and higher costs of investment funds consisting partly of equity. In such cases, capital flows from the domestic economy to the foreign economy, thereby reducing the foreign interest rate, discouraging foreign saving and stimulating foreign investment. The cases in which $dr*/d\pi = 0$ consist of situations in which inflation discourages domestic saving and domestic investment equally, thereby requiring no international capital movement in order to maintain capital balances—and, consequently, no change in the foreign interest rate.

In each of these scenarios the underlying logic is the same. First, the ability of foreign lenders to deduct foreign exchange losses forces domestic nominal

interest rates to rise one-for-one with inflation. Second, the degree to which domestic inflation penalizes domestic saving relative to domestic investment then determines whether capital enters or leaves the inflating country and the extent to which foreign interest rates are affected.

6.4   Efficiency Consequences of Inflation in a Small Open Economy

A consistent analysis of the efficiency consequences of inflation in open economies includes consideration of the deadweight losses generated by inflation together with the implications of inflation for tax revenue. Higher rates of inflation typically, though not uniformly, generate greater tax revenue while exacerbating tax distortions. Since tax revenue is valuable to governments whose alternative sources of revenue are distortionary, the costs of inflation-induced distortions must be weighed against the benefits of greater tax revenue. Additionally, inflation affects economic efficiency and tax revenue in two ways: through its interaction with the personal income tax and through its interaction with the corporate income tax. Consequently, a consistent welfare analysis has four components: $d\mathrm{DWL}_p/d\pi$, $d\mathrm{DWL}_c/d\pi$, $d\mathrm{REV}_p/d\pi$, and $d\mathrm{REV}_c/d\pi$, where p, for personal, denotes the effect of interactions between inflation and personal income taxes and c, for corporate, denotes the effect of interactions between inflation and corporate income taxes.

This section derives expressions for the home and world welfare effects of inflation in open economies, in the process demonstrating that the world efficiency impact of inflation is a function of disparities between domestic and rest-of-world inflation rates. The revenue impact of inflation in a small open economy is then integrated with deadweight loss considerations to generate overall welfare effects of inflation. The analysis then estimates these effects for realistic cases using a modified version of the methodology employed by Feldstein (chap. 1 in this volume).

6.4.1   Deadweight Loss Due to Inflation-Induced Capital Flows

The efficiency consequences of inflation-induced international capital movements appear even in the very simplified case analyzed earlier. Specifically, consider again the case in which domestic and foreign firms finance their investments entirely with debt ($b = b^* = 1$), domestic and foreign tax systems provide economic depreciation allowances ($\delta = \delta^* = 0$), and all tax rates are equal ($\theta = \tau = \tau^* = \theta^*$). The effect of inflation on the welfare of a small open economy can be decomposed into the effect of inflation on the allocation of consumption and the effect of inflation on the allocation of investment.

It is useful to consider intertemporal consumption distortions in a two-period framework in which individuals save in the first period to finance consumption in the second. In the home country, the after-tax real price of second-period consumption (p_2^a), measured in first-period units, is $p_2^a = 1/[1 + r(1 - \theta) - \pi]^T$, where T is the number of years that elapses between first-period

saving and second-period consumption. The before-tax real price of second-period consumption (p_2^b), measured in first-period units, is $p_2^b = 1/(1 + r - \pi)^T$. The difference between these two prices represents the wedge introduced by the tax system and its interaction with inflation.

The effect of inflation on the efficiency of intertemporal consumption is represented by the interaction of inflation-induced compensated changes in demand for second-period consumption with the tax wedge identified above. As always in analyzing tax-induced deadweight loss, it is important to use compensated rather than uncompensated demand schedules; more specifically, as noted by Feldstein (1978), the compensated demand derivative with which the tax wedge is properly interacted is that for second-period consumption rather than that for saving. Denoting the derivative of compensated demand for second-period consumption by dC_2/dp_2^a, the domestic deadweight loss from the consumption reallocation that accompanies a small change in inflation is $-(dC_2/dp_2^a)(dp_2^a/d\pi)(p_2^a - p_2^b)$. Imposing $dr/d\pi = 1$, this deadweight loss can be expressed as

$$(16) \quad \frac{d\mathrm{DWL_p}}{d\pi} = -\frac{dC_2}{dp_2^a}\frac{dp_2^a}{d\pi}(p_2^a - p_2^b) \cong -T\theta\frac{dC_2}{dp_2^a}p_2^a(p_2^a - p_2^b),$$

in which the approximation is valid at low after-tax real interest rates.[12]

Interactions between inflation and the corporate income tax also carry welfare implications. Equations (3) and (5) together imply a value for the marginal product of capital: $f' = r - \pi/(1 - \tau)$. Hence the difference between the marginal product of capital and the pretax real rate of return $f' - (r - \pi)$ equals $-\tau\pi/(1 - \tau)$ in this special case. This negative tax wedge may at first seem paradoxical because, in a world without inflation, the effective tax rate is zero if tax systems provide economic depreciation deductions and marginal investments are financed by debt. The negative effective tax rate reflects that inflation subsidizes investment by increasing deductible nominal interest payments.

The welfare effect of a change in inflation equals the product of any inflation-induced investment change and the difference between the after-tax and before-tax marginal products of capital. Accordingly,

$$(17) \quad \frac{d\mathrm{DWL_c}}{d\pi} = \frac{\gamma\tau^2\pi}{(1 - \tau)^2}.$$

Adding this to the deadweight loss generated by the personal income tax yields[13]

12. Formally, $dp_2^a/d\pi = \theta Tp_2^a/[1 + r(1 - \theta) - \pi]$, which approximates θTp_2^a if the after-tax real interest rate is close to zero.

13. Note that it is appropriate to sum deadweight losses from interactions between inflation and personal taxes and inflation and corporate taxes because the benchmark real rate of interest, $r - \pi$, is common to both calculations. In a closed economy, such a calculation corresponds to measuring the sizes of two pieces that together make up the Harberger triangle. In an open economy the calculation is somewhat more complicated because inflation-induced changes in saving need not equal changes in investment.

(18) $$\frac{d\text{DWL}}{d\pi} = \frac{\gamma\tau^2\pi}{(1-\tau)^2} - T\theta\frac{dC_2}{dp_2^a}p_2^a(p_2^a - p_2^b),$$

which is unambiguously positive. Inflation reduces the efficiency of domestic resource allocation both in consumption, by discouraging second-period consumption that is already penalized by the tax system, and in investment, by encouraging investment that (in the case of pure debt financing and economic depreciation) is already subsidized by the tax system.

In this scenario, inflation improves the quality of resource allocation in foreign countries. Inflation increases foreign saving and reduces foreign investment; since the foreign tax system penalizes saving and subsidizes investment, each of these changes reduces deadweight loss in the foreign country. Specifically, domestic inflation changes foreign deadweight loss by

(19) $$\frac{d\text{DWL}^*}{d\pi} = T\tau p_2^{a^*}(p_2^{a^*} - p_2^{b^*})\frac{dC_2}{dp_2^{a^*}} - \frac{\gamma\tau^{*2}\pi^*}{(1-\tau^*)^2}.$$

Note that this expression is independent of ψ, the ratio of the sizes of the rest of the world and the domestic economy. Intuitively, higher values of ψ imply that domestic inflation has a smaller effect on foreign interest rates but that the impact of higher interest rates applies to a larger world economic base, thereby generating an equivalent deadweight loss.

The same terms appear (with opposite signs) in both equations (18) and (19), thereby suggesting that world welfare might not be affected by inflation. While it is true that domestic inflation reduces deadweight loss in the rest of the world, it does not follow that this reduction is of the same magnitude as the positive impact of inflation on deadweight loss in the home country. This can be illustrated by adding equations (18) and (19) and imposing equality between the tax and behavioral patterns of the two countries other than their inflation rates (so that, for example, $r^* - \pi^* = r - \pi$):

(20)

$$\frac{d(\text{DWL} + \text{DWL}^*)}{d\pi} = \frac{\gamma\tau^2}{(1-\tau)^2}(\pi - \pi^*)$$

$$+ T\tau\frac{dC_2}{dp_2^a}[p_2^{a^*}(p_2^{a^*} - p_2^{b^*}) - p_2^a(p_2^a - p_2^b)].$$

Inspection of equation (20) verifies that $d(\text{DWL} + \text{DWL}^*)/d\pi = 0$ when $\pi = \pi^*$, since the first term on the right-hand side is zero, as is the second term, by virtue of the equalities $p_2^a = p_2^{a^*}$ and $p_2^b = p_2^{b^*}$. This is a sensible result, since the foreign and domestic economies are identical when $\pi = \pi^*$, making the world equivalent to a large closed economy. Darby (1975) and Feldstein (1976) show that inflation does not reduce the welfare of a closed economy with debt-financed investments and economic depreciation because inflation does not change after-tax real interest rates and borrowing costs.

In order to characterize the global welfare properties of inflation, it is useful to differentiate both sides of equation (20) with respect to π:

(21)
$$\frac{d^2(\text{DWL} + \text{DWL}^*)}{d\pi^2} = \frac{\gamma\tau^2}{(1 - \tau)^2} + T^2\tau^2 \frac{dC_2}{dp_2^a}$$

$$\left\{ \frac{1}{\psi}\left[(p_2^{a*})^{1+1/T}p_2^{b*} + \frac{p_2^{a*}(p_2^{b*})^{1+1/T}}{1 - \tau} - 2(p_2^{a*})^{2+1/T} \right] \right.$$

$$\left. + \left[(p_2^a)^{1+1/T}p_2^b - 2(p_2^a)^{2+1/T} \right] \right\}.$$

The first term on the right-hand side of equation (21) is positive, and since $dC_2/dp_2^a < 0$, the second term is also positive if the expression in braces is less than zero. In evaluating the sign of this expression, it is useful to note that $p_2^a > p_2^b$, $p_2^{a*} > p_2^{b*}$, and, if $\pi > \pi^*$, $p_2^a > p_2^{a*}$ while $p_2^b > p_2^{b*}$. As a result, an upper bound of the absolute value of the expression in braces can be obtained by evaluating the expression if $p_2^a = p_2^b = p_2^{a*} = p_2^{b*}$:

(22)
$$\frac{d^2(\text{DWL} + \text{DWL}^*)}{d\pi^2} \geq \frac{\gamma\tau^2}{(1 - \tau)^2}$$

$$+ T^2\tau^2 \frac{dC_2}{dp_2^a}(p_2^a)^{2+1/T}\left[\frac{1}{\psi}\left(\frac{1}{1 - \tau} - 1 \right) - 1 \right].$$

The term in brackets on the right-hand side of equation (22) is less than zero as long as $\tau < \psi/(1 + \psi)$. Since the rest of the world is taken to be large relative to the inflating economy, this condition is equivalent to the realistic case of tax rates less than 100 percent. Consequently, both terms on the right-hand side of equation (22) are positive, and $d^2(\text{DWL} + \text{DWL}^*)/d\pi^2 > 0$.

Figure 6.1 depicts the relationship between deadweight loss and inflation differences. The $d(\text{DWL} + \text{DWL}^*)/d\pi$ schedule is upward sloping and takes a value of zero at $\pi = \pi^*$. Accordingly, as is evident from the figure, $d(\text{DWL} + \text{DWL}^*)/d\pi$ takes the same sign as $\pi - \pi^*$. The deadweight loss function is also nonlinear in π, generally taking a convex form (as pictured).

Equation (20) indicates that the aggregate welfare cost of domestic inflation depends on existing disparities between national inflation rates. In the scenario under consideration, greater domestic inflation improves world welfare if the rest of the world has a higher rate of inflation.[14] Conversely, if the domestic inflation rate exceeds the world inflation rate, higher domestic inflation reduces world welfare. The international reallocations that accompany inflation stem

---

14. It is worth emphasizing that this result depends on the values of relevant parameters. There exist scenarios in which higher domestic inflation reduced world welfare, even though world inflation rates exceed the domestic rate.

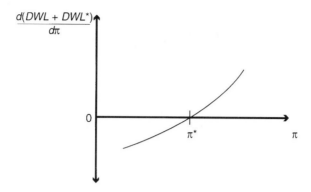

Fig. 6.1   World welfare and inflation disparities
Note: The figure depicts the relationship between disparities in inflation rates ($\pi - \pi^*$) and the effect of inflation on world welfare. It is evident from the figure that $d(\text{DWL} + \text{DWL}^*)/d\pi$ takes the same sign as $\pi - \pi^*$.

from the fact that foreign lenders deduct exchange losses when calculating their taxable incomes. Domestic inflation increases nominal interest rates by the same amount that it reduces expected exchange gains of foreign lenders. Consequently, domestic inflation does not generate any additional tax liabilities for foreign lenders. But domestic lenders, who are taxed on their nominal interest receipts without any adjustments for inflation, face lower after-tax real interest rates and therefore save less as inflation rises. Domestic corporations deduct nominal interest payments and therefore invest more at higher rates of inflation. As a result, capital flows from noninflating countries to inflating countries.

These international capital reallocations are costly because they imply that too little saving and too much investing take place in inflating countries relative to noninflating countries. It is noteworthy that the nonzero deadweight loss derivative in equation (20) appears in a scenario—one in which firms finance their marginal investments with debt and governments provide depreciation allowances that do not erode with inflation—in which inflation would not generate deadweight loss if the economy were closed. All of the deadweight loss described in equation (20) comes from international capital movements and associated effects.

In the more general case in which governments provide historic cost depreciation and investments are financed at least in part by equity, the expression for the component of deadweight loss generated by personal taxation is unchanged from equation (16). The expression for the component of deadweight loss generated by corporate taxation does, however, change, as the expressions for the preexisting tax wedge and inflation-induced change in domestic investment become somewhat more complicated. Taking $c = \theta$ for simplicity, the domestic deadweight loss due to interactions between inflation and corporate taxation systems is

(23) $\quad \dfrac{d\text{DWL}_c}{d\pi} = \dfrac{\gamma}{(1 - \tau)^2}\{(\delta - \tau b)[r\tau(1 - b) + \pi(\delta - \tau)]\}.$

This expression can be understood as the product of the investment response, represented by $\gamma(\delta - b\tau)/(1 - \tau)$, and the preexisting distortion, represented by $[r\tau(1 - b) + \pi(\delta - \tau)]/(1 - \tau)$. Relative values of δ and $b\tau$ dictate whether inflation encourages or discourages domestic investment. The sign of the preexisting distortion indicates whether effective tax rates are positive or negative. Their product determines whether deadweight losses are positive or negative. For example, if the effective tax rate is positive and inflation discourages domestic investment, equation (23) is positive. If the effective tax rate is negative and inflation encourages domestic investment, equation (23) is again positive.

Expressions for foreign deadweight loss in the general case are slightly more complicated than that in equation (19). Deadweight losses generated by interactions between inflation and foreign corporate and personal taxes are

(24) $\quad \dfrac{d\text{DWL}_p^*}{d\pi} = T\dfrac{dr^*}{d\pi}(1 - \theta^*)p_2^{a*}(p_2^{a*} - p_2^{b*})\dfrac{dC_2^*}{dp_2^{a*}},$

(25)
$$\dfrac{d\text{DWL}_c^*}{d\pi} = \dfrac{\gamma^*}{(1 - \tau^*)^2}[r^*\tau^*(1 - b^*)$$
$$+ \pi^*(\delta^* - \tau^*)]\dfrac{dr^*}{d\pi}(1 - b^*\tau^*),$$

where $dr^*/d\pi$ is as represented in equation (15).

6.4.2 The Revenue Impact of Inflation

Inflation rates influence tax collections, which in turn have welfare implications since alternative sources of tax revenue are generally distortionary. The impact of inflation on the present value of personal income tax revenue is

(26) $\quad \dfrac{d\text{REV}_p}{d\pi} = \dfrac{dp_2^a}{d\pi}C_2 + (p_2^a - p_2^b)\dfrac{dC_2}{dp_2^a}\dfrac{dp_2^a}{d\pi}.$

The first term in equation (26) reflects revenue obtained by changing the price of retirement consumption, while the second term reflects the revenue effect of changes in retirement consumption, holding its price constant. In general, the sign of equation (26) is indeterminate. The impact of inflation on corporate tax revenue is similarly

(27) $\quad \dfrac{d\text{REV}_c}{d\pi} = \dfrac{df'}{d\pi}K - [f' - (r - \pi)]\dfrac{df'}{d\pi}\gamma.$

In order to unify the analysis of deadweight loss and revenue effects of inflation, it is necessary to assign a shadow value to government revenue equal to

$1 + \lambda$, in which a value of $\lambda > 0$ reflects the deadweight loss that accompanies alternative sources of tax revenue. Accordingly, the overall effect of inflation on social welfare is

$$(28) \qquad \frac{d\text{SW}}{d\pi} = \lambda \frac{d\text{REV}}{d\pi} - \frac{d\text{DWL}}{d\pi},$$

where SW denotes social welfare.

6.4.3 Estimation of the Welfare Impact of Inflation

In order to estimate magnitudes of equation (28) it is helpful to use the empirical framework sketched by Feldstein (chap. 1 in this volume). Interactions between inflation and the personal income tax generate deadweight loss given by

$$(29) \qquad \frac{d\text{DWL}_p}{d\pi} = -(p_2^a - p_2^b)\frac{dC_2}{dp_2^a}\frac{dp_2^a}{d\pi},$$

where

$$\frac{dp_2^a}{d\pi} = T\left[1 - \frac{dr}{d\pi}(1 - \theta)\right]p_2^a\frac{1}{1 + r(1 - \theta) - \pi}$$

and T is the number of years in a period. Equation (29) can be transformed into a direct analogue of Feldstein's equation (4):

$$(30) \qquad \frac{d\text{DWL}_p}{d\pi} = (p_2^a - p_2^b)\left(\frac{1}{p_2^a}\right)^2\frac{dp_2^a}{d\pi}S_2(1 - \eta_{Sp} - \sigma),$$

in which S_2 is saving in preretirement years, η_{Sp} is the uncompensated elasticity of saving with respect to the price of retirement consumption, and σ is the propensity to save out of exogenous income. Further manipulation yields an expression that is easily calibrated. Taking $\eta_{Sp} = 0$, $\sigma = 0.12$, and $S_2 = 0.09\text{GDP}$,[15] equation (30) becomes

$$(31) \qquad \frac{d\text{DWL}_p}{d\pi} = (p_2^a - p_2^b)\left(\frac{1}{p_2^a}\right)^2\frac{dp_2^a}{d\pi}(0.0792\text{GDP}).$$

In order to evaluate this expression, it is useful to assume that 30 years elapse between periods and to consider the case that $r = 0.07$, $\pi = 0.02$, and $\theta = 0.35$ in a small open economy in which $dr/d\pi = 1$. Under these assumptions, $d\text{DWL}_p/d\pi = 0.4115\text{GDP}$, which is similar to estimates reported by Feldstein (chap. 1 in this volume).[16]

---

15. This value of preretirement saving is derived by linking preretirement saving with national income account measures of personal saving as in Feldstein (chap. 1 in this volume).

16. This estimate implies that a 2 percent reduction in inflation produces an efficiency gain of 0.823 percent of GDP per year; Feldstein estimates the gain to be 0.730 percent of GDP per year.

A similar procedure can be used to estimate the revenue consequences of domestic inflation. Equation (26) can be transformed to yield

$$(32) \quad \frac{d\text{REV}_p}{d\pi} = \frac{dp_2^a}{d\pi} \frac{1}{p_2^a} S_2 \left[1 - (p_2^a - p_2^b) \frac{1}{p_2^a} (1 - \eta_{Sp} - \sigma) \right].$$

Assuming the uncompensated elasticity of saving with respect to the after-tax interest rate to be zero and taking $r = 0.07$, $\pi = 0.02$, and $\theta = 0.35$, it follows that $d\text{REV}_p/d\pi = 0.5100\text{GDP}$. With $\lambda = 0.4$, the overall welfare impact of interactions between inflation and personal income taxes is $d\text{SW}_p/d\pi = -0.2075\text{GDP}$.[17]

The distinguishing difference between inflation-induced deadweight losses in open and closed economies lies in values of $dr/d\pi$ and, consequently, $dp_2^a/d\pi$. In an open economy, $dr/d\pi = 1$ due to arbitrage in the world capital market, while in a closed economy, $dr/d\pi$ varies with the underlying parameters of the economy. The appendix presents an analogous closed economy model for which it derives $dr/d\pi$. Table 6.3 illustrates the difference between closed and open economies by presenting estimates of $dr/d\pi$ in closed economies and using these values to estimate the components of the welfare effect of interactions between inflation and personal income taxes in closed economies: $(d\text{DWL}_p/d\pi)^{\text{closed}}$ and $(d\text{REV}_p/d\pi)^{\text{closed}}$. These values are then used to construct ratios of welfare losses from personal income taxes in open and closed economies.

The first line of table 6.3 evaluates the Feldstein-Darby case of 100 percent debt financing and economic depreciation allowances. The closed economy is not distorted by inflation because the nominal interest rate rises sufficiently to generate no change in the after-tax price of retirement consumption. Since inflation is responsible for deadweight loss in small open economies, the ratio of deadweight losses in open and closed economies, provided in column (7), is infinite. Realistic alternative scenarios with some nondebt financing and departures from economic depreciation offer additional information. The ratio of deadweight losses in open and closed economies varies directly with values of $(dr/d\pi)^{\text{closed}}$. Intuitively, the ratio of deadweight losses in open and closed economies equals unity when $(dr/d\pi)^{\text{closed}} = 1$. If $(dr/d\pi)^{\text{closed}} > 1$, then $(dp_2^a/d\pi)^{\text{closed}} < (dp_2^a/d\pi)^{\text{open}}$, which implies that the efficiency costs of interactions between inflation and personal income taxes are more modest in closed economies than in open economies. Alternatively, if $(dr/d\pi)^{\text{closed}} < 1$, then

---

17. There is considerable dispute over the correct value of λ for the U.S. economy. Ballard, Shoven, and Whalley (1985) estimate values of λ between 0.17 and 0.56, on the basis of which (in addition to other calculations) many authors use $\lambda = 0.40$ as a baseline for deadweight loss calculations. For considerably higher estimates of λ, see Feldstein (1995).

It is possible to calculate the implied values of λ for the model by comparing marginal tax revenue and marginal deadweight losses as tax rates vary. At baseline parameter values, the model implies $\lambda = 0.22$ if corporate taxes are the marginal source of funds and $\lambda = 0.81$ if personal taxes are the marginal source of funds. Hence, $\lambda = 0.40$ appears to be a reasonable baseline case.

Table 6.3 Deadweight Loss and Revenue of Domestic Inflation in Open and Closed Economies: Personal Income Taxation

	$\left(\dfrac{dr}{d\pi}\right)^{closed}$	$\left(\dfrac{dp_2^a}{d\pi}\right)^{closed}$	$\left(\dfrac{dDWL_p}{d\pi}\right)^{closed}$	$\left(\dfrac{dREV_p}{d\pi}\right)^{closed}$	$\left(\dfrac{dDWL_p}{d\pi}\right)^{open}$	$\left(\dfrac{dREV_p}{d\pi}\right)^{open}$	$\dfrac{dSW_p^{open}}{d\pi} / \dfrac{dSW_p^{closed}}{d\pi}$
	(1)	(2)	(3)	(4)	(5)	(6)	(7)
$b = 1.0$							
$\delta = 0.0$	1.5385	0.0000	0.0000GDP	0.0000GDP	0.4115GDP	0.5100GDP	$-\infty$
$\delta = 0.1$	1.3849	1.3721	0.1174	0.1455	0.4115	0.5100	3.5044
$\delta = 0.2$	1.2313	2.7440	0.2348	0.2929	0.4115	0.5100	1.7524
$b = 0.5$							
$\delta = 0.0$	1.2127	2.9102	0.2490	0.3085	0.4115	0.5100	1.6523
$\delta = 0.1$	1.0917	3.9908	0.3414	0.4321	0.4115	0.5100	1.2049
$\delta = 0.2$	0.9708	5.0711	0.4339	0.5376	0.4115	0.5100	0.9482
$b = 0.2$							
$\delta = 0.0$	1.0761	4.1302	0.3534	0.4378	0.4115	0.5100	1.1643
$\delta = 0.1$	0.9689	5.0886	0.4354	0.5394	0.4115	0.5100	0.9450
$\delta = 0.2$	0.8616	6.0468	0.5173	0.6410	0.4115	0.5100	0.7952

Notes: Col. (1) indicates the responsiveness of nominal interest rates to inflation in a closed economy. Col. (2) presents inflation-induced changes in after-tax prices of retirement consumption in closed economies. Col. (3) presents inflation-induced changes in portions of deadweight losses corresponding to intertemporal consumption distortions. Col. (4) presents inflation-induced changes in personal income tax revenues in closed economies corresponding to intertemporal consumption distortions. Col. (5) presents inflation-induced changes in deadweight losses in open economies corresponding to intertemporal consumption distortions. Col. (6) presents inflation-induced changes in personal income tax revenues in open economies. Col. (7) presents ratios of changes in domestic welfare arising from intertemporal consumption distortions in open and closed economies.

The parameter b denotes the fraction of domestic investment financed at the margin by debt, and δ is a measure of the degree to which depreciation accounting for tax purposes is sensitive to inflation ($\delta = 0$ corresponds to zero sensitivity, or economic depreciation). The calculations take the domestic tax rate on interest income to be equal to the domestic tax rate on capital gains ($\theta = c$). The domestic inflation rate, π, is assumed to be 2.0 percent, and the nominal interest rate, r, is assumed to be 7.0 percent. The calculations also assume a zero elasticity of saving with respect to the real rate of return ($\eta_{Sr} = 0$) and that the shadow value of tax revenue is 1.4 ($\lambda = 0.4$).

$(dp_2^a/d\pi)^{closed} > (dp_2^a/d\pi)^{open}$ and the efficiency costs of interactions between inflation and personal taxes in closed economies exceed those in open economies. In a reference case in which $b = 0.5$ and $\delta = 0.1$, open economies are characterized by 20 percent greater deadweight losses from interactions with personal taxation than are closed economies.[18]

Inflation is responsible for the following deadweight losses through its interaction with corporate taxes:

$$(33) \qquad \frac{d\text{DWL}_c}{d\pi} = [f' - (r - \pi)]\frac{df'}{d\pi}\gamma.$$

The associated revenue consequences are

$$(34) \qquad \frac{d\text{REV}_c}{d\pi} = \frac{df'}{d\pi}K - [f' - (r - \pi)]\frac{df'}{d\pi}\gamma,$$

where

$$\frac{df'}{d\pi} = \frac{1}{1 - \tau}\left[\frac{dr}{d\pi}(1 - b\tau) - (1 - \delta)\right].$$

In order to calibrate γ, we assume that the economy has a Cobb-Douglas production function and corresponding unit elasticity of capital demand. In order to make the results comparable with the analysis of intertemporal consumption distortions, we further assume the capital stock to be twice the size of GDP.

Distinctions between open and closed economies are reflected in values of $dr/d\pi$ and $df'/d\pi$. In a closed economy with zero uncompensated saving elasticity, inflation does not affect the size of the capital stock. However, in calculating the welfare consequences of inflation, it is important to incorporate the fact that if individuals are compensated for real income changes due to inflation, the size of the capital stock will change. Accordingly, deadweight loss calculations must be performed in a setting in which inflation affects the size of the capital stock in a closed economy—even though the uncompensated saving elasticity is zero. In open economies, the interaction between corporate taxes and inflation generates further distortions through international capital flows. Table 6.4 provides estimates of equations (33) and (34) under different scenarios in a manner comparable to the presentation in table 6.3.

Column (1) of table 6.4 indicates the responsiveness of the marginal product of capital to inflation and, as such, reflects whether investment flows into or out of the inflating economy. The entries correspond to those presented in table 6.1 in that their signs depend on the relative magnitude of δ and the product of b and τ. Column (2) indicates the size of the existing tax wedge, $f' - (r - \pi)$. Signs of entries in columns (1) and (2) of table 6.4 determine the sign of the

---

18. Auerbach (1978) calculates a value of $\delta = 0.23$ for the U.S. tax system in the 1970s. Subsequent U.S. tax changes have reduced the inflation sensitivity of the present value of depreciation allowances, making $\delta = 0.10$ a reasonable base case.

Table 6.4   Deadweight Loss and Revenue of Domestic Inflation in Open and Closed Economies: Corporate Income Taxation

	$\left(\dfrac{df'}{d\pi}\right)^{open}$	$f' - (r - \pi)$	$\left(\dfrac{dDWL_c}{d\pi}\right)^{closed}$	$\left(\dfrac{dREV_c}{d\pi}\right)^{closed}$	$\left(\dfrac{dDWL_c}{d\pi}\right)^{open}$	$\left(\dfrac{dREV_c}{d\pi}\right)^{open}$	$\dfrac{dSW_c^{open}}{d\pi}\Big/\dfrac{dSW_c^{closed}}{d\pi}$
	(1)	(2)	(3)	(4)	(5)	(6)	(7)
b = 1.0							
δ = 0.0	−0.5385	−0.0108	0.0000GDP	0.0000GDP	0.2956GDP	−1.3725GDP	−∞
δ = 0.1	−0.3846	−0.0077	−0.0001	0.0006	0.1399	−0.9091	−1518.1529
δ = 0.2	−0.2308	−0.0046	−0.0001	0.0012	0.0469	−0.5085	−424.4788
b = 0.5							
δ = 0.0	−0.2692	0.0081	0.0002	0.0013	−0.0749	−0.4636	−364.8884
δ = 0.1	−0.1154	0.0112	0.0004	0.0017	−0.0421	−0.1887	−108.3006
δ = 0.2	0.0385	0.0142	0.0006	0.0022	0.0170	0.0599	27.0485
b = 0.2							
δ = 0.0	−0.1077	0.0194	0.0007	0.0018	−0.0602	−0.1552	−86.0827
δ = 0.1	0.0462	0.0225	0.0010	0.0022	0.0286	0.0637	28.6728
δ = 0.2	0.2000	0.0256	0.0013	0.0026	0.1352	0.2648	100.3005

Notes: Col. (1) indicates the responsiveness of marginal products of capital to inflation in open economies. Col. (2) presents tax and inflation-induced differences between marginal products of capital and pretax real rates of return. Col. (3) presents inflation-induced changes in portions of deadweight losses in closed economies corresponding to investment distortions. Col. (4) presents inflation-induced changes in corporate tax revenues in closed economies. Col. (5) presents inflation-induced changes in portions of deadweight losses in open economies corresponding to investment distortions. Col. (6) presents inflation-induced changes in corporate tax revenues in open economies. Col. (7) presents ratios of inflation-induced changes in social welfare due to corporate taxation in open and closed economies.

The parameter b denotes the fraction of domestic investment financed at the margin by debt, and δ is a measure of the degree to which depreciation accounting for tax purposes is sensitive to inflation ($\delta = 0$ corresponds to zero sensitivity, or economic depreciation). The calculations take the domestic tax rate on interest income to be equal to the domestic tax rate on capital gains ($\theta = c$). The domestic inflation rate, π, is assumed to be 2.0 percent, and the nominal interest rate, r, is assumed to be 7.0 percent. The calculations also assume a zero elasticity of saving with respect to the real rate of return ($\eta_{Sr} = 0$) and that the shadow value of tax revenue is 1.4 ($\lambda = 0.4$).

impact of inflation on investment efficiency. Common signs indicate either that the effective tax wedge is negative and inflation is associated with greater investment or that the effective tax wedge is positive and inflation is associated with reduced investment. In either of these cases, higher rates of inflation are associated with greater deadweight loss. Given the small size of inflation-induced deadweight loss in the closed economy, the ratio of deadweight losses from corporate taxes in open and closed economies approximates $\pm\infty$. In the base case of $b = 0.5$ and $\delta = 0.1$, the signs of the two components of deadweight loss differ (there is a positive effective tax wedge while higher inflation rates increase investment), so higher rates of inflation reduce deadweight loss.

Table 6.5 summarizes the results of tables 6.3 and 6.4. Note that the ratios in column (5) typically exceed unity and that the deadweight losses due to taxes in open economies range from 0.2006GDP to 1.0522GDP. These values suggest that the efficiency gain from reducing inflation by 2 percent is bounded by 0.40 percent of GDP per year and 2.10 percent of GDP per year. In the base case of $b = 0.5$ and $\delta = 0.1$, the inflating economy experiences 40 percent greater inflation-induced welfare loss when open relative to when it is closed to the rest of the world. In this context, it is noteworthy that the closed economy deadweight losses from inflation, with the exception of the case of all-debt financing and economic depreciation, are not trivial. The results in tables 6.3, 6.4, and 6.5 are not sensitive to the assumption of a foreign inflation rate as equations (30), (32), (33), and (34) are functions of $dr/d\pi$ and not π^*.

Table 6.6 outlines the relevant welfare considerations for the rest of the world. Columns (1), (2), and (3) detail the welfare impact of distortions to intertemporal consumption choices. These results are directly linked to the results on $dr^*/d\pi$ presented in column (2) of table 6.2.[19] Note that when the foreign nominal interest rate rises with domestic inflation ($dr^*/d\pi > 0$), the foreign after-tax price of consumption declines ($dp_2^{a*}/d\pi < 0$) and, consequently, foreign welfare improves. Foreign parameters match the base case of the inflating economy ($b^* = 0.5$, $\tau^* = 0.35$, $\delta^* = 0.1$, and $\theta^* = 0.35$). At these parameter values, there exists a positive investment tax wedge, and signs of the figures in column (4) correspond to the direction of investment flows in response to domestic inflation. Column (7) aggregates the world welfare consequences of inflation in open and closed economies. In the base case, the impact of inflation on world welfare is 49 percent greater when the inflating economy is open than when it is closed.

6.5   Imperfect Capital Mobility

The validity of the assumption that capital is perfectly mobile internationally is frequently questioned on the basis of the persistent correlation between

---

19. Note that the values of $dr^*/d\pi$ presented in table 6.2 are based on calculations using uncompensated saving elasticities, while the values of $dr^*/d\pi$ used in the welfare analysis are based on calculations using compensated saving elasticities. Implied values of $dr^*/d\pi$ only differ slightly between these two cases.

Table 6.5 Welfare Effects of Domestic Inflation in Open and Closed Economies: Summary Table

	$\left(\dfrac{dSW_p}{d\pi}\right)^{closed}$	$\left(\dfrac{dSW_c}{d\pi}\right)^{closed}$	$\left(\dfrac{dSW_p}{d\pi}\right)^{open}$	$\left(\dfrac{dSW_c}{d\pi}\right)^{open}$	$\dfrac{dSW^{open}}{d\pi}\Big/\dfrac{dSW^{closed}}{d\pi}$
	(1)	(2)	(3)	(4)	(5)
$b = 1.0$					
$\delta = 0.0$	0.0000GDP	0.0000GDP	-0.2075GDP	-0.8446GDP	-∞
$\delta = 0.1$	-0.0592	0.0003	-0.2075	-0.5035	12.0756
$\delta = 0.2$	-0.1184	0.0006	-0.2075	-0.2503	3.8859
$b = 0.5$					
$\delta = 0.0$	-0.1256	0.0003	-0.2075	-0.1105	2.5387
$\delta = 0.1$	-0.1722	0.0003	-0.2075	-0.0334	1.4013
$\delta = 0.2$	-0.2188	0.0003	-0.2075	0.0069	0.9177
$b = 0.2$					
$\delta = 0.0$	-0.1782	0.0000	-0.2075	-0.0019	1.1751
$\delta = 0.1$	-0.2196	-0.0001	-0.2075	-0.0031	0.9588
$\delta = 0.2$	-0.2609	-0.0003	-0.2075	-0.0293	0.9066

Notes: Col. (1) presents inflation-induced changes in social welfare due to personal taxation in closed economies. Col. (2) presents inflation-induced changes in social welfare due to corporate taxation in closed economies. Col. (3) presents inflation-induced changes in social welfare due to personal taxation in open economies. Col. (4) presents inflation-induced changes in social welfare due to corporate taxation in open economies. Col. (5) presents the ratios of inflation-induced changes in social welfare due to personal and corporate taxation in closed and open economies.

The parameter b denotes the fraction of domestic investment financed at the margin by debt, and δ is a measure of the degree to which depreciation accounting for tax purposes is sensitive to inflation ($\delta = 0$ corresponds to zero sensitivity, or economic depreciation). The calculations take the domestic tax rate on interest income to be equal to the domestic tax rate on capital gains ($\theta = c$). The domestic inflation rate, π, is assumed to be 2.0 percent, and the nominal interest rate, r, is assumed to be 7.0 percent. The calculations also assume a zero elasticity of saving with respect to the real rate of return ($\eta_{Sr} = 0$) and that the shadow value of tax revenue is 1.4 ($\lambda = 0.4$).

Table 6.6   Effects of Domestic Inflation on Foreign Economy and World Welfare

	$\dfrac{d\text{DWL}^*_p}{d\pi}$ (1)	$\dfrac{d\text{REV}^*_p}{d\pi}$ (2)	$\dfrac{d\text{SW}^*_p}{d\pi}$ (3)	$\dfrac{d\text{DWL}^*_c}{d\pi}$ (4)	$\dfrac{d\text{REV}^*_c}{d\pi}$ (5)	$\dfrac{d\text{SW}^*_c}{d\pi}$ (6)	$\left.\dfrac{d(\text{SW}^{\text{open}}+\text{SW}^*)}{d\pi}\right/\dfrac{d\text{SW}^{\text{closed}}}{d\pi}$ (7)
$b = 1.0$							
$\delta = 0.0$	−0.3244GDP	−0.4019GDP	0.1636GDP	0.1965GDP	−0.0881GDP	−0.2317GDP	−∞
$\delta = 0.1$	−0.2318	−0.2873	0.1169	0.1404	−0.0630	−0.1656	12.9025
$\delta = 0.2$	−0.1393	−0.1727	0.0703	0.0844	−0.0378	−0.0995	4.1343
$b = 0.5$							
$\delta = 0.0$	−0.1626	−0.2014	0.0820	0.0985	−0.0441	−0.1161	2.8112
$\delta = 0.1$	−0.0701	−0.0869	0.0354	0.0425	−0.0190	−0.0501	1.4869
$\delta = 0.2$	0.0223	0.0276	−0.0113	0.0135	0.0061	0.0159	0.8963
$b = 0.2$							
$\delta = 0.0$	−0.0656	−0.0813	0.0331	0.0397	−0.0178	−0.0469	1.2524
$\delta = 0.1$	0.0268	0.0332	−0.0135	−0.0162	0.0073	0.0192	0.9332
$\delta = 0.2$	0.1192	0.1477	−0.0601	−0.0722	0.0324	0.0852	0.8108

Notes: Col. (1) presents inflation-induced changes in portions of deadweight loss in the rest of the world corresponding to intertemporal consumption distortions. Col. (2) presents inflation-induced changes in personal income tax revenues in the rest of the world. Col. (3) presents inflation-induced changes in foreign welfare arising from intertemporal consumption distortions. Col. (4) presents inflation-induced changes in the portions of deadweight loss in the rest of the world corresponding to investment distortions. Col. (5) presents inflation-induced changes in corporate tax revenue in the rest of the world. Col. (6) presents inflation-induced changes in social welfare in the rest of the world arising from corporate taxation. Col. (7) presents the ratios of inflation-induced changes in world welfare when inflating economies are open and closed.

The parameter b denotes the fraction of domestic investment financed at the margin by debt, and δ is a measure of the degree to which depreciation accounting for tax purposes is sensitive to inflation ($\delta = 0$ corresponds to zero sensitivity, or economic depreciation). The calculations take the domestic tax rate on interest income to be equal to the domestic tax rate on capital gains ($\theta = c$). The domestic inflation rate, π, is assumed to be 2.0 percent, and the nominal interest rate, r, is assumed to be 7.0 percent. The calculations also assume a zero elasticity of saving with respect to the real rate of return ($\eta_{Sr} = 0$) and that the shadow value of tax revenue is 1.4 ($\lambda = 0.4$). Foreign parameters are fixed at $\pi^* = 0$ percent, $b^* = 0.5$, $\delta^* = 0.1$, $\tau^* = 35$ percent, and $\theta^* = 35$ percent.

saving and investment for a variety of countries and the widespread home bias in domestic portfolios.[20] The economic significance of imperfect capital mobility is a matter of some dispute. In the present context, it suggests that capital might not flow in sufficient volume to inflating countries in order to maintain local before-tax real interest rates at world levels. Such a failure to equate real interest rates implies a failure of arbitrage that is consistent with profit-maximizing behavior only if lenders incur some costs associated with international capital flows. In order to examine the implications of imperfect international capital mobility, this section analyzes a model in which such costs are present.

The most convenient way to introduce the model of imperfect capital mobility is to specify the reaction of domestic interest rates to inflation. Specifically, suppose that

$$(35) \qquad \frac{dr}{d\pi} = 1 + \mu,$$

in which μ is a free parameter that is zero if capital is perfectly mobile internationally and is nonzero if capital mobility is limited by some kind of transactions cost. The value of μ takes the same sign as the value of $dr/d\pi - 1$ in an otherwise equivalent closed economy. Of course, μ is not a choice variable but instead a function of transactions costs as well as the supply and demand conditions for world capital. For the moment, it is useful to take μ to be a given parameter that represents costs associated with information gathering or a reduction in return attributable to gains from diversification.[21]

The effect of domestic inflation on domestic saving is then no longer represented by equation (10), instead becoming

$$(36) \qquad \frac{dS}{d\pi} = \frac{dS}{dr}[(1 - \theta)(1 + \mu) - 1] = \frac{dS}{dr}[-\theta + \mu(1 - \theta)].$$

In a similar manner, the effect of domestic inflation on domestic investment becomes a function of μ. Combining equations (4), (5), and (35) yields

$$(37) \qquad \frac{dK}{d\pi} = -\gamma\left[\frac{\delta - \beta}{1 - \tau} + b - \frac{(1 - b)(c - \theta)}{(1 - \tau)(1 - \theta)} + \frac{\mu(1 - \tau b)}{1 - \tau}\right].$$

20. On the saving-investment correlation, see Feldstein and Horioka (1980) and Frankel (1991). French and Poterba (1991), Tesar and Warner (1994, 1995), and Cooper and Kaplanis (1994) provide evidence of the home bias phenomenon. These studies assess possible causes of limited international diversification—such as high transactions costs or the desire to hedge against deviations from PPP—and reject these hypotheses.

21. Note that this specification of the transactions costs associated with international capital mobility does not parallel the "iceberg" models of international trade but rather posits that transactions costs are current instead of capital costs. Furthermore, the costs are assumed to be tax deductible—which is sensible if, for example, the costs take the form of payments to market analysts or reduced risk-adjusted returns.

Equilibrium in the capital market requires equality of world inflation-induced capital supply and capital demand changes, which in turn requires that equation (15) be modified in the presence of imperfect capital mobility to

$$\frac{dr*}{d\pi} =$$

(38)
$$\frac{1}{\psi}\left[\frac{(\theta - \mu(1 - \theta))\dfrac{dS}{dr} - \gamma\left(\dfrac{\delta - b}{1 - \tau} + b + \dfrac{(1 - b)(c - \theta)}{(1 - \tau)(1 - \theta)} + \dfrac{\mu(1 - \tau b)}{1 - \tau}\right)}{\dfrac{dS}{dr}(1 - \theta*) + \dfrac{\gamma}{1 - \tau*}(1 - b*\tau*)}\right].$$

This value of $dr*/d\pi$ in turn determines $dK*/d\pi$, $dS*/d\pi$, and the welfare effects associated with the behavioral responses.

Comparing equation (36) with equation (10), (37) with (6), and (38) with (15), it is clear that the introduction of imperfect capital mobility limits the reduction in domestic saving and the change in domestic investment associated with inflation. Furthermore, imperfect capital mobility reduces the effect of domestic inflation on the world interest rate. This analysis of capital immobility is comparable with the closed economy analysis of Feldstein (1976). In the context of economic depreciation, equal tax rates, and all-debt financing ($\tau = \theta$, $b = 1$, and $\delta = 0$), μ is bounded between 0, for perfectly mobile capital markets, and $\tau/(1 - \tau)$, for closed economies. When $\mu = \tau/(1 - \tau)$, the economy is effectively closed, and as a result, domestic saving and investment are unaffected by inflation.

Imperfect international capital mobility introduces two other potentially important differences to the welfare analysis of inflation. The first is that inflation may have a first-order effect on the terms at which a country can borrow and consequently may be responsible for income redistribution between foreigners and domestic residents. The second is that the transactions costs associated with international capital mobility must be incorporated into the welfare analysis since inflation that reallocates capital internationally is responsible for these additional costs.

The real rate of interest paid on borrowing by the home country is $r - \pi$, so the effect of inflation on the home country's real borrowing cost is $dr/d\pi - 1 = \mu$. As the home country borrows net capital equal to $K - S$ from the rest of the world, a small change in domestic inflation is responsible for a wealth transfer from home country residents of an amount equal to $\mu(K - S)$. Foreign lenders do not receive all of this amount, however, since the return on their inframarginal lending rises by $(dr*/d\pi)(K - S)$. The parameter μ differs from $dr*/d\pi$ due to the deadweight losses that accompany saving and investment distortions as well as the adjustment costs incurred as a result of inflation-induced changes in net international lending.

Putting these pieces together, the impact of inflation on domestic welfare is in part given by equations (16) and (23), properly modified to incorporate the behavioral effects described by equations (36) and (37). In addition, if the home country is a capital importer, domestic residents lose $\mu(K - S)$ with every unit change in inflation. Hence the effect of inflation on welfare in the home country is given by

(39)
$$\frac{d\text{DWL}}{d\pi} = \frac{\gamma}{(1 - \tau)^2}[\delta - \tau b + \mu(1 - \tau b)][r\tau(1 - b) + \pi(\delta - \tau)]$$

$$-T[1 - (1 + \mu)(1 - \theta)]p_2^a \frac{dC_2}{dp_2^a}(p_2^a - p_2^b) + \mu(K - S),$$

in which the last component, $\mu(K - S)$, represents a wealth transfer and not inefficiency.

In order to examine the impact of imperfect capital mobility on the welfare of the rest of the world, it is necessary to specify the costs associated with imperfect capital mobility. The equilibrium condition is that small changes in inflation in a small open economy cannot affect net-of-adjustment-cost real rates of return available to foreign lenders. Hence, it must be the case that marginal adjustment costs equal the difference between real rates of return at home and abroad, $(r^* - \pi^*) - (r - \pi)$, and the change in adjustment costs for which a small change in inflation is responsible equals

(40)
$$\left(\frac{dK}{d\pi} - \frac{dS}{d\pi}\right)[(r - \pi) - (r^* - \pi^*)].$$

The reduction in foreign welfare that accompanies a domestic inflation is in part given by equations (24) and (25), properly modified to incorporate equation (38). In addition, foreign residents gain an amount after adjustment costs equal to

(41)
$$\mu(K - S) - \left(\frac{dK}{d\pi} - \frac{dS}{d\pi}\right)[(r - \pi) - (r^* - \pi^*)].$$

Additional restrictions on the form of adjustment costs permit equation (41) to be further simplified. Consider, for example, the case of quadratic adjustment costs, in which $\mu = \zeta(\pi - \pi^*)$. This specification implies that $(r - \pi) - (r^* - \pi^*) = (\mu/2)(\pi - \pi^*)$, so the inflation-induced income transfer to foreigners, net of adjustment costs, is

(42)
$$\mu\left[(K - S) - \left(\frac{dK}{d\pi} - \frac{dS}{d\pi}\right)\frac{\pi - \pi^*}{2}\right].$$

For small values of μ and π, $dK/d\pi$ and $dS/d\pi$ are unaffected by π, and $K - S \cong (dK/d\pi - dS/d\pi)(\pi - \pi^*)$. Imposing this approximation implies

that half of the income transfer to foreigners is lost in transactions costs, and the net welfare gain for foreign residents from domestic inflation is given by

$$
\frac{d\mathrm{DWL}^*}{d\pi} = T\frac{dr^*}{d\pi}(1 - \theta^*)p_2^{a*}(p_2^{a*} - p_2^{b*})\frac{dC_2^*}{dp_2^{a*}}
$$

(43)
$$
+ \frac{\gamma^*}{1 - \tau^*}[r^*\tau^*(1 - b^*) + \pi^*(\delta^* - \tau^*)]\frac{dr^*}{d\pi}(1 - b^*\tau^*)
$$

$$
- \frac{\mu}{2}(K - S),
$$

in which the last piece, $(\mu/2)(K - S)$, is the income transfer to foreigners, and $dr^*/d\pi$ is given by equation (38). Imperfect capital mobility has an indeterminate effect on world welfare. There are important scenarios in which imperfect capital mobility reduces inflation-induced capital reallocations and associated deadweight losses. At the same time, however, capital immobility reflects transactions costs for which inflation may be partly responsible. As a result, the net welfare effects of inflation-tax interactions with imperfect capital mobility are case specific.

6.6   Foreign Direct Investment

The analysis to this point considers investments that are financed through a combination of equity held by domestic residents and debt that may be held by either domestic or foreign residents. Consequently, the only form in which international investment is undertaken is by cross-border portfolio lending. There are at least two other important possibilities. The first is cross-border individual investing in equities. International investment seldom takes this form, and as Gordon (1986) notes, the effect of inflation on equilibrium capital flows with cross-border equity holdings is unlikely to differ significantly from the effect of inflation when international capital flows are limited to portfolio investments. Consequently, little realism is lost by abstracting from the ability of investors to hold foreign equities.

The second important alternative possibility is that some foreign investments are undertaken by domestic firms with controlling interests in their foreign operations. Foreign direct investment of this type may have different financial characteristics than local operations in foreign countries and typically receives different tax treatment from home countries.[22] It is, however, important to note that foreign direct investments almost uniformly receive the same tax treatment from host countries as do local firms. Consequently, the significance of foreign direct investment to the effect of inflation on international capital flows and associated welfare costs is that its financing may differ from

---

22. See Hines (1997) for a review of the practice and effect of taxing foreign direct investment.

the financing arrangements of local firms. Given the small size of foreign direct investment relative to portfolio capital flows and the modest difference between its incentives and those of portfolio investors, treating all cross-border investment as portfolio flows offers a reasonable approximation to a complete treatment of cross-border investment.

6.7 Conclusion

The results reported in this paper indicate that there are important efficiency implications of the international dimensions of inflation-tax interactions. In particular, inflation in one country can generate sizable international capital flows with attendant changes in domestic and foreign welfare. The central mechanism for these flows is the ability of foreign savers to convert the inflation component of their nominal interest receipts into a foreign exchange loss, while domestic savers do not have the ability to do so. As a consequence, inflation discourages domestic saving and encourages domestic investment by reducing the after-tax rate of return, and foreign saving must finance the resulting difference.[23] The translation of these capital flows into efficiency terms indicates that inflation-tax interactions yield distortions of possibly much greater magnitude in open economies than they do in closed economies. In part, this difference reflects the greater mobility of capital in an open economy and the larger deadweight loss that therefore accompanies any given tax-induced distortion.

This analysis of inflation-tax interactions in open economies departs from the earlier work of Hartman (1979) in three ways. The first is to note that capital need not flow to inflating countries, since the direction of capital flow depends on the details of an inflating country's tax system. The second is to stress the related idea that as a consequence of these flows, domestic inflation influences world interest rates. Even though the size of a small economy's effect on world interest rates is barely perceptible, the resulting welfare effect may be quite large because the world interest rate influences an extremely large base of capital. The third departure is to measure the impact of inflation-induced capital flows on economic welfare at home and in the rest of the world.

The paper does not analyze certain consequences of inflation. The analysis does not include estimates of the lump-sum income redistributions that accompany unanticipated changes in inflation, nor does it include the effects of possible disruptions to import and export markets that may react sluggishly to real exchange rate changes. The one-sector model does not capture distortions created by subsidizing specific assets, such as owner-occupied housing. In addition, the analysis considers only permanent changes in inflation rates. Transitory inflation changes current costs of holding assets without necessarily

---

23. Desai (1997) offers evidence that this open economy result may explain the empirical regularity, noted by Romer (1993), that more open economies have lower inflation rates.

changing future costs, thereby generating deadweight losses that differ from those analyzed in the paper. The analysis does not incorporate any of the costs associated with the credibility of future monetary policy for which inflation may be responsible and abstracts entirely from the macroeconomic effects of inflation.

In spite of these omissions, the results in the paper identify an important possible motivation for monetary and fiscal policy coordination between countries. The welfare consequences of domestic inflation are greatly amplified if the home country's inflation rate exceeds world levels and are reduced as inflation rates are equalized across countries. It may not, however, be in the perceived interest of all countries to harmonize their inflation rates because deviations from a common inflation rate may improve the welfare of deviating countries at the expense of others. As an empirical matter, countries typically select different inflation targets. The point of this paper is to explore the welfare consequences of such heterogeneous inflation experiences in open economies. The results indicate that the effects of inflation in open economies may be far more dramatic, both for home countries and for the world, than are the equivalent welfare effects of inflation in closed economies.

Appendix

The purpose of this appendix is to identify the closed economy model that is the basis of the welfare comparisons presented in section 6.4. Using the same notation introduced earlier in the paper, capital market equilibrium in a closed economy implies that any inflation-induced saving changes are matched exactly by inflation-induced investment changes:

$$(A1) \qquad \frac{dS}{d\pi} = \frac{dK}{d\pi},$$

which in turn implies

$$(A2) \quad \frac{dS}{d\pi}\left[\frac{dr}{d\pi}(1-\theta)-1\right] = -\gamma\left\{\frac{dr}{d\pi}\frac{1-b\tau}{1-\tau} - \left[\frac{(1-b)(1-c)}{(1-\tau)(1-\theta)} - \frac{\delta-b}{1-\tau}\right]\right\}.$$

This equality implies an effect of inflation on nominal interest rates in a closed economy:

$$(A3) \quad \left(\frac{dr}{d\pi}\right)^{closed} = \frac{\dfrac{\gamma}{1-\tau}\left[\dfrac{(1-b)(1-c)}{1-\theta} - \delta + b\right] + \dfrac{dS}{dr}}{\dfrac{dS}{dr}(1-\theta) + \dfrac{\gamma(1-b\tau)}{1-\tau}}.$$

In order to identify the distortions associated with the interaction of inflation and personal taxation in a closed economy, equation (A3) can be used to indicate the effect of inflation on the after-tax price of retirement consumption:

$$(\text{A4}) \quad \left(\frac{dp_2^a}{d\pi}\right)^{\text{closed}} = T\left[1 - \left(\frac{dr}{d\pi}\right)^{\text{closed}}(1 - \theta)\right]p_2^a \frac{1}{1 + r(1 - \theta) - \pi}.$$

Similarly, the distortions associated with the interaction of inflation and corporate taxation in a closed economy depend on the effect of inflation on marginal products of capital:

$$(\text{A5}) \quad \left(\frac{df'}{d\pi}\right)^{\text{closed}} = \frac{1}{1 - \tau}\left[\left(\frac{dr}{d\pi}\right)^{\text{closed}}(1 - b\tau) - (1 - \delta)\right].$$

The values of $(dp_2^a/d\pi)^{\text{closed}}$ and $(df'/d\pi)^{\text{closed}}$ implied by equations (A4) and (A5) can then be used to determine the relevant welfare components of the effect of inflation—as in $d\text{DWL}_p/d\pi$ in equation (31), $d\text{DWL}_c/d\pi$ in equation (33), $d\text{REV}_p/d\pi$ in equation (32), and $d\text{REV}_c/d\pi$ in equation (34)—in a closed economy.

References

Abuaf, Niso, and Philippe Jorion. 1990. Purchasing power parity in the long run. *Journal of Finance* 45:157–74.

Auerbach, Alan. 1978. Appendix: The effect of inflation on the tax value of depreciation. In Inflation and taxes in a growing economy with debt and equity finance, by Martin Feldstein, Jerry Green, and Eytan Sheshinski. *Journal of Political Economy* 86, no. 2, pt. 2 (April): S68–S69.

Auerbach, Alan J., and James R. Hines Jr. 1988. Investment tax incentives and frequent tax reforms. *American Economic Review* 78 (2): 211–16.

Ballard, Charles L., John B. Shoven, and John Whalley. 1985. General equilibrium computations of the marginal welfare costs of taxes in the United States. *American Economic Review* 75:128–38.

Bayoumi, Tamim, and Joseph Gagnon. 1996. Taxation and inflation: A new explanation for capital flows. *Journal of Monetary Economics* 38 (2): 303–30.

Commission of the European Communities. 1992. *Report of the Committee of Independent Experts on Company Taxation*. Luxembourg: Office for Official Publications of the European Communities.

Cooper, Ian, and Evi Kaplanis. 1994. What explains the home bias in portfolio investment? *Review of Financial Studies* 7 (1): 45–60.

Darby, Michael. 1975. The financial and tax effects of monetary policy on interest rates. *Economic Inquiry* 13:266–76.

Desai, Mihir. 1997. Inflation, taxation and openness. Cambridge, Mass.: Harvard University. Manuscript.

Feldstein, Martin. 1976. Inflation, tax rules, and the rate of interest: A theoretical analysis. *American Economic Review* 66:809–20.

———. 1978. The welfare cost of capital income taxation. *Journal of Political Economy* 86, no. 2, pt. 2 (April): S2–S51.

———. 1983. *Inflation, tax rules, and capital formation.* Chicago: University of Chicago Press.

———. 1995. Tax avoidance and the deadweight loss of the income tax. NBER Working Paper no. 5055. Cambridge, Mass.: National Bureau of Economic Research.

Feldstein, Martin, Jerry Green, and Eytan Sheshinski. 1978. Inflation and taxes in a growing economy with debt and equity finance. *Journal of Political Economy* 86, no. 2, pt. 2 (April): S53–S70.

Feldstein, Martin, and Charles Horioka. 1980. Domestic saving and international capital flows. *Economic Journal* 90:314–29.

Fisher, Irving. 1930. *The theory of interest.* New York: Macmillan.

Frankel, Jeffrey A. 1991. Quantifying international capital mobility in the 1980s. In *National saving and economic performance,* ed. B. Douglas Bernheim and John B. Shoven. Chicago: University of Chicago Press.

French, Kenneth R., and James M. Poterba. 1991. Investor diversification and international equity markets. *American Economic Review* 81 (2): 222–26.

Froot, Kenneth A., Michael Kim, and Kenneth Rogoff. 1995. The law of one price over 700 years. NBER Working Paper no. 5132. Cambridge, Mass.: National Bureau of Economic Research.

Gordon, Roger. 1986. Taxation of investment and savings in a world economy. *American Economic Review* 76:1086–1102.

Gordon, Roger, and Hal Varian. 1989. Taxation of asset income in a world securities market. *Journal of International Economics* 26:205–26.

Graham, Edward M., and Paul R. Krugman. 1991. *Foreign direct investment in the United States.* Washington, D.C.: Institute for International Economics.

Hansson, Ingemar, and Charles Stuart. 1986. The Fisher hypothesis and international capital markets. *Journal of Political Economy* 94:1330–37.

Hartman, David. 1979. Taxation and the effects of inflation on the real capital stock in an open economy. *International Economic Review* 20:417–25.

Hines, James R., Jr. 1997. Tax policy and the activities of multinational corporations. In *Fiscal policy: Lessons from economic research,* ed. Alan J. Auerbach. Cambridge, Mass.: MIT Press.

Howard, David, and Karen Johnson. 1982. Interest rates, inflation, and taxes: The foreign connection. *Economics Letters* 9:181–84.

International Monetary Fund (IMF). 1991. *Determinants and systemic consequences of international capital flows.* Washington, D.C.: International Monetary Fund.

———. 1997. *International financial statistics.* Washington, D.C.: International Monetary Fund.

Johnson, David R. 1990. Co-integration, error correction, and purchasing power parity between Canada and the United States. *Canadian Journal of Economics* 23 (November): 839–55.

Levi, Maurice. 1977. Taxation and "abnormal" international capital flows. *Journal of Political Economy* 85:635–46.

Mishkin, Frederic S. 1992. Is the Fisher effect for real? *Journal of Monetary Economics* 30:195–215.

Mundell, Robert. 1963. Inflation and real interest. *Journal of Political Economy* 71: 280–83.

Romer, David. 1993. Openness and inflation: Theory and evidence. *Quarterly Journal of Economics* 108 (4): 869–903.

Sinn, Hans-Werner. 1991. The non-neutrality of inflation for international capital movements. *European Economic Review* 34:1–22.
Sorenson, Peter Birch. 1986. Taxation, inflation, and asset accumulation in a small open
economy. *European Economic Review* 30:1025–41.
Tesar, Linda L., and Ingrid M. Werner. 1994. International equity transactions and U.S.
portfolio choice. In *The internationalization of equity markets,* ed. Jeffrey A. Frankel.
Chicago: University of Chicago Press.
———. 1995. Home bias and high turnover. *Journal of International Money and Fi-
nance* 14 (4): 467–92.
Tobin, James. 1965. Money and economic growth. *Econometrica* 33:671–84.
Wahl, Jenny Bourne. 1989. Tax treatment of foreign exchange gains and losses and the
Tax Reform Act of 1986. *National Tax Journal* 42:59–68.
Wei, Shang-Jin, and David C. Parsley. 1995. Purchasing power *dis*-parity during the
floating rate period. Cambridge, Mass.: Harvard University. Working paper.
World Bank. 1995. *World tables 1995.* Baltimore: Johns Hopkins University Press.

Comment   Jeffrey A. Frankel

The paper by Mihir Desai and James Hines is a welcome contribution to
knowledge at the intersection of international finance and tax analysis, an un-
derstudied area that we international economists have largely left to the public
finance people by default. One might suppose that the major lessons here have
to do with international differences in tax rates. But as I read this literature,
the public finance economists have concluded, correctly, that interaction of the
tax parameters with international differences in inflation rates and interest rates
can dwarf the effects of the simple tax differences. The Desai-Hines paper
concludes that inflation in open economies reallocates capital internationally,
with large adverse implications for efficiency. The result that inflation might
be more harmful in an open economy than a closed economy would be an
example of the "theory of the second best": eliminating one distortion (capital
controls) is not necessarily good if there exist other distortions (taxes and inflation). The surprising aspect of the model is that capital can flow into the
inflating country.

The approach follows Hartman (1979), an open economy version of the
analysis of the effect of inflation on nominal interest rates. The Feldstein-
Darby (closed economy) answer to that question was that the nominal interest
rate rises *more* than the increase in the inflation rate, a nonneutrality. The reason is that savers demand no less: otherwise they would suffer a loss in the
after-tax real rate of return. But what does it mean that savers demand no loss?
What would they substitute into if the after-tax real rate of return were to fall?

Jeffrey A. Frankel is a member of the President's Council of Economic Advisers. He is on leave
from the University of California, Berkeley, and from the National Bureau of Economic Research,
where he directed the program on International Finance and Macroeconomics.

In closed economies, the answer is that they would save less or else shift into real assets. But these are not perfect substitutes. For example, in the 1970s, the after-tax real return was in fact negative. Savers were simply not able to protect themselves.

In an open economy, there is another, potentially more complete, escape: savers can take their money abroad. Does this then give us the Feldstein-Darby result (the "modified" or "tax-adjusted" Fisher effect)? Not necessarily: savers are also taxed on their foreign earnings, and the foreign inflation rate is not directly relevant to the domestic resident's purchasing power. The effect, rather, comes indirectly, via the foreign interest rate and exchange rate. In Hartman's open economy model, the Feldstein-Darby effect apparently vanishes because world capital markets apparently tie down the real interest rate. We are back to neutrality (the "traditional" Fisher effect).

Desai and Hines advance the analysis substantially by working out the inflation interactions of three kinds on nonneutralities: capital gains on exchange rate changes, the tax deductibility of nominal interest payments, and nominal depreciation allowances. This analysis is more complete than the earlier approaches.

I would like to raise a question about the fundamental framework, in which real interest rates would be equalized in the absence of tax factors. We know that real interest rates are not in fact equalized internationally. (Mishkin 1984 is one among many references cited in Frankel 1991.) U.S. real interest rates were above Japanese real rates in the 1980s, for example, and the same is probably again true now. Consider two possible explanations: imperfect capital mobility, defined as an observed discrepancy between the nominal interest differential and the expected rate of depreciation of the domestic currency, and a failure of purchasing power parity (PPP), defined as a discrepancy between the expected rate of depreciation of the domestic currency and the expected inflation differential.

Desai and Hines consider the imperfect mobility case in section 6.5, so let us begin there. They cite evidence of home bias in equity holdings, though I would rather cite the Feldstein-Horioka evidence on correlations between national saving and investment, and other evidence on the failure to equalize rates of returns. They have the Feldstein-Darby effect reemerging, presumably because savers can take their money abroad. The nominal interest rate rises by more than the inflation rate, with the difference denoted by μ. But μ is simply assumed: I would rather it be derived. This could be done by modeling the international flow of capital (or the stock of foreign holdings, in a portfolio balance model) as a function of the differential in expected returns. One must be careful to recognize that the decision of a resident about what assets to hold depends on how he or she is taxed on domestic versus foreign assets (not on the tax rate paid by domestic residents versus foreign residents). This means that under certain circumstances, tax rates can drop out, as can inflation rates.

Desai and Hines do it right for the case of perfect capital mobility. But the analysis is not shown for the case of imperfect capital mobility, so one cannot judge.

The authors do not consider the implications of the possible failure of PPP. Not surprising for public finance economists, but I as a macroeconomist tend to think in such terms. Some examples can illustrate why I think this macroeconomic dimension could be important. Consider a monetary expansion. The idea behind the Desai-Hines approach is that the inflation rate rises, leading to a large increase in the nominal interest rate and a capital inflow. But in monetary expansions I can recall (Japan in the late 1980s), interest rates fell, and capital flowed out, not in. In monetary contractions I can recall (the United Kingdom in 1979, the United States in 1980–82, Germany in 1991), interest rates rose, and capital flowed in, not out.

The interaction of the tax and macroeconomic effects could be modeled. Equation (1) is still right; but the expected rate of change of the exchange rate could be specified in either of two ways. It could be given by the change in the relative price of traded goods versus nontraded, as in the long-term postwar trend in the yen brought about by rapid Japanese productivity growth. Alternatively, the exchange rate could be expected to move in the direction of a long-term real equilibrium from which it has temporarily overshot, as in the Dornbusch overshooting model. The outcome would likely be that monetary expansion is associated with a low real interest rate, real depreciation of the currency, and net capital outflow, rather than a high real interest rate and net capital inflow.

The ready defense of the Desai-Hines model (and the other internationalized work of public finance economists) is that they are talking about the long run and that deviations from PPP disappear in the long run. It should be noted, however, that the short run can last longer than one thinks. The period over which a country's real interest rates can be high or low for pure monetary reasons can easily be as long as the period over which its tax parameters remain at a particular setting.

I agree with the paper's bottom line, that inflation can have bigger effects in an open economy than a closed one. But I am inclined to think it is because savers can take their money *out* of the country, rather than in.

References

Frankel, Jeffrey. 1991. Quantifying international capital mobility in the 1980s. In *National saving and economic performance,* ed. D. Bernheim and J. Shoven, 227–60. Chicago: University of Chicago Press.

Hartman, David. 1979. Taxation and the effects of inflation on the real capital stock in an open economy. *International Economic Review* 20:417–25.

Mishkin, Frederic. 1984. Are real interest rates equal across countries? An empirical investigation of international parity conditions. *Journal of Finance* 39:1345–58.

Discussion Summary

In response to the discussant's remarks, *Jim Hines* stated that he would like to remind the participants that he is not completely unaware of what international economists think, as his wife teaches international finance. When he first told her about this paper, she said, "You have got to be kidding." International economists think of at least six different channels through which inflation can affect capital flows, of which the inflation-tax interaction is the last. Whereas this may be justified for countries with very high inflation rates, for well-functioning economies Hines suggested that the inflation-tax interaction may play a prominent role.

Laurence Ball wondered whether it is possible to resolve empirically the question of the effect of inflation on capital flows, noting the recent paper by Bayoumi and Gagnon. The authors responded that Bayoumi and Gagnon look at OECD countries and assert that, empirically, capital flows are related to inflation in the same way that is predicted in the Desai-Hines model. However, the empirical evidence is not conclusive because it is difficult to control for the many other factors that influence capital flows.

Alan Auerbach asked the authors to clarify how it is possible that as capital flows get less elastic (as measured by the parameter μ) the deadweight loss increases. The authors responded that there are already distortions when capital flows are impeded in the initial situation. They presume that this is the source of the increase in deadweight loss.

Glenn Hubbard asked for an explanation of the parameter ψ in the Desai-Hines calculations. The authors responded that the parameter ψ is the ratio of the size of the rest of the world to the domestic economy, and this ratio is assumed to equal 10 in the simulations. A bigger ψ means that the effect of disinflation in the domestic economy on the world real interest rate is smaller but it will affect a larger world capital market. These opposing effects make the influence of ψ on the inflation effect on world welfare theoretically ambiguous.

Benjamin Friedman noted that the springboard for the analysis is the fact that a foreign lender can deduct from taxation the expected exchange rate depreciation caused by inflation in the domestic country. What happens if foreign countries also change their inflation rate? The authors responded that the welfare effects in the open economy case really depend on inflation differentials. If all countries inflate at the same rate, the analysis is the same as the closed economy analysis, assuming that tax systems are the same in all countries.

Andrew Abel inquired whether, in reality, one is taxed for transactions in the forward currency exchange market. The authors responded that after the Tax Reform Act of 1986, nominal exchange rate gains are taxed at the same rate as other interest income. Hence, in the model's notation, $\theta = g$. Most foreign countries try to do the same.

7 Identifying Inflation's Grease and Sand Effects in the Labor Market

Erica L. Groshen and Mark E. Schweitzer

7.1 Introduction

Monetary authorities around the industrialized world achieved a major disinflation during the late 1980s and early 1990s. Now they must select implicit or explicit inflation goals for the future. On the real side of the economy, the choice boils down to weighing inflation's purported benefits as it "greases the wheels" of the labor market against the expected costs imposed by its simultaneous tendency to disrupt ("add sand to") wage and price adjustments.[1] Empirical guidance for this choice is scant because of the paucity of modern experience with low inflation rates. This paper and its companion study (Groshen and Schweitzer 1996) are intended to help fill that gap.

Grease and sand effects can both arise from nominal rigidities in wages or prices in the face of shocks. Beyond that shared characteristic, however, the effects are theoretically and empirically distinct. The grease effect arises from downward-rigid wages (usually attributed to money illusion, social standards of fairness, or pervasive nominal contracts) in an economy with real economic shocks. Inflation, then, facilitates real intermarket price adjustments, reducing the extent to which the nominal rigidities bind and depress employment and output.

By contrast, the sand effect arises from errors (due to uncertainty and main-

Erica L. Groshen is assistant vice president and head of the Domestic Research Function at the Federal Reserve Bank of New York. Mark E. Schweitzer is an economist at the Federal Reserve Bank of Cleveland.

The authors thank Karen Schiele and Christy Rollow for excellent and timely research assistance. The views expressed in this paper are those of the authors and are not necessarily reflective of views at the Federal Reserve Banks of New York and Cleveland, or the Federal Reserve System. Any errors or omissions are the responsibility of the authors.

1. For further articulation of the grease and sand effects, respectively, see contrasting lectures—both titled "Inflation and Unemployment"—by James Tobin (1972) and Milton Friedman (1977).

tained for a contract period) or idiosyncratic nominal rigidities (due to menu costs or timing constraints) in the face of aggregate nominal shocks. Hence, inflation—when not universally recognized by market participants—raises the variance of intramarket wage or price adjustments, changing relative prices and wages, which misdirects resources and lowers output below potential. As inflation rises, these grease and sand effects offset each other in a welfare sense. When inflation is low, their net impact may be positive. However, at higher rates, the grease effect is bounded (by the size of real shocks), so sand effects are expected to dominate.

Individual empirical tests for grease and sand effects (the former in labor markets, the latter primarily in retail markets) yield mostly affirmative results. However, except for this paper and its companion study (Groshen and Schweitzer 1996), these studies have two crucial weaknesses that limit their usefulness for policy. First, each paper focuses on only grease or sand, omitting consideration of the offsetting effect and yielding no estimate of net impact.[2] Second, the studies largely rely on out-of-sample projections to predict the impact of low inflation because of the scarcity of recent low-inflation episodes. The latter is problematic because relationships estimated under moderate or high inflation may not carry over to low rates. In particular, inflation itself lowers incentives to relax rigid wages. Under persistent low inflation, competition should pressure employers to adopt more flexible practices (such as contingent contracts or bonus and incentive pay), which could mitigate inflation's grease or sand effects.

Our two studies are the only ones to include coverage of low-inflation years (in the 1950s, 1960s, and 1990s) and to estimate and compare simultaneous grease and sand effects. We find empirical evidence of both effects in the labor market, and that the net impact of inflation is positive but statistically indistinguishable from zero at low levels of inflation, turning negative at rates of over 5 percent.

This study has two aims: to further test the identification strategy for grease and sand used in Groshen and Schweitzer (1996) and to expand our understanding of the impact of low inflation by adding four low-inflation years (1993–96) to the data. We ask whether sand effects are actually distinguishable from grease effects and large enough (even at low to moderate rates of inflation) to offset estimated grease effects. We also use the most relevant evidence available (the late 1950s, early 1960s, and 1992–96) to focus on the labor market effects of low inflation in the United States.

We proceed as follows: Section 7.2 relates the formal model of grease and sand presented in Groshen and Schweitzer (1996) to wage-setting procedures in large firms and then summarizes that paper's strategy and main findings. Section 7.3 describes the updated data set. Section 7.4 presents a decomposi-

---

2. Another exception, Kahn (1997), notes evidence of "menu cost" (sand) effects but focuses on the grease effects.

tion of wage changes and examines the distribution of those components under high and low inflation. Section 7.5 reestimates the basic statistical model from Groshen and Schweitzer (1996) on the extended sample and tests for the sensitivity of the results to the following: separating inflation from productivity, adding controls for trend and unemployment, and splitting inflation into its expected and unexpected components. Section 7.6 evaluates net unemployment implications of our results and compares our results to two previous grease-only studies. The final section concludes.

7.2 Grease, Sand, and Wage-Setting Practices under Low Inflation

This section discusses how inflation acts on wage setting in large U.S. firms to produce the grease and sand effects and reviews findings from Groshen and Schweitzer (1996) in order to set the stage for the empirical work that follows.

7.2.1 A Narrative Model of Inflation's Impact on Large Firms' Wage Adjustments

Groshen and Schweitzer (1996) develops a simple formal model to demonstrate that inflation could simultaneously raise both intentional and distortionary wage changes. The model also motivates empirical tests of the effects. Here we show how the model incorporates institutional wage-setting practices that salary surveys (such as the one analyzed here) were designed to inform. This description is based on discussions with personnel executives, compensation textbook descriptions of the process, and compensation managers' responses to surveys conducted by Levine (1993) and others.[3]

The main elements of the Groshen and Schweitzer (1996) model are simply listed: The starting point is a standard efficiency wage model (where firms optimize over both labor and wages), in the context of inflation and distinct occupational labor markets. Grease and sand effects result from two added complications: (1) Inflation causes firms to commit and correct errors as they set annual wage levels. (2) Nominal wages are rigid downward, despite the presence of relative wage shocks among occupations. The net result is that if the sand effect exists, it can be detected as an inflation-induced increase in interemployer wage-change variation. Similarly, if the grease effect exists, inflation raises interoccupational wage-change variation.

To see how the model's elements correspond to observable features of salary administration, it is crucial to recognize that most large U.S. firms use a two-step process to set annual wages. In the first step, senior management sets the average nominal adjustment for the workforce—using inflation forecasts, labor market salary surveys, and financial, sales, and product price projections. In the second step, the annual "pool" for raises is divided among workers.

---

3. Examples of compensation policy references that describe and recommend these practices include Hills (1987), Milkovich and Newman (1990), and Wallace and Fay (1988).

During each phase, a different layer of management aims to maintain the company's profitability by not over- or underpaying employees, to prevent both unwanted turnover and excessively high labor costs.

To guide their decisions, many employers share wage information through community, industry, and occupational wage surveys.[4] A Conference Board study (Freedman 1976) found that while compensation executives considered diverse factors in their determination of wage adjustments, area salary surveys and cost-of-living measures were particularly prominent.

At the first step of the process, employers usually pursue their wage-setting goals by maintaining parity with other employers they consider comparable. The organizational behavior literature describes a firm as choosing a long-term labor market "position." This stable wage differential between the firm and alternative employers yields a workforce quality or effort differential consistent with the firm's overall production strategy. This wage-setting behavior closely mimics that described in the efficiency wage literature. Indeed, the efficiency wage hypothesis is most often used to link wages and job characteristics in large, bureaucratic workplaces. Furthermore, the model's prediction that alternative wage movements feed directly into the firm's wage adjustments is consistent with descriptions of firm wage-setting exercises found in textbooks for practitioners.

The Groshen and Schweitzer (1996) model represents sand with a single inflation-correlated term. This term can reflect employers' deviations from their intended wage differentials because they disagree on the expected rate of local wage inflation.[5] That is, firms' compensation administrators err more often in calculating the "correct" adjustments as inflation rises because their uncertainty rises simultaneously.

This assumption is consistent with the observed tendency of inflation to raise forecast and actual goods price-change dispersion (Ball and Cecchetti 1990; Lach and Tsiddon 1992; respectively). Indeed, it is implausible that firms' wage-change forecasts would be more accurate than their other price-change forecasts, since there would be strong incentives and little cost to sharing such information within the firm. Furthermore, uncertainty in market wage adjustments may well exceed that of goods markets due to the limited samples, retrospective nature, and infrequency of salary surveys. Widespread reliance on employer salary surveys (rather than direct measures of inflation—such as the consumer price index, CPI) confirms compensation managers' concerns over matching competitors' actions rather than matching some simple, easily observed level of goods inflation.[6] Of course, if a region's employers agreed on

---

4. See Groshen (1996) for a description of salary surveys and their use in research.

5. By contrast, if employers were to agree on some expected inflation rate that proved incorrect, this rate would effectively operate as the true rate and would not distort relative wages among the individual firms.

6. This focus makes sense because of regional divergence in wage levels and relativities (and the lack of precision of local CPIs) and because goods-price movements understate average nominal wage changes by the growth of labor productivity.

some expected inflation rate that proved incorrect, this rate would effectively operate as the true rate and not distort relative wages among the individual firms.

Supplementing the effect of errors, employers may also differ in their menu costs of adjustment because of differences in their salary administration rules, fiscal year calendars, or length of union contracts. Or some may face cash or other constraints that temporarily prevent them from adjusting fully. These variants yield idiosyncratic lags that are also captured by the inflation-correlated term in the model.

Since these lags or mistakes and corrections affect the firm's entire salary budget, the existence of the sand effect is indicated by growing dispersion among employers' wage adjustments (controlling for skill mix) as inflation rises. These unintended variations alter firms' wages relative to the market, which can reduce profitability via high labor costs, unnecessary layoffs, workforce dissatisfaction, or quits. Note also that any idiosyncratic errors or lags that affect the next step (when the budget is divided among occupations) would tend to cancel out across employers, so they do not raise interoccupational wage-change dispersion.

Employers could also respond to uncertain inflation by raising their wage-change frequency, allowing use of more current information. However, this is costly, particularly for bureaucratic firms or those with union or other fixed-term contracts. Similarly, the desire to avoid inflation-induced fluctuations may encourage companies to spend extra money gathering information to improve their decisions. These avoidance strategies also misdirect resources from their most productive uses and suggest that our metric may underestimate true sand effects.

By contrast, inflation's grease effects (its purported benefits) are conferred during the second step of the wage-setting process—the decentralized step. At this stage, corporate divisions allocate their shares of the total salary budget among workers, to match market wages and reward performance.

Divisions adjust wage differences among the occupations they employ to reflect shifts in training needs, working conditions, technology, product prices, demographics, or other input prices. In a well-functioning market, these interoccupational wage changes influence people's job search and training decisions. However, the division's annual decision may be altered by two constraints: the financial requirement that they not overspend their budget and a social (or bureaucratic) restriction on cutting the wages of good performers who face unfavorable labor market conditions—even when inflation is low. The reasons posited for this "downward wage rigidity" are money illusion, personnel practices designed to promote fairness, and the importance of fixed dollar payments in workers' expenditures.

For simplicity, the Groshen and Schweitzer (1996) model imposes complete downward nominal wage rigidity in a single-step process. This assumption could be relaxed in several ways without loss of generality. For example, in some situations the lowest acceptable raise may exceed zero. The higher the

floor, the larger the grease effect. Alternatively, some portion of pay or the workforce may not be subject to downward rigidity. As long as the flexible component is small relative to the size of normal shocks or the workforce, the results obtained hold.

Even more generally, downward-rigid rules may also constrain wage *raises* during periods of low inflation. When the compensation budget binds, it limits wage adjustments to those that can be balanced by restraint on another's raise. While the traditional story of rigid wages stresses the unemployment consequences, a firm might choose to limit higher than average desired increases rather than lay off workers, particularly in the short run.

As an illustration, suppose the firm had two workers, each earning the same amount, but real wages for one worker's occupation were rising by 1 percent per year while the other's were falling by 1 percent. Suppose also that the wage bill was restricted to grow at the rate of inflation and firm policy prevented pay cuts. Then under zero inflation, neither worker would get a raise—if this can be done without inducing quits. Indeed, the employer might lay off the worker in the declining occupation, if there were no complementarities in production. By contrast, in a year with 1 percent inflation, the worker in the slow-wage-growth job would get no raise while the other would receive a 2 percent hike, and there would be no incentive for layoffs.

Thus low-inflation environments reduce the variance of occupational wage adjustments in two ways. First, they eliminate some wage cuts in declining occupations. Second, they restrain increases for other workers—in order to balance the compensation budget. Such restrictions will be evident in intentional components of wages that require occasional, substantial adjustments. The obvious candidate is occupational wage adjustments. If wage rigidity simply eliminated wage changes below a cutoff, a test for truncation would adequately verify rigidity. However, the realistic complications described above or differences in firms' inflation expectations could distort that implication. For this reason, and to maintain symmetry in our analysis, we look for wage rigidity's effect on the standard deviation of occupational adjustments, because truncation always implies a reduced variance.

In social welfare terms, the grease effect predicts that higher inflation allows divisions to lower real wages for workers facing unfavorable market conditions. That is, inflation avoids costly alternatives such as layoffs, lowering other workers' raises (risking quits), maintaining prices above competitors paying the market wage (risking market share), and accepting lower profits. Then wage signals travel more rapidly throughout the economy, reducing layoffs and providing accurate incentives to workers choosing training and career paths.

A final realistic feature of our model is that it recognizes that general increases in labor productivity can substitute for inflation in both the grease and sand stories. Since broad-based productivity growth shifts out market demand for labor, firms must match other employers' productivity-based adjustments—along with inflation—in their average nominal wage adjustments. In

light of this, we measure external wage change as the change in output prices plus the general increase in labor productivity. Ceteris paribus, this sum approximates the average nominal wage growth in the economy.

Thus the main features of the formal model accord well with large firms' actual wage-setting practices. This supports confidence in the identification strategy generated by the model—that inflation's negative effects can be distinguished from its positive effects because they affect different components of wage changes. On the negative side, inflation adds unintended variation to firmwide salary adjustment budgets (sand). On the positive side, it frees divisions from downward nominal wage rigidity, allowing firms to adjust wages more rapidly to reflect market conditions for particular occupations (grease). In the following subsection, we summarize the measures of these effects obtained in Groshen and Schweitzer (1996).

7.2.2   Summary of Previous Results

Groshen and Schweitzer (1996) distinguishes inflation's positive labor market effects from its negative ones in the wage changes observed in a unique, long-lived panel of occupations and employers from the Federal Reserve Bank of Cleveland Community Salary Survey (CSS).

The analysis begins by characterizing wage changes in the CSS and extracting common occupational and employer components in each city and year. As confirmation of the consistency of the model with observables, we find the following: (1) As predicted, annual mean wage adjustments are highly correlated with external measures of inflation and productivity growth. (2) An ANOVA of annual wage changes verifies that employer and occupation components both play statistically strong, independent roles. (3) Over time, the dispersion of employer and occupation adjustments display a correlation coefficient of only .48; these two components of wage-change dispersion often move independently.

Next we regress the standard deviation of the estimated occupation and employer components on external nominal wage growth (inflation plus productivity growth). Since productivity growth, unlike inflation, has other unambiguous benefits and is not a direct monetary policy target, we focus on implications for inflation policy.

The empirical results suggest that potentially beneficial grease (as measured by the standard deviation of occupational wage adjustments) shows a diminishing relationship with nominal wage growth. These potential benefits taper off after inflation rates of about 3 to 4 percent (assuming labor productivity growth of 1.5 percent, the average rate over the period observed). By contrast, disruptive sand from additional inflation (as measured by the standard deviation of employer wage adjustments) rises about twice as quickly as occupational variation with respect to inflation and shows less evidence of a turndown at inflation levels over 7 percent. The robustness of these results is confirmed by nonparametric, filtered, and panel versions of the tests.

We then combine the two gross results to consider the net (i.e., grease minus sand) impact of inflation. This is possible if the two effects are measured in the same units on the same data, are equally well identified, and subject firms to symmetric losses. Assuming productivity growth of 1.5 percent, net benefits peak at 2.5 percent inflation. Maximum net benefits amount to about a tenth of the gross benefits and are not statistically different from zero. At inflation levels above 5 percent, the disruptive effects of inflation on the labor market overwhelm the positive impacts and net benefits turn negative. Thus, in contrast to many grease-only studies, we conclude that the labor market provides little guidance on the preferred inflation goal at the low end of the range.

7.3   The Community Salary Survey

This study uses an updated version of the annual private salary survey data described in Groshen and Schweitzer (1996). The Federal Reserve Bank of Cleveland has conducted the CSS in Cleveland, Cincinnati, and Pittsburgh since 1927 to assist its annual salary budget process. The analysis data set reports wages for detailed occupations, by employer, from 1956 through 1996.

The data set has three major selling points for this study. First, the wages recorded here are less prone to random reporting error than household data because they derive from administrative records. Second, the data are longer lived than any source previously investigated. Third, because employer data record wages in the way most meaningful to firms, they are preferable to household or aggregate data for studying impacts on firms' wage setting. This perspective appropriately reflects the strategies used by firms to adjust wage bills (e.g., promotions, reassignments, or reorganization), but not the potentially confounding means used by workers individually to adjust their earnings (e.g., taking second jobs or changing hours).

Table 7.1 describes the dimensions of the CSS wage-change data set. From wage levels, we compute 75,765 annual wage changes for occupation-employer ("job") cells observed in adjacent years.[7] Each observation gives the change in the log of the mean or median salary for all individuals employed in an occupation-employer cell.[8] Cash bonuses are included as part of the salary, although fringe benefits are not.

---

7. Job-year observations where the calculated change in log wages exceeds 0.50 in absolute value are deleted from the sample on the assumption that most of these arise from reporting or recording errors. Over 1,000 observations are imputed from cases where job cells are observed two years apart. The imputed one-year changes are simply half of the two-year differences. Many of the results reported here were also run without the imputed observations. Their inclusion does not affect the results.

8. Only means were recorded before 1974. Since medians should be more robust to outliers, our results use means through 1974 and medians for the years thereafter. Comparison of the coefficients estimated separately for means and medians for some years where both were available (1974 and 1981–90) suggests that they are highly correlated (correlation coefficients of .97 to .99). However, coefficients estimated with medians show more variation than those estimated on means and are more highly correlated over time, consistent with medians being a more robust measurement of central tendency.

Table 7.1   **Description of the Annual Wage Adjustment Data Set Drawn from the Updated CSS, 1956–96**

Characteristic	Value
Total number of job-cell wage adjustments observed	75,765
Number of years of changes	40
Average number of observations per year	1,894
Mean log wage adjustment	0.048
Standard deviation of log wage adjustment	0.084
Number of occupation*city*year observations	6,187
Average number of occupation*city observations per year	155
Number of employer*year observations	3,002
Average number of employers per year	75

Source: Authors' calculations from the Federal Reserve Bank of Cleveland Community Salary Survey.

Note: All numbers reported are for the first-differenced data set.

Participants in each city are chosen to be representative of large employers in the area. Until 1995, the number of companies participating trended up from 66 to over 80 per year (see table 7.2). On average, they stay in the sample for almost 13 years each. Since each participant judges which establishments to include in the survey, depending on its internal organization, we use "employer," a purposely vague term, to mean the employing firm, establishment, division, or collection of local establishments for which the participating entity chooses to report wages.[9] The industries included vary widely, although the emphasis is on obtaining employers with many employees in the occupations surveyed.[10]

The occupations surveyed (43 to 100 each year) are exclusively nonproduction jobs that are found in most industries, with relatively high interfirm mobility, and well-developed markets.[11] Many occupations are divided into grade levels, reflecting responsibility and experience. In the analysis, to avoid unnecessary restrictions, we consider each occupational grade in each city to be a separate occupation. Thus the total number of "occupations" in table 7.2 exceeds the number surveyed. For example, 83 occupational grades were surveyed in 1996, yielding 240 occupations across the three cities. On average, each employer reports wages for about 27 occupations.

Although the CSS is conducted annually, the month surveyed has changed

9. Some include workers in all branches in the metropolitan area; others report wages for only the office surveyed. Since a participant's choice of the entities to include presumably reflects those for which wage policies are actually administered jointly, the ambiguity here is not particularly troublesome.

10. The employers surveyed include government agencies, banks, manufacturers, wholesalers, retailers, utilities, universities, hospitals, and insurance firms.

11. They include office (e.g., secretaries and clerks), maintenance (e.g., mechanics and painters), technical (e.g., computer operators and analysts), supervisory (e.g., payroll and guard supervisors), and professional (e.g., accountants, attorneys, and economists) occupations. Job descriptions for each are at least two paragraphs long.

Table 7.2   **Description of CSS Data by Year**

| End Year | Number | | | Mean Log Wage Adjustment | | |
	Job Cells	Occupations[a]	Employers	Cleveland	Cincinnati	Pittsburgh
1957	1,336	94	73	0.051	0.046	0.045
1958	1,557	94	83	0.049	0.054	0.050
1959	1,714	103	88	0.040	0.048	0.070
1960	1,669	103	86	0.036	0.032	0.034
1961	1,701	103	88	0.039	0.035	0.036
1962	1,881	109	93	0.024	0.022	0.024
1963	1,910	112	90	0.019	0.026	0.024
1964	2,032	113	96	0.026	0.022	0.023
1965	2,123	124	95	0.021	0.026	0.010
1966	1,965	125	89	0.040	0.045	0.038
1967	1,967	125	89	0.037	0.042	0.035
1968	2,128	124	94	0.046	0.044	0.042
1969	1,972	114	97	0.066	0.050	0.049
1970	853	49	36	0.068	—[b]	—[b]
1971	854	49	36	0.061	—[b]	—[b]
1972	1,262	66	38	0.061	—[b]	—[b]
1973	1,477	90	57	0.056	0.095	—[b]
1974	1,335	96	73	0.126	0.084	0.139
1975	1,379	101	73	0.074	0.063	0.090
1976	1,391	104	72	0.065	0.057	0.078
1977	789	60	72	0.030	0.021	0.052
1978	1,674	197	68	0.052	0.063	0.066
1979	2,418	267	75	0.064	0.071	0.069
1980	2,689	295	79	0.095	0.074	0.087
1981	2,196	186	83	0.086	0.089	0.059
1982	2,185	193	82	0.072	0.092	0.078
1983	2,013	190	75	0.050	0.055	0.073
1984	2,274	213	80	0.047	0.058	0.063
1985	2,272	212	79	0.040	0.044	0.042
1986	2,396	220	82	0.042	0.044	0.037
1987	2,437	226	80	0.031	0.037	0.038
1988	2,401	222	82	0.036	0.037	0.023
1989	2,407	225	81	0.045	0.041	0.036
1990	2,505	222	84	0.052	0.046	0.024
1991	2,536	223	89	0.038	0.045	0.035
1992	2,398	223	84	0.039	0.042	0.043
1993	2,355	223	89	0.032	0.026	0.040
1994	2,128	223	84	0.027	0.029	0.025
1995	1,841	241	69	0.027	0.031	0.019
1996	1,345	240	51	0.040	0.032	0.030
Total	75,765	6,187	3,002	0.049	0.048	0.048

Source: Authors' calculations from the Federal Reserve Bank of Cleveland Community Salary Survey, 1956–96.

[a]Occupations are counted separately for each city.

[b]In 1970–72, the CSS is missing Cincinnati; in 1970–73, the CSS is missing Pittsburgh.

several times. Throughout the paper, results for any year refer to the time between the preceding survey and the one conducted in that year—usually a 12-month span, but occasionally not. All data merged in have been adjusted to the extent possible to reflect time spans consistent with those in the CSS.

We also incorporate standard measures of inflation and national output per hour in our analysis (see table 7.3). As a measure of general inflation experienced in the country, we use percentage changes in the monthly averages of the Consumer Price Index for All Urban Workers (CPI-U). Our labor productivity measure is the Nonfarm Business Sector Output per Hour Worked (pre-chain-weights).

Mean log wage changes among the three cities are highly correlated and closely track national wage trends. Figure 7.1 shows the strong correspondence between the CSS three-city mean log wage change and our simple measure of nominal wage change (labeled CPI+), which equals the sum of inflation (CPI-U) and aggregate labor productivity movements. The new observations (1993–96) are all years in which the mean wage change in these three cities did not keep pace with CPI+. However, Groshen and Schweitzer (1996) shows that correlations between mean CSS wage adjustments and the CPI-U and CPI+ (.84 and .74, respectively) are quite high. The wages in the CSS largely adhere to national trends and thus may enlighten us about the behavior of wages in the nation as a whole.

Table 7.3   Means and Standard Deviations of CSS Wage Adjustment Components and Other Economic Indicators

Variable	Mean	Standard Deviation
Standard deviation of employer wage adjustment components	0.030	0.011
Standard deviation of occupation wage adjustment components	0.023	0.009
Current U.S. CPI-U[a]	0.046	0.034
ΔOutput/hour[b]	0.016	0.018
CPI+[c]	0.062	0.026
Unemployment rate[d]	0.061	0.014
Expected inflation[e]	0.046	0.024
Inflation surprise[f]	−0.001	0.022

Sources: Authors' calculations from the Federal Reserve Bank of Cleveland Community Salary Survey, 1956–96; U.S. Bureau of Labor Statistics; Surveys of Consumers, Survey Research Center, University of Michigan.

Note: Total number of observations is 113.

[a]The annual change in the BLS Consumer Price Index for All Urban Workers (CPI-U) for the United States.

[b]The annual change in the BLS Nonfarm Business Sector Output per Hour Worked for the United States.

[c]CPI-U plus Δoutput/hour.

[d]U.S. civilian unemployment rate.

[e]Taken from the Michigan Survey of Inflation Expectations.

[f]CPI-U minus expected inflation.

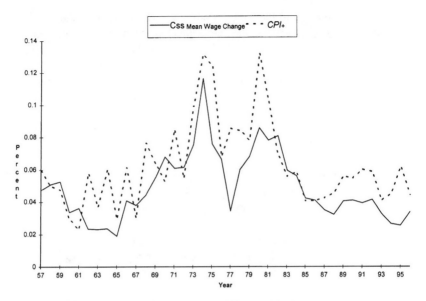

Fig. 7.1   CSS mean wage change versus CPI+, 1957–96

7.4   Wage Adjustment Components

7.4.1   ANOVA of CSS Wage Changes

Table 7.4 presents an analysis of variance (ANOVA) of wage adjustments in the updated CSS sample to verify the existence of distinguishable employer and occupation components. The following fixed effects regression model is used to decompose log wage changes (w_{fj}):

(1) $w_{fj} = \alpha + \beta D_f + \gamma D_j + \mu_{fj}$ for each locality and year,

where β and γ are coefficient vectors for matrices of dummy variables (D_f and D_j) referring to the cell's firm and occupation, respectively. The β-vector measures deviations from the mean wage change across the firm's complement of occupations, that is, the general pricing deviation developed above (sand). The γ-vector represents average occupational wage adjustments made in the market.

The results are little changed by the addition of the new data. Columns (1) and (2) list sources of variation and their associated degrees of freedom. Control for mean annual changes in three cities absorbs 112 degrees of freedom. To allow occupational wage patterns to diverge in the cities, occupation and city are interacted, accounting for 6,186 degrees of freedom. Employers' mean annual wage movements absorb another 3,001 degrees of freedom.

Column (3) lists each source's marginal contribution to the model sum of squares (over the contributions of the sources listed above it on the table). We

Table 7.4   ANOVA of Annual Wage Adjustments in the CSS, 1957–96

Source of Variation (1)	Degrees of Freedom (2)	Marginal Contribution to Sum of Squares (3)	Percentage of Total Sum of Squares (4)	Percentage of Model Sum of Squares (5)	Stepwise F-Statistic (6)
City	2	0.3	0.0	0.1	12.3
Year	39	30.6	5.8	21.1	119.7
Year*city	71	3.4	0.6	2.3	7.2
Occupation*year*city	6,186	45.2	8.5	31.1	1.2
Employer*year	3,001	65.9	12.4	45.4	4.3
Model	9,299	145.3	27.4	100.0	
Residual	66,465	385.2	72.6		
Total	75,764	530.5	100.0		

Source: Authors' calculations from the Federal Reserve Bank of Cleveland Community Salary Survey.
Note: The three cities are Cleveland, Cincinnati, and Pittsburgh. The years are 1956/57 through 1995/96.

choose this method of presentation—similar to a stepwise regression—because of its parsimony when the data are unbalanced (i.e., the occupations in each firm vary). Since the joint effects in wage-change variation between occupation and employer are minuscule, the order of presentation is unimportant.

All together, the model accounts for 27.4 percent of the variation in annual wage adjustments. The residual variation is presumably due to compositional changes, individual merit raises, and, perhaps, commingled grease and sand effects. Column (5) of the table shows that slightly more than one-fifth of the equation's explanatory power stems from changes common to all job cells in each year. Intercity differences account for little variation. Occupation-wide changes, on the other hand, constitute more than one-quarter of observed variation. By far the strongest effect is employer-wide changes, which account for close to half of the explained variation and 12.4 percent of total variation. F-statistics for these five sources of variation are all significant at the 1 percent level.

This decomposition suggests that the institutional model described above fits the data: occupation-wide and employer-wide variations in wage changes are large and statistically distinguishable from each other. In particular, the firmwide wage movements are interesting because employer wage differentials are quite stable over long periods of time (Groshen 1989). Thus variation here suggests errors and corrections.

7.4.2   Inflation's Impact on the Distribution of Wage Change Components

Since the grease hypothesis is based on downward (one-sided) wage rigidity while the sand hypothesis posits symmetrical rigidities, inflation may affect the distribution (as well as the variance) of occupation and employer wage

components differently. In particular, there is no reason to think that the distribution of employer deviations under low inflation would not be symmetric, simply showing thinner tails than the distribution of changes under high inflation. By contrast, downward wage rigidity under low inflation implies left-hand truncation of occupational wage changes, which may vary among firms. This effect suggests that low-inflation environments will skew the distribution to the right, with little impact on the right-hand tail—to the extent that the lack of cuts is not balanced by corresponding restraint in raises.

Figures 7.2*A* and 7.2*B* plot the distribution of employer and occupation

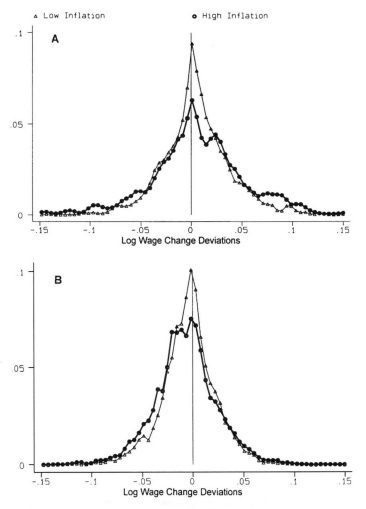

Fig. 7.2   Density of wage adjustments during high- and low-inflation years
Note: A, CSS employer adjustments; B, CSS occupational adjustments.

wage adjustments during years of high (over 5 percent) and low (under 3 percent) inflation. Consistent with our previous results, in both panels higher inflation is associated with higher variation. Indeed, Kolmogorov-Smirnov tests resoundingly reject equality between the high- and low-inflation distributions. Second, we note that the two sets of distributions do not look the same—providing more evidence of a difference between the two components.

Third and most important, the density plot for employers (A) shows thinning in both tails as the level of inflation falls. By contrast, the density plot for occupations (B) shows a marked, asymmetrical loss of small negative adjustments under low inflation, consistent with truncation. The tails are virtually unaffected. The fact that inflation affects the components' distributions differently, in ways consistent with the identification strategy, helps bolster confidence in both the strategy and the existence of grease and sand effects.

7.5   Regression Results

In this section, we further examine links between price changes and the variability of the β- and γ-vectors (the firm and occupation coefficients estimated in eq. [1] and summarized in table 7.4), through regressions of their job-cell-weighted standard deviations on the level of inflation. The sand and grease hypotheses predict that the standard deviations of the β- and γ-vectors (respectively) increase with the level of inflation. A priori, we also expect the standard deviation of occupational wage changes to be bounded by the size of usual shocks to the labor market, whereas disruptive firm variation may be unbounded under high inflation.[12] The regressions reported in this section all take the following form:

$$(2) \qquad \left.\begin{array}{c} \text{stdoc}_t \\ \text{stdem}_t \end{array}\right\} = \psi + \phi_1(\Delta X)_t + \phi_2(\Delta X)_t^2,$$

where stdoc_t and stdem_t (occupation and employer wage-change dispersion, respectively) are regressed independently on some proxy (or proxies) for annual wage movement, represented here by ΔX.[13] The simple two-term quadratic expansions allow curvature in these estimates while remaining easily interpretable. To further aid interpretation, the bottom row of each table below also reports the implied value of the independent variable at the maximum.

After considering the impact of expanding the sample, we compare a variety of specifications. Then we consider the likelihood that inflation might aid the intended adjustment of firm (rather than occupation) wage differentials.

---

12. Expanding indexation could bound the sand effect, as suggested by Drazen and Hamermesh (1986).

13. While the two-stage nature of this procedure may raise standard errors in eq. (2), it will not influence coefficient estimates unless the first-stage estimation errors are correlated with our measures of inflation. We have no a priori reason to suspect such a correlation.

Table 7.5   **Basic Regressions of the Standard Deviation of Employer and Occupation Wage Adjustments on Wage Inflation: Original and Extended Samples**

	Dependent Variable: Standard Deviation of Wage Adjustment Components			
	Employer		Occupation	
Model	1957–92 (1)	1957–96 (2)	1957–92 (3)	1957–96 (4)
Intercept	0.012	0.015	0.004	0.007
	(0.007)	(0.006)	(0.005)	(0.005)
CPI+	0.394	0.323	0.458	0.427
	(0.198)	(0.177)	(0.136)	(0.137)
Squared CPI+	−1.475	−1.104	−2.293	−2.301
	(1.227)	(1.120)	(0.843)	(0.865)
Adjusted R^2	0.138	0.121	0.151	0.089
N	101	113	101	113
F-statistic for joint test, 1% cutoff ≤ 4.8	9.0	8.7	9.9	6.5
Implied CPI+ maximum (%)	13.4	14.6	10.0	9.3

Source: Authors' calculations from the Federal Reserve Bank of Cleveland Community Salary Survey, 1956–96.

Note: Numbers in parentheses are standard errors.

7.5.1   The Effect of Sample Extension

Table 7.5 shows the impact of the new observations, using the CPI+ measure of external nominal wage change. Columns (1) and (3) report basic regression results from the original Groshen and Schweitzer (1996) sample. Columns (2) and (4) report results from the extended sample.

The qualitative results (inverted U-shaped relationships, with an earlier peak for occupation) are unchanged, but some interesting effects are evident. First, the employer (sand) effect now peaks at an even higher inflation rate, while the occupation (grease) effect tops out at slightly lower inflation rate than before. Thus the contrast between the two is more marked. Second, however, the explanatory power (R^2) of both equations has fallen (particularly for the occupation/grease effect) suggesting that extrapolations from the quadratic form may not fit well at the current low inflation rates.

Figures 7.3A and 7.3B plot the new estimated relationships, along with nonparametric (smoothed) versions of the same relationships.[14] The smoothing is

---

14. We use the LOWESS smoother with a bandwidth of one, recommended by Cleveland (1979), for its robustness with respect to both axes. Various bandwidths from 0.2 to 1 were tried, with little variation in effect.

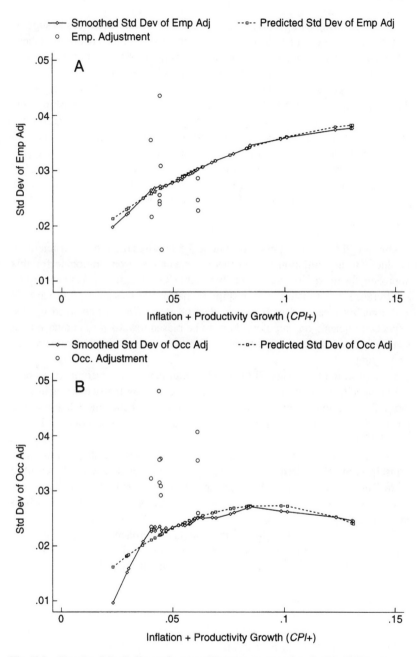

Fig. 7.3   Standard deviations of wage adjustments associated with CPI+ on extended sample: nonparametric and regression predictions

Note: A, CSS employer adjustments; *B,* CSS occupational adjustments. In each case, the smooth line is the fitted quadratic relationship, while the kinked line is the nonparametric version of the same relationship.

similar to allowing a large number of quadratic terms and continues to suggest that the parsimonious models in table 7.5 capture most of the curvature in these relationships. The frequency of observations is indicated (except for overlaps) by the density of tick marks for the smoothed estimates.

The two figures also show tick marks for the new observations. In figure 7.3*B*, the marks are concentrated far above the predicted relationship. This pattern indicates that interoccupational wage flexibility has consistently exceeded the levels that would be expected by extrapolation off the historical relationship. No similar evidence is noticeable for employer adjustments in figure 7.3*A*. These results support the hypothesis that downward wage rigidity has relaxed recently in large employers—precisely the segment of the labor market where wages would tend to be the most rigid.

7.5.2   Freeing the Coefficients on CPI and Productivity

Use of CPI+ in the regressions in table 7.5 imposes the same coefficient on productivity and inflation. While theory provides a strong rationale for this approach, the restriction is empirically testable. One practical reason to suspect a difference in estimated relationships is that productivity is highly variable and arguably measured with a great deal of error. Thus, when freed up, we expect coefficients on output per hour to be biased toward zero and have high standard errors. Table 7.6 reports results for some variants that separate the two underlying series.

Specification (1) repeats CPI+ results from table 7.5 for comparison purposes. Specification (2) shows the impact of separating the two series in quadratic form. Employer wage-change dispersion is no better modeled with the terms separate than together, while the separation more than doubles the adjusted R^2 of the model of occupational adjustments. But specification (3)—CPI-U and its square alone—suggests that in both cases, the shape of the relationship is mostly determined by inflation: output per hour contributes little extra. The implied maxima shown at the bottom suggest that it is in their relationship to the CPI-U that the employer and occupational adjustments differ most strikingly.

The final model shown takes an intermediate approach. It assumes that the difference between the results for output per hour and CPI-U stems mostly from poor output measurement. In both cases, the fit improves and the coefficient is negative, suggesting that the term may absorb some of the downward bias caused by productivity mismeasurement.

These decompositions of the impact of mean nominal wage change are consistent with poor measurement of productivity growth. Since the problem is not easy to fix and theory is unambiguous about productivity's role in generating grease, we continue to prefer specifications that include both inflation and productivity changes.

Table 7.6   Regressions of the Standard Deviation of Employer and Occupation Wage Adjustments on CPI and Output/Hour Separately

Dependent Variable: Standard Deviation of Wage Adjustment Components

	Employer				Occupation			
	(1)	(2)	(3)	(4)	(1)	(2)	(3)	(4)
Intercept	0.015	0.021	0.024	0.014	0.007	0.017	0.015	0.006
	(0.006)	(0.003)	(0.003)	(0.006)	(0.005)	(0.002)	(0.002)	(0.004)
CPI+	0.323			0.403	0.427			0.589
	(0.177)			(0.182)	(0.137)			(0.129)
Squared CPI+	−1.104			−1.683	−2.301			−3.480
	(1.120)			(1.162)	(0.865)			(0.823)
CPI-U		0.119	0.136			0.219	0.293	
		(0.097)	(0.090)			(0.068)	(0.065)	
Squared CPI-U		0.456	−0.108			−0.771	−1.377	
		(0.723)	(0.570)			(0.513)	(0.415)	
ΔOutput/hour		0.224		−0.096		0.085		−0.197
		(0.146)		(0.057)		(0.103)		(0.040)
Squared Δoutput/hour		−3.716				−4.559		
		(3.101)				(2.204)		
Adjusted R^2	0.121	0.122	0.119	0.136	0.089	0.233	0.189	0.246
F-statistic joint test, 1% cutoff ≤ 4.8	8.7	4.9	8.6	6.9	6.5	9.5	14.0	13.2
Implied maximum (%)								
CPI+	14.6			12.0	9.3			8.5
CPI		∞	63.0			14.2	10.6	
ΔOutput/hour		3.0				0.9		

Source: Authors' calculations from the Federal Reserve Bank of Cleveland Community Salary Survey, 1956–96.
Note: Numbers in parentheses are standard errors. Number of observations is 113.

7.5.3   Adding Controls for Trend and Unemployment

Cyclical factors or secular trends could augment the level of employer wage-change dispersion or the pace of occupational adjustment, and these could be correlated with measures of inflation. Thus table 7.7 reports the result of adding controls for time trend and the unemployment rate.

Specification (4) repeats the results from the last specification of table 7.6 for comparison purposes. Model (5) adds a time trend and its square. While taking account of the trend improves the fits substantially (by about double), the implied maxima and the shape of the CPI+ relationships are stable—the grease and sand effects are independent of the trends. The estimated coefficients on trend imply that the average pace of adjustment in both these components is rising. For the occupation component, this result suggests growing wage flexibility or, perhaps, increased frequency or size of shocks. Ultimately, such changes would be expected to alter grease or sand relationships.

Results of adding the unemployment rate vary more between components. Employer wage-change dispersion is unaffected by the unemployment rate: fit worsens and the sand coefficients are unchanged. While the grease coefficients are also unchanged, occupational adjustments clearly respond strongly to cyclical factors, pointing to another intriguing difference in behavior between the occupation and employer components.

This result rules out a compositional interpretation of our findings. Reder (1955) argues that employers hire lower quality workers during expansions than recessions. If three additional conditions hold (i.e., low-quality workers receive lower wage changes within cell, inflation level and unemployment rate are negatively correlated, and these quality differences vary by employer or occupation), our results could reflect systematic variations in worker quality. However, if this were the correct interpretation of our results, then including the jobless rate—a better measure of labor market conditions—would reduce the size and significance of the estimated coefficients on CPI+. The strong association between occupational adjustments and joblessness supports Reder's hypothesis. Nevertheless, unemployment's lack of impact on the grease coefficients constitutes strong evidence that this hypothesis cannot explain our results.

Thus, while trend and cyclical factors influence the variance of both components of wage adjustments, their omission does not appear to bias the grease and sand estimates. This result increases our confidence in the grease and sand interpretation of our findings and justifies our preference for the parsimonious basic model for exposition.

7.5.4   Inflation Surprises versus Expected Inflation

The grease effect results from the leeway provided by expected or experienced inflation, but not by inflation surprises. On the other hand, price level surprises are sufficient to cause the sand effect in the presence of timing

Table 7.7 Regressions of the Standard Deviation of Employer and Occupation Wage Adjustments on CPI+ and Unemployment and Trend Controls

	Dependent Variable: Standard Deviation of Wage Adjustment Components					
	Employer			Occupation		
	(4)	(5)	(6)	(4)	(5)	(6)
Intercept	0.014	78.899	0.013	0.006	68.852	−0.024
	(0.006)	(34.162)	(0.016)	(0.004)	(20.078)	(0.010)
CPI+	0.403	0.658	0.407	0.589	0.471	0.589
	(0.182)	(0.185)	(0.187)	(0.129)	(0.109)	(0.119)
Squared CPI+	−1.683	−2.974	−1.709	−3.480	−2.435	−3.593
	(1.162)	(1.155)	(1.191)	(0.823)	(0.679)	(0.761)
ΔOutput/hour	−0.096	−0.185	−0.096	−0.197	−0.147	−0.209
	(0.057)	(0.059)	(0.058)	(0.040)	(0.034)	(0.039)
Trend		0.084			0.073	
		(0.036)			(0.021)	
Squared trend/1,000		0.022	0.019		0.073	
		(0.010)	(0.006)		(0.021)	
Unemployment			0.037			0.813
			(0.436)			(0.279)
Squared unemployment			−0.344			−4.821
			(3.361)			(2.149)
Adjusted R^2	0.136	0.223	0.120	0.246	0.534	0.374
F-statistic joint test, 1% cutoff ≤ 4.8	6.9	7.4	4.0	13.2	26.7	14.4
Implied CPI+ maximum (%)	12.0	11.1	11.9	8.5	9.7	8.3

Source: Authors' calculations from the Federal Reserve Bank of Cleveland Community Salary Survey, 1956–96.

Note: Numbers in parentheses are standard errors. Number of observations is 113.

rigidities. Thus separating expected inflation from surprises provides another check on the identification strategy. A priori, we expect occupation wage-change variation to rise mostly with expected inflation. Inflation surprises should have their primary effect on employer wage adjustments.

Our measure of firms' inflation expectations is the (beginning of the period) University of Michigan Surveys of Consumers' mean inflation expectations. This series provides a consistent measure over the entire sample period and has been shown to be an unbiased predictor of future price increases (Bryan and Gavin 1986).

Table 7.8 splits the grease and sand effects between expectations and surprises. Model (1) repeats results from specification (3) of table 7.6 for comparison purposes. Models (2), (3), and (4) show the impact of expected and surprise inflation separately and together. Looking at the significance of the coefficients, the R^2s, and the implied maxima, the results are quite stark. As predicted, a surprise sharply raises employer wage-change dispersion, whereas expectations dominate for the occupational adjustments. Also, the expected-surprise distinction clearly improves the fit of the employer regression while contributing no explanatory power for occupational adjustments. Finally, these estimates strongly suggest that the sand effects caused by inflationary surprises may be unbounded, while any impact on occupational adjustments is quickly exhausted.

Because they are very difficult to explain otherwise, these results provide particularly strong support for the grease and sand interpretation of our findings.

7.5.5   Might Inflation Also Speed Intended Firm Adjustments?

An important possibility to consider is whether employers' inflation-induced wage-change variation may be intentional, rather than sand. This would be the case if inflation allowed firms more scope to reduce average wage differentials in response to negative shocks. For example, they might intend to induce quits to allow shrinkage, or to reduce shared rents. We consider such an interpretation inconsistent with our findings for the following reasons.

First, prior studies lead us to expect sand effects among firms. The sand literature for product markets finds consistent evidence of inflation-induced price-change variation (for the closest example, see Lach and Tsiddon 1992). If inflation has no similar effect on wages, information must be better in labor markets, or menu costs or other sources of rigidity must be lower. None of these is likely. Certainly, if better inflation forecasts were available in corporate personnel offices, it would be shared with their sales offices. Menu costs in salary administration are high enough that salaries are rarely reviewed more than annually, while many product prices are changed much more often. So there is good reason to expect a sand effect for wages among firms.

Second, the circumstances under which inflation would play a grease role between firms are quite limited. As we discuss above, it is unusual for a firm

Table 7.8   Regressions of the Standard Deviation of Employer and Occupation Wage Adjustments on Inflation Expectations and Surprises Separately

| | Dependent Variable: Standard Deviation of Wage Adjustment Components | | | | | | | | | |
| | Employer | | | | | Occupation | | | | |
Model	(1)	(2)	(3)	(4)	(5)	(1)	(2)	(3)	(4)	(5)
Intercept	0.024	0.033	0.030	0.034	0.031	0.015	0.013	0.023	0.013	0.016
	(0.003)	(0.004)	(0.001)	(0.004)	(0.004)	(0.002)	(0.003)	(0.001)	(0.003)	(0.003)
CPI-U	0.136					0.293				
	(0.090)					(0.065)				
Squared CPI-U	-0.108					-1.377				
	(0.570)					(0.415)				
Expected inflation		-0.241		-0.246	-0.225		0.330		0.326	0.306
		(0.145)		(0.137)	(0.137)		(0.106)		(0.105)	(0.105)
Squared expected inflation		2.981		3.067	3.208		-1.790		-1.668	-1.803
		(1.230)		(1.185)	(1.181)		(0.897)		(0.911)	(0.903)
Inflation surprise			0.173	0.218	0.268			0.046	0.081	0.033
			(0.062)	(0.061)	(0.070)			(0.049)	(0.047)	(0.053)
Squared inflation surprise			0.238	-1.546	-1.832			0.463	-0.991	-0.718
			(1.198)	(1.317)	(1.322)			(0.959)	(1.013)	(1.012)
ΔOutput/hour					0.106					-0.101
					(0.070)					(0.053)
Adjusted R^2	0.119	0.071	0.112	0.175	0.185	0.189	0.143	0.011	0.152	0.208
F-statistic joint test, 1% cutoff ≤ 4.8	8.6	5.30	8.08	6.94	6.08	14.0	10.38	1.60	6.01	5.63
Implied maximum (%)										
CPI-U	63.0					10.6				
Expected inflation		∞		∞	∞		9.2		9.8	8.5
Inflation surprise			∞	7.1	7.3			∞	4.1	2.3

Source: Authors' calculations from the Federal Reserve Bank of Cleveland Community Salary Survey, 1956–96.

Note: Numbers in parentheses are standard errors. Number of observations is 113.

to want to change its market position. Indeed, in these data, autocorrelations for employers' fixed wage effects one and ten years apart are .93 and .62, respectively (Groshen and Levine 1998). Most effort is directed at maintaining, not adjusting, the market position. However, firms under severe duress do cut nominal wages (Bewley and Brainard 1993; Blinder and Choi 1990; Levine 1993). Thus the conditions under which a firm would resort to using inflation to adjust relative wages are rather narrow: a shock large enough to fundamentally alter its labor market strategy but not big enough for it to openly admit the problem and cut nominal wages.

Even then, it is unclear why a firm in these intermediate circumstances would reduce wages for all workers (risking a general decline in effort) rather than those of the particular occupations it needed to shed.

If, however, such circumstances were common enough to drive many of firms' inflation-induced wage changes in the CSS, there would be no reason to expect markedly different employer and occupation wage responses to inflation. For example, the effect of inflation on wage-change densities and standard deviations should be similar for the two components, not distinctly different. In particular, since downward wage rigidity would be a factor, we should see evidence of truncation in the low-inflation employer density in figure 7.2A—which we do not. Also, the later peak in firms' standard deviation regressions would be unexpected. Finally, inflation surprises should not raise firms' wage-change variation at all—let alone *more* than expected inflation.

Thus labor market sand effects are anticipated, and the circumstances under which inflation would relax a constraint imposed by downward wage rigidity on firm differentials are likely to be rare. Indeed, if they are not rare, we have a puzzle: what explains the striking differences between employer and occupational adjustment patterns under inflation? By contrast, these differences are fully explicable, indeed expected, under the identification strategy. Therefore, our findings are consistent with a sand interpretation for inflation-induced firm wage shifts and inconsistent with a grease interpretation.

7.6   Implications of Results

This section considers the net impact of inflation on the economy. We motivate the question by examining the aggregate relationship between inflation and joblessness. Next we present two approaches to estimating the extent to which grease and sand effects estimated here offset each other. Finally, we contrast our approaches and conclusions with those contained in two recent studies of inflation's grease effect.

7.6.1   The Aggregate Relationship between Inflation and Unemployment

As a first pass at considering the net impact of grease and sand we plot the aggregate relationship between inflation and unemployment. While other factors beyond grease and sand undoubtedly influence this relationship, it is

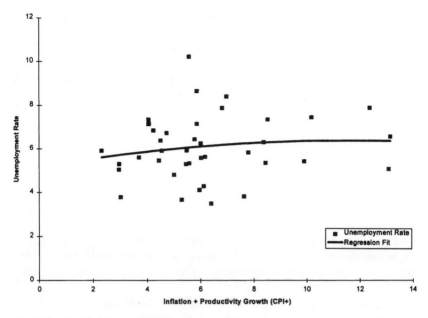

Fig. 7.4   Aggregate relationship between U.S. unemployment rate and CPI+, 1956–96

useful to apprise ourselves of the historical correspondence in the United States before proceeding to more direct estimates of the net impact of inflation on unemployment. In particular, has higher inflation been associated with lower U.S. unemployment—as would be the case, ceteris paribus, if the grease effect dominated the sand effect? Or higher joblessness, if sand effects dominate?

Figure 7.4 plots U.S. civilian unemployment against CPI+ from 1956 through 1996. The fitted regression line makes it clear that what little relationship exists between the two series suggests that more inflation is associated with higher, not lower, rates of unemployment. This aggregate relationship is fully consistent with the results obtained here and with long-run cross-country correlations of GDP growth and inflation across OECD countries (Andrés and Hernando, chap. 8 in this volume).

However, figure 7.4 stands in direct contradiction to the predictions of grease-only estimates. Thus the grease effect must either be offset by sand— as our findings suggest—or small relative to other factors that drive the relationship between unemployment and inflation.

7.6.2   Net Impact of Grease and Sand Effects—General Approach

We offer two ways to translate our results into an indication of inflation's net impact on the economy. The first approach derives from the assumption that

employers find any deviation from their intended wage rates costly, both in ways that increase the unemployment rate and in ways that do not. The second way simulates unemployment consequences of the two effects, for comparability to previous studies.

Our first approach uses inflation-induced wage variation to measure the welfare consequences of inflation. The reasoning follows directly from the model used in Groshen and Schweitzer (1996) and has the advantage of including the full range of impacts on firms. Whatever their source (lack of grease or too much sand), variations from intended wage changes are costly for firms. If the wages are too high, these costs take the form of decreased profits, retained earnings, or investment or lower production and market share (as the result of laying off overpaid workers). If wages are set too low, the costs come from undesired turnover, extended vacancies, or lower morale and productivity. For firms and workers the losses from mispricing are symmetric across the two effects. That is, the impact differs by whether the deviation is up or down, but not by whether its source is lack of grease or too much sand. Hence, the two impacts of inflation can be compared if they are measured equally well, in the same units, in the same market.

Therefore, our first approach simply nets the inflation-induced impacts on wage variation. Figure 7.5 plots these net benefits using the extended data.

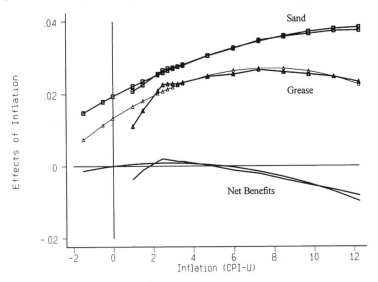

Fig. 7.5   Estimated net effects of inflation, using extended CSS sample (assuming productivity growth of 1.5 percent)

Note: In each case, the smooth line is the fitted quadratic relationship, while the kinked line is the nonparametric version of the same relationship. The vertical axis measures effects of inflation on the standard deviation of log wage changes. The grease effect is assumed to be beneficial because the adjustments are intended responses to changing labor market conditions among occupations. The sand effect is disruptive because it reflects unintended deviations from parity with other employers—due to errors or lags. Net benefits also assume that gross benefits and costs of inflation are zero when the inflation rate is zero.

The horizontal axis measures inflation (controlling for productivity), while the vertical axis measures the standard deviation of log wage changes. For grease, sand, and net benefits two lines are drawn: a smooth line for the fitted quadratic relationship and a kinked line for the nonparametric version of the same relationship. The sand (employer) and grease (occupation) lines are identical to those shown in figures 7.3A and 7.3B, respectively. Grease effects are taken as positive, while the sand effect is negative (although plotted in the positive quadrant for consistency with fig. 7.3A).

Net benefits are calculated assuming that gross benefits and costs of inflation are zero when the inflation rate is zero, and that productivity growth is 1.5 percent, using the following relationship (suppressing the time subscript):

$$\text{(Net benefits} \mid \Delta\text{Prod} = .015) = (\text{Grease} \mid \Delta\text{Prod} = .015)$$

$$- (\text{Sand} \mid \text{Prod} = .015)$$

$$(3)$$

$$= [\text{stdoc(CPI}+) - \text{stdoc}(.015)]$$

$$- [\text{stdem(CPI}+) - \text{stdem}(.015)],$$

where stdem and stdoc are the predicted standard deviations of the employer and occupation components (using cols. [2] and [4] of table 7.5, respectively).

As in the original sample, these estimates suggest a small net benefit for inflation rates below 5 percent. The peak remains at 2.5 percent, and net benefits at the peak remain an order of magnitude less than gross grease benefits. Bootstrapped standard errors around the net benefits estimate are wide enough that they never rule out a net loss from inflation, or a higher gain. However, they conclusively rule out both equality between gross and net benefits and flat (rather than declining) net benefits at higher rates of inflation.

From this exercise we conclude that while inflation's net benefits are maximized at low levels of inflation, the impact is modest at best. This is because rising sand effects mostly offset the gross grease benefits, leaving little net improvement. Although this approach to calculating net benefits does not directly map into more common metrics, such as output or job losses, it has the distinct advantage of accounting for all costs imposed on firms and workers. While some of the above-mentioned costs of unintended wage variation will affect unemployment, others may not. Particularly if workers' human capital is very firm specific, employers and employees have less incentive to sever relationships over a short-lived deviation. Thus impacts on profitability, morale, and productivity may well be larger than observed unemployment effects. Hence, as the best summary of our findings, we prefer this formulation because it does not unduly confine the measurement of impacts.

7.6.3   Net Impact of Grease and Sand Effects—Simulated Unemployment

However, for policy purposes and for comparison with previous studies, an estimate of the unemployment impact of the grease and sand effects measured in the CSS is desirable. This section first explains why such an estimate cannot

be derived directly from the CSS and then describes the simulation we use to address the question.

The statistical model in Groshen and Schweitzer (1996) is designed to detect wage rigidity and uncertainty effects, not employment impacts. Several of the model's features are not suited to a direct translation of our results into joblessness. First, the structure of the data does not allow a reliable measurement of aggregate employment effects. For example, in most years the population of workers in the occupation cells is unknown. Second, the identification strategy does not completely determine all sources of wage variation. Indeed, the approximately 70 percent of wage-change variation remaining in the residual might include unidentified grease and sand effects. Third, unemployment depends on total wage deviations from equilibrium wages, so all components should be accumulated before any impact can be discerned. Thus unemployment effects cannot be estimated directly from the CSS. However, the parameters of the CSS can be used to craft a simulation that illuminates unemployment effects.

To clarify the underlying source of wage-change variation that could account for data like the CSS, we generate artificial data consistent with key features of the CSS. The appendix describes the simulation in more detail. The simulated data mimic the CSS in three dimensions: an identical firm, occupation, and city structure; the same levels of overall variation by year, city, occupation, firm, and residual; and regression coefficients approximately matching those in the CSS.

Having simulated the data, we next build on the assumption that job losses occur when grease or sand effects drive workers' final wage changes away from equilibrium. The size and frequency of these deviations (combined with elasticities of labor demand and supply) determine the unemployment rate. For truncated wage changes, only the labor demand elasticity comes into play because truncation can only raise wage adjustments. Drawing on Hamermesh (1993), we apply a range of uncompensated demand elasticities from -0.1 to -0.5. For sand effects, which can be either positive or negative, supply elasticities also matter. We use uncompensated labor supply elasticities from 0.0 to 0.6, reflecting widely varying implied estimates when both men and women are in the market (Pencavel 1986; Killingsworth and Heckman 1986).

Figure 7.6 shows simulated total unemployment effects of inflation due to grease and sand. The horizontal axis measures CPI+, while the vertical axis reports percentage points of unemployment. The data are sparse at high and low inflation. Therefore, ends of the curves are determined by the average effect for extreme observations, which are plotted as corresponding to the average lowest and highest CPI+ values of 2.8 and 11.8 percent, respectively.[15]

15. To construct these endpoints, we aggregate all observations with CPI+ of less than 3.5 or more than 9.5 and estimated mean grease and sand effects. In fig. 7.6, these mean effects are assigned to CPI+ values of 2.9 and 11 percent, respectively—because these are the mean CPI+ values for the extreme observations.

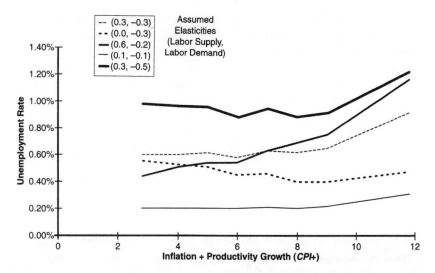

Fig. 7.6   Simulated net effects of CPI+ on unemployment, based on CSS results

Note that a CPI+ value of 2.8 percent corresponds to a very low rate of inflation (near 1 percent), once productivity growth of 1.5 percent (the average over
this period) and any positive biases in the CPI are accounted for.

Over the range in which inflation has net beneficial effects, the line will
slope down: the steeper the slope, the greater the benefits. Net disruptive effects will be seen as a positive slope. The five lines on the figure correspond to
different assumed supply and demand elasticities. As a baseline, we consider
a symmetric case (0.3 labor supply elasticity, −0.3 labor demand elasticity),
seen as the thin dashed line in figure 7.6. At low rates of inflation, the downward wage rigidity underlying the grease effect causes unemployment. As inflation rises, the grease effect lowers unemployment. However, inflation also
raises sand-induced joblessness. Thus the line shows a mild U-shape. Over the
downward-sloping portion (from CPI+ of 2.8 to 6 percent), there is little net
unemployment impact (less than 0.1 percentage points) of inflation. Beyond
that, the grease-effect unemployment reductions become trivial and sand effects continue to grow. There is no evidence of a strong nonlinearity as inflation
gets very low.

Higher elasticities of labor demand raise inflation-related unemployment because employers are more likely to lay off workers in response to higher than
notional wages (see the line for supply elasticity of 0.3 and demand elasticity
of −0.5). The net effect line shifts up fairly uniformly because both grease and
sand effects rise, leading to more unemployment at high and low levels of
inflation. The slope of the line (which is the net effect of additional inflation
on unemployment) remains almost flat, except at high levels.

Labor supply elasticity, on the other hand, affects only sand-induced jobless-

ness. More elastic supply emphasizes the sand effects. The less elastic is supply, the smaller the sand effect, so grease effects dominate. However, even the extreme example shown in figure 7.6 (perfectly inelastic supply with demand elasticity of -0.3) generates only a 0.2 percentage point drop in unemployment for a 5 percentage point increase in inflation (from CPI+ of 2.8 to 8.0).

To sum up: In this section we simulate a wage-change-generating process modeled on the structure of the CSS. Simulated observations allow us to estimate unemployment impacts of grease and sand. The exercise shows that even under extreme assumptions about the elasticities of labor demand and supply, grease and sand effects almost fully offset each other at low to moderate rates of inflation. In particular, under a wide range of elasticities of labor supply and demand, we find no evidence that very low rates of inflation raise unemployment noticeably.

7.6.4 Comparison of Results with Recent Wage Rigidity Studies

How do these results compare with recent studies of inflation's effect on wage setting? We focus on Akerlof, Dickens, and Perry (1996, hereafter AD&P) and Card and Hyslop (1995, hereafter C&H), since they are very recent studies.[16]

We begin by listing three important ways in which our work differs from both studies. First, neither AD&P nor C&H considers offsetting sand effects. Second, our analysis and model are tightly linked to actual wage adjustment procedures. Our firm-level data allow us to identify and interpret wage rigidities unobservable in household surveys. Third, neither study analyzes microlevel wage changes spanning the range of years (and thus the range of inflation rates) covered in the CSS. In particular, neither study includes low-inflation years in the 1950s, 1960s, and 1990s. Thus implications they derive about low inflation are largely out-of-sample extrapolations.

Nevertheless, broadly speaking, our empirical results for the grease effect are consistent with findings in both studies: downward wage rigidity binds more at low rates of inflation, so higher inflation has some beneficial gross effects. We now contrast our study with the two others in turn.

AD&P has three main sections. The first examines wide-ranging, new and old empirical evidence of downward nominal wage rigidity. Next it models and emulates grease effects to show that (for plausible values of parameters) this rigidity could raise unemployment substantially at low inflation rates. Third, it converts the simulation model to one that can be estimated on aggregate data and shows that out-of-sample predictions from the model can emulate Depression era unemployment patterns. Thus AD&P concludes that low inflation is very costly in the labor market.

---

16. Other fairly recent studies of the grease effects include Kahn (1997), McLaughlin (1994), and Lebow, Stockton, and Wascher (1995). All three perform microlevel tests of downward wage rigidity.

In the empirical section, AD&P considers the spike at zero in the density of wage changes to be key evidence of downward wage rigidity. We argue that while the spike is a likely prediction, it may not be either necessary or sufficient. It is not necessary evidence if constrained workers are laid off. It is not sufficient because zero is a double rounding point (in even dollars and percentage points), potentially creating a large spurious concentration at zero. For those reasons, we consider inflation's impact on wage-change variation a preferable measure (particularly in the CSS, which does not report individual wages). Nevertheless, our findings agree with AD&P's qualitative conclusion that the grease effect exists.

The contrast with our study centers on unemployment effects in our simulation exercises. The marked difference in conclusions reflects divergent structures for wage-change variation. To explicitly consider the effect of errors and other randomness, we observe and thus generate firm-based wage variation (0.036 log points when CPI+ is 5 percent) that rises with inflation, plus a constant residual variation (0.080 log points). To reflect persistent market shocks, we add constant occupation variation (0.028 log points). By contrast, AD&P's underlying structure is constant with respect to inflation, has a single component (the firm), and generates a much smaller standard deviation of log wage-changes (0.028) than we observe in the CSS. AD&P's firm effects are most comparable to our occupation effects in size and in variance with inflation. Their demand shocks affect firms, while ours act on both firms and skills. Thus AD&P implicitly assumes that there are no distinct occupational markets, or that firms employ only one occupation at a time.

The AD&P simulation also assumes a fairly high rate of truncation for constrained wages—not much different from ours. At low rates of inflation, the CSS data on which we base our simulation show no sign of nonlinearity. By contrast, AD&P's extrapolated simulation produces a highly nonlinear region at low inflation rates. Indeed, this is the range on which they base their strongest policy conclusions.

C&H performs a more detailed analysis of the effect of wage rigidity in the March Current Population Survey (CPS), 1979–93, and the Michigan Panel Study of Income Dynamics, 1976–79 and 1985–88. They consider the impact that wage rigidity would have on the distribution of changes, accounting for errors and rounding. Then they generate a counterfactual, unconstrained distribution to gauge the effects of wage rigidity. Despite some assumptions that might bias down their estimated effect, they detect evidence of substantial wage rigidity under low inflation. In contrast to the CSS sample used here, C&H has no information on firms and few low-inflation years.

The final part of C&H detects little or no macroimpact of a net grease effect at the market level. A state-level comparison of the relationship between nominal wage changes and unemployment (using CPS files from 1976 to 1992) yields only a small, statistically insignificant relationship. Although C&H offer little explanation for the apparent contradiction between their individual and

aggregate results, their findings can be easily explained by the existence of the sand effect, which they do not measure at the microlevel. Indeed, their findings, if not their interpretations, are compatible with those presented above.

Thus the evidence for the grease effect in the CSS is consistent with microlevel findings in AD&P and C&H. In addition, our simulated unemployment results can explain the lack of relationship between inflation and state-level unemployment rates found in C&H. By contrast, our findings suggest that the AD&P simulations—which predict a strong unemployment cost for low inflation—appear to be largely an artifact of extrapolation in a model that ignores sand effects.

7.7 Conclusions

Our companion study finds evidence that inflation stimulates both beneficial intermarket and distortionary intramarket wage changes. The identification strategy for this conclusion is that inflation-induced occupational adjustments represent beneficial grease, while inflation-induced wage changes among employers reflect distortionary sand in the labor market. This paper examines 40 years of CSS data in order to judge the appropriateness of this key identification strategy. We also check whether downward wage rigidity has relaxed in recent years, reducing our need for inflation's grease.

One form of support for the assumption is that many important institutional features of the wage-setting process accord well with the formal model used to generate the hypotheses tested. In addition, we present a variety of independent empirical findings that all provide further support. Table 7.9 summarizes these findings. Probes 4 and 5 are more fully described in our companion paper. The others are presented above.

No single probe can be fully convincing on its own. However, the combined weight of these varied findings sustains the validity of the identification strategy. Indeed, these findings (such as inflation expectations being the sole source of the inflation-induced occupation effects, while surprises matter more for employer effects) are very difficult to explain if the strategy is not valid. Thus the grease and sand interpretation of inflation-induced occupation and employer wage adjustments holds up well to close scrutiny.

The second question—whether wage rigidity has relaxed in recent years—finds the following support:

- The pace of occupational wage adjustments in past years is consistently much higher than would be predicted based on the historical relationships and the current level of inflation. The same does not hold true for employer wage-change dispersion.
- Over time, occupational wage-change dispersion shows a statistically significant upward trend, with a lot of explanatory power. While this is also true among employers, it explains much less variation over time.

Table 7.9   Summary of Evidence in Support of Identification Strategy

Probe	Finding	Consistent with Grease and Sand Interpretation?
1. Test wage changes for *independent* employer and occupation components.	Employer and occupational wage changes are almost fully separable and distinguishable statistically, even though data are unbalanced.	*Yes.* Consistent with two-stage wage-setting procedure.
2. Plot *densities* of low- versus high-inflation occupational and employer wage changes.	Occupational adjustments show evidence of truncation under inflation. No such effect for employer wage changes; lower inflation simply thins both tails.	*Yes.* Consistent with downward rigidity constraining wage cuts for occupations under low inflation, and reducing errors or lags by firms.
3. Compare *peak* of occupation and employer effects.	The pace of occupational adjustments slows at inflation rates above 5%. Employer wage-change dispersion shows a higher (perhaps unbounded) peak. Finding is robust over all specifications examined.	*Yes.* Consistent with a grease effect bounded by the size of real shocks to skill groups, while inflation-induced disagreement among employers has no limit without indexation.
4. *Filter* to obtain low-frequency occupation changes and high-frequency employer adjustments.	Little qualitative impact. The shape of the employer relationship is driven by short-term changes; the shape of the occupation relationship is driven by long-term adjustments.	*Yes.* Consistent with occupation adjustments reflecting long-term market movements and employer deviations being errors and corrections.
5. Use *panel* specification to control for lags and employer and occupation fixed effects.	Little qualitative impact. Occupation adjustments peak somewhat earlier, employer effects peak later, if at all.	*Yes.* Rules out spurious autocorrelations and fixed effects as the source of the estimated relationships.
6. Divide CPI between inflation *surprises* and *expectations*.	The pace of occupational adjustments rises only with inflation expectations—not with surprises. Inflation surprises matter more than expectations for raising employer disagreement.	*Yes.* Consistent with expected inflation providing leeway for intended occupational adjustments, while price level surprises cause more unintended adjustments among employers.
7. Control for cyclical *unemployment* and secular *time* trend.	Little qualitative impact. But, independent of inflation, occupational adjustments rise strongly with unemployment, while employer adjustments are unaffected.	*Yes.* Rules out interpretations of the results as the product of time, business cycles, or trends correlated with the level of inflation, such as worker quality fluctuations.

Although it would be premature to claim that this evidence constitutes proof of the U.S. economy's reduced need for inflationary grease, our findings do point in that direction. This result is particularly intriguing because large firms are precisely the segment of the labor market where wages are thought to be most rigid. More research is clearly warranted in this area.

What implications do these findings have for policy? Both buttress the conclusion that low-inflation regimes may not raise unemployment or impair the smooth functioning of labor markets. Even if one accepts previous estimates of the grease effect at full face value, our results suggest that the net labor market benefits of inflation are an order of magnitude smaller because of inflation's simultaneous sand effect. And they may be shrinking further. Thus the labor market provides little guidance on which inflation goal to choose in a low-inflation regime.

Appendix
Description of Unemployment Simulation Exercise

This section describes the process used to arrive at the unemployment simulations results reported in the text and figure 7.6. We generate artificial data consistent with various key features of the CSS.

The simulated data are constructed to mimic the CSS in three ways: (1) a firm, occupation, and city structure identical to that shown in tables 7.1 and 7.2, so that any limitations on the identification strategy due to the number of cells with given characteristics is replicated; (2) the same levels of overall variation by year, city, occupation, firm, and residual, as seen in table 7.4; and (3) regression coefficients approximately matching the basic (stage 2) estimates shown in table 7.5. From these results we calculate unemployment impacts for grease and sand, using labor supply and demand elasticities estimated elsewhere.

Underlying wage changes are assigned a trend equal to inflation plus productivity growth. Around that trend, we allow the following five sources of variation: occupation, firm (uncorrelated with inflation and general productivity growth), firm uncertainty, city, and residual (which accounts for all other sources of wage-change variation). If the total wage change sums to less than zero, it is truncated with a fixed probability.

The parameterization we use parallels results in stages 1 and 2 of the CSS statistical model. In any year, both firm and occupation effects are allowed to vary 12 percent as much as total wage changes. Firm variation also rises with inflation and productivity (CPI+). The slope of the relationship—0.18—was chosen so that the sand component accounts for half of total firm variation.

Variation in the raw (pretruncated) residual is set slightly greater than the total CSS variation, so that ANOVA results for posttruncation simulated data resemble those observed in stage 1. Independent city variation is set to zero because the firm variation already generates comparable city effects. Firms truncate the wages of workers with negative total (raw) wage changes 75 percent of the time. This frequency of truncation replicates stage 2 grease estimates.

References

Akerlof, George A., William T. Dickens, and George L. Perry. 1996. The macroeconomics of low inflation. *Brookings Papers on Economic Activity,* no. 1: 1–59.

Ball, Laurence, and Stephen G. Cecchetti. 1990. Inflation and uncertainty at short and long horizons. *Brookings Papers on Economic Activity,* no. 1: 215–54.

Bewley, Truman, and William Brainard. 1993. A depressed labor market, as explained by participants. New Haven, CT: Yale University, Cowles Foundation, February. Mimeograph.

Blinder, Alan S., and Don H. Choi. 1990. A shred of evidence on theories of wage stickiness. *Quarterly Journal of Economics* 105, no. 4 (November): 1003–15.

Bryan, Michael F., and William T. Gavin. 1986. Models of inflation expectations formation. *Journal of Money, Credit, and Banking* 18, no. 4 (November): 539–44.

Card, David, and Dean Hyslop. 1997. Does inflation "grease the wheels of the labor market"? In *Reducing inflation: Motivation and strategy,* ed. Christina Romer and David Romer, 71–114. Chicago: University of Chicago Press.

Cleveland, William S. 1979. Robust locally weighted regression and smoothing scatter plots. *Journal of the American Statistical Association* 79:829–36.

Drazen, Allan, and Daniel S. Hamermesh. 1986. Inflation and wage dispersion. NBER Working Paper no. 1811. Cambridge, Mass.: National Bureau of Economic Research, January.

Freedman, Audrey. 1976. *The new look in wage policy and employee relations.* Report no. 865. New York: The Conference Board.

Friedman, Milton. 1977. Nobel lecture: Inflation and unemployment. *Journal of Political Economy* 85 (3): 451–72.

Groshen, Erica L. 1989. Do wage differences among employers last? Working paper no. 8906. Cleveland: Federal Reserve Bank of Cleveland, June (revised 1991).

———. 1996. American employer salary surveys and labor economics research: Issues and contributions. *Annales d'Economie et de Statistique,* no. 41/42: 414–42.

Groshen, Erica L., and David I. Levine. 1998. The rise and decline(?) of U.S. internal labor markets. Research Paper no. 9819. New York: Federal Reserve Bank of New York, July.

Groshen, Erica L., and Mark E. Schweitzer. 1996. The effects of inflation on wage adjustments in firm-level data: Grease or sand? Staff Report no. 9. New York: Federal Reserve Bank of New York, January (latest version December 1996).

Hamermesh, Daniel S. 1993. *Labor demand.* Princeton, N.J.: Princeton University Press.

Hills, F. S. 1987. *Compensation decision making.* Hinsdale, Ill.: Dryden.

Kahn, Shulamit. 1997. Evidence of nominal wage stickiness from microdata. *American Economic Review* 87, no. 5 (December): 993–1008.

Killingsworth, Mark R., and James J. Heckman. 1986. Female labor supply: A survey. In *Handbook of labor economics,* ed. O. Ashenfelter and R. Layard, 103–204. Amsterdam: North Holland.

Lach, Saul, and Daniel Tsiddon. 1992. The behavior of prices and inflation: An empirical analysis of disaggregated price data. *Journal of Political Economy* 100 (2): 349–89.

Lebow, David E., David J. Stockton, and William L. Wascher. 1995. Inflation, nominal wage rigidity, and the efficiency of labor markets. Finance and Economics Discussion Series, no. 94-45. Washington, D.C.: Board of Governors of the Federal Reserve System, October.

Levine, David I. 1993. Fairness, markets, and ability to pay: Evidence from compensation executives. *American Economic Review* 83, no. 5 (December): 1241–59.

McLaughlin, Kenneth J. 1994. Rigid wages? *Journal of Monetary Economics* 34 (3): 383–414.

Milkovich, George, and J. M. Newman. 1990. *Compensation.* Homewood, Ill.: BPI-Irwin.

Pencavel, John. 1986. Labor supply of men: A survey. In *Handbook of labor economics,* ed. O. Ashenfelter and R. Layard, 3–102. Amsterdam: North Holland.

Reder, Melvin. 1955. The theory of occupational wage differentials. *American Economic Review* 45, no. 5 (December): 833–52.

Tobin, James. 1972. Inflation and unemployment. *American Economic Review* 62, no. 1 (March): 1–18.

Wallace, M. J., and C. H. Fay. 1988. *Compensation theory and practice.* Boston: PWS-Kent.

Comment   Laurence Ball

Groshen and Schweitzer do two things in their paper. First, they provide new evidence about an important nonneutrality of inflation: its effects on relative wages. Second, they use this evidence to address the policy question of whether the United States should move to price stability. I think the first part of the paper is excellent: we learn a lot from Groshen and Schweitzer's novel data set, and from their clever identifying assumptions. I am more skeptical about the policy analysis.

The Paper's Contributions

The paper establishes that inflation raises the variability of relative wages, both variability across employers and variability across occupations. The evidence is more conclusive than that of previous studies because the authors' salary surveys measure wages more accurately than standard data sets such as the Panel Study of Income Dynamics.

The paper also makes an important contribution by introducing the distinc-

Laurence Ball is professor of economics at Johns Hopkins University and a research associate of the National Bureau of Economic Research.

tion between grease and sand. Many previous studies ask whether inflation raises the overall variability of wages or prices. Groshen and Schweitzer make it clear that this is not the right question because wage variability is like cholesterol: we need to distinguish between the good kind and the bad kind. Good variability is caused by microeconomic forces, while bad variability arises from varying reactions to inflation.

The paper's key assumptions are that wage variability across occupations is the good kind of variability and variability across employers is the bad kind. Are these assumptions convincing? The assumption about occupational variability is plausible, but I am not sure that employer variability is all bad. It is likely that some employers, such as those in declining industries, need to cut relative wages to maintain employment. If the grease effect of inflation allows this adjustment, the resulting variability is good. So I suspect that wage variability across employers has some grease mixed in with the sand. Nonetheless, the paper's decomposition of variability is very useful.

A final strong point of the paper is that its evidence concerns grease and sand effects that we have observed historically. Much previous work, by contrast, relies on out-of-sample predictions about the effects of price stability. For example, Akerlof, Dickens, and Perry (1996) argue that reducing inflation will greatly reduce relative wage flexibility, but not until inflation falls below 2 percent. Their argument assumes that the nominal rigidity we have observed in recent decades, when inflation exceeded 2 percent, will remain if inflation falls. As discussed by Mankiw (1996) this assumption is dubious: downward rigidity may decrease when lower inflation makes it more common for equilibrium wages to fall. In contrast to Akerlof et al., Groshen and Schweitzer do not rely on assumptions about hypothetical inflation rates. They show that inflation has already fallen low enough to detect a decrease in the grease effect.

The Case for Price Stability

After measuring the grease and sand effects, Groshen and Schweitzer add them together to determine the desirability of moving to price stability. They conclude that the two effects roughly cancel out, so their results do not provide a strong argument either for or against price stability. In my view, there are several problems with this argument.

First, it is not obvious that the welfare effect of inflation is given by the unweighted sum of grease and sand. Why must a unit increase in wage variability across employers have the same effect as a decrease in variability across occupations? I do not understand the claim that the two effects can be summed because they "are measured in the same units." We need more work to determine the welfare effects of grease and sand.

Second, even if the two effects can be summed, the paper's finding of a small net effect is fragile. The point estimates imply that both grease and sand effects are large, but they are almost equal so the net effect is much smaller. This

canceling out is a knife-edge result. If we change one of the point estimates by a standard error or two, the net effect can be the same order of magnitude as the gross effects, and it can have either sign. We should conclude that both gross effects are important but more work is needed to pin down their relative sizes.

There is also a broader problem with the paper's policy analysis. Even if we accept the point estimates of grease and sand effects, it does not follow that there is little net difference between price stability and low inflation. In analyzing welfare, it is crucial to distinguish between the average level of inflation and inflation variability. Recognizing this, Groshen and Schweitzer present evidence that these variables have different effects on wage adjustment. The level of inflation is the main determinant of grease, while variability creates sand because it leads to mistakes in wage setting. These results imply that the best policy is to minimize the variance of inflation but not the mean: to aim for steady positive inflation, which yields grease without sand. Such a policy is close to ones actually practiced in some countries. In Australia, for example, policy attempts to keep inflation close to a target of 2.5 percent.

Finally, in assessing whether the United States should move to price stability, Groshen and Schweitzer face the same basic problem as previous researchers: it's hard to say what will happen at price stability because we haven't been there yet. As discussed above, Akerlof et al. claim that large distortions will arise when inflation falls below 2 percent. There is little hard evidence that this will happen, but there is also little evidence that it will not happen. The distortions caused by downward wage rigidity might rise dramatically if eliminating inflation makes rigidity more binding. One of the paper's strengths—that it provides within-sample evidence of grease effects—is also a weakness when we analyze the out-of-sample policy of price stability.

How might we gain reliable evidence on the effects of price stability? One possibility is to examine experiences in countries other than the United States. It is not clear, however, whether such evidence is convincing. Mankiw (1996) cites Germany's experience to argue that reducing inflation is benign, but Germany has not reached true price stability. Krugman (1996) blames low inflation for high unemployment in Canada and France, but this unemployment may be the cyclical result of disinflation rather than a steady state effect. Perhaps the recent period of near-stable prices in Japan will provide useful evidence.

References

Akerlof, George A., William T. Dickens, and George L. Perry. 1996. The macroeconomics of low inflation. *Brookings Papers on Economic Activity,* no. 1: 1–59.

Krugman, Paul. 1996. Stable prices and fast growth: Just say no. *Economist,* 31 August, 15–18.

Mankiw, N. Gregory. 1996. Comment on "The macroeconomics of low inflation," by G. A. Akerlof, W. T. Dickens, and G. L. Perry. *Brookings Papers on Economic Activity,* no. 1: 66–70.

Discussion Summary

Anna Schwartz noted that the Bureau of Labor Statistics also gathers wage data for detailed occupation groups and sectors at the city level and asked in what respect these data differ from the wage data used by the authors. The authors responded that the main difference is that the Bureau of Labor Statistics does not report wage data at the establishment level whereas the data from the Federal Reserve Bank of Cleveland Community Salary Survey does. However, the correlation between these two data sources is very high, .95 to .97.

Benjamin Friedman said he is skeptical about the authors' interpretation of wage variability within occupations as "sand" (cost of inflation) and the interpretation of wage variability across occupations as "grease" (benefits of inflation). The reason for his skepticism is that this is a ceteris paribus argument. For example, if a firm increases its X-efficiency, it will offer higher wages to attract workers, which increases wage variability within occupations. This seems to be a good thing, which should not be interpreted as a cost of inflation. Similarly, why does the role of forecast errors not also bear on interoccupational shifts?

Stanley Fischer noted that inflation also increased price variability in the goods market but that the right underlying level of price variability is not obvious. He said he wondered why the sand and grease interpretation should be compelling in the labor market whereas few would find it compelling in the goods market.

Matthew Shapiro remarked that inflation caused by supply shocks rather than by demand shocks may change relative prices. For example, an oil shock would have different effects on the wages offered by oil firms in Texas and by financial firms in the same state. However, this does not correspond to harmful sand effects. Shapiro also concurred with a comment by Laurence Ball that it is not clear whether it is correct to subtract sand costs from grease benefits to obtain a net effect. The main reason for this is that grease effects arise from expected inflation whereas sand effects are caused by unexpected inflation. Finally, Shapiro remarked that table 7.8 is hard to interpret because of the squared inflation term.

Martin Feldstein noted that many highly paid employees already experience reductions in nominal earnings but that these reductions take place through cuts in bonuses rather than through reductions of base salaries. Under price stability, bonuses are likely to become much more prevalent throughout the wage distribution in order to allow reductions in compensation without nominal salary cuts. Feldstein asked the authors to comment on the effects of sand and grease on unemployment.

Erica Groshen and Mark Schweitzer, in response to these questions, began by noting (particularly in response to the issue raised by Friedman) that the intraoccupational wage variability is calculated after controlling for occupation fixed effects and the interoccupational wage variability is calculated after con-

trolling for employer fixed effects. Moreover, not all intraoccupational wage variability is the effect of sand, only the component that is induced by inflation, and similarly, only the inflation-induced component of interoccupational wage variability is the effect of grease. The inclusion of employer fixed effects is important, and the employer fixed effects are highly persistent over time. Because of these controls the authors do not feel uncomfortable about the results.

Replying to Stanley Fischer, they noted that the effect of inflation on product market price variability has been studied by Lach and Tsiddon. However, grease effects are only important for labor markets because product prices generally do not exhibit nominal downward rigidity.

The authors reported that their data do include bonuses and that their results are consistent with increased wage flexibility in the most recent low-inflation years, suggesting that wage flexibility does indeed increase in a low-inflation regime. The authors also note that they looked at the more mobile occupations such as secretaries and computer specialists. For these occupations, firms can expect to lose workers if they set a wage below the going wage.

Mark Schweitzer emphasized that their panel spans a long period, from 1957 to 1996, which encompasses periods of both high and low inflation. If the results were spurious, one would not expect similar results in all periods. The authors acknowledged that separating sand and grease effects ultimately is a very difficult task. However, they worked through their analysis very carefully and performed many checks that they believe support the validity of their approach.

Many models including efficiency wage models imply that firms want to set their wage as close as possible to the market wage and that any deviation, whether due to sand or grease, is costly. For this reason sand and grease effects can be compared.

The authors chose to look only at U.S. data because labor market institutions in other countries are too different to make inferences that are relevant for the United States.

The authors agreed that it is worthwhile to try to make a distinction between the variability of inflation and the level of inflation. However, it is very difficult to pin down exactly the contemporaneous disagreement among employers about inflation expectations, and empirically this disagreement can be captured best by the current level of inflation.

Martin Feldstein said that he accepts that at a hand-waving level, grease and sand effects can be compared but would like to know how they affect unemployment. The effect on unemployment is especially interesting because it would allow a comparison with the paper by Akerlof, Dickens, and Perry.

Mark Schweitzer stated that it is extremely difficult to map a given set of wage mismatches into welfare statements or unemployment effects. One way of doing this may be the model used by Akerlof et al., but this is very speculative. *Erica Groshen* added that the Akerlof et al. model has some peculiar features that the authors are hesitant to accept. The model is inconsistent with the

distribution of wage changes that Akerlof et al. take as evidence of nominal downward wage rigidity. Another problem is that firms can take a wide variety of responses to wage mismatches. For example, employers may curtail the wage increase of good performers because they cannot cut wages of bad performers due to the downward nominal wage rigidity. While this may lead to unemployment in the long run, the authors do not believe that it actually causes unemployment in the short run. This illustrates that one needs very heroic assumptions to translate grease and sand effects into unemployment.

8 Does Inflation Harm Economic Growth? Evidence from the OECD

Javier Andrés and Ignacio Hernando

8.1 Introduction

From 1973 until 1984 OECD economies underwent a period of macroeconomic distress in which inflation escalated to reach an average rate of 13 percent, three times as high as in the previous decade. Since then, achieving low and stable inflation has become the main goal of monetary policy in western economies. This move in monetary policy making rests on the belief, firmly rooted in many economists' and politicians' minds, that the costs of inflation are nonnegligible, so that keeping inflation under control pays off in terms of faster sustainable growth in the future.

The shortage of theoretical models explicitly addressing the issue of the long-run effects of inflation has not prevented many researchers from trying to estimate the costs of inflation. A series of recent papers have tried to assess the long-run impact of current inflation within the framework of *convergence equations*. These equations can be derived from a theoretical model of economic growth, and although the precise channels through which inflation affects growth are not always made explicit, they have several advantages for the purposes at hand. First and foremost, an explicit model reduces the risk of omitting relevant variables. Second, convergence equations allow for a variety of effects of inflation, including those that reduce accumulation rates and those that undermine the efficiency with which productive factors operate. Finally, in this framework a clear distinction can be made between *level* and *rate-of-*

Javier Andrés is professor of economics at the University of Valencia and an economist in the Research Department of the Banco de España. Ignacio Hernando is an economist in the Research Department of the Banco de España.

The authors are grateful to Palle Andersen, Sean Craig, Juan Dolado, Rafael Doménech, Angel Estrada, Frederic Mishkin, Teresa Sastre, Javier Vallés, José Viñals, and conference participants for their comments and to Francisco de Castro for his excellent research assistance. Javier Andrés acknowledges financial support by DGICYT grant SEC96-1435-C03-01.

growth effects of inflation; this difference matters as regards the size and the timing of the costs of inflation. We stick to this methodology, whose main shortcoming is that it focuses on long-run issues, disregarding the short-run costs associated with disinflation, the *sacrifice ratio*. Our purpose is to study the correlation between growth and inflation at the OECD level and to discuss whether this correlation withstands a number of improvements in the empirical models, which try to address the most common criticisms of this evidence. In particular, we aim to answer the following questions: Is this correlation explained by the experience of high-inflation economies? Are the estimated costs of inflation still significant once country-specific effects are allowed for in the empirical model? Can the observed negative correlation be dismissed on the grounds of reverse causation (from GDP to inflation)?

The rest of the paper is organized as follows. Section 8.2 briefly summarizes the literature dealing with the costs of inflation, the empirical model, and the data used. In section 8.3 we present the estimated convergence equations augmented with the rate of inflation, and in section 8.4 the empirical model is further augmented to allow for cross-country heterogeneity. In these two sections, we test the sensitivity of the results to the exclusion of high-inflation countries. In section 8.4 we also estimate the long-run benefits of a permanent disinflation and address the issue of whether the cost of inflation varies with the level of inflation or not. In section 8.5 standard causality tests are applied to the inflation-growth relationship. Section 8.6 concludes with some additional remarks. The main results of the paper can be summarized as follows. Even low or moderate inflation rates (such as the ones we have witnessed within the OECD) have a negative temporary impact on long-term growth rates; this effect is significant and generates a permanent reduction in the level of per capita income. Inflation not only reduces the level of investment but also the efficiency with which productive factors are used. The estimated benefit of a permanent reduction in the inflation rate by a percentage point is an increase in the steady state level of per capita income that ranges from 0.5 to 2 percent. Although the size varies somewhat across specifications (as well as across different levels of inflation), the correlation between inflation and future income is never found to be positive. This result holds across different subsamples (even excluding high-inflation countries) and is also robust to alternative econometric specifications. In particular, inflation Granger-causes income and the current and lagged correlation between these two variables remains significant when we control for country-specific variables (such as accumulation rates) and time-invariant effects.

8.2   Theoretical Framework

8.2.1   International Evidence

The negative effects of inflation have been studied in the context of models of economic growth in which the continuous increase of per capita income is the outcome of capital accumulation along with technological progress.[1] The uncertainty associated with high and volatile unanticipated inflation has been found to be one of the main determinants of the rate of return on capital and investment (Bruno 1993; Pindyck and Solimano 1993). But even fully anticipated inflation may reduce the rate of return of capital given the nonneutralities built into most industrialized countries' tax systems (Jones and Manuelli 1995; Feldstein 1997). Besides, inflation undermines the confidence of domestic and foreign investors about the future course of monetary policy. Inflation also affects the accumulation of other determinants of growth such as human capital or investment in R&D; this channel of influence is known as the *accumulation* or *investment effect* of inflation on growth.

But over and above these effects, inflation also worsens the long-run macroeconomic performance of market economies by reducing total factor productivity. This channel, also known as the *efficiency channel,* is harder to formalize in a theoretical model;[2] nonetheless, its importance in the transmission mechanism from inflation to lower growth cannot be denied. A high level of inflation induces frequent changes in prices that may be costly for firms (*menu costs*) and reduces the optimal level of cash holdings by consumers (*shoe leather costs*). It also generates larger forecasting errors by distorting the information content of prices, encouraging economic agents to spend more time and resources in gathering information and protecting themselves against the damage caused by price instability, hence endangering the efficient allocation of resources. Although some theoretical models analyze the components of the efficiency channel in more detail, it is difficult to discriminate among them in aggregate empirical growth equations. Thus we shall not pursue this issue further here. We shall turn our attention to the empirical evidence.

Several authors have found a negative correlation between growth and inflation. Kormendi and Meguire (1985) estimate a growth equation with cross-sectional data and find that the effect of inflation on the growth rate is negative, although it loses explanatory power when the rate of investment is also included in the regression. This would indicate that the effect of inflation mainly manifests itself in a reduction in investment but not in the productivity of capital. Grier and Tullock (1989) estimate a model that excludes the rate of investment and includes several measures of nominal instability (such as the inflation

---

1. See Orphanides and Solow (1990), De Gregorio (1993), and Roubini and Sala-i-Martin (1995) among others.
2. Briault (1995) surveys the literature on these effects.

rate, the acceleration of prices, and the standard deviation of inflation). The results differ according to the group of countries considered, but for the OECD only the variability of inflation seems to have a significant and negative effect on growth.

More recently, the study of the long-run influence of inflation has progressed within the framework of convergence equations developed by Barro and Sala-i-Martin (1991).[3] Fischer (1991, 1993) reports a significant influence of several short-term macroeconomic indicators, in particular inflation, on the growth rate. Cozier and Selody (1992) estimate cross-sectional convergence equations for different samples and find a fairly large negative effect of inflation on income at the OECD level. These authors conclude that inflation affects the level rather than the growth rate of productivity and that the impact of inflation variability is weak.[4] This finding coincides with the result obtained more recently for a sample of 120 countries by Barro (1995, 1996), who reports a negative long-run effect of inflation using alternative instruments to correct for the endogeneity of inflation. The general conclusion of these and other studies (De Gregorio 1992a, 1992b, 1996; Motley 1994) is consistent with the negative correlation between inflation and income in the long run suggested in the theoretical literature. However, the consensus in this respect is far from absolute, and several authors have criticized these findings, arguing that the lack of a fully developed theoretical framework makes it difficult to interpret the empirical correlations and that even these are not robust to changes in the econometric specification. The latter argument is developed by Levine and Renelt (1992), Levine and Zervos (1993), and Clark (1997). Levine and Renelt carry out an exhaustive sensitivity analysis among a broad set of regressors in growth equations and conclude that the statistical significance (and even the sign) of most of these variables (inflation among them) is not invariant under changes in the information set.[5] Nor do these results, in turn, escape criticism. Sala-i-Martin (1994) argues that the problem of finding a macroeconomic variable whose effect is invariant under alternative specifications of the convergence equation should not be taken to mean that this influence is absent, but should instead be viewed as a sign of the difficulty of finding indicators that can adequately capture this effect for any period and group of countries. Gylfason and Herbertsson (1996) find that the inflation rate is robust to changes in the

3. Several exceptions, however, are worth noting: the studies of Grimes (1991) for the OECD, Smyth (1994) for the United States, Cardoso and Fishlow (1989), who use a panel of five-year averages for 18 Latin American countries, Burdekin et al. (1994), and Bruno (1993). In all these studies, a significant negative effect of inflation on growth is reported. On the other hand, Bullard and Keating (1995) find that the long-run output response to permanent inflation shocks in a structural vector autoregressive model is zero for most advanced economies.

4. Judson and Orphanides (1996) measure the variability of inflation as the variance of the quarterly rate for each country and find that it is negatively correlated with growth. These authors also find a significant negative effect of the level of inflation.

5. McCandless and Weber (1995) conclude also that the cross-country correlation between inflation and growth is zero.

conditioning set, whereas Andrés, Doménech, and Molinas (1996) show that for the OECD as a whole, short-run macroeconomic variables are at least as robust as rates of accumulation in explaining economic growth and that this holds for alternative conditioning sets as well as across different time periods.

8.2.2   Effect of Inflation in Convergence Equations

There are a number of advantages in approaching the correlation between inflation and growth within the framework of convergence equations as proposed by Barro and Sala-i-Martin (1991), which represent the main empirical proposition of growth models with constant returns.[6] In this paper we do not intend to test any particular model of economic growth, nor does the use of convergence equations mean that the exogenous growth model is the only possible representation of the evolution of OECD economies in the long run. As Gylfason and Herbertsson (1996) have pointed out, these equations might encompass the empirical implications of many endogenous growth models. The main advantage of this specification is that it systematically captures most of the factors that have usually been considered determinants of growth, reducing the risk of omitting relevant regressors entailed in ad hoc specifications.[7] The technology is represented by the following production function of constant returns (Mankiw, Romer, and Weil 1992):

$$(1) \qquad Y_t = (A_t L_t)^\beta K_t^\alpha H_t^\gamma.$$

Total factor productivity (A_t) grows at the constant exogenous rate ϕ, whereas fixed capital (K) and human capital (H) grow in proportion to the output assigned for their accumulation.[8] Assuming that the depreciation rates of both factors are the same, it is possible to derive the following equation of growth between two moments in time:

$$(2) \qquad y_{T+\tau} - y_T = \phi\tau + (1 - e^{-\lambda\tau})(\Omega^c + y_T^* - y_T),$$

where y represents the logarithm of per capita income in the period indicated by the subscript and y^* represents its steady state value. Expression (2) indicates that the growth rate of an economy will have a component determined by the growth in factor productivity, ϕ, and another resulting from the economy's propensity to move to its steady state level if, for some reason (shocks, initial conditions, etc.), it lies outside. The parameter λ is the rate at which the econ-

---

6. De Gregorio (1993) and Roubini and Sala-i-Martin (1995) provide more elaborate models of the interaction between inflation and growth.

7. In particular, unlike those equations that do not include the catching-up component, convergence equations provide a way of controlling the level of per capita income when analyzing the determinants of its growth rate. This turns out to be of crucial importance in obtaining a significant correlation between growth and inflation.

8. In the original formulation of Solow (1956), the rate of technological progress is exogenous, although in more recent models it can be explained by the set of resources assigned to research, market size, learning-by-doing, etc.

omy closes the gap between its current income and its potential or steady state level.[9] This level is, in turn, determined by the parameters of the production function and by the rates of accumulation of the productive factors:

$$(3) \quad y_T^* = \Omega^s + \phi T + \beta^{-1}[\alpha s_{Tk}^* + \gamma s_{Th}^* - (\alpha + \gamma)\log(n_T^* + \phi + \delta)],$$

where s_k^* is the logarithm of the rate of investment, s_h^* represents the logarithm of the rate of accumulation of human capital, and n^* is the growth rate of the population, all evaluated at their steady state levels; δ is the depreciation rate of capital, which will be assumed equal to 3 percent, while the two constants combine different parameters of the model and the starting level of technology (A_T).

This structure allows us to test the different hypotheses considered in this paper. First, the presence of the rates of factor accumulation in equation (3) is useful to discriminate between the two channels through which macroeconomic imbalances can affect the growth rate. Thus, if inflation reduces total factor productivity, we could expect a significant coefficient of the rate of inflation in equation (5), below. In this case, the productivity index (A_t) might be assumed to evolve as in equation (4) (Cozier and Selody 1992), which reflects the influence of the inflation rate (π) and its variability (σ):

$$(4) \quad A_t = A_0 \exp(\phi t)\exp(\mu_1 \pi_t)\exp(\mu_2 \sigma_t).$$

The empirical specification is then given by

$$(5) \quad y_{T+\tau} - y_T = \phi \tau + (1 - e^{-\lambda \tau})[\Omega - y_T + \phi T + \mu_1 \pi_T \\ + \mu_2 \sigma_T + \beta^{-1}(\alpha s_{Tk}^* + \gamma s_{Th}^* - (\alpha + \gamma)\log(n_T^* + \phi + \delta))].$$

However, if inflation influenced growth solely through its impact on investment (s_k), its coefficient in equation (5) would not be significant.[10] Unless it is necessary we shall not impose the parametric restrictions in the previous equations; we shall focus on the linear version (5′) instead:

$$(5') \quad y_{T+\tau} - y_T = \psi_0 + \psi_1 T + \psi_2 y_T + \psi_3 s_{Tk}^* + \psi_4 s_{Th}^* \\ + \psi_5 \log(n_T^* + \phi + \delta) + \psi_6 \pi_T + \psi_7 \sigma_T.$$

Second, the exogenous growth model specifies the determinants of both the long-run level of per capita income and the sustained growth rate. Inflation can affect one or the other, although the implications in terms of welfare are different.[11] According to the specification of equation (4), the impact of inflation basically impinges on the potential level of income but not on sustained

---

9. This rate can be written as $\lambda = (1 - \alpha - \gamma)(n^* + \phi + \delta)$.

10. In this case, the impact of inflation on growth in the long run should be evaluated by estimating investment equations.

11. See Thornton (1996) for a discussion of this issue.

growth (represented by ϕ). To examine the latter possibility, we shall also consider an alternative specification, (4′), which allows for the influence of inflation on the long-run growth rate:[12]

(4′)
$$A_t = A_0 \exp[(\phi + \phi'\pi)t]\exp(\mu_1 \pi)$$

such that the equation to be estimated would be represented by

(6)
$$y_{T+\tau} - y_T = (\phi + \phi'\pi)\tau + (1 - e^{-\lambda\tau})[\Omega - y_T + (\phi + \phi'\pi)T$$
$$+ \mu_1 \pi_1 + \beta^{-1}(\alpha s_{Tk}^* + \gamma s_{Th}^* - (\alpha + \gamma)\log(n_T^* + \phi + \delta))].$$

In section 8.3 we estimate the elasticity of growth with respect to inflation in models (5), (5′), and (6).

Our observations are four-year averages of OECD annual variables. Our data set is described at length by Dabán, Doménech, and Molinas (1997), who use OECD 1990 purchasing power parities to homogenize OECD national accounts from 1960 to 1992. When making real income comparisons among a set of countries, we must be aware of the properties of the data elaborated for that purpose. In particular, the more transitive we want our comparisons to be, the more the reference basket of goods has to depart from the most representative sample of items for each country. Since we restrict the analysis to the OECD, we avoid the use of data sets designed to homogenize information from a much larger set of countries (such as the one in the Penn World Tables, Mark 5, PWT 5; Summers and Heston 1991).

8.3   Estimation of the Effect of Inflation

Tables 8.1 and 8.2 show the instrumental variables estimates of the steady state and convergence equations, using one- and two-period-lagged regressors as instruments. The results are quite robust, both in the linear and in the nonlinear specifications, as regards the effect of inflation. Linear models (eq. [5′]) are shown in table 8.1. The models in columns (1) and (2) of table 8.1 correspond to different versions of the convergence equation. As predicted by the neoclassical model, the parameter of initial per capita income is negative and highly significant, both when steady state variables are included (conditional convergence) and when they are not (unconditional convergence). In column (2), the coefficients of the input accumulation rates have the expected sign, although the one for human capital is nonsignificant. The estimated parameter of the trend, which according to the theoretical model is approximating the rate of technological progress, has an unexpected negative sign.[13] On the other

---

12. This is the specification proposed by Motley (1994). The variability of inflation is excluded in order to simplify the expression.

13. A possible interpretation for this result is that the trend may be capturing the process of sustained reduction in the rate of growth of per capita income suffered by OECD countries during part of the sample period. We have tried alternative characterizations of technological progress:

Table 8.1   Linear Models: Equation (5′)

	Dependent Variable			
	Δy (1)	Δy (2)	y^* (3)	y^* (4)
ψ_0	0.348 (8.68)	−0.241 (1.08)	2.314 (25.49)	−1.044 (0.96)
ψ_1	−0.010 (3.35)	−0.010 (3.08)	0.076 (5.22)	0.050 (3.41)
ψ_2	−0.073 (4.40)	−0.089 (5.08)		
ψ_3		0.045 (1.97)		0.161 (1.44)
ψ_4		0.030 (1.02)		0.630 (4.78)
ψ_5		−0.123 (1.66)		−0.052 (0.14)
ψ_6	−0.002 (2.94)	−0.001 (1.73)	−0.024 (8.50)	−0.014 (4.34)
R^2	0.30	0.36	0.37	0.52
σ	0.055	0.053	0.299	0.259

Note: Estimation method is instrumental variables. Instruments are constant, trend and first- and second-order lags of the regressors, and second lag of the dependent variable. Numbers in parentheses are absolute *t*-ratios.

hand, the trend coefficient has the expected positive sign in the steady state equation (cols. [3] and [4]), but the values of the coefficients of the accumulation rates suggest a far too large share of human capital in the production function.

When the inflation rate and its variability (proxied by the coefficient of variation) are included, the rest of the parameters do not change significantly. The coefficient of the inflation rate is negative and significant, both in the convergence and in the steady state equation, whereas no significant effect is found from the variability of inflation. Thus the equations presented hereafter exclude this variable. When the factor accumulation rates are included (cols. [2] and [4]) the size of the inflation effect is smaller than when they are omitted (cols. [1] and [3]), but it is still significant. These results suggest that there are two channels by which inflation influences growth: first, through a reduction in the propensity to invest and, second, through a reduction in the efficiency in use of inputs.

Nonlinear models (eq. [5]) are shown in table 8.2. The estimated parameters

---

first, including time dummies instead of the linear trend and, second, imposing a rate of technological progress of 2 percent. The estimated coefficients, including that of inflation, do not change significantly. These results are omitted to save space.

Table 8.2   **Nonlinear Models: Equation (5)**

		Dependent Variable		
	y^*	Δy	Δy	Δy
	(1)	(2)	(3)	(4)
Ω^s	−2.22			
	(2.46)			
Ω^c		−4.09	−1.97	−0.19
		(2.84)	(1.61)	(0.13)
α	0.09	0.27	0.23	0.35
	(1.31)	(2.87)	(2.56)	(3.45)
γ	0.31	0.27	0.21	0.11
	(6.30)	(3.18)	(2.54)	(1.13)
ϕ_{ss}	0.051			
	(3.35)			
ϕ_c		−0.09	−0.05	−0.05
		(2.57)	(1.79)	(1.91)
ϕ'				0.005
				(2.10)
μ_1	−0.013	−0.011	−0.025	−0.22
	(4.00)	(2.03)	(3.95)	(2.38)
λ		0.027	0.032	0.031
R^2_{ss}	0.50			
R^2_c		0.37	0.39	0.27
σ_{ss}	0.266			
σ_c		0.053	0.050	0.057

Note: Estimation method: see note to table 8.1. Numbers in parentheses are absolute *t*-ratios.

of the accumulation rates in the steady state equation (col. [1]) are quite far from those usually obtained in the empirical literature, the low value of α being particularly remarkable. The effect of inflation is negative and significant. The estimated coefficients in the convergence equation (col. [2]) look more reasonable, pointing toward a technology of similar factor shares ({1/3, 1/3, 1/3}), with an implicit rate of convergence around 2.7 percent. Again, the effect of inflation is negative and significant.

Additionally, some tests of the sensitivity of the inflation coefficient to the sample definition have been performed in order to ascertain whether the negative correlation between inflation and income is driven by the presence of some high-inflation countries. The most noticeable change in the estimated coefficient takes place when Iceland is excluded from the sample. In this case (col. [3] of table 8.2) the correlation between inflation and growth is almost twice as high as when it is included. This is not surprising because Iceland, the country with the second highest average inflation within the OECD, is also a high-income fast-growth economy, which may be generating a downward bias in the absolute value of the growth-inflation correlation. We have proceeded to estimate the model for different subsamples according to their average infla-

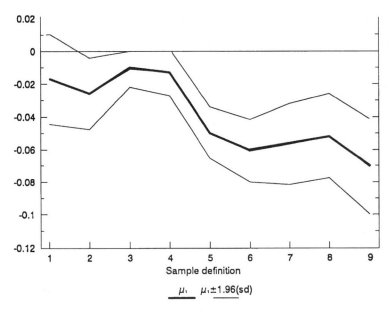

Fig. 8.1   Sensitivity of inflation coefficient to sample definition: basic model

Note: The figure depicts the estimated coefficient (μ_1) for inflation in model (5) as well as the 95 percent confidence intervals (± 1.96 standard deviation band) for different sample definitions.

Sample Definition: 1—High-inflation countries (above OECD average). 2—High-inflation countries (excluding Iceland). 3—OECD. 4—OECD excluding Turkey. 5—OECD excluding Turkey and Iceland. 6—OECD excluding Turkey, Iceland, and Portugal. 7—OECD excluding Turkey, Iceland, Portugal, and Greece. 8—OECD excluding Turkey, Iceland, Portugal, Greece, and Spain. 9—Low-inflation countries (below OECD average).

tion. The results, depicted in figure 8.1, indicate that if anything, the coefficient of inflation in the convergence equation is higher (in absolute value) and more significant for low-inflation countries.

The negative effect of inflation on per capita income seems to be robust both in the steady state and in the convergence equation. Although the negative influence of inflation on per capita income is well established, its effect on the sustainable growth rate is less clear. If the inflation rate is a determinant of steady state per capita income (y^*) it should also appear in the convergence equation. But it is not clear whether the negative coefficient in this equation points to an effect on the level or on the growth rate of output. To discriminate between these effects we have estimated equation (6), allowing for an effect of inflation both on the steady state level of income (μ) and on the permanent component of the growth rate (ϕ'). Both these coefficients are negative and significant when they are introduced individually, but when they are jointly included in the model (col. [4] of table 8.2) the effect on the trend component takes an unexpected positive sign. This would indicate that the negative effect of inflation impinges on the level of per capita income but not on the sustain-

able rate of growth of the economy. Thus the impact on the growth rate is transitory (in the medium run) as long as convergence is under way.

Summing up, the analysis in this section, in accordance with other studies, provides evidence of an adverse influence of inflation on growth. As regards the size of this effect, if we take the coefficient in column (3) of table 8.2 as a reliable estimate of the long-run effect of inflation on growth, an increase in average inflation by 1 percentage point reduces per capita growth by 0.08 points per year. This fall in the growth rate is not permanent, but it lasts for a long period, leading to a permanent reduction in steady state per capita income of 2.5 percent.[14] However, before drawing any policy implications from these numbers it is convenient to take a closer look at the relationship between inflation and growth, trying to correct for some biases that might arise in specifications like the ones studied so far.

8.4   Country-Specific Effects and the Cost of Inflation

There are several reasons to include individual effects in convergence equations estimated with multicountry data sets. Most empirical analyses of economic growth have relied on the use of information for wide groups of countries. This makes it possible to focus on low-frequency properties of the data, taking time-series averages and still avoiding a severe shortage of degrees of freedom. However, this approach imposes a very strong restriction, namely, that the data for all the economies of the sample stem from the same theoretical distribution (i.e., the technological parameters are homogeneous across countries). This assumption is seldom explicitly tested, although its empirical implications may be very important (see Pesaran and Smith 1995). The existence of technological differences in the rates of technical progress or, as is more likely, in the initial conditions of each country would lead to the presence of idiosyncratic effects in growth equations. If these and other country time-invariant characteristics affect the growth-inflation relationship, the lagged regressors would be rendered inappropriate as instruments in growth equations (Barro 1996). The consideration of individual effects in the constant term (Knight, Loayza, and Villanueva 1993; Islam 1995) or in a more general way (Andrés, Boscá, and Doménech 1996) might then alter significantly some of the main results of the empirical growth literature.

In this section, we test whether the estimated negative effect of inflation on growth is biased by the omission of these country-specific (time-invariant) effects. The main results are summarized in table 8.3. In column (1), the linear model (eq. [5']) has been estimated under the assumption that the omitted individual effects are not correlated with the regressors. The random effects estimates, and in particular the coefficient of the inflation rate, resemble very much those of the basic model depicted in column (2) of table 8.1. Nevertheless,

14. When Iceland is included in the sample, these figures are 0.03 and 1.1 percent, respectively.

Table 8.3   **Convergence Equation with Individual Effects: Equation (5′)**

	Dependent Variable: Δy				
	(1)	(2)	(3)	(4)	(5)
ψ_0	−0.26	1.54	1.18	1.24	1.07
	(1.22)	(2.03)	(6.44)	(2.95)	(3.22)
ψ_1	−0.01	0.04	0.03	0.02	0.02
	(2.96)	(3.16)	(3.26)	(3.04)	(3.26)
ψ_2	−0.08	−0.65	−0.48	−0.43	−0.40
	(5.15)	(4.70)	(5.44)	(5.45)	(6.99)
ψ_3	0.05	−0.16		−0.03	−0.04
	(2.34)	(1.54)		(0.84)	(1.24)
ψ_4		−0.019		−0.010	−0.02
		(0.28)		(0.25)	(0.70)
ψ_5	−0.16	−0.21		−0.007	−0.007
	(2.34)	(0.98)		(0.07)	(0.11)
ψ_6	−0.001	−0.001	−0.002	−0.002	−0.003
	(1.90)	(1.16)	(2.29)	(2.47)	(3.99)
R^2	0.36	0.35	0.50	0.48	0.48
σ	0.053	0.054	0.047	0.048	0.048
ψ_6 (LI)[a]		−0.008		−0.011	
		(2.01)		(5.18)	
ψ_6 (HI)[a]		−0.001		−0.001	
		(0.84)		(0.87)	
ψ_6 (HI-ICL)[a]		−0.002		−0.002	
		(1.83)		(1.88)	

Note: Estimation method in col. (1) is random effects (instrumental variables); instruments are first and second lags of the regressors. Estimation method in cols. (2)–(5) is country-dummies instrumental variables; instruments are as in table 8.1 plus country dummies and inflation variability. Dummy variables included: Cols. (2) and (3), one for each country except Australia. Col. 4, one for each of the following countries: Canada, Switzerland, Germany, Spain, the United Kingdom, Finland, Greece, Ireland, Iceland, Luxembourg, New Zealand, Portugal, Turkey, and the United States. Col. (5), one for each of the following countries: Iceland, Spain, Greece, and Turkey; and one for each of the following country groups: Ireland and Portugal; Canada and Germany; Switzerland, Luxembourg, and the United States; and Finland, New Zealand, and the United Kingdom. Numbers in parentheses are absolute t-ratios.
[a]HI—sample of six countries with inflation rates above the OECD average; LI—OECD excluding HI countries; HI-ICL—HI countries excluding Iceland.

the reasons to include country-specific effects in the model suggest that the assumption of noncorrelation among these and the regressors might not be appropriate in this setting. Thus, in what follows, we focus on the fixed effects estimates, which we compute including dummies in the linear convergence equation. All the models have been estimated by instrumental variables. When we add a dummy variable for each country (col. [2]) the explanatory power of most regressors changes, as compared with the models in the previous section. In particular, while inflation still has a negative effect on income, its t-statistic

is now lower (-1.16).[15] The changes in the rest of the model are far more radical, though. First, whereas the negative trend coefficient was an unappealing feature of the models in section 8.3, this coefficient now becomes positive and significant, with a reasonable point estimate of 0.04. Second, the point estimates of the technological coefficients are now either nonsignificant or wrongly signed. In fact, excluding the accumulation rates from the equations, the negative correlation between growth and inflation becomes highly significant with a t-statistic of -2.29 (col. [3]). Finally, several country dummies are not different from zero, which means that the model might be overparametrized.

The search for a more parsimonious specification proceeds along the following steps. Starting from the model with a dummy variable for each country, the nonsignificant dummy variables are removed, setting aside the one with the lowest t-statistic each time. As a second step, these excluded variables are added again, one at a time, retaining those with t-ratios greater than 1.5.[16] Every time a dummy variable is added back into the model, the process is reinitiated. This procedure does not involve the analysis of every single possible specification according to all the combinations of country-specific constants. However, it provides a model selection procedure that allows us to test, at least twice, the marginal significance of each dummy variable: first against a more general model (with all the country-specific dummies) and next against a more restricted one. The model in column (4) summarizes the final outcome of this specification process. The results do not change very much from those in column (1), except in that now the coefficient of the inflation rate is negative and significant and its size is similar to that obtained for the model without individual effects. Furthermore, this result is quite robust to the set of country-specific dummies included in the regression. The same search process has also been carried out for different subsamples with different average inflation rates. The point estimates of the inflation coefficient, along with its confidence interval, are depicted in figure 8.2. The coefficient of inflation turns out to be larger and more significant whenever high-inflation countries are not considered. Hence, as was the case in models without country dummies, the estimated correlation between inflation and growth (or income) does not depend on the presence of a group of high-inflation countries in the sample.

Taking column (4) of table 8.3 as a starting point, in the model in column (5) individual dummies are clustered into country-group dummy variables. The

15. It must be noted that the fixed effect estimate of the coefficient of inflation is still significant at the 5 percent level if we focus on the low-inflation countries (LI). This coefficient is lower and weakly significant for the subsample of all countries but Iceland (HI-ICL) with inflation above the OECD average.

16. If the threshold level of the t-ratio is 2.0, the final specification is more parsimonious. Nevertheless, the estimated long-run coefficient of inflation does not depart very much from that in col. (4).

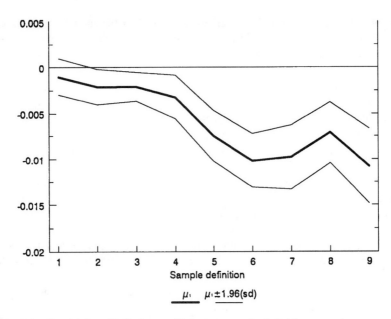

Fig. 8.2   Sensitivity of inflation coefficient to sample definition: country dummies (restricted model)

Note: The figure depicts the estimated coefficient (μ_1) for inflation in model (5) as well as the 95 percent confidence intervals (± 1.96 standard deviation band) for different sample definitions.

Sample Definition: 1—High-inflation countries (above OECD average). 2—High-inflation countries (excluding Iceland). 3—OECD. 4—OECD excluding Turkey. 5—OECD excluding Turkey and Iceland. 6—OECD excluding Turkey, Iceland, and Portugal. 7—OECD excluding Turkey, Iceland, Portugal, and Greece. 8—OECD excluding Turkey, Iceland, Portugal, Greece, and Spain. 9—Low-inflation countries (below OECD average).

t-statistic of the inflation rate increases again (up to -3.99).[17] It is quite remarkable that the negative and highly significant influence of inflation on growth during rather long periods survives all these changes in the specification. In fact, it turns out to be, along with initial per capita GDP, the most robust variable of the model. The country groups in column (5) have been defined according to the size of the individual effect. Greece shows an individual effect that is clearly negative (-0.31) as compared with the excluded countries,[18] followed by Turkey (-0.29), Ireland and Portugal (-0.22), Spain (-0.15), and Finland, New Zealand, and the United Kingdom (-0.05). On the other hand, Canada and Germany (0.04), Iceland (0.08), and Switzerland, Luxembourg, and the United States (0.1) display positive individual effects on the growth

17. As in col. (2), the coefficients for the input accumulation rates are not significant. The exclusion of these variables does not worsen substantially the fit of the equation and further increases the significance level of the inflation rate.

18. Australia, Austria, Belgium, Denmark, France, Netherlands, Italy, Japan, Norway, and Sweden.

rate. The estimated individual effects reveal a systematic pattern that, if ignored, could have led to a bias in the estimated effect of inflation. The individual effect is strongly correlated with the level of per capita income achieved at the end of the sample period. Thus, omitting the individual effect, the model would underestimate the growth of the richest countries and overestimate that of the poorest countries. Since there is a negative correlation at the OECD level between per capita income in 1993 and the average inflation rate, excluding the individual effects is a source of potential upward bias in the estimation of the effect of inflation. Indeed, although the estimated coefficient of inflation remains largely unchanged, compared with that in table 8.1, there is nevertheless a significant change in the point estimate of the long-run effect of inflation once country-specific dummies are included in the model. The coefficient of initial GDP is now almost five times as large as the one in tables 8.1 and 8.2, thus the estimated long-run cost of inflation is now lower. A permanent increase of 1 percentage point leads to a 0.75 percent permanent fall in output. This time, though, the transition period is much shorter because a higher coefficient of initial GDP means that convergence to the steady state is much faster too.

Although OECD economies have certain common institutional features, their inflation performances are rather different. Once we have a more accurate estimate of the long-run cost of inflation we can address the issue of whether this cost varies according to the level of inflation or not. The different perspectives adopted to analyze the linearity of the inflation effect have led to contradictory results. For instance, Barro (1995), estimating different coefficients for different levels of inflation, finds a greater effect of inflation on growth the greater the inflation level.[19] Motley (1994), estimating the growth model for different subsamples, concludes the opposite. We have tried these two approaches in equation (5′) and found that they also yield somewhat different results for the OECD, although the coefficients of inflation in different subsamples were not very precisely estimated. In general, though, the coefficient corresponding to lower inflation rates tends to be higher, although with a lower t-ratio. This would indicate that the benefits of lower inflation are indeed higher at low rates, although the functional form might be inappropriate to capture this result. As an alternative, we have estimated the basic model allowing for a nonlinear effect of inflation on growth. When π and π^2 are included, both coefficients are significant while the positive coefficient on π^2 indicates that the marginal cost of inflation is positive but decreasing with its level. Two alternative specifications that allow for a falling marginal cost of inflation have also been tried. In these, inflation is represented by log π and the ratio $\pi/(1 + \pi)$,[20] respectively. In all the specifications tried (with country dummies, excluding Iceland, and so on) these equations perform better than the ones with the level of inflation.

---

19. Although the null of linearity cannot be rejected (see also Barro 1996).
20. Gylfason and Herbertsson (1996) propose this nonlinear transformation.

Table 8.4   **Linearity of the Inflation Effect**

Inflation Level	Elasticity of Income with Respect to Inflation in Estimates of Linear Version of Convergence Equation
A. Whole Sample Estimates with Specific Inflation Coefficients[a]	
Low inflation	−0.091
	(2.33)
Medium inflation	−0.061
	(2.58)
High inflation	−0.066
	(4.23)
B. Subsample Estimates[b]	
Low inflation	−0.052
	(2.59)
High inflation	−0.034
	(2.15)
Very low inflation	−0.036
	(1.82)
Very high inflation	−0.046
	(1.61)

Note: Estimation method: see note to table 8.1. Numbers in parentheses are absolute *t*-ratios.

[a]Low inflation—observations with inflation lower than 6 percent; medium inflation—observations with inflation between 6 percent and 12 percent; high inflation—observations with inflation greater than 12 percent.

[b]Low inflation—countries with average inflation lower than the median; high inflation—countries with average inflation greater than the median; very low inflation—eight countries with the lowest inflation; very high inflation—eight countries with the highest inflation.

A further test for linearity has been carried out in the model in log π. In panel A of table 8.4, a different coefficient is allowed for log π depending on its level. These elasticities are always negative and significant but not statistically different. As an alternative approach, the homogeneity assumption may be relaxed by estimating the convergence equation for different subsamples. This approach allows all the parameters, and not only the coefficient of inflation, to vary across subsamples. The results are summarized in panel B of table 8.4. The effect of inflation is negative and significant both for low (and very low) as well as for high (and very high) inflation countries, and the coefficient of log π is similar across different subsample specifications.[21] The results of these two approaches lead us to conclude that the elasticity of income with respect to inflation does not change significantly with the level of inflation. If anything, this tells us that it pays more in a low-inflation country than in a high-inflation one to reduce the inflation rate by a given amount. By the same

21. The coefficient of initial GDP is also similar across the specifications in table 8.4, panel B. Thus the hypothesis of homogeneity in the long-run elasticity cannot be rejected either.

Table 8.5   **Long-Run Effect of Inflation on Per Capita Income (percent)**

Model[a]	OECD		OECD Excluding Iceland	
	Low π	High π	Low π	High π
π, π^2	0.80	0.40	1.10	0.60
$\pi/(1 + \pi)$	0.45	0.30	0.70	0.50
$\log \pi$	2.00	0.30	2.20	0.40
π	0.75	0.75	0.75	0.75

Note: The long-run effect is calculated as the coefficient of inflation divided by the coefficient on initial income in the convergence equation augmented with country dummies. Low π—reducing inflation from 4 to 3 percent. High π—reducing inflation from 20 to 19 percent. Initial GDP is noninstrumented.

[a]The variables in the first column indicate the way in which inflation enters in each model.

token, it is more costly for a low-inflation country to concede an additional (and permanent) point of inflation than it is for a country with a higher starting rate.[22]

Table 8.5 shows the long-run impact on income of a 1 percentage point permanent reduction of inflation for a variety of specifications of the effect of inflation. All models include country-specific constants, and we report results for the OECD as a whole and also excluding Iceland. The estimated long-run benefit of a reduction of inflation from 20 to 19 percent varies between 0.30 and 0.75 percent, with an average value of 0.5 percent. At lower inflation levels (a reduction from 4 to 3 percent), the benefit is higher, with an average 1 percent increase in steady state income. These estimated values are all rather similar except for the specification in logs, which overrates the benefits of disinflation at low inflation levels.

These benefits seem lower than others reported in the literature, but it must be noted that they are obtained in equations displaying a higher than usual 2 to 3 percent convergence rate. This is most important because it means that the transition period until the increase in GDP actually takes place is shorter; thus it would not take the representative economy much time to reap the full benefits of a sustained disinflation. In table 8.6 we compare the cost of inflation

22. The exercises in table 8.4 have been carried out for different inflation regimes and also for different specifications of the equation and the inflation term. The overall picture that emerges from these exercises is the same. The coefficient of the inflation term is negative in most cases, and it tends to be bigger (in absolute value) at low inflation rates, although with lower t-statistics as well. In a few specifications the coefficient for very low inflation rates (below 3 to 4 percent) is positive, although never significant. This issue deserves more careful scrutiny because it might well be that inflation ceases to be costly at all at very low levels. Since we have very few data points with inflation under 3 percent in our sample, we have not been able to pursue this further. Sarel (1996) concludes that the cutoff point might be at an 8 percent rate of inflation. However, both the model and the data used differ from ours in several respects.

Table 8.6   **Per Capita Income Gain from Reducing Inflation: Steady State and Present Value (percent)**

	Basic Model	Country Effects
Steady state per capita income gain	2.5	0.75
λ	2.5	13
Half-life per capita income gain	1.25[a]	0.375[b]
Present value:[c] discount rate 4%	0.32	0.29
Present value:[c] discount rate 5%	0.23	0.27

[a]Half-life is 30 years.
[b]Half-life is 7 years.
[c]Discounted present value of half-life gain (expressed in percentage points of steady state per capita income).

estimated in the basic model (col. [3], table 8.2) with that obtained in the model with country-specific effects (col. [4], table 8.3). The estimated benefit from a permanent reduction in the inflation rate by 1 percentage point is higher in the former (2.5 vs. 0.75 percent). Nevertheless, since this is a steady state effect and the convergence rates also differ across models (2.5 vs. 13 percent), the relevant comparison should be made in present value terms, which makes the outcome depend on the discount rate. According to the figures in this example, for discount rates slightly above 4 percent the benefit of disinflation is larger in models with faster dynamics, despite the lower coefficient of the inflation rate in the convergence equation. Hence, the present value of the per capita income gain might well be within the range of those found in other studies.

8.5 Analysis of Causality

The models studied in previous sections can generate a nonnegligible bias in the estimation of the influence of inflation on growth by focusing on the contemporaneous correlation between these two variables. Inflation and growth are the joint outcome of the way an economy responds to different shocks. If demand shocks predominate, a positive association between GDP growth and inflation can be expected, whereas the association will be negative in response to supply shocks. Also, even if we consider the possibility of a true influence of one variable over the other, the theoretical literature presents arguments in favor of causality in both directions. For this reason, the contemporaneous correlation between growth and inflation may not be very informative as to the existence and magnitude of a real cost associated with inflation.

In fact, it might be the case that the estimated negative correlation between inflation and growth is driven by the predominance of negative supply shocks during the sample period. To test this possibility we have estimated the linear version of the convergence equation for two periods: 1961–72 and 1989–92, during which demand shocks predominated, and 1973–88, during which

Table 8.7   **Inflation Effect for Different Periods**

Estimation	Coefficient of Inflation in Linear Version of Convergence Equation[a]
A. Demand Shocks Predominance Period: 1961–72 and 1989–92	
Ordinary least squares	−0.002
	(2.33)
Instrumental variables[b]	−0.003
	(2.52)
B. Supply Shock Predominance Period: 1973–88	
Ordinary least squares	−0.004
	(3.85)
Instrumental variables[b]	−0.003
	(2.14)

Note: Numbers in parentheses are absolute *t*-ratios.

[a]Eq. (5′) excluding the trend.

[b]Instruments are constant, first- and second-order lags of the regressors, and second lag of the dependent variable.

supply shocks were probably more significant.[23] The results of this split are shown in table 8.7, where we present only the coefficient on inflation for both the ordinary least squares (OLS) and the instrumental variables (IV) estimations. As expected, the IV coefficient is higher (lower), in absolute value, than the OLS coefficient for the first (second) period given the nature of the expected bias in each case. But in all cases, the coefficients are negative and significant, meaning that the negative supply shocks that hit the OECD economies during most of the second half of the sample period are not primarily responsible for the estimated negative correlation between inflation and growth. If this had been the case, we ought to find a positive coefficient for the first period, at least in the OLS estimation. The finding of negative coefficients for both periods strengthens the view that there is indeed a genuine negative effect of inflation on growth that does not rely on the existence of supply shocks determining simultaneously inflation and growth.

In order to pursue this issue more thoroughly, this section analyzes the statistical causality, as formulated by Granger, of inflation to growth and vice versa. This perspective is broader than that of convergence equations in several ways. First, the analysis of causality focuses on the study of noncontemporaneous effects of one variable on the other. This is precisely the influence of inflation on growth predicted by the theoretical models: an influence that does not operate in the short run but that takes time to show instead. Second, in using a more flexible specification, we avoid the imposition of the parametric restrictions of the neoclassical growth model, which might make the correlation that concerns

23. Similar results were obtained when we split the period up in other two parts: 1961–76, for demand shock predominance, and 1977–92, for supply shock predominance.

us here less clear. The analysis of causality carried out in this section does not put theoretical growth models aside. Economic theory suggests a series of growth determinants that can be incorporated into the information set in the tests of causality.

To analyze the causality from the rate of inflation to the level of per capita income,[24] a test is run on the joint significance of $\{d_1, \ldots, d_p\}$ in the model:

$$(7) \qquad y_t = A + C(L)y_t + D(L)\pi_t + G(L)X_t + u_t,$$

where y_t and π_t are (24×1) vectors of current observations of the logarithm of per capita GDP and of the rate of inflation, respectively, for the 24 member countries of the OECD; X_t is a vector of additional regressors, suggested by growth theory; and A is a (24×1) vector of constants. $C(L)$, $D(L)$, and $G(L)$ are (24×24) matrices in which elements off the main diagonal are zero and elements on the main diagonal are lagged polynomials of order p such as (for $C(L)$, e.g.)

$$c_1 L + c_2 L^2 + c_3 L^3 + \cdots + c_p L^p.$$

The rejection of the null hypothesis that the d_j are zero indicates that current inflation helps to reduce the mean-squared error in the prediction of per capita income and, therefore, that π causes y in the Granger sense. Likewise, the causality from the growth rate to inflation is tested through the joint significance of $\{e_1, \ldots, e_p\}$ in

$$(8) \qquad \pi_t = B + E(L)\Delta y_t + F(L)\pi_t + H(L)X_t + \varepsilon_t,$$

where $E(L)$, $F(L)$, and $H(L)$ are matrices of a structure similar to $C(L)$ and B is a (24×1) vector of constants. The rejection of the null hypothesis that the coefficients e_j are zero indicates that Δy causes π.

The elements of the matrices A and B, as well as the coefficients of the lagged polynomials (in $C(L)$, $D(L)$, $E(L)$, $F(L)$, $G(L)$, and $H(L)$), will be assumed to be homogeneous among countries unless expressly stated otherwise. The estimation of equations (7) and (8) raises several methodological issues,[25] the most important being the possibility that some variables are nonstationary, in which case exclusion tests do not have a standard distribution. In the case at

24. Testing the causality from the rate of inflation to the growth rate only entails adding a linear restriction on the coefficients in $C(L)$ and writing per capita income in first differences. The results of the causality tests to the growth rate are quite similar to those of the causality tests to the level of per capita income and will be omitted here to save space.

25. Since this section applies annual data relating to the variables of interest for the 24 OECD countries, it departs from the traditional approach in the empirical literature on growth, which avoids using annual information. Nevertheless, an increasing number of studies tend to use raw annual data. Moreover, in the dynamic analysis of causality, models based on time averages can be considered as restricted versions of models that use annual data. As regards the role of individual effects in multicountry regressions, we shall take them into account in this section by considering several specifications in which vectors A and B include a different constant for each country (a_i, b_i).

Table 8.8   **Causality from Inflation to Per Capita Income**

	Negative[a]			Positive[a]
	Significant at 5% Level	Significant at Level between 5% and 10%	Nonsignificant	
Causality[b]	15 (6)	10 (2)	22 (2)	0
Noncausality[b]	0	0	3 (0)	0

Note: Each cell reports the number of specifications in that case. In parentheses is the number of specifications corresponding to the model with individual effects, lagged accumulation rates, and lagged macroeconomic indicators.

[a]Sign of the t-statistic for the sum of the coefficients of the inflation lags.

[b]Causality (noncausality): The null hypothesis that the inflation coefficients are jointly nonsignificant is (is not) rejected at the 5 percent level.

hand, both per capita income and the rate of inflation are, for most countries in the sample, nonstationary. There are several ways in which the hypothesis of causality between integrated variables can be tested making use of statistics with asymptotic standard distribution. These procedures basically consist of a reparametrization of the model in order to obtain stationary regressors (see Sims, Stock, and Watson 1990). The method proposed by Dolado and Lütkepohl (1996) does not require a search for possible cointegration vectors, which is quite often a hazardous task in panel data models. These authors propose the estimation of a vector autoregression (VAR) in levels of order $p + 1$. The exclusion test performed on the p first lags is thus distributed asymptotically as an F, whereby the loss of efficiency by the overparametrization of the model is compensated by the test's consistency and simplicity.[26] The application of this method requires knowing the true order, p, of the VAR. In this paper, rather than discussing the structure of the lags in detail, we present results for a range of lags broad enough to ensure the stationarity of the residuals.

The exclusion test in equation (7) has been performed for 10 different structures of lags (p going from 3 to 12) and for five sets of additional regressors (X_t).[27] Thus the causality from the rate of inflation to the level of per capita income has been tested in 50 specifications. Table 8.8 summarizes the results of these tests, which can be read as follows. In 47 cases, the null hypothesis that the inflation coefficients are jointly nonsignificant, and hence that inflation does not cause income, can be rejected at the 5 percent level. Furthermore, the

26. For an application of this method, see Andrés, Boscá, and Doménech (1996).

27. These five sets are the following: (1) includes neither additional regressors ($g_j = 0$) nor constant individual effects; (2) includes individual constant effects so that A is a vector of different constants, one for each country; (3) incorporates, in addition to individual effects, several other regressors such as a linear trend, the saving ratio, the rate of schooling, and the growth rate of the population, all of them contemporaneous; (4) as the previous set, but with the first lag of (instead of the current) accumulation rates; and (5) as the previous set plus current export growth and the first lag of money growth, export growth, public consumption, and public deficit as a percentage of GDP.

sum of the lagged coefficients of inflation is negative in all 50 cases. This would imply that higher inflation today anticipates lower income in the future. However, the evidence of a long-run effect of inflation on income is not unequivocal because the sum of the coefficients of the inflation lags is significantly different from zero (at the 10 percent level) in just half of the cases. This is worrisome because a nonsignificant long-run coefficient can be interpreted as if the effect of inflation on growth is not permanent, casting some doubts on the validity of the correlation found in previous sections.

Table 8.8 indicates in parentheses the number of specifications corresponding to the model with the largest set of additional regressors: individual effects, lagged accumulation rates, and several macroeconomic variables. Many authors have studied the relationship between long-term growth and the short-term performance of economies.[28] The main argument on which this relationship rests is that the shocks hitting an economy or the way economic policy is conducted influences agents' accumulation decisions and the way markets operate. Thus a succession of negative shocks or an inadequately designed fiscal or monetary policy may have effects that go beyond the short term, affecting potential output and sustained growth. If this argument is correct, the causal interpretation of the estimated correlation between inflation and growth could be called into question. The estimated correlation between growth and inflation could be due simply to the fact that inflation approximates the impact of other macroeconomic variables with which it is strongly correlated. Those specifications that include other macroeconomic indicators allow for an analysis of the influence of inflation on growth while isolating it from the effect of other shocks. The numbers in parentheses indicate that after taking into account the effect of fiscal and monetary policy and export performance, the existence of causality of a negative sign from inflation to economic growth becomes more apparent. The null hypothesis that inflation does not help to improve the prediction of the future growth rate is clearly rejected in all cases. The statistic associated with the sum of the coefficients of the inflation lags is negative in all cases and statistically significant in most of them.[29]

Although the results of these causality tests are not fully conclusive, their importance is enhanced if we compare them with similar tests relating growth to other variables, such as investment in physical and human capital or public spending. Several recent attempts to corroborate the statistical causality from investment in physical capital to growth and income[30] have concluded that even though it cannot be rejected that a high rate of current investment could be explained by rapid growth in the past, the existence of causality in the opposite direction is far less conclusive. Blömstrom, Lipsey, and Zejan (1996) show that

28. See Levine and Renelt (1992), Fischer (1993), and Andrés, Doménech, and Molinas (1996), among others, for alternative views of the influence of macroeconomic shocks on growth.

29. In eight out of ten cases at a 10 percent significance level, and in six of them at the 5 percent level.

30. Correlations that are among the main findings of the empirics of convergence.

Table 8.9   **Causality from Growth to Inflation**

		Positive		
	Negative	Nonsignificant	Significant at Level between 5% and 10%	Significant at 5% Level
Causality	0	3 (0)	2 (0)	45 (10)
Noncausality	0	0	0	0

Note: See notes to table 8.8.

growth always precedes investment, rather than the other way round. A similar result is obtained by Carrol and Weil (1993) for the OECD sample. Andrés, Boscá, and Doménech (1996) also find that investment does not help to improve the prediction of income or of its growth rate in practically any of the specifications studied. Moreover, when investment appears to cause income, the negative sign makes this result hard to interpret. A similar effect is obtained in relation to other determinants of growth—the rate of schooling, among others. What these authors find is that most of the observed positive correlation between investment and growth (or income) can be attributed to reverse causation. Reasoning on similar grounds, many authors suspect that something of this kind might be behind the correlation between inflation and growth (Kocherlakota 1996).

Interestingly enough, unlike what happens with investment and schooling, in this case the causality running from income growth to inflation is indeed significant but with a sign that weakens, rather than strengthens, the case for reverse causality. As can be seen in table 8.9, causality from growth to inflation is not rejected in any of the 50 specifications analyzed; thus we may conclude that current growth rates help to explain the future course of the inflation rate. The *t*-statistic of the long-run coefficient is always positive, and significantly so (at the 5 percent significance level) in 90 percent of the cases.[31] Economic theory proposes several reasons why rapid growth is associated with higher inflation in the more or less immediate future. On the one hand, it could be a movement along a negatively sloped Phillips curve, as prices respond after a period of rapid expansion in demand. Another interpretation is derived from the so-called Balassa-Samuelson effect (Balassa 1964; Samuelson 1964). According to these authors, rapid economic growth is associated with rapid expansion in the productivity of a country's tradable goods sector, in turn leading to an appreciation of its currency. Insofar as the nominal exchange rate is not adjusted to produce this appreciation, domestic prices will grow faster. This leading correlation of a positive sign indicates that the risk of a simultaneity

31. Again, the results are even more clear-cut if we focus on the specifications with the largest set of additional regressors. In all 10 of those cases, the null hypothesis of noncausality is rejected and the sum of the inflation lags is positive and significant.

downward bias in the estimation of inflation costs is considerable.[32] As a result, the contemporaneous correlation in the convergence equations could be regarded as a lower bound of the costs of inflation, which would have to be adjusted upward in absolute value.

In the light of this evidence, the results presented in this section have an unequivocal interpretation. The current rate of inflation provides relevant information on income prospects in OECD countries. In particular, ceteris paribus, higher inflation never anticipates a higher level of income in the medium and long run. This effect is robust to alternative specifications and, most notably, survives even when accumulation rates and individual effects are included among the set of regressors. Moreover, it can be rejected that this leading correlation between inflation and income is spurious and produced by the coincidence of inflationary tendencies and slow growth in some economies. Therefore, even though the magnitude of the negative effect of inflation might be questioned, the results of this section tell us that inflation does not appear to be neutral in the long run and that in no case does the persistence of inflationary tensions favor rapid economic growth in the future.

8.6   Concluding Remarks

In this paper we have tried to assess the long-run costs of inflation, within an explicit theoretical framework stemming from the growth literature: the convergence equation. Despite its shortcomings, this approach is well suited to test the robustness of the correlation between growth and inflation in low-inflation economies with reasonably well working markets, such as the OECD countries during the 1960–92 period. The specific results are described at length in each section and will not be repeated here. The main finding is that current inflation has never been found to be positively correlated with income per capita over the long run.

In fact, in most, though admittedly not all, specifications tried we obtained a significant negative correlation between inflation and income growth during rather long periods. This negative correlation survives the presence of additional regressors, such as the investment rate, population growth, and schooling rates, and the imposition of the theoretical restrictions implied by the technology of constant returns. What is most remarkable is that the negative coefficient of inflation in growth equations remains significant even after allowing for country-specific time-invariant effects in the equations. This is striking because, as is well known in the empirical growth literature, few regressors in convergence equations withstand the explanatory power of country dummies.

---

32. Andrés, Hernando, and Krüger (1996) show that when observations under fixed exchange rates are excluded from the sample, the size and the significance level of the coefficient of inflation in OECD convergence equations increase substantially.

The analysis of causality gives less clear-cut results, but it is also noteworthy that causality from inflation to growth is always significant and never positive. Again, this result shows up more clearly whenever the influence of country dummies, accumulation rates, and the effect of other macroeconomic variables is controlled for.

Inflation not only reduces the level of investment but also the efficiency with which productive factors are used. It has a negative temporary impact on long-term growth rates, which, in turn, generates a permanent fall in income per capita. Our results suggest that the marginal cost of inflation diminishes with the inflation rate. The estimated benefit of a permanent reduction of inflation by 1 percentage point depends on the starting level of inflation. Thus reducing the inflation rate from , say, 20 to 19 percent may increase output by 0.5 percent in the long run. This benefit increases with further reductions in inflation and might be twice as large when inflation reaches a low 5 percent. These benefits seem to be lower than others reported in the literature, but some evidence suggests that they might be underestimated since there is a positive causation running from growth to inflation, in particular for economies with fixed exchange rates. It must also be noted that these estimates are obtained in models displaying a fast convergence rate, so that the present value of the benefits of disinflation might be quite sizable. Overall, these results indicate that the long-run costs of inflation are nonnegligible and that efforts to keep inflation under control will sooner or later pay off in terms of better long-run performance and higher per capita income.

References

Andrés, J., E. Boscá, and R. Doménech. 1996. Testing the neoclassical growth model: A causality approach. Mimeograph.

Andrés, J., R. Doménech, and C. Molinas. 1996. Macroeconomic performance and convergence in OECD countries. *European Economic Review* 40:1683–1704.

Andrés, J., I. Hernando, and M. Krüger. 1996. Growth, inflation and the exchange rate regime. *Economics Letters* 53:61–65.

Balassa, B. 1964. The purchasing power parity doctrine: A reappraisal. *Journal of Political Economy* 72:584–96.

Barro, R. 1995. Inflation and economic growth. *Bank of England Economic Bulletin* 35 (May): 1–11.

———. 1996. Determinants of economic growth: A cross-country empirical study. NBER Working Paper no. 5698. Cambridge, Mass.: National Bureau of Economic Research.

Barro, R., and X. Sala-i-Martin. 1991. Convergence across states and regions. *Brookings Papers on Economic Activity*, no. 1: 107–82.

Blömstrom, M., R. Lipsey, and M. Zejan. 1996. Is fixed investment the key to economic growth? *Quarterly Journal of Economics* 111:269–76.

Briault, C. 1995. The costs of inflation. *Bank of England Economic Bulletin* 35 (February): 33–45.
Bruno, M. 1993. Inflation and growth in an integrated approach. NBER Working Paper no. 4422. Cambridge, Mass.: National Bureau of Economic Research.
Bullard, J., and J. Keating. 1995. The long-run relationship between inflation and output in postwar economies. *Journal of Monetary Economics* 36:477–96.
Burdekin, R., T. Goodwin, S. Salamun, and T. Willett. 1994. The effects of inflation on economic growth in industrial and developing countries: Is there a difference? *Applied Economic Letters* 1:175–77.
Cardoso, E., and A. Fishlow. 1989. Latin American economic development: 1950–1980. NBER Working Paper no. 3161. Cambridge, Mass.: National Bureau of Economic Research.
Carrol, C., and D. Weil. 1993. Saving and growth: A reinterpretation. NBER Working Paper no. 4470. Cambridge, Mass.: National Bureau of Economic Research.
Clark, T. E. 1997. Cross-country evidence on long run growth and inflation. *Economic Inquiry* 35:70–81.
Cozier, B., and J. Selody. 1992. Inflation and macroeconomic performance: Some cross-country evidence. Working Paper no. 92-06. Ottawa: Bank of Canada, Department of Monetary and Financial Analysis.
Dabán, T., R. Doménech, and C. Molinas. 1997. International and intertemporal comparisons in OECD countries: A growth sensitivity analysis. *Review of Income and Wealth* 43:33–48.
De Gregorio, J. 1992a. Economic growth in Latin America. *Journal of Development Economics* 39:59–84.
———. 1992b. The effects of inflation on economic growth: Lessons from Latin America. *European Economic Review* 36:417–25.
———. 1993. Inflation, taxation, and long-run growth. *Journal of Monetary Economics* 31:271–98.
———. 1996. Inflation, growth and central banks: Theory and evidence. Policy Research Working Paper no. 1575. Washington, D.C.: World Bank.
Dolado, J., and H. Lütkepohl. 1996. Making the Wald test work for cointegrated VAR systems. *Econometric Review* 15:369–86.
Feldstein, M. 1997. The costs and benefits of going from low inflation to price stability. In *Reducing inflation: Motivation and strategy,* ed. C. Romer and D. Romer, 123–56. Chicago: University of Chicago Press.
Fischer, S. 1991. Growth, macroeconomics, and development. In *NBER macroeconomics annual,* 329–64. Cambridge, Mass.: MIT Press.
———. 1993. The role of macroeconomic factors in growth. *Journal of Monetary Economics* 32:485–512.
Grier, K., and G. Tullock. 1989. An empirical analysis of cross-national economic growth, 1951–80. *Journal of Monetary Economics* 24 (2): 259–76.
Grimes, A. 1991. The effects of inflation on growth: some international evidence. *Weltwirtschaftliches Archiv* 127 (4): 631–44.
Gylfason, T., and T. Herbertsson. 1996. Does inflation matter for growth? CEPR Discussion Paper no. 1503. London: Centre for Economic Policy Research.
Islam, N. 1995. Growth empirics: A panel data approach. *Quarterly Journal of Economics* 110:1127–70.
Jones, L., and R. Manuelli. 1995. Growth and the effects of inflation. *Journal of Economic Dynamics and Control* 19:1405–28.
Judson, R., and A. Orphanides. 1996. Inflation, volatility and growth. Finance and Economics Discussion Series, no. 96-19. Washington, D.C.: Board of Governors of the Federal Reserve System.

Knight, M., N. Loayza, and D. Villanueva. 1993. Testing the neoclassical theory of economic growth: A panel data approach. *IMF Staff Papers* 40:512–41.

Kocherlakota, N. 1996. Commentary. *Federal Reserve Bank of St. Louis Review* 78 (May/June): 170–72.

Kormendi, R., and P. Meguire. 1985. Macroeconomic determinants of growth: Cross-country evidence. *Journal of Monetary Economics* 16 (2): 141–63.

Levine, R., and D. Renelt. 1992. A sensitivity analysis of cross-country growth regressions. *American Economic Review* 82:942–63.

Levine, R., and S. Zervos. 1993. What have we learned about policy and growth from cross-country regressions? *American Economic Review* 83:426–30.

Mankiw, N., D. Romer, and D. Weil. 1992. A contribution to the empirics of economic growth. *Quarterly Journal of Economics* 107 (May): 407–38.

McCandless, G., and W. Weber. 1995. Some monetary facts. *Federal Reserve Bank of Minneapolis Quarterly Review* 19 (summer): 2–11.

Motley, B. 1994. Growth and inflation: A cross-country study. Working Paper no. 94-08. San Francisco: Federal Reserve Bank of San Francisco.

Orphanides, A., and R. Solow. 1990. Money, inflation and growth. In *Handbook of monetary economics,* vol. 1, ed. B. M. Friedman and F. Hahn. Amsterdam: North Holland.

Pesaran, M. H., and R. Smith. 1995. Estimating long-run relationships from dynamic heterogeneous panels. *Journal of Econometrics* 68:79–113.

Pindyck, R., and A. Solimano. 1993. Economic instability and aggregate investment. NBER Working Paper no. 4380. Cambridge, Mass.: National Bureau of Economic Research.

Roubini, N., and X. Sala-i-Martin. 1995. A growth model of inflation, tax evasion and financial repression. *Journal of Monetary Economics* 35:275–301.

Sala-i-Martin, X. 1994. Cross-sectional regressions and the empirics of economic growth. *European Economic Review* 38:739–47.

Samuelson, P. 1964. Theoretical notes on trade problems. *Review of Economics and Statistics* 46:145–54.

Sarel, M. 1996. Nonlinear effects of inflation on economic growth. *IMF Staff Papers* 43:199–215.

Sims, C., J. Stock, and M. Watson. 1990. Inference in linear time series models with some unit roots. *Econometrica* 58:113–44.

Smyth, D. 1994. Inflation and growth. *Journal of Macroeconomics* 16 (spring): 261–70.

Solow, R. 1956. A contribution to the theory of economic growth. *Quarterly Journal of Economics* 70:65–94.

Summers, R., and A. Heston. 1991. The Penn World Table (Mark 5): An expanded set of international comparisons, 1950–1988. *Quarterly Journal of Economics* 106 (2): 327–68.

Thornton, D. 1996. The costs and benefits of price stability: An assessment of Howitt's rule. *Federal Reserve Bank of St. Louis Review* 78 (March/April): 23–38.

Comment   Frederic S. Mishkin

The paper by Andrés and Hernando is excellent and significantly advances the literature on the relationship between inflation and growth. There are several reasons why I take this view.

Strengths of the Paper

The core analysis in the paper makes use of a standard convergence equation framework, which I find attractive for two reasons. First, it enables the econometric analysis to distinguish between two important alternatives: (1) the effect of inflation on growth is temporary, yet there is a permanent effect on the level of output, and (2) the effect of inflation on growth is permanent. Second, the standard convergence equation framework is a sensible theoretical construct that allows straightforward interpretation of the results.

Another important strength of the paper is that the econometric analysis is very careful. The authors pay serious attention to potential biases of coefficients by allowing for individual country effects and using instrumental variables estimation techniques. Furthermore, the authors expend substantial effort checking the robustness of their results, an extremely important attribute of good empirical research. They do this by exploring different specifications and different subsamples as well as by allowing for country dummies in their regressions.

The most important strength of the paper and what sets it apart from the earlier literature on inflation is the choice of the data set. The data set restricts itself to OECD countries, rather than including a wider range of countries as in earlier studies. This choice of data is desirable for two reasons. First, there has always been a question whether earlier results with the sample dominated by developing countries is meaningful for industrialized countries like the United States. Andrés and Hernando deal with this problem because their OECD data set makes the results particularly relevant for policymakers in industrialized countries. Since I am currently in this position, I find the results in this paper particularly valuable. Second, the choice of data set also has the advantage of having mostly low-inflation countries in the sample, which makes the results directly applicable to low-inflation countries. This is important because earlier results with samples that include high-inflation countries may not provide as clear a picture of the inflation-growth relationship when inflation is low.

Frederic S. Mishkin is the A. Barton Hepburn Professor of Economics at the Graduate School of Business, Columbia University, and a research associate of the National Bureau of Economic Research. When this comment was written, he was director of research at the Federal Reserve Bank of New York.

Any views expressed in this comment are those of the author only and not those of the National Bureau of Economic Research, Columbia University, the Federal Reserve Bank of New York, or the Federal Reserve System.

Results

The paper has several important findings. The primary result, which is very robust, is that there is a negative relationship between inflation and growth and this is true even in the industrialized countries that make up the OECD. A secondary finding, which is quite surprising, is that the inflation effect is larger when inflation is low; that is, the positive effect on growth is larger when inflation declines from 5 to 4 percent than when it declines from 20 to 19 percent. This result contrasts with other papers in the literature. For example, Bruno and Easterly (1995) find that the negative relationship between inflation and growth is no longer significant when inflation rates are below 40 percent, while Sarel (1996) finds that the inflation effect on growth disappears when inflation is below 8 percent. In contrast, the results in this paper suggest that the negative effect of inflation on growth is especially strong for low-inflation countries. These results are extremely important for people like me who are policymakers at central banks in countries with low inflation because the results justify our focus on price stability as the primary long-run goal of monetary policy.

As I mentioned earlier, because the empirical analysis is based on a standard convergence equation framework, it is able to determine whether the inflation effect is temporary rather than permanent. The analysis produces what I consider to be an eminently sensible finding: in the OECD countries, the inflation effect is temporary, with a 1 percent decline in inflation leading to a rise in the *level* of per capita income by 0.5 to 2 percent. The fact that the impact of inflation in the long run is on the level of output rather than the growth rate is entirely consistent with the analysis in other papers in this volume that focus on the costs of inflation.

Another interesting finding in the paper is that higher inflation reduces growth by its negative effects not only on the accumulation of capital but also on total factor productivity. Results like these may help us sort out which theoretical models better describe the relationship between inflation and growth.

The bottom line is that the paper has produced an important set of results that are highly relevant to important policy issues. Clearly, the results in this paper cannot settle the issue of whether the pursuit of low inflation enhances economic growth. Particularly important in this regard are the always present questions about causality: whether it runs from inflation to growth or the other way around, or whether a third driving factor is generating the inflation-growth correlation. Indeed, all that good empirical work can do is to move or strengthen priors and this is what the paper does. It strengthens my priors for what I like to refer to as the central bank mantra: price stability should be the primary long-run goal of monetary policy.

A Minor Quibble

No discussant worth his salt can leave a paper totally unscathed: he or she must find something to criticize. I have one minor quibble with the paper. I did

not find the Granger causality results in section 8.5 very useful. My criticisms here are the standard ones about the use of Granger causality tests to make inferences about true causal relationships. Granger causality is an atheoretical technique that only tells us about predictive relationships and not about causality. Therefore, it is hard to interpret Granger causality tests unless there is a theoretical model that has implications in terms of the predictive relationships that are the focus of Granger causality tests.

It is true that the Granger causality results are consistent with the results in the paper using the standard convergence equation framework, so there really is no harm done. However, because they are hard to interpret, in contrast with the results earlier in the paper using the convergence equation setup, I do not think they add much and may even detract from the valuable results earlier in the paper.

Implications for Policy

This paper provides important ammunition in defense of the pursuit of price stability, even in low-inflation countries, and this is has important implications for the conduct of monetary policy. However, the paper does not answer a question of critical importance to central bankers in industrialized countries at the present time: how should price stability be defined? Or stated alternatively: what is the optimal level of inflation that should be the goal of monetary policy?

Answers to this question are particularly important for two reasons. First, many OECD countries are now in the enviable position of experiencing inflation below 5 percent. Yet policymakers still need to know whether inflation should be even lower. For example, in the United States the inflation rate has been running around the 3 percent level for the past five years. Should the Federal Reserve try to drive down inflation further?

Second, a new framework for the conduct of monetary policy has been gaining support in recent years: inflation targeting (see Bernanke and Mishkin 1997, and the references therein). A key element of inflation targeting is that it picks a specific numerical inflation goal for monetary policy and so necessarily requires a decision as to what the optimal inflation rate should be. Thus I would characterize the question of what the optimal inflation rate should be as a $64,000 question. It is probably the key question that faces many monetary policymakers at the present time.

My comment that the paper does not answer this question is really not a criticism because there is nothing the authors could do about it. There are several reasons why this paper is unable to address the $64,000 question. First, as is mentioned in footnote 22 of the paper, very few data points in the sample have inflation rates below 3 percent. Yet almost all the economists and monetary policymakers whom I know take the view that the optimal inflation rate is likely to be below 3 percent. The problem is, then, that any information about

the question of the optimal inflation rate that comes from this paper must be obtained by extrapolating the results outside of the sample range. As is well known in the econometrics fraternity, this is a dangerous exercise. Extrapolation outside of sample ranges can produce misleading and at best highly uncertain results. Therefore, because so little of the sample in this paper includes data with inflation rates below 3 percent, the paper can tell us little on how much below 3 percent inflation should go.

There is a further reason why the paper cannot tell us what the optimal inflation rate is. There are good theoretical reasons for believing that the relationship between inflation and growth is highly nonlinear as inflation declines. Indeed, I think it is unlikely that the inflation effect on growth remains favorable as inflation drops to zero. This view relates to recent literature on why the optimal inflation rate is above zero.

In a much-discussed recent article, Akerlof, Dickens, and Perry (1996) point out that if nominal wages are rigid downward, a possibility they argue is consistent with the evidence, then reductions in real wages can occur only through inflation in the general price level. Very low inflation, therefore, effectively reduces real wage flexibility and hence may worsen the allocative efficiency of the labor market; indeed, the authors perform simulations suggesting that inflation rates near zero would permanently increase the natural rate of unemployment. Groshen and Schweitzer (chap. 7 in this volume) provide some support for the Akerlof-Dickens-Perry view that higher inflation provides "grease" for the labor market that increases its efficiency. However, Groshen and Schweitzer also argue that higher inflation puts "sand" in the labor market and so the Akerlof-Dickens-Perry results are overstated. Groshen and Schweitzer argue that low inflation has benefits in the labor market because lower levels of inflation are associated with less uncertainty and hence better allocations of labor. Although their work indicates that the benefits of inflation estimated by Akerlof, Dickens, and Perry (1996) are overstated, this line of research suggests that pursuing the goal of zero inflation may be undesirable.

A second reason why the optimal rate of inflation might be above zero is that with a goal of zero, shocks to the economy are more likely to produce deflation in which the price level is actually falling. As pointed out in the literature on financial crises, deflation—particularly if unanticipated—can create serious problems for the financial system, interfering with its normal functioning and precipitating a severe economic contraction (Bernanke and James 1991; Mishkin 1991). Deflation can be particularly dangerous if the financial system is already in a weakened state. Thus avoiding deflation may be so important that shooting for a zero inflation rate may not be desirable.

A key point is that both of these reasons for having an inflation target above zero are based on strong nonlinearities in the inflation-growth relationship. The Akerlof-Dickens-Perry view suggests that the costs of low inflation only become significant at inflation rates below 3 percent; while the view stemming

from the dangers of deflation suggests that high costs only occur when inflation is so low that it is highly likely the economy will at times be tipped into deflation.

As a practical matter, countries that have adopted inflation targets have all chosen targets that are above zero, even with the inflation rate corrected for possible measurement bias. This suggests that practicing policymakers also have some concern about nonlinearities of the type described here.

Conclusion

The paper by Andrés and Hernando is very valuable because it tells us that low inflation is important to healthy growth in industrialized countries and so provides support for a position close to any central banker's heart, that price stability should be the primary long-run goal of monetary policy. The paper also provides ammunition for the view that the optimal inflation rate is below 3 percent. However, through no fault of its own, the paper is unable to tell us whether the optimal inflation rate is zero or some number slightly higher than this. Clearly, we need more research to tell us specifically what inflation rate policymakers should shoot for; this is exactly what this conference is all about.

References

Akerlof, George, William Dickens, and George Perry. 1996. The macroeconomics of low inflation. *Brookings Papers on Economic Activity,* no. 1: 1–59.

Bernanke, Ben, and Harold James. 1991. The gold standard, deflation, and financial crisis in the Great Depression: An international comparison. In *Financial markets and financial crises,* ed. R. G. Hubbard. Chicago: University of Chicago Press.

Bernanke, Ben, and Frederic S. Mishkin. 1997. Inflation targeting: A new framework for monetary policy? *Journal of Economic Perspectives* 11, no. 2 (spring): 97–116.

Bruno, Michael, and William Easterly. 1995. Inflation crises and long-run growth. NBER Working Paper no. 5209. Cambridge, Mass.: National Bureau of Economic Research, August.

Mishkin, Frederic S. 1991. Asymmetric information and financial crises: A historical perspective. In *Financial markets and financial crises,* ed. R. Glenn Hubbard, 69–108. Chicago: University of Chicago Press.

Sarel, Michael. 1996. Nonlinear effects of inflation on economic growth. *IMF Staff Papers* 43 (March): 199–215.

Discussion Summary

In response to the discussant's remarks about Granger causality, the authors noted that while the Granger causality tests do not prove causality, they protect the findings against the possible criticism that they are a result of reverse causation. The authors stated that their approach is intermediate between time-series and cross-sectional analysis.

Laurence Meyer noted that in the time-series charts shown by the authors, there is a clear negative correlation between inflation and growth because of the 1973 productivity slowdown. Is it possible that all the results are driven by the 1973 experience? The authors responded that the Granger causality tests are meant to deal with this possibility. Meyer suggested that one can test whether the 1973 experience drives the results by testing whether the results are robust to removing the years around 1973. The authors noted that this was done in a paper by Stanley Fischer and that his results were robust to removing the episode around 1973. *Martin Feldstein* noted that Stanley Fischer used a sample with many more countries, so that the robustness of his findings is not conclusive for the robustness of the current findings. *Frederic Mishkin* remarked that the identification also comes from the cross-sectional variation but acknowledged that there is a slight risk that the 1973 experience pollutes the results. Another participant suggested that the inclusion of country fixed effects that vary over time may alleviate some of the concerns.

Edmund Phelps noted that there are many other taxes besides the inflation tax and found it surprising that the authors find such a clear relation between inflation and growth while the literature has found no relation between growth and other taxes. He suggested that the authors may wish to include other taxes as controls in the growth equations. Phelps also asked what the relation between inflation and growth is in a pure cross section. The authors replied that this relation is strongly negative and emphasized that it is important to find the right balance between cross-sectional and time-series identification.

A participant inquired to what extent the productivity slowdown is taken into account in the analysis. The authors replied that both the size and significance of coefficients decrease if they add time dummies to the model. However, these dummies may capture many other things, and it is therefore hard to find the right mix of controls.

Laurence Ball expressed the opinion that Frederic Mishkin was too "soft" on the causality issue in his discussant's remarks. According to Ball the model in the paper is simply not identified, and therefore, the final results are not convincing. There are numerous factors that may lead to a negative correlation between inflation and growth. Though it is a boring remark to make, it is important to realize that Granger causality is not equivalent to true causality. Splitting the sample would be good but does not solve the fundamental identification issue. Ball apologized for the nihilism of this remark but warned that these data simply cannot conclusively identify the effect of inflation on growth.

Benjamin Friedman noted that it is striking that the present value calculations in the paper are so small compared to Martin Feldstein's results. *Martin Feldstein* replied that the annual GDP level effects of inflation are actually larger in the current paper than in his own analysis but warned that the calculations are not comparable because the calculations in the current paper are in terms of GDP whereas his calculations are in terms of welfare. *Friedman* stated

that it would be helpful if the two measures somehow could be made comparable, or at least reconciled explicitly.

Anna Schwartz, referring to the discussant's remarks, noted that financial stability is indeed very important but disagreed that deflation causes financial instability. Instead, financial instability is caused by financial agents taking large bets on inflation expectations. *Mishkin* responded that deflation causes transfers from borrowers to creditors leading to information problems in financial markets. Although the deflationary harm also depends on the state of financial institutions, deflation can nevertheless be dangerous to financial stability.

Stephen Cecchetti emphasized the importance of the identification issue. According to Cecchetti, one needs a model that makes the source of the shocks explicit. It is well known that supply shocks cause a negative correlation between growth and inflation whereas demand shocks cause a positive correlation. Perhaps supply shocks were simply more prevalent in the sample period, which would explain the authors' findings of a negative effect of inflation on growth. *Matthew Shapiro* suggested that it may be valuable to use a longer time series, for example, the Maddison data. With respect to the discussion on financial instability, he noted that is it is unexpected disinflation that causes problems, not deflation as such. *Mishkin* said that this point is well taken but also expressed his amazement at how slowly some financial institutions adapt to new inflation regimes. *Martin Feldstein* disagreed with the suggestion to use long time series on the grounds that the economy has changed and that, therefore, very old data is not informative for the current economy.

Karl-Heinz Tödter said that the sample is homogenous in one respect but heterogeneous in another respect, namely, the size of countries. He wondered whether a weighted regression reflecting the countries' sizes would be more appropriate. The authors stated that they could do this, but Xavier Sala-i-Martin found in related work that weighting did not matter. *James Hines* explained that results may be stronger if the weights are GNP based rather than GDP based because the GNP weights also capture investment inflows.

Contributors

Andrew B. Abel
Department of Finance
Wharton School
2315 Steinberg-Dietrich Hall
3620 Locust Walk
University of Pennsylvania
Philadelphia, PA 19104

Javier Andrés
Departamento de Analisis Economico
Universitat de Valencia
Campus de los Naranjos
Avenida do los Naranjos
Edificio Departamental Oriental
E-46011 Valencia, Spain

Alan J. Auerbach
Department of Economics
University of California, Berkeley
549 Evans Hall
Berkeley, CA 94720

Hasan Bakhshi
Monetary Analysis
Bank of England
Threadneedle Street
London, EC2R 8AH United Kingdom

Laurence Ball
Department of Economics
Johns Hopkins University
Baltimore, MD 21218

Darrel Cohen
Board of Governors of the Federal
    Reserve System
Washington, DC 20551

Mihir A. Desai
Morgan 363
Harvard Business School
Soldiers Field
Boston, MA 02163

Juan J. Dolado
Department of Economics
Universidad Carlos III de Madrid
c/ Madrid 126
E-28903 Getafe Spain

Rudiger Dornbusch
Department of Economics, E52-357
Massachusetts Institute of Technology
Cambridge, MA 02139

Martin Feldstein
NBER
1050 Massachusetts Avenue
Cambridge, MA 02138

Stanley Fischer
International Monetary Fund
700 19th Street NW
Room 12-300F
Washington, DC 20431

Jeffrey A. Frankel
Council of Economic Advisers
Room 315 OEOB
Washington, DC 20502

José M. González-Páramo
Banco de España
Alcala, 50
E-28014 Madrid, Spain

Erica L. Groshen
Domestic Research
Federal Reserve Bank of New York
33 Liberty Street
New York, NY 10045

Andrew G. Haldane
Bank of England
Threadneedle Street
London, EC2R 8AH United Kingdom

Kevin A. Hassett
American Enterprise Institute
1150 17th Street NW
Washington, DC 20036

Neal Hatch
Bank of England
Threadneedle Street
London, EC2R 8AH United Kingdom

Ignacio Hernando
Research Department
Banco de España
Alcala, 50
E-28014 Madrid, Spain

James Hines Jr.
University of Michigan Business School
701 Tappan Street
Ann Arbor, MI 48109

R. Glenn Hubbard
Graduate School of Business
Uris Hall 609
Columbia University
New York, NY 10027

Frederic S. Mishkin
Graduate School of Business
Uris Hall 619
Columbia University
New York, NY 10027

Mark E. Schweitzer
Federal Reserve Bank of Cleveland
1455 East 6th Street
Cleveland, OH 44101

Karl-Heinz Tödter
Research Department
Deutsche Bundesbank
Wilhelm-Epstein-Strasse 14
D-60431 Frankfurt am Main, Germany

José Viñals
Jefe de Estúdios Monetários y
    Financieros
Banco de España
Alcala, 50
E-28014 Madrid, Spain

Gerhard Ziebarth
Division of Public Finance
Deutsche Bundesbank
Wilhelm-Epstein-Strasse 14
D-60431 Frankfurt am Main, Germany

Author Index

Abel, A., 153, 181, 184–85, 200, 225
Abuaf, Niso, 238n2
Akerlof, George, 5, 42, 47n2, 53n12, 127n28, 141n17, 142n19, 193, 302–4, 309, 345
Albi, E., 106, 111n18
Almeida, A., 135n3
Altshuler, Rosanne, 206
Andrés, J., 100, 319, 325, 335n26, 336n28, 337, 338n32
Argimón, I., 108
Ariznavarreta, J. L. García, 106
Attanasio, O. P., 84, 150
Auerbach, Alan, 17, 62, 107, 199, 204, 205, 211, 212, 218, 220, 223, 224, 240n6, 255n18

Bailey, Martin J., 32, 49, 119, 134n2, 135n4, 165, 199n1
Balassa, Bela, 337
Ball, Laurence, 10, 37, 53, 56n21, 100, 137–39, 141, 142–43, 200, 276
Ballard, Charles, 20, 22, 23, 32, 110, 152–53, 253n17
Banco de España, 105, 106n11, 108, 113n21
Banks, J. W., 150, 154
Barro, Robert J., 4, 47, 134, 135n4, 318, 319, 325, 329
Bayoumi, T., 151, 201n5, 203n7, 237
Beaudry, T., 84
Bernanke, Ben, 344, 345
Bewley, Truman, 296
Bianchi, M., 135
Black, R., 57

Blanchard, Olivier, 83n61
Blinder, Alan, 20n23, 134n1, 296
Blömstrom, M., 336
Blundell, R., 150, 176
Bond, S., 148, 149, 174
Boscá, E., 325, 335n26, 337
Boskin, Michael, 20n23, 136n6, 151
Bradford, David F., 204
Brainard, William, 296
Breedon, F. J., 166
Briault, C. B., 133, 317n2
Bruno, Michael, 4, 317, 318n3, 343
Bryan, Michael F., 294
Bullard, J., 318n3
Burdekin, R., 318n3

Cagan, Philip, 34n39
Card, David, 302–4
Cardoso, E., 318n3
Carrol, C., 337
Cecchetti, S. G., 138n9, 276
Chadha, J., 166n56, 168
Chapple, B., 138n9, 141n16
Chari, V. V., 70n53
Choi, Don H., 296
Christiano, L. J., 70n53
Clark, T. E., 318
Cleveland, William S., 28n14
Commission of the European Communities, 239n4
Cooley, T. F., 135, 169
Cooper, Ian, 260n20
Cozier, B., 318, 320

Crawford, A., 136n6
Croushore, D., 47, 53n11, 68n48
Cummins, J. G., 175, 176, 207n13, 208, 220
Cunningham, A. W. F., 136

Dabán, T., 321
Darby, Michael, 60n30, 199, 237, 248
De Gregorio, J., 317n1, 318, 319n6
Denny, K., 174
Desai, Mihir, 264n23
Devereux, M., 146n25, 148, 149, 173, 174
Dickens, William, 5, 42, 47n2, 53n12,
    127n28, 141n17, 142n19, 193, 302–4,
    309, 345
Dicks-Mireau, Louis, 16n9
Dilnot, A., 154
Dolado, Juan J., 97, 99n2, 335
Doménech, R., 319, 321, 325, 335n26,
    336n28, 337
Döpke, J., 69, 70n52
Dotsey, M., 135, 166n57, 169
Drazen, Alan, 287n12
Driffill, J. J., 133

Easterly, William, 4, 343
Edey, M., 57, 61n34
Einaudi, L., 79
Estrada, A., 108
Evans, C. L., 101
Evans, O., 20n23

Fay, C. H., 275n3
Fazzari, S. M., 176
Feenberg, Daniel, 23
Feldstein, Martin, 1n1, 2, 6, 9nn1, 2, 10, 11,
    13n6, 16n9, 17nn13, 15, 20n23, 21n25,
    23, 32n37, 34n39, 38, 45, 48–49, 60n30,
    62, 66n46, 90t, 96, 101, 103, 108, 109,
    112, 120, 122, 124t, 126, 128, 134, 135,
    136, 139–41, 144–45, 152–55, 158, 163,
    166–67, 169, 170, 180–81, 183, 199–
    200, 201n5, 224, 225, 237, 239n5, 247,
    248, 253n17, 260n20, 261, 317
Fischer, Stanley, 4, 13n6, 41, 43n1, 47n2, 52,
    57, 83n61, 96, 133, 135nn3, 4, 166,
    199n1, 318, 336n28
Fisher, Irving, 201n5, 236
Fisher, P. G., 151, 166
Fishlow, A., 318n3
Flaig, G., 84
Frankel, Jeffrey, 238n2, 260n20, 269
Freedman, Audrey, 276

Freeman, H., 148, 149
French, Kenneth R., 260n20
Friedman, Milton, 33, 70, 119, 273n1
Froot, Kenneth, 238n2
Fry, M. J., 135n3
Fuhrer, J., 143n22
Fullerton, D., 49n4, 153, 173, 174, 210, 224,
    225
Fundación BBV, 112n19, 114

Gagnon, Joseph, 201–2n5, 203n7, 237
Gallego, M., 113
Gavin, William T., 294
González-Páramo, J. M., 106n10, 108
Goodhart, C. A. E., 53n12, 135n3
Gordon, Roger H., 199, 238n3, 263
Graham, Edward M., 235
Green, Jerry, 17n13, 49n4, 199, 237
Greenspan, Alan, 48
Grier, K., 317
Grimes, A., 57n26, 318n3
Groshen, Erica L., 5, 273, 274, 275, 276, 277,
    279, 280, 283, 285, 288, 296, 298, 300,
    345
Gylfason, T., 128, 318, 319, 329n20

Hagen, J. von, 52
Haldane, A. G., 166n56, 168
Hall, Robert E., 20n23, 151, 174, 209
Hall, S., 134n1
Hallman, J. J., 50
Hamermesh, Daniel, 287n12, 300
Hansen, G. D., 135, 169
Hansson, I., 153, 201n5, 204n11, 238
Harris, Trevor, 205n12
Hartman, David, 17n15, 201–2n5, 203n7, 237,
    238, 239, 242, 264, 268
Hassett, K. A., 175, 176, 205n12, 208, 218,
    220, 225
Heckman, James J., 300
Henderson, Y. K., 153
Henry, S. G. B., 159
Herbertsson, T. Thor, 128, 318, 319, 329n20
Hernando, I., 338n32
Herrmann, H., 53
Heston, A., 321
Hills, F. S., 275n3
Hills, J., 160n44
Hines, James R., Jr., 203n8, 206, 240n6,
    263n22
Horioka, Charles, 260n20
Howard, David, 237

Howitt, P., 77n58
Hubbard, R. G., 175, 176, 199n1, 203n8,
    205n12, 206, 207n13, 208, 220, 225
Hyslop, Dean, 302–4

Institute for Fiscal Studies, 172
Instituto Nacional de Estadistica, 114
International Monetary Fund (IMF), 235,
    244n10
Ireland, P., 135, 166n57, 169
Islam, N., 325
Issing, O., 48, 50nn7, 8, 51t, 52n9, 56n22, 79

Jackman, R., 142n19
Jaén, M., 114
Jahnke, W., 55
James, Harold, 345
Janssen, N., 166n56, 168
Johnson, Karen, 237
Jones, L., 317
Jorgenson, Dale, 174, 209
Jorion, Philippe, 238n2
Judson, R., 318n4

Kahn, Shulamit, 274n2, 302n16
Kaplanis, Evi, 260n20
Karayannis, Marios, 224
Kay, J. A., 146
Keating, J., 318n3
Kehoe, P. J., 70n53
Kehoe, T., 110
Kemsley, Deen, 205n12
Kennedy, Jim, 225
Killingsworth, Mark R., 30
Kim, Michael, 238n2
King, M. A., 49n4, 56n21, 57, 105, 135, 146,
    173, 174, 205, 210
King, R., 97
Knight, M., 325
Kocherlakota, N., 337
Konieczny, J. D., 47–48
König, R., 52n9
Kormendi, R., 317
Krüger, M., 338n32
Krugman, Paul R., 235, 310

Lach, Saul, 276, 294
López-Salido, D., 97, 99n2
Laxton, D., 141
Layard, R., 142n19
Leal, J., 113n20

Le Blanc, François, 79
Lebow, David E., 302n16
Leigh-Pemberton, R., 134
Levi, Maurice D., 204n11, 239n4
Levine, David I., 275, 296
Levine, R., 318, 336n28
Lipsey, R., 336
Loayza, N., 325
Low, H., 154
Lucas, Robert E., Jr., 49, 56, 121, 167–68
Lütkepohl, H., 335

McCallum, Bennett, 166
McCandless, G., 318n5
Macklem, T., 57
McLaughlin, Kenneth J., 302n16
Madigan, B., 143n22
Makin, John, 20n23
Mankiw, N. Gregory, 20n23, 141, 309, 310,
    319
Manuelli, R., 317
Marchante, A., 108n16
Mayes, D., 138n9, 175
Meguire, P., 317
Meredith, G., 141
Mestre, R., 100
Meyer, Laurence H., 201–2n5, 214n18
Miles, D., 159
Milkovich, George, 275n3
Mishkin, Frederic, 17n15, 62, 201–2n5, 238,
    269, 344, 345
Mizon, G. E., 133
Modigliani, Franco, 96, 133
Molina, A., 114
Molinas, C., 319, 321, 336n28
Motley, B., 318, 321n12, 329
Muellbauer, J., 151
Mulligan, Casey, 121, 168
Mundell, Robert, 236
Murphy, A., 151

Neumann, M. J. M., 52
Newlon, T. Scott, 206
Newman, J. M., 275n3
Nickell, S., 142n19
Nordhaus, William, 136n6

Oliver, J., 108, 111n18
Organization for Economic Cooperation and
    Development (OECD), 107
Orphanides, A., 317n1, 318n4

Pain, D. L., 159
Pain, N., 159
Parsley, David C., 238n2
Pencavel, John, 300
Perry, George, 5, 42, 47n2, 53n12, 127n28,
    141n17, 142n19, 193, 302–4, 309, 345
Persson, M., 128
Persson, T., 128
Pesaran, M. H., 325
Petersen, B. C., 176
Phelps, Edmund, 34, 70n53, 167
Pindyck, R., 317
Poloz, S., 57
Porter, R. D., 50
Poterba, James, 16n9, 26n28, 27nn29, 30,
    199n1, 205n12, 260n20
Prakken, Joel L., 201–2n5, 214n18
Pujolar, D., 108

Ramsey, F. P., 140
Randolph, William C., 206
Raymond, J. L., 108
Reder, Melvin, 292
Reimers, H.-E., 51
Renelt, D., 318, 336n28
Rippe, Richard, 16
Robinson, W., 158–59
Robson, M., 139n13, 147
Rogers, Diane Lim, 224, 225
Rogoff, Kenneth, 238n2
Rolsán, J. M., 108
Romer, David, 83n61, 141, 236n1, 264n23,
    319
Rose, D., 141
Rosen, Harvey, 26, 30
Roubini, N., 317n1, 319n6
Rudebusch, G. D., 135

Sala-i-Martin, Xavier, 121, 167, 317n1, 318,
    319
Samuelson, Paul A., 337
Samwick, Andrew, 16n9
Sanz, J. F., 107
Sarel, Michael, 4, 135, 343
Scarth, W., 52, 78n59
Scharnagl, M., 50n7, 51
Schelde-Andersen, P., 53, 54, 55n17
Schwab, R. M., 134n1
Schweitzer, Mark E., 5, 273, 274, 275, 276,
    277, 279, 280, 283, 288, 298, 300, 345
Selody, J., 318, 320
Shapiro, M. D., 136n6

Sheshinski, Eytan, 17n13, 49n4, 199, 237
Shiller, Robert, 133, 193
Shoven, John, 20, 22, 23, 32, 110, 152–53,
    253n17
Sidrauski, M., 153, 181
Sievert, O., 49n4
Silberberg, Eugene, 63n42, 81n60
Sims, C., 335
Sinn, Hans-Werner, 49n4, 237
Skinner, T., 158–59
Small, D. H., 50
Smith, J., 135
Smith, R., 325
Smyth, D. J., 135n3, 318n3
Sociedad de Tasación, 113, 114
Solimano, A., 317
Solow, R., 317n1, 319n8
Sorenson, Peter Birch, 237
Stock, J., 335
Stockton, David J., 302n16
Stuart, C. E., 153, 201n5, 204n11, 238
Summers, L. H., 43n1, 143n22, 205n12
Summers, R., 321
Svensson, L. E. O., 128

Tanzi, Vito, 49n4
Tesar, Linda L., 260n20
Thornton, D. L., 77n58, 320n11
Tobin, James, 81, 237, 273n1
Tödter, K.-H., 50n8, 51
Tower, E., 135n4
Tsiddon, Daniel, 276, 294
Tullock, G., 317

Ulph, A., 133

Vallés, J., 100
Varian, Hal, 63n42, 238n3
Varvares, Chris P., 201–2n5, 214n18
Vega, J. L., 97, 99n2
Villanueva, D., 325
Viñals, José, 103

Wahl, Jenny Bourne, 239n4
Wallace, M. J., 275n3
Walsh, M., 134n1
Wardlow, A., 140
Warner, Ingrid M., 260n20
Wascher, William L., 302n16
Watson, M., 97, 335
Weber, G., 84
Weber, W., 318n5

Wei, Shang-Jin, 238n2
Weil, D., 319, 337
Westaway, P., 159
Whalley, John, 20, 22, 23, 32, 110, 152–53, 253n17
Whitley, J. D., 151
Wilcox, D. W., 135, 136n6
Wincoop, E. van, 84
Woolwich Building Society, 159

World Bank, 244n10
Wright, C., 20n23

Yates, A., 134n1, 141nn16, 17
Young, G., 175

Zejan, M., 336
Zervos, S., 318

Subject Index

Capital: factors influencing user cost of, 201–20; impact of tax system on user cost of, 231–32; variation in user cost of, 211

Capital flows, international: imperfect mobility of, 257, 260–63; open economy inflation-induced, 246–51, 264; tax-inflation distortion of, 4

Community Salary Survey (CSS), Federal Reserve Bank of Cleveland, 279–84

Consumption: effect in Spain of inflation on, 103–11; effect of German tax system–inflation interaction on, 57–67; effect of inflation-induced capital flows, 246–57; effect of lower inflation on, 220–23; inflation effect on intertemporal allocation of, 12–26; with inflation in United Kingdom, 144–57; in Sidrauski model of welfare effect, 181–83. *See also* Revenue; Saving

Consumption, retirement: effect of inflation in Spain on, 103–5; effect of inflation on, 13–19; with inflation in United Kingdom, 144–50; overlapping generations model for Germany, 82–88; price in relation to inflation rates, 15–19

Convergence equations: to assess long-run impact of inflation, 315–16, 318–19, 342; estimation of inflation's effect, 321–25; estimation with individual country effects, 325–32; model of growth and inflation correlation, 319–21

Data sources: for analysis of inflation-consumption behavior in United Kingdom, 145–46; in assessing inflation's distortions, 135; Community Salary Survey (CSS), 279–84; evidence for effect of inflation on OECD economic growth, 321, 325, 342

Deadweight losses: changes from reduced inflation, 223–25; from demand for U.S. housing services, 26–35; in German tax system–inflation interaction, 57–67; from inflation-induced capital flows, 246–51; of inflation in open and closed economies, 253–57; model of distortion of consumption causing, 13–26, 41–42; triangles and trapezoids resulting from, 2, 10, 134

Debt service: cost in United States, 11–12; with reduction of inflation in Spain, 122; related to inflation in Germany, 72–73; related to inflation in United Kingdom, 169–70; related to inflation in United States, 35–36

Disinflation: cost and benefits of, 2, 9–10; costs in Germany of, 49–56; costs in Spain of, 97–103; costs in United Kingdom, 137–44; differences in gains related to tax rules, 3; Howitt's rule, 77–78; optimal rate in Germany, 79–80; optimal rate of, 77–79. *See also* Sacrifice ratio

Economic and Monetary Union (EMU) convergence criteria, 95

Economic growth: Balassa-Samuelson effect, 337; causality tests of impact of inflation on OECD, 332–38; correlation between inflation and, 4–5, 319–25; evidence of inflation's effect on, 4–5, 134–35, 317–19

Economic shocks: response of economy to, 332–33; response of government to, 11; in Spanish economy, 101

Efficiency: effect of inflation in open economy on, 246–57; effect of inflation on efficiency channel, 317; effect of tax distortions on, 2

Feldstein trapezoids. *See* Trapezoids

Fiscal channels, Germany, Spain, and United Kingdom, 180–81

Fisher effect: in closed and open economies, 204–7; correlation of nominal interest rates and inflation rate, 17, 236–37, 242–46; German interest rates and price effects, 60; modified, 237; in open and closed economies, 253–55; tax-adjusted, 202, 204–7, 211, 215, 219f, 221f, 222f; on worldwide saving and investment in open economy, 238–46

Harberger triangles. *See* Triangles

Household behavior: with change in inflation rate, 10; nonsavers, 23–24. *See also* Consumption; Saving

Housing, owner-occupied: demand in Germany for, 67–70; demand in Spain for, 3, 111–19; inflationary distortion of demand in United States, 26–32; mortgage interest relief in United Kingdom, 157–65

Howitt's rule, 77–78

Income: inflation's impact on OECD per capita, 331–32; tax on investment, earned, and retirement, 21–26

Income tax: effect of inflation on, 15–19; indexation of capital income, 43; treatment of owner-occupied housing, 26–32

Indexation: as alternative in Germany to price stability, 66; in Spain, 102; of U.K. capital gains tax, 140, 171; of U.S. tax system for inflation, 6, 10

Inflation: aggregate relationship between unemployment and, 296–97; convergence equations, 315–16; cost of servicing national debt with reduced, 35–36; costs of high levels of, 317; cost to shift to price stability from, 38; distortion of demand for money, 32–35; distortion of demand for owner-occupied housing, 26–32; effect on allocation of capital, 223–25; effect on consumption of lower, 220–23; effect on cost of owner-occupied housing, 26–35; effect on domestic and foreign investment incentives, 239–46; effect on efficiency in open economy, 246–57; effect on occupation and employer wage components, 285; effect on tax distortions, 2, 10; effect on user cost of capital, 211–22; evidence of effect on economic growth, 4–5, 134–35, 317–19; impact on OECD growth, 325–38; model of effect on large-firm wage setting, 275–79; negative effects of, 317–18; net impact of effects on labor market, 297–99; targeting of, 344–45; triangle and trapezoid distortions, 2, 10. *See also* Disinflation; RPIX inflation, United Kingdom; Trapezoids; Triangles

Inflation, Germany: welfare gain from reducing, 3

Inflation, Spain: gain from reduction in, 3; relation to unemployment (1964–95), 97–99

Inflation, United Kingdom: gain from reduction in, 3–4; house prices with, 157; RPIX inflation, 136

Inflation rate: benefit of zero, 73–75; effect in OECD countries, 316; effect of differences on capital flows, 235–36; effect of high, 2; effect on revenues, 21–22; EU annual, 96; excess burden associated with, 47; G-7 countries (1963–95), 48; Howitt's rule, 77–78; optimal, 48; for price stability in United States, 1; relation to price of retirement consumption, 15–19; sacrifice ratio as cost to correct, 47

Inflation-tax interaction: in closed and open economy, 236–46; effect on international capital flows, 4; in Germany, 3, 56–79; trapezoids in, 173–74; in United Kingdom, 3–4, 144–57; in United States, 2–3

Interest rates: effect of capital inflows on, 237–38, 242; Fisher's hypothesis related to inflation, 17, 60–63, 236–37; obeying Fisher effect ($dr/d\pi = 1$), 239, 242–57

Investment, business: effect in open economy of inflation on, 239–46; effect of corporate taxes on incentives for, 209–10; ef-

fect of inflation on, 317–18; effect of inflation on user cost in open economy, 213–19; foreign direct investment, 263–64; relation to inflation in United Kingdom, 173–75

Labor market: inflation's cost and benefit impact, 273–74, 297–304, 309–10; low inflation's cost and benefits to, 275–80; wage adjustment under high and low inflation, 284–96; wage data for occupations, 280–84

MIRAS. *See* Mortgage interest relief at source (MIRAS), United Kingdom
Monetary policy: Bundesbank targeting strategy, 51–52; Federal Reserve goal for, 1, 6–7; goals of future European System of Central Banks, 95–96; implications of inflation's effect on OECD countries, 344–46; inflation targeting, 344–45; price stability as target for, 47; related to inflation in Germany, 49–50
Money demand: effect of reducing inflation on, 32–35; Harberger analysis, 70–71; related to inflation in United Kingdom, 165–69; related to seigniorage in Germany, 70–72
Mortgage interest relief at source (MIRAS), United Kingdom, 157–65, 171–72

OECD countries: causality tests of inflation-growth correlation, 332–38, 343–44; estimated long-run cost of inflation, 325–32; estimation of inflation's effect on growth, 4–5, 321–38, 343; inflation rate (1963–95), 48
Okun's law, 53, 79, 81, 99, 134, 197–98
Open economy: efficiency consequences of inflation, 246–57; Fisher effect with taxation, 238–39; interaction of inflation and taxation in, 236–46

Phillips curve. *See* Unemployment
Price stability: absolute, 11; advantages of, 5–6, 10–12; benefits in Germany of, 56–79; benefits in Spain for policy of, 103–11, 122–25; cost of going from low inflation to, 2; estimates of German tax system–inflation interaction on, 63–67; as goal of European System of Central Banks, 95–96

Revenue: with reduction in inflation, 10, 120; from seigniorage, 11, 32–35, 120–22; from taxes with change in inflation, 10; welfare effect of changes in, 22–23
Revenue effect: of domestic inflation on foreign economy, 257, 259t; on housing with move to price stability in United Kingdom, 163–65; of inflation in open economy, 251–52; of inflation on housing subsidy, 30–32; from lower inflation in Spain, 116–19; of lower inflation rates on, 21–22; with move to price stability in United Kingdom, 152–57; of reduced demand for money in United States, 34–35; of reduced money demand in Germany, 71–72; with rise in capital stock in United Kingdom, 175–76; of tax treatment for German owner-occupied housing, 70
RPIX inflation, United Kingdom, 136, 140

Sacrifice ratio: defined, 47, 316; empirical estimates for, 54–55; estimated for Spanish economy, 97–103; as measure of cost of disinflation, 193–94; for OECD countries, 53; Okun gap, 53, 79, 81, 99–100; output and unemployment, 53–54; related to reduced inflation in Germany, 49–56; in United Kingdom, 137–44
Saving: effect in open economy of inflation and taxation, 239–46; effect of German tax system–inflation interaction on, 57–67; effect of inflation-induced capital flows, 246–57; effect of inflation on, 12–26; with inflation in United Kingdom, 144–52; relation to inflation levels in Spain, 103–11; U.S. and U.K. ratios (1990), 150–51
Seigniorage: as advantage of inflation, 11; loss with reduction in inflation, 32–35, 120–22; in relation to demand for money in Germany, 70–72; in relation to demand for money in Spain, 119–22; in relation to demand for money in United States, 32–35

Tax, corporate: effect on user cost of capital, 209–10
Tax Reform Act (1986): depreciation schedules, 231; investment tax credit, depreciation, and corporate tax rate under, 208, 226–27

Tax revenue. *See* Revenue

Tax system: distortions caused by, 2, 10; effect of differential taxation, 223–25; effect on user cost of capital with inflation, 201–13; impact on user cost of capital, 231–32; indexation for inflation, 6, 10; reform proposals to gain price stability, 6; role in model of inflation's effect on consumption, 12–26, 41–42. *See also* Inflation-tax interaction

Tax system, Germany: effect on consumption and saving, 57–67; interaction with inflation, 56–79; treatment of owner-occupied housing, 67–70

Tax system, Spain: effect with inflation, 103–11; treatment of owner- and non-owner-occupied housing, 111–16

Tax system, United Kingdom: advanced and mainstream corporation tax, 146; differences in, 3–4; effect of interaction with inflation, 144–57; incentives in mortgage interest relief, 157–63

Tax wedge: with inflation-induced capital flows, 246–47; Spain, 106; United Kingdom, 144, 148, 171, 173–75

Trapezoids: in analysis of money demand in Germany, 70–71; in analysis of U.K. business investment–inflation interaction, 173–74; deadweight loss of inflation, 2, 10, 59, 135–36; to measure welfare effect of price stability, 79, 81–82, 135–36

Triangles: from deadweight loss of inflation, 2, 10, 134; Harberger's deadweight loss of taxation, 58–59, 135; to measure welfare effect of price stability, 79, 81–82, 134–36; welfare benefits in United Kingdom, 172

Unemployment: aggregate relationship between inflation and, 296–97; effect of inflation on downward wage inflexibility, 42; German sacrifice ratio related to, 52–56; with low U.S. inflation, 5–6; related to disinflation in United Kingdom, 141–44; relation in Spain to inflation (1964–95), 97–99; with shift to price stability, 5; simulated effects of inflation-induced wage adjustment on, 299–302

Wage adjustment, large-firm: analysis of variance (ANOVA), 284–85; from Commu-

nity Salary Survey (CSS), 280–84; comparison among studies of inflation-induced, 302–4; density in high- and low-inflation years, 285–87; model of inflation effect on, 275–79

Welfare effect: comparing move to price stability in Spain and United States, 125–30; cross-country comparison with 2 percent inflation cut, 191–93; discounting gains, 9; with distortion of demand for money, 33–34, 119–22; gain from move to price stability, 2–3, 10–11; gain from negative rate of inflation, 6–7; gain from reduced distortion of demand for housing, 27–31; gain from reduced intertemporal distortion, 14–21; gain from reducing rate of inflation, 2, 9–10, 12t, 22–23, 36–38; Howitt's rule of choice of inflation rate, 77–78; of inflation in open and closed economies, 246–58; losses related to allocation of consumption, 12–26; loss from inflation and tax distortions, 2, 38; of lost seigniorage, 32–35; of reduced distortions in consumption, 103–11; related to costs of government debt service, 35–36, 72–73; related to demand for money, 70–72; Sidrauski model applied to Germany, Spain, and United Kingdom, 181–91; of U.K./U.S. tax and inflation distortions, 135–38. *See also* Deadweight losses

Welfare effect, Germany: gain from reducing inflation, 3; of price stability, 57–67; tax system–inflation interaction, 57–67

Welfare effect, Spain: demand for money distortion, 119–20; gain from reducing inflation, 3; gains related to housing demand, 111–16; of moving to price stability, 122–25

Welfare effect, United Kingdom: consumption and saving with move to price stability, 154–57; gain from reducing inflation, 3–4; of inflation, 144–57; of inflation distortions on money demand, 165–69

Welfare gains. *See* Welfare effect

Welfare loss. *See* Welfare effect

Welfare programs: effect of lower inflation on, 12t, 36–38, 41